DATE DUE

International Studies
of the
Committee on International Relations
University of Notre Dame

International Studies

DIPLOMACY IN A WHIRLPOOL

Hungary between Nazi Germany and
Soviet Russia

DIPLOMACY IN A WHIRLPOOL

Hungary between Nazi Germany and Soviet Russia

by

STEPHEN D. KERTESZ

University of Notre Dame Press
Notre Dame, Indiana

Library of Congress
Catalog Card Number
53-7349

To the memory of Andor Szentmiklóssy
Secretary General of the Hungarian Ministry for Foreign Affairs
in 1943-1944
(† Dachau, February, 1945)

PREFACE

The geographical position of Hungary has made it a meeting place of expansive forces which on several occasions in her history became a swirling whirlpool. To survive in this critical zone of Europe a different kind of statesmanship has been necessary from that practiced in nations more favored by geography. When the stage was set for the Second World War, Hungarian statesmen had to choose, not between good and bad, but rather between evil and lesser evil. They could not freely choose their course of actions, but did—rightly or wrongly—what they considered necessary for the survival of their nation. The main actors in this drama have disappeared from the public scene. A few of them have perished in Germany, others in the Soviet Union. Many were executed. Count Paul Teleki committed suicide in protest against the things to come. Some are scattered around the globe. Although the events which inflicted this vast misfortune belong to contemporary history, they seem nearly as remote as the period of the Turkish occupation of Hungary.

In dealing with the foreign political aspects of these past regimes, I have tried to establish facts accurately, but do not pretend to be authoritative or complete. Within the limited scope of this book, I have not tried to explore basic social tensions or to appraise systematically all the trends of Hungarian foreign policy.

Before the German and during the Soviet occupation of Hungary, a considerable number of Hungarian documents had been deposited abroad. Yet the Hungarian source material is far from complete. The Nuremberg trials revealed some additional data, and the Ciano diaries and diplomatic papers furnished valuable information. The British and German documents thus far published are incomplete, since they terminate in early 1939. Other official publications cover only certain selected events. The unevenness of the available, and not infrequently contradictory, evidence caused a certain disproportion in exposition. In dealing with more recent events, I have used some of my own observations and experiences.

Since political thinking in Eastern Europe is closely related to events of even the distant past, the introductory chapter contains some background material. In the later chapters it was thought necessary to explain certain aspects of the internal changes in Hungary and to discuss the economic problems which confronted the nation, because these problems were closely connected with the entirely changed international scene after the Second World War.

The maps and their accompanying data were prepared by Professor Géza Teleki and Mr. N. F. W. Thrower of the Virginia Geographical Institute. I am greatly indebted for all their work. I enjoyed the most generous cooperation of many other scholars, statesmen and diplomats whose contributions are acknowledged in a special note dealing with my sources.

Notre Dame, Indiana   S.D.K.

ACKNOWLEDGMENTS AND NOTE ON SOURCES

When I arrived in the United States in 1948, I was greatly depressed because of the turn of events along the Danube. In order not to revive painful memories I began to work on some general problems of contemporary diplomacy. Professor Philip E. Mosely of Columbia University urged me to write a book on Hungary's foreign relations in recent times—a topic which would enable me to use my personal experiences. Professor Waldemar Gurian, Chairman of the Committee on International Relations at the University of Notre Dame, gave me the final impulse. I extend my thanks to both of them for their encouragement. I also wish to express my deep appreciation to my colleagues on the Committee on International Relations, especially M. A. Fitzsimons, for their sympathetic interest and assistance. Some chapters of the book were read by Hans Kohn of the City College of New York, Robert Ferrell of Michigan State College and Thomas Stritch of Notre Dame University. Professor A. S. Ryan was very helpful concerning stylistic matters. I am grateful to all my research assistants and especially to Charles Poinsatte who is also responsible for the index. I am deeply indebted to several officials of the United States Government who kindly helped me establish some of the facts relating to the diplomacy of the Allies during and following the Second World War.

Although many Hungarian documents were at my disposal, the lack of regular archives made difficult the complete clarification of some events. I tried to overcome this shortcoming by consulting participants in Hungarian public life. Baron George Bakách-Bessenyey, formerly Hungarian Minister to Yugoslavia, France and Switzerland, Aladár Szegedy-Maszák, former head of the political division of the Hungarian Foreign Ministry and later Hungarian Minister to the United States, Professor Géza Teleki, former Minister of Religion and Public Instruction, Loránd D. Schweng, former Secretary of State in the Ministry of Finance, and Monsignor Gedeon Péterffy, former head of the Hungarian Papal Institute in Rome, read most parts of the manuscript and greatly assisted in the clarification of many facts. Information received from Professor Teleki was the basis for the material pertaining to the activities of the first Hungarian armistice delegation in Moscow. Paul Auer, former Hungarian Minister to France, reviewed the passage concerning his contacts with Czechoslovak statesmen in the 1930's. Paul Balla, former under-Secretary of State, gave me information regarding the tragic events of

Zsablya and Ujvidék which he investigated in his official capacity in 1943-1944. I am most grateful for the generous assistance of all the persons who cooperated in my research. I have established the final text after considering all the facts and information at my disposal, and I alone am responsible for all evaluations, interpretations and possible errors.

LIST OF ABBREVIATIONS

British Documents—

Documents on British Foreign Policy 1918-1939, edited by E. L. Woodward and Rohan Butler, *Third Series,* Volumes II, III and IV, (London, 1949-1951).

Bulletin—

The Department of State Bulletin, U. S. Government Printing Office, (Washington, D. C.).

DGFP—

Documents on German Foreign Policy 1918-1945, Series D, Volumes II and IV, (Washington, D. C., 1949 and 1951).

HFR—

Papers and Documents Relating to the Foreign Relations of Hungary. Vol. I, 1919-20. Edited by Francis Deák and Dezsö Ujváry. Vol. II, January to August, 1921, edited by Dezsö Ujváry. Published by the Royal Hungarian Ministry for Foreign Affairs. (Budapest, 1939 and 1946).

Hungary and the Conference of Paris, Vol. II—

Hungary's International Relations Before the Conference of Paris; Hungaro-Czechoslovak Relations Papers and Documents Relating to the Preparation of the Peace and to the Exchange of Population Between Hungary and Czechoslovakia. Published by the Hungarian Ministry for Foreign Affairs, (Budapest, 1947).

Hungary and the Conference of Paris, Vol. IV—

Hungary at the Conference of Paris, Papers and Documents Relating to the Czechoslovak Draft Amendments Concerning the Transfer of 200,000 Hungarians from Czechoslovakia to Hun-

gary. Published by the Hungarian Ministry for Foreign Affairs, (Budapest, 1947).

La Hongrie et La Conférence de Paris, Tome 1er—

Les Rapports Internationaux de la Hongrie Avant la Conférence de Paris. Notes Introductives. — Notes Concernant les Relations Hungaro-Roumaines. —Protection des Minorités.—Notes Adressées au Conseil des Ministres des Affaires Étrangères. Published by the Hungarian Ministry for Foreign Affairs, (Budapest, 1947).

Selected Documents—

Paris Peace Conference, 1946, Selected Documents, published by the Department of State, (Washington, no date).

Table of Contents

LIST OF MAPS

Part I

Background and Developments until 1945

I. STRUGGLE ALONG THE DANUBE.

Eastern European affairs have been vital to the security of the Western World. The history of this area had been one of almost continuous turmoil, dating from the glories of the old Roman Empire down to the erection of the Iron Curtain. Dividing lines of two worlds have been drawn more than once across this region full of small nationalities which remember intensely their glories of yore and cherish embittered nationalistic feelings, if not hatred against their neighbors. In modern times powerful external forces have repeatedly used the conflicting national aspirations of the small nations for their own purposes. It is not by pure accident that the sparks of two world wars were ignited in Eastern Europe.

In this region lie the Carpathian mountains, the easternmost bulwark of western civilization. With its compact form and a readily defensible mountain arc, the Carpathian or Middle Danube Basin controls the two main gateways between the Russian steppes and Western Europe.[1] In this danger zone the Danubian pillar of European security, the Austrian-Hungarian Monarchy, was destroyed in the First World War.

The European state system was based on the coexistence of great powers, one of which was located strategically in the Danubian area. Its dissolution in 1918 fatally weakened the power structure of central Eastern Europe. The path lay open for a Central European Power to move toward the East and for an Eastern Power to move toward Western Europe.

Since time immemorial, the Danubian region has been a highway of migrating peoples and a focus of conflicts. The frontiers of the Roman Empire once reached the Danube. After the apocalyptic days of the Empire's disintegration, at least a dozen major nations lived in and fought for this valuable area during the period of the great migrations.[2]

The Magyars crossed the Carpathian mountains at the end of the ninth century and, after a period of adventures, during the course of which some of the tribes roamed as far as the Pyrenees, they created a well organized state in the Middle Danube basin. Since the Magyars were ethnically different from their neighbors, they formed a wedge between the various groups of the Northern and Southern Slavs, and Hungary became a buffer state between Germans, Slavs and eventually Rumanians. Historic Hungary enjoyed natural geographic boundaries, for the Carpathians have proved to be one of the most enduring frontiers in Europe.[3]

THE SITUATION AND ROLE OF THE CARPATHIANS IN THE DEFENSE OF EUROPE AGAINST EASTERN IMPERIALISM

1. First strategic defense line of Europe.
2. Second strategic defense line of Europe.
3. Third strategic defense line of Europe.
4. Important gaps in defense lines.
5. Main strategic attack lines of the Soviet Union.
6. Lines of attack by the Soviet after breaking through first defense line.
7. Naval attack lines of the Soviet Union.
8. Important cities (marked by their first letters.
9. Straits of strategic importance.
10. The Carpathian mountain arc (solid black).
11. Other important mountain areas (dotted).
12. "F" stands for the Door of Focsani, 45 miles broad between the Carpathians and the Danube marshlands close to its estuary.
13. "W" stands for Warsaw, the strategic city governing the 300-miles-broad-gap between the Carpathians and the Baltic Sea (Gdansk-Warsaw-Krakow Gap).
14. "M" stands for Moscow, center of Soviet imperialism.

The first strategic defense line was broken by the Soviet Union in World War II. The possession of the Carpathian Basin now enables the Soviet:

    a. to attack at any time the second defense line with its strategic points: The Skagerrak, the Rhine region, the Ljubljana-Trieste Gap, the Strait of Otranto (here the Soviet stands already through the occupation of Albania) and the Straits (Dardanelles and Bosporus) .

    b. to close, more effectively, the Gap of Warsaw and the Door of Focsani.

4

Shortly after the foundation of the state, the Hungarians were forced to take sides in the great competition between Eastern and Western ideologies and political systems.

Throughout the tenth century Byzantine religious and political influence was strong in Hungary. However, the still Pagan ruler Géza and especially his son, the first Hungarian King, St. Stephen, turned their people definitely westward. Hungary embraced Christianity and King Stephen, in the year 1000, obtained the Holy Crown from Pope Sylvester II. The attachment to Rome created a lasting connection with the West and Hungary became and remained an outpost of Western culture.[4]

The prosperous Hungarian Kingdom had to defend itself against Byzantium from the south,[5] German and Venetian pressure from the west, and recurring invasion from the east.[6] Since the twelfth century Croatia, as an associated state, was attached to the Crown of St. Stephen. The Roman Catholic religion and similar political institutions greatly facilitated the union of and cooperation between Croatia and Hungary proper.

East and south from Hungary's frontiers the Orthodox world began. North from Hungary Poland formed a bulwark of Western European culture and civilization. To the northwest, Bohemia played an important role in Central European politics. The histories of Hungary, Poland and Bohemia are somewhat similar, although, due largely to geography, their fate differed. The existence of these strong powers in this critical zone proved to be a benefit to the whole of Europe. Hungary with her solid frontiers maintained complete independence toward East and West and did not become a member of the Holy Roman Empire. After an era of generally favorable developments, which lasted from the eleventh to the sixteenth century, Hungary, like Bohemia and much later Poland, suffered a decline of political and social leadership.[7]

During this period of decline Southeastern Europe became a battlefield between Western Christianity and Islam. The wars fought by Hungary against the Ottoman Empire lasted more than three centuries. In the fifteenth century the Ottoman Empire reached the lines of the Danube and Save rivers and consolidated its rule in the lower Danube valley. After the capture of Constantinople in 1453, the Sultan attacked the important Hungarian outpost, Nándorfehérvár, the present day Belgrade. At the time the Turks were repelled and Hungarians remained free for another generation.[8] However, in the following century, under the renewed aggression of Islam, Hungary collapsed.

Louis Jagiello, King of Hungary and Bohemia, died in the fateful battle of Mohács fought against the Turks in 1526. After his death the

Habsburg family successfully claimed both the Hungarian and Bohemian thrones. Another consequence of the battle of Mohács was the Turkish occupation of two-thirds of Hungary. Buda was under Turkish yoke for nearly 150 years. The Great Hungarian Plain became a Turkish province, and Upper and Western Hungary together with Croatia passed under Habsburg rule; Transylvania, in recent times the bone of contention between Hungary and Rumania,[9] existed as a semi-independent principality, generally tributary to the Sultan.[10]

The political dismemberment of Hungary was undoubtedly aggravated by religious dissension. The majority of the Hungarian nobility and their serfs had become Calvinist by the end of the sixteenth century. Even after the successful Counter-Reformation lead by Péter Cardinal Pázmány in the seventeenth century, a substantial percentage of Hungarians remained Protestant. Calvinism considered itself "the Hungarian religion" in the face of the pro-Habsburg Catholic Church. But religious intolerance generally was not as exaggerated in Hungary as in the Western European countries. In this troublesome period the Catholic and Protestant political leaders of the Hungarian nation cooperated most of the time on basic national issues. An outstanding example of such cooperation was the relationship between the leader of the Counter-Reformation in Hungary, Péter Cardinal Pázmány, and the Calvinist ruler of Transylvania, Gabriel Bethlen. In a famous letter Pázmány asked for Bethlen's goodwill "lest the German spit under our collar."

The Turkish wars had been fought mostly in the plains and on the hillsides, densely populated by Magyars. Consequently, many centers of Magyar culture were annihilated. The inhabitants were killed or taken as slaves to Asia Minor. Towns, villages and forests burned to ashes, and fertile lands became as deserts. Areas inhabited by non-Magyars were of a more peripheral location, mostly in the mountainous regions, and were far less damaged. The destroyed Magyar population was replaced by Serbs and Rumanians, particularly in the southern districts. They could move freely, for under Turkish rule no frontier or obstacle of any kind existed between the Balkans and Hungary.

Hungary ultimately survived the Turkish wars and occupation, but was so gravely weakened that she never recovered her former power and independence. The Hungarian constitution provided opportunities for some opposition to the Habsburgs. This opposition occasionally resulted in open resistance, plots and uprisings. None was successful. Even the great insurrection of Francis Rákóczi II, failed.[11]

The liberated territories in southern Hungary were administered directly from Vienna and the Viennese Government directed a large-scale colonization policy. Immigrants and settlers came from all over

Europe, and Slovaks from Upper Hungary.[12] The majority consisted of Germans, Rumanians and Slovaks, but also included in the migratory group were French, Italian, Catalan, Armenian, Bulgarian and other settlers. Some immigrants were granted huge properties in the liberated territories, creating a new non-Magyar aristocracy. In the course of the gradual destruction of the Turkish conqueror, the Austrian Empire thus acquired and populated new territories. Her position along the banks of the Danube was no longer threatened from the Balkan peninsula.

The growth of nationalism in Hungary began with the use of the vernacular. Until the early nineteenth century Latin was the official language of administration. But the Hungarian Diet in 1830 passed a law requiring officials to know the Magyar language, and in 1844 Magyar replaced Latin altogether, and became the exclusive language of the legislature and administration.

In the reform period (1830-1848), the Diet gradually transformed Hungary into a modern state. The Acts of 1848 swept away many remainders of feudalism and established a government responsible to parliament. Liberal legislation and establishment of constitutional government, however, did not satisfy the national aspirations of the non-Magyar peoples in Hungary.[13] Nor could these reforms be tolerated by the absolutistic Austrian Empire. In this complex situation Vienna became the ally of the non-Magyar nationalities and incited them against the new Hungarian regime established under the leadership of Lajos Kossuth. In the ensuing armed conflict the Croats, Serbians, and Rumanians took a stand against Hungary. The Hungarian Parliament dethroned the Habsburgs and issued a Declaration of Independence on April 14, 1849. Kossuth became president. Although the majority of the Slovaks and Ruthenians supported Kossuth or remained indifferent in the struggle, and some other nationalities, especially Poles, fought for a free Hungary, eventually the Austrian Empire with the aid of a Russian army crushed Hungarian independence.[14]

The Hungarian war of independence was watched with sympathy in the western world. Notwithstanding, Kossuth's Hungary did not receive any effective political support from the West. Only the United States of America intended to recognize Kossuth's regime as a *de facto* government but independent Hungary was destroyed before the American agent reached the country.[15] The general western European attitude toward Hungary was expressed by Lord Palmerston, who in the course of a debate in the House of Commons concerning the Russian invasion of Hungary had declared, on July 21, 1849, that Austria was a most important element in the balance of European power, and explained that:

7

Austria stands in the center of Europe, a barrier against encroachment on the one side, and against invasion on the other. The political independence and liberties of Europe are bound up, in my opinion, with the maintenance and integrity of Austria as a great European Power; and therefore anything which tends by direct or even remote contingency to weaken and to cripple Austria, but still more to reduce her from the position of a first-rate power to that of a secondary state, must be a great calamity to Europe, and one which every Englishman ought to deprecate and try to prevent.[16]

Kossuth went into exile in Turkey. In the West he was considered a champion of liberty and democratic ideas, and was especially popular in the English speaking countries. In 1851 he was invited to the United States, and left Turkey on an American gunboat. After a successful speaking tour in Great Britain, he sailed to New York where he met with great popular enthusiasm and official honors, as Lafayette had before him. During his stay in the United States he was presented to the Senate and to the House of Representatives. In Washington numerous official receptions were organized in his honor. Altogether, Kossuth delivered over three hundred public addresses throughout the United States.[17] Later he settled down in Italy and sought in vain to direct the winds of European politics into the sails of Hungarian independence.[18]

Activities and plans of an exile had no influence whatever on developments in Danubian Europe. Russia loomed increasingly as a formidable great power, and the Slav nationalities of the Danubian Empire looked to her for help and encouragement. The development of Pan-Slav nationalist ideas afforded a convenient vehicle for unofficial Russian intervention.[19] Prior to the nineteenth century the Turkish danger had created a common interest in defense among the peoples of the Monarchy. In the course of the gradual disappearance of this threat nationalism developed along the Danube, and Holy Russia came to be considered by most of the Slavs in a somewhat romantic way as a benevolent "Big Brother" and not as a danger.[20]

Meanwhile the center of gravity of the Habsburg Monarchy was definitely shifted to the East. After Austria suffered defeat at the hands of the combined Italian and French forces on the battlefield of Solferino (1859), and at the hands of the Prussians at Sadowa (1866), she was ejected from both Italy and Germany. In the course of the unification of the German States, her place as a power in the West was taken by Prussia.

After these defeats the territory of Austria became smaller than that of Hungary, and under the new power conditions the importance of the strategic location of the latter was more fully recognized than ever. One of the consequences of this new development was the famous *Ausgleich,* the compromise of 1867, which established the Dual Monarchy.[21] The Kingdom of Hungary was placed on a par with Austria. The basis of this compromise was the establishment of three common services; foreign policy, war and finance. A minister common to both countries was appointed to control each of the three ministries, and was responsible to delegations elected annually by the respective parliaments of Austria and Hungary.

The new constitutional arrangement gave a definite advantage to the Germans and Magyars in political matters. This fact, coupled with the anachronistic political structure of the Monarchy, was the chief cause of the growing dissatisfaction which existed particularly among the Slav and Rumanian nationalities. The intransigeance of Hungarian nationalism contributed to the weakening of the Monarchy and, in the decades preceding 1918, was a serious obstacle to all large-scale reforms along federative lines.

In Hungary the Nationalities Law of 1868 was a very liberal legislative measure. "It is certainly one of the best nationality laws that have ever been drafted; the League of Nations Minority Treaties which have drawn very largely upon it for inspiration, fall far short of it in generosity." [22] The provisions of the law, however, were only partly carried out. And irrespective even of the non-execution of the law, the minority nationalities were not satisfied because the law guaranteed only individual rights to the members of the various nationality groups and did not grant the desired local autonomies and other corporate rights. Later a policy of Magyarization was followed and the spirit of the Nationality law was applied even less than its letter.[23] The fact that Rumanian and Slav irredentist movements were fomented abroad did not incite the Hungarian governments to a more liberal nationality policy.[24]

Russia supported the Slav nationalist movements both in Austria and Hungary with increasing vigor, for the Habsburg Empire had been one of the chief stumbling blocks to Russian expansion in the Balkans. At the Congress of Berlin the Austrian-Hungarian Monarchy in cooperation with the Western powers prevented establishment of Russian predominance in the Balkans. But then the German *Drang nach Osten* policy sought to make the Danubian and Balkan regions the first stepping stones toward the Middle-East. The Berlin-Bagdad railway was one of the primary aims of German expansion. This in turn threatened British control of India. The expansion of the German navy challenged

9

Great Britain even more.

With the formation of the Triple Alliance and the Triple Entente, a rigid bi-polar balance of power—a "two-power world"—appeared in Europe. Tension increased dangerously after the annexation of Bosnia-Herzegovina and a conflagration became almost inevitable. Neither the traditional means of diplomacy nor the personal relations between the monarchs could prevent the outbreak of the First World War. The self-destruction of the western state system began.

II. CONSEQUENCES OF THE FIRST WORLD WAR.

One of the momentous results of the First World War was the dismemberment of the Austrian-Hungarian Monarchy. The peacemakers of 1919, instead of reforming the antiquated political structure of the Danubian Empire on a democratic and federative basis, created small successor states dominated by jingo-nationalism. At the peace table the Allied and Associated Powers, still under the spell of their own wartime propaganda, did not even endeavor to maintain the unity of the Danubian area in one form or another. The subsequent unfortunate situation in this region was only the natural consequence of this territorial dismemberment and of the lip service paid at the peace settlement to some of the principles of President Wilson. This destruction of the Eastern bastion of the European state system not only proved foolhardy for the victors of 1918, but was, eventually, catastrophic for all the nations of Western civilization.

By virtue of the peace treaties of St. Germain and Trianon, the territory was divided among Austria, Czechoslovakia, Yugoslavia, Italy, Hungary, Poland and Rumania. Some of these states inherited much of the complex nationality pattern of the Monarchy, but none of the states possessed the fallen Monarchy's economic advantages. The new settlement opened the door to political and economic nationalism on a scale unheard of before. The roles changed. German and Magyar supremacy was wiped out and some of the oppressed peoples became the oppressors.

The dismemberment of the Monarchy was a flagrant contradiction to the general trend of world evolution which favored economic integration, a necessary consequence of the growing interdependence of nations. Destruction of the Danubian Empire created a vacuum of power in the Danubian area, thereby flinging open a strategic gateway of Europe.[1] In the light of the political events of the last thirty years, it is commonplace to say that its destruction, without adequate substitution, was probably one of the greatest diplomatic errors in modern history.[2] Winston Churchill was fully justified in calling the complete break-up of the Empire a "cardinal tragedy." [3] Anthony Eden recently expressed the opinion that: "The collapse of the Austro-Hungarian Empire was a calamity for the peace of Europe. If the countries that formed it could one day find some arrangement that would allow them to work together again in a happy association, how welcome this would be." [4] Such statements emanating from outstanding British statesmen are all the more significant since the secret treaties concluded by Great Britain and

11

France during the First World War and the wartime policy and propaganda of the same powers were instrumental, if not decisive, in bringing about the collapse of the Monarchy and the establishment of a small state system in the Danubian area.

Although Oscar Jászi, a distinguished student of the nationality problems of Austria-Hungary, has written that the dissolution of the Monarchy was not a mechanical but an organic process,[5] and although many facts support this view, there are some facts to the contrary.[6] A fundamental reorganization of the Monarchy, along democratic and federative lines, would, in any event, have been necessary.[7] Although in the last period of the war the discontent of the nationalities was stirred up by various means, important cohesive forces still existed. The armies of the Monarchy everywhere stood on foreign soil. With the exception of a considerable part of the Czech army groups, the nationalities of the Monarchy by and large fought well, despite war-weariness, economic hardships, growing Allied propaganda and Allied preponderance.[8] Although composed of many nationalities, the administration and especially the foreign service fulfilled their task loyally until the last.[9]

In the light of these and some other evidences, then, one might say that the collapse of the Monarchy was not entirely self-inflicted. Social and political reforms and federalization probably could have revitalized the Monarchy. Serious discontent existed, and revolutionary movements were encouraged and fomented from outside, but the change of attitude by the victorious Western powers was the decisive factor.[10] The leaders of the various nationalities received encouragement, support, and even instructions from abroad. The chance of being able to switch from the defeated camp to that of the victorious powers had a strong appeal to all nationalities. Under these conditions and prospects the discontented nationalities themselves had no particular reason to remain with the old Monarchy. It is therefore somewhat understandable that most of the nationalities, irrespective of other political considerations, eventually preferred to belong to the victorious Allied nations.[11]

In Hungary the government declared on October 16, 1918, that the dual system with Austria had ended and that only personal union existed between the two countries. Soon revolutionary movements broke out and a National Council formed. King Charles, on October 31, appointed Count Michel Károlyi as Prime Minister. Károlyi was a rich aristocrat but a staunch left-wing politician with an outspoken pro-Entente and anti-German record. He attempted to bring about a compromise with the nationalities, within a democratic Hungarian state. His minister of nationalities, Oscar Jászi, advocated the formation of an "Eastern Switzerland" in historic Hungary. In this spirit the new regime tried to persuade the nationalities to live together in a commonwealth.[12] These actions came too late, for the victorious great powers had promised complete independence to them.

The Croat Parliament at Zagreb decided, on October 29, to sever constitutional relations with Hungary and Austria. A National Assembly of the Rumanians in Alba Julia (Gyulafehérvár) decided, on December 1, upon the unification of all Rumanians in one state.[13]

King Charles surrendered the reins of government on November 13, 1918, but did not abdicate. Hungary was proclaimed a "People's Republic" on November 16, 1918, and the Hungarian National Council elected Count Michel Károlyi President of the Republic in January, 1919.

In a recent publication, a British historian has remarked, concerning Károlyi's failure, that "Unfortunately for Hungary and for Central Europe, Károlyi was not Masaryk: he had not carried his peoples with him." [14]

Nevertheless, in the cases of Károlyi and Masaryk, popular support was not the primary or decisive factor. Masaryk enjoyed the full support of the Allied powers, and this Allied support—rather than the opinion of the Czech people—assured Czechoslovakia the status of a victorious nation. Károlyi, however, was openly rebuffed and humiliated by the Entente powers and could not give anything to the Magyars, or, for that matter, to the other nationalities. The occupation of Hungarian territories by the successor states was authorized by the Supreme Council of the Allied powers in Paris. The Rumanian, Yugoslav, and Czech armies violated even these prescriptions by advancing beyond the demarcation lines. This situation foreshadowed the territorial provisions of the Treaty of Trianon, that is, the loss of considerable territories inhabited by Magyars.

Károlyi frankly admitted that his confidence in the Entente powers and in the principles of President Wilson had been misplaced and, in desperation, he resigned his office of President of the Hungarian Republic. The succeeding Communist regime of Béla Kun (March-July, 1919) created general fear of the spread of Bolshevism all over Europe.[15] In addition, the Communist Republic, to win popular support, lost no time in organizing an army, which overran a substantial part of Slovakia and attacked the Rumanians. All these happenings, particularly the Bolshevist rule and subsequent reaction, did not make Hungary popular in Western Europe.[16]

Although at the peace settlement the Monarchy was destroyed in the name of the self-determination of peoples, this principle was grossly violated in practice. None of the nationalities living within the former

13

Monarchy was allowed to express its will through a plebiscite. Only the treaty of St. Germain provided for a plebiscite in a small area of Carinthia. The Slovene majority there decided to join with defeated Austria, instead of with the newly created victorious state of the Serbs, Croats and Slovenes.[17] This case did not justify the principle of nationality solemnly proclaimed at Paris as the principle of the new *status quo*. The Hungarian peace delegation futilely proposed plebiscites in territories to be detached from Hungary by the peace treaty.

In an answer given in the name of the Allies on May 5, 1920, Premier Millerand of France explained that plebiscites were unnecessary because their result would not be substantially different from the condition established by the peacemakers.[18]

Eventually the peace treaties shifted 38,000,000 of the 52,000,000 inhabitants of the Monarchy into countries belonging to the victors. Only small Austria (6,289,380) and Hungary (7,615,117) were considered as defeated states, and treated as such. Winston Churchill characterized the absurd situation as follows: "Two soldiers have served side by side sharing in common cause the perils and hardships of war. The war is ended and they return home to their respective villages. But a frontier line has been drawn between them. One is a guilty wretch, lucky to escape with life the conqueror's vengeance. The other appears to be one of the conquerors himself." [19]

The internal political structure of Austria-Hungary was obsolete, but the Empire still held advantages. It was located in the most strategically important region of Europe, and comprised an area greater than that of any European state, save Russian, with a common tariff and currency. Thus the 52,000,000 inhabitants of the Monarchy could trade freely over an area of 267,239 square miles.[20] In the ten years preceding the first World War, the money income in Austria increased by 86 percent and in Hungary by 92 percent: the increase in the real income per head was 63 percent in Austria and 75 percent in Hungary. This rate of increase was much more rapid than in Great Britain or Germany.[21] Despite many adverse political factors, the advantages of the great internal market and the natural division of labor among the different parts of the Empire resulted in a rapid rise in wealth, shared in by all nationalities.

But the nationality struggle in the Danubian Empire was a serious and baffling problem to Western observers. Under the impact of this complicated and often ugly picture, it was rather easy to forget wider horizons, and to overlook the fact that the existence of a Danubian great power was both a benefit to its own people and a necessity for the European state system. In June, 1946, the late Jan Masaryk was to tell

14

Sir Alfred Duff Cooper, then British Ambassador to France, that "Czechoslovakia had never been so happy as when forming part of the Austro-Hungarian Empire." Sir Alfred Duff Cooper thought this a tragic admission on the part of the son of Thomas Masaryk, commenting: "Time has given it proof. It is surely now generally recognized that the disappearance of the Austro-Hungarian Empire has proved to be one of the major calamities of this disastrous century." [22]

From the point of view of the European state system the victorious powers committed a fundamental mistake in failing to compel the new Danubian states to form a federal state not incompatible with the re-establishment of an independent Poland. This would have enabled the Danubian peoples and the Poles, together, later to resist pressure or invasion by outside forces. At that time the potential opponents of such a scheme, the neighboring great states of Germany and Russia, did not exist as power factors. Thus the victorious Western powers had practically a free hand in Eastern Europe. Of course the extreme nationalism of the leaders of the new states still remained an obstacle to any new form of integration. But the peacemakers had the necessary means at their disposal to check the intransigent nationalism of the governments of the new states. It would not have been difficult to make their recognition and support dependent on the maintenance of Danubian unity in one form or another. The lack of foresight of the victorious allies paved the way for Hitler's aggressive policy in Eastern Europe and eventually opened wide the door for Russian penetration.

All the newly created Danubian states, whether victorious or defeated, besides falling into political chauvinism, followed the policy of an exaggerated protectionism. They erected high tariff walls and engaged, from time to time, in economic wars. The general result was a rise in unemployment and the cost of living, and a decline in national income. As Frederick Hertz later pointed out, "progress achieved in one field was as a rule offset by retrogression in another." [23]

There were a few vague endeavors towards integration but these did not prove successful. Certain sections of the Treaty of St. Germain, and of the Treaty of Trianon opened the way for negotiating preferential trade agreements,[24] but in the hostile political atmosphere these negotiations proved fruitless, as did Tardieu's endeavors in 1932, which promised France's financial assistance in the event of preferential trade agreements being concluded between the Danubian States.

Co-operation in the sphere of agriculture, proposed at the Bucharest Conference of 1930 between Yugoslavia, Rumania and Hungary; the attempt at economic collaboration by the member states of the Little Entente according to the provisions of an agreement reached in February,

15

1933; and the Rome Protocols signed by Austria, Hungary and Italy in March, 1934, should all be considered short-lived expedients brought about by momentary exigencies. These agreements could not achieve tangible and lasting success. They could not substitute for true economic collaboration between the Danubian countries. The failure of such endeavors as these made it clear that, without a reasonable settlement of basic political issues, durable cooperation in economic fields could not be established.

Politically, it has often been claimed that Soviet Russia easily conquered and transformed the Danubian area because she found there a vacuum of power. The vacuum of power was created in 1919. The new political system established along the banks of the Danube was a weak superstructure, without solid foundation, and could not fill either the political or the economic place of the Monarchy in the international community. The expectations attached to the creation of small national states in the Danubian Valley did not materialize. The new states could not develop sufficient cohesive force, could not bring about an effective cooperation among themselves, and were swept away.[25]

Though American intervention in the first World War was accompanied by a proclamation of lofty political ideas—"to make the world safe for democracy"—the new Danubian order, sometimes called the Balkanization of the Danubian area, did not help toward establishing political democracies.[26] In some of the successor states retrograde political conditions and corruption reached a point altogether unknown in the Monarchy. In Yugoslavia, for example, the leader of the Croatian opposition party, Stefan Raditch, and two other Croatian deputies, actually were shot while in a session of Parliament in June, 1928. In most of the successor states, political democracy remained meaningless to the masses, which were ruled by pseudo-parliamentary regimes or by outright dictatorships. Only Czechoslovakia was considered in the West as a notable exception in this respect. This country received the lion's share of the Monarchy and considerable financial support from abroad. But while the balanced economic and social conditions, the well-known administrative qualities of the Czechs, and the industrial skill of the Sudeten Germans facilitated the functioning of democratic political institutions, political democracy alone could not assure the independence and survival of Czechoslovakia in the serious crises of 1938 and 1944-48.[27]

Despite the existence of the League of Nations, which was to end alliance-making throughout the world, alliances multiplied in Eastern Europe. France attempted to consolidate the new territorial settlement by her alliance with Poland and by supporting the alliance concluded between Czechoslovakia, Yugoslavia and Rumania, known as the Little

Entente. Opposition to this alliance resulted in close cooperation among Austria, Hungary, and Italy. The Little Entente, the Balkan Entente and the Hungaro-Italo-Austrian combination, however, could not survive the soon resurgent and overwhelming outside force from Germany and Russia.[28]

The fact that jingo-nationalist, but internally weak and quarrelling, small states would not be able to check the overwhelming outside forces was disregarded by the peacemakers after the First World War. The might of Germany and Russia existed potentially even in the 1920's. Perhaps Austrian and Hungarian statesmanship had made a poor showing in the decades preceding the destruction of the Dual Monarchy, but the peacemakers of 1919 and the leaders of the successor states between the World Wars certainly surpassed them in political shortsightedness. This has been demonstrated *ad oculos* by the outcome of their policies in the Danubian area.

The political structure of the multi-national Empire may have been antiquated, but the new order proved to be less stable and offered less security for the Danubian people and for the whole of Europe. In one man's lifetime the Danubian nations experienced the destruction of three international and domestic orders. *Peccatur intra muros et extra muros.* In the course of these events, almost all nationalities committed errors and mistakes. Although one cannot turn back the wheels of history, the positive and negative teaching of these manifold experiences, if examined with mutual understanding and humility, might suggest some solutions for the future. Probably the advantages of a great political and economic unit combined with the benefits of democratic equality, extended to all nationalities, might open the door for better developments after the ordeal of the present period.

III—HUNGARY BETWEEN THE WORLD WARS.

The Peace Treaty

Hungary's status after the first World War was particularly difficult. After the defeat and disintegration of the Red Army of Béla Kun, Rumanian troops occupied Budapest and the major part of the country.[1] The occupation was accompanied by extensive looting, which caused damages of almost three billion gold crowns.[2] This was followed by a disastrous peace treaty. As Francesco Nitti put it: "By a stroke of irony the financial and economic clauses inflict the most serious burdens on a country which had lost almost everything: which has lost the greatest number of men proportionately in the war, which since the war has had two revolutions, which for four months suffered the sackings of Bolshevism—led by Béla Kun and the worst elements of revolutionary political crime—and, finally, has suffered a Rumanian occupation, which was worse almost than the revolutions of Bolshevism." [3]

Negotiations with Hungary did not precede the peace settlement; the provisions of the treaty were established by the victorious states. Subsequently the Hungarian peace delegation was merely heard on one occasion. The Treaty of Trianon made Hungary the most dissatisfied of all the Danubian states.[4] The Peace Conference decided the claims of the neighboring states put forward against Hungary, but did not consider the cumulative effect of these claims on the new Hungary itself. As one outstanding chronicler of the Peace Conference, Harold Nicolson, points out, the Conference "approached its problems in terms, not of the enemy Powers, but of the respective 'claims' of the succession and smaller States." [5] Dealing with the problem of the Territorial Committees, Nicolson noted the defects in their proceedings, pointing out that the main task of the Committees was not to recommend a general territorial settlement, but to pronounce on the particular claims of certain states.[6] The adverse effects of such a procedure are obvious.

The American recommendations concerning Hungary's frontiers were more favorable than the final provisions of the Trianon Treaty.[7] A member of the American Peace Commission, Professor Archibald C. Coolidge of Harvard, visited Hungary in January of 1919 and prepared a very objective report on the conditions in Hungary and the repercussions to be expected from the projected peace settlement.[8] And as Lloyd George himself pointed out in a memorandum of March 25, 1919, "There will never be peace in Southeastern Europe if every little state now coming into being is to have a large Magyar irredenta within its

18

borders." Therefore he recommended that the different races should be allocated to their motherlands, and that this criterion "should have precedence over considerations of strategy or economics or communications, which can usually be adjusted by other means." [9]

Such considerations were discarded. The frontiers of the new Hungary were fixed principally according to Rumanian, Czechoslovak, and Yugoslav demands, and after consideration of their geographical, strategic, economic and ethnographic arguments. Territories inhabited by Magyars figured as a sort of "no man's land".[10] A remark attributed to Beneš was characteristic of the general atmosphere of the conference. "I am alarmed" Beneš said to a friend, "when I see that they give me everything that I ask for. It is too much." [11]

The upshot of the matter was that the peace settlement was incomparably more severe for Hungary than for Germany or Bulgaria. True, Austria lost even more than Hungary, but Austria was a frequently changing federation of heterogeneous territories gradually acquired by the House of Habsburg and the Germans formed only a little over one-third of its population. Hungary had existed for centuries as a unitary state which demonstrated a remarkable degree of stability and stamina through the vicissitudes of history. The Treaty of Trianon reduced Hungary proper to less than one-third of her former territory and about two-fifths of her population.[12] Over three million Magyars were attached, against their wishes, to the neighboring states. The Hungarian peace delegation vainly proposed a plebiscite for the territories in dispute.[13]

As a result of the territorial changes effected under the peace treaty the population of Hungary decreased to a figure considerably less than the actual number of Magyars residing in Southeastern Europe, while the population of Czechoslovakia, Rumania and Yugoslavia became, in every case, considerably greater than the actual number of any of their respective national groups. This situation is especially evident in the light of the 1910 and 1920 censuses, but it can also be clearly seen from the 1930 censuses which were least favorable to the Magyars.[14]

It is generally known that because of the complication of ethnographic conditions in the Danube Valley it was impossible to establish completely satisfactory frontiers. However, about one and a half million Magyars who lived in compact blocks along the new frontiers were detached from Hungary. This artificial separation could not be justified, even in the eyes of a disinterested observer, let alone to the Hungarian people themselves.

The dissolution of the Monarchy in itself had a very unfavorable effect on the economy of Hungary. The great internal market and balanced economy suddenly ceased to exist. Most of the factories and industrial areas remaining in Hungary were deprived of their markets and were cut off from their sources of raw materials within the neighboring states. In addition, the Trianon frontiers produced a whole series of special economic difficulties. For example, the new frontiers cut in half the areas of twenty-four flood control companies. As a result of the uncooperative attitudes of Czechoslovakia and Rumania, Hungary became exposed to grave risk of floods on the lower reaches of her rivers without being able to establish sufficient protection against them. A careless deforestation policy in both countries increased the flood danger to Hungary. The major part of Hungary is a lowland, and nearly one quarter of the productive area of the country consists of land which had been protected against inundations only at an enormous cost in money and labor. In many cases such troubles could have been avoided by minor frontier rectifications or other suitable arrangements, if Hungary's case had been seriously considered and Hungarian experts had been consulted at the peace settlement.

The general economic difficulties created by the peace settlement were increased by the refugee problem. More than 350,000 Magyars were forced to leave the neighboring states and move to the reduced territory of Hungary. These homeless masses, largely middle-class people, greatly increased Hungary's economic and social difficulties. They also became, as a matter of course, the moving spirits of revisionist movements.

The situation created by the peace treaty would have been unacceptable to any self-respecting people, but the Magyars were particularly proud of having organized and maintained a state on one of the most dangerous spots of Europe for a thousand years. Their bitterness was made even greater by their conviction that after Hungary had defended the whole of Europe against invasions in the past—a claim asserted by a number of the countries of Eastern Europe—the West had, so to speak, "stabbed them in the back."

The Magyars looked with great confidence to the United States and especially to the principles promulgated by President Wilson.[15] However, the vindictive peace settlement imposed by the victors in the name of democracy gave that term a rather doubtful meaning to many Magyars. It seemed to them that, at the peace table, the lofty principles were applied only against them and never in their favor. Trianon had a harmful effect in domestic politics as well. It gave an evil connotation to the term "democracy", and indirectly retarded democratic forces in the country.

Consolidation of the Status Quo.

After the upheavals of the revolutionary years of 1918-1919, the National Assembly, in March, 1920, elected Admiral Nicholas Horthy as Regent.[16] Hungary remained a monarchy with the kingship in abeyance. The Treaty of Trianon was signed on June 4, 1920, and ratified by Hungary under pressure from the great powers on November 13, 1920.

The period preceding the ratification of the peace treaty was eventful in Hungarian foreign politics. Early in 1920 confidential parleys took place between France and Hungary.[17] These were followed by formal negotiations. French foreign policy endeavored to bring about a Danubian integration. In connection with this plan France was inclined to support Hungarian claims aimed at correcting some of the territorial provisions of the Trianon Treaty.[18] The French High Commissioner in Budapest, Maurice Fouchet, declared that France was determined to base her whole policy in Southeastern Europe upon Hungary as a pivot.[19] In return Hungary was expected to give important concessions to France. These included leasing the Hungarian State Railways and Railway Locomotive Works, the exploitation of navigation on the Danube by a French concern, the building of a Danube port in Budapest by Schneider-Creusot, and the transfer of control over the Hungarian Credit Bank to a French financial syndicate. This bank owned a considerable part of Hungarian industry. The French negotiator, Maurice Paléologue, secretary general of the Quai d'Orsay, was supported by Prime Minister Millerand, but many influences worked at cross purposes. The Franco-Hungarian negotiations provoked Italian and British protests, and Hungary's neighbors were greatly alarmed.

Since official French documents have not yet been published, the ultimate French objectives in these negotiations are not quite clear. Isolated Hungary obviously hoped that an understanding with France might improve her international situation. Paléologue gradually played down the prospects of a long-term Franco-Hungarian *rapprochement* and promised assistance to Hungary in negotiating with her neighbors for friendly settlements. Eventually the pro-Hungarian French policy in Danubian Europe was abandoned. Paléologue resigned in September, 1920. His successor, Philip de Berthelot, energetically supported a maintenance of the *status quo*. This remained thereafter the main line of French foreign policy.

One of the results of the Franco-Hungarian *rapprochement* may have been the vague promise inserted in the Covering Letter of Millerand which was transmitted to the Hungarian peace delegation with the draft peace treaty on May 6, 1920.[20] But the Hungarian public greatly

21

overestimated the extremely cautious passage of the letter which mentioned possible revision of the frontiers, and disappointment was great when the commissions of delimitation later recommended only a few minor frontier rectifications.

Another important development of the postwar years was the formation of the Little Entente, an alliance system almost completely encircling Hungary. The creator of the Little Entente was Eduard Beneš, who foresaw the Hungarian reactions to the Trianon settlement and began negotiations with Yugoslav and Rumanian representatives as early as the end of 1918. Yugoslavia and Rumania shared Beneš' feelings towards Hungary, but were reluctant at first to conclude a formal alliance with Czechoslovakia. A treaty of alliance concluded between Czechoslovakia and Yugoslavia on August 14, 1920, and directed against Hungary, was the first success of Beneš' policy. Two attempts by King Charles to return to the Hungarian throne gave impetus to the movement among Hungary's neighbors for further integration.[21]

The concept of the Little Entente was not viewed with sympathy by re-established Poland—a state which was to become an important factor in Eastern Europe. Marshal Joseph Pilsudski, President of Poland, and the Polish Foreign Minister, Prince Eustace Sapieha, would have preferred a Polish-Hungarian-Rumanian *rapprochement* with French blessing.[22] Such developments had some chance of success during the Russo-Polish war, which broke out in February, 1920. Even before the outbreak of the war, the Polish Government, anticipating a Bolshevik attack, inquired as to whether the munition factory at Csepel could supply Poland with ammunition.[23] The Hungarian Government reacted positively and later the Minister of National Defense put at Poland's disposal the army's whole reserve of ammunition and instructed the factory at Csepel that for fourteen days, all production should be for the benefit of Poland.[24] Beyond this material assistance, the negative Czechoslovak attitude excluded large-scale military cooperation between Hungary and Poland. Sub-Carpathian Ruthenia was attached to Czechoslovakia, and thus Hungary and Poland had no common frontier. The Poles especially asked for twenty to thirty thousand cavalry troops, which Hungary was not able to supply. But other troops of considerable strategic value were offered.[25] Negotiations continued, but there were great difficulties to overcome. Irrespective of the unfriendly Czech attitude, the disarmament clauses of the peace treaty made major Hungarian assistance an impossibility, and Hungary's neighbors were reluctant to modify the pertinent treaty provisions. Polish diplomacy cautiously supported Hungary and a special Hungarian diplomatic-military mission was dispatched to Paris to obtain French endorsement. The French were inclined to comply with the Hungarian request, but they made their decision conditional upon the approval of the Rumanians and the Czechoslovaks who refused to give their consent. Sapieha informed the Hungarian Government that the chief reason why the Allied Powers declined Hungary's assistance against the Bolsheviks was the refusal of Czechoslovakia to permit the transportation of Hungarian troops. He explained that the Allied Powers were unable to force their will upon Czechoslovakia, thus they preferred to adopt a position of intransigeance toward Hungary rather than to admit their impotency.[26] Eventually it was decided to send Hungarian legions of volunteers to Poland, but due to the favorable turn of the military operations against the Bolsheviks, this plan was not carried out.[27]

The Polish victory over the Red Army in August, 1920, followed by an armistice in October, and the peace treaty of Riga the following March, made military cooperation between Hungary and Poland superfluous. Although relations between the two states remained cordial throughout the interwar period, their international positions and political interests were really widely divergent. While Hungary was the greatest loser of the peace settlement and consequently almost inevitably a revisionist state, Poland was quite naturally a *pro-status-quo* power and an ally of Rumania and France. The manifest political difficulties notwithstanding, however, Polish diplomacy endeavored several times to bring about a reconciliation between Hungary and Rumania. But these attempts met with little success.

The return of King Charles to Hungary in March, 1921, soon further troubled the already difficult waters of Hungary's foreign relations. Charles received French encouragement[28] and appeared unexpectedly in Hungary on March 26, and remained until persuaded to leave the country by Regent Horthy on April 5 of the same year. Nevertheless, the damage was done. Czechoslovakia and Yugoslavia threatened armed intervention, and the great powers lodged protests. Italy also strongly supported the anti-Habsburg campaign.[29] The Hungarian Government considered the return of Charles a matter which concerned Hungary exclusively, but obviously Hungary was not in a position to resist the whole of Europe.

Under the impact of Charles' return, Rumania signed a treaty of alliance with Czechoslovakia on April 23, and with Yugoslavia on June 17, 1921.[30] Charles returned to Hungary for a second time on October 21, 1921, and marched with some Hungarian army units on Budapest. As the military threat of the neighboring states was even more serious than in March, the Hungarian Government resisted by force and interned the King. The Allied powers exiled him to the island of Madeira

23

where he died shortly thereafter. Hungary was, however, obliged to enact a law declaring the dethronement of the House of Habsburg.

The two attempts of Charles to return to the Throne of St. Stephen complicated Hungary's foreign relations in many other respects, and especially increased suspicion among the neighboring countries. Following the signing of the peace treaty the government of Count Paul Teleki succeeded in stabilizing somewhat the internal conditions of the country, and sought to improve relations with the neighboring states. On March 14 and 15, 1921, Prime Minister Count Paul Teleki and Foreign Minister Gustave Gratz negotiated with Beneš in Bruck.[31] The two delegations discussed certain problems connected with the execution of the peace treaty and the larger aspects of political relations between Hungary and Czechoslovakia. The possibility of territorial revisions of the Trianon Treaty was also discussed, and Beneš made interesting suggestions.[32] But, after these negotiations, relations deteriorated between the two countries, although Masaryk himself visualized a close cooperation and even an alliance between Hungary and Czechoslovakia.[33] Negotiations took place again in Marienbad on June 23 and 24, between Beneš and the new Hungarian foreign minister, Count Nicholas Bánffy, but these were restricted to certain technicalities connected with the execution of the peace treaty.[34] Meanwhile, political events in Danubian Europe began to take a course which excluded a sincere reconciliation between Hungary and Czechoslovakia. Masaryk maintained a friendly attitude toward Hungary throughout his presidency and was disposed to make important concessions, including territorial revisions, but Beneš resolutely opposed such a policy.[35]

After the Trianon Treaty became effective, Yugoslavia finally withdrew her troops from the occupied territories in southern Hungary in July, 1921. At the same time, the ratification of the treaty gave rise to an acute tension between Hungary and another neighbor, Austria. Rumania, Czechoslovakia, and Yugoslavia occupied the Hungarian territories promised to them by the principal Allied powers at the close of hostilities, but western Hungary (*Burgenland*) remained under Hungarian administration. Hungary was obliged to transfer this territory to Austria within a month after the treaty entered into force. This placed the government in an extremely embarrassing position, since the Hungarian public bitterly resented this territorial claim, particularly since the war had been fought with Austria as an ally, and the Hungarian Prime Minister, Count Stephen Tisza, was the only leading statesman in the Monarchy who energetically opposed in July, 1914 those diplomatic steps which lead to war.

It was true that the overwhelming majority of the population was

German, but Burgenland had belonged to Hungary for a thousand years. Under pressure from the principal Allied powers Hungary evacuated the region in August, 1921, but immediately after the evacuation irregular detachments took over the territory and ejected Austrian *gendarmerie.*

Italian mediation helped to solve the ensuing deadlock. Under the presidency of the Italian foreign minister, Marchese della Torretta, Hungarian and Austrian representatives met in Venice and signed a protocol providing for a plebiscite in the city of Sopron and in eight small villages. The plebiscite took place and resulted in 15,334 votes for Hungary and 8,227 votes for Austria.[36] Thus occurred the first territorial revision of the Trianon Treaty. After the settlement of this question relations between Austria and Hungary gradually improved.

Meanwhile, following the first attempt of King Charles to recover the Hungarian throne, Count Paul Teleki resigned in April, 1921, and Count Stephen Bethlen took over the government, which he subsequently headed for more than ten years. Bethlen continued the work of internal and external consolidation began by Teleki. They suppressed the counter-revolutionary extremist movements.[37]

Since relations with her neighbors improved to some extent in 1923, Hungary was able to begin financial reconstruction with the help of the League of Nations.[38] A reconstruction loan was floated abroad, the currency was stabilized and the budget balanced. An American citizen, Jeremiah Smith of Boston, became the League's Commissioner-General in Budapest. With his energetic cooperation Hungary made rapid progress on the road to economic recovery.

The government adopted a protective tariff and especially supported the development of textile and manufacturing industries. Increased industrialization was a necessity because Hungary, as an agricultural state, was overpopulated. But the Government failed to carry out an adequate agrarian reform. A large scale agrarian reform was a foremost social necessity; however, this alone could not have solved the economic problems of the country. Bethlen's idea was first to develop an industry and then to carry out an agrarian reform, when the necessary capital had been made available by the Hungarian industry.

Bethlen's conservative administration was supported by a strong parliamentary majority. The franchise was restricted and balloting was secret only in towns, being open in the countryside. Considerable progress was made in the fields of social legislation and public education. Intercultural relations were greatly developed, particularly with western countries, and hundreds of students were sent to foreign universities with the aid of government scholarships.[39]

Hungary gradually concluded a network of commercial and other treaties, and in September, 1922, became a member of the League of Nations. Despite the assistance the League gave in connection with the financial reconstruction of the country, it never became popular in Hungary. The Hungarian political scene was dominated by the idea of revision, and the League was considered, with some justification, as the guardian of the *status quo*. Article XIX of the Covenant theoretically made possible the revision of treaties and the consideration of international conditions whose continuance might endanger the peace of the world, but actually this provision remained a dead letter.

Another cause of dissatisfaction was connected with the fate of the Magyars in the neighboring states. Immediately following the occupation of Hungarian territories, the successor states began to apply oppressive measures against them. These continued with varying intensity throughout the interwar years. The Magyar minority was almost completely cut off from Hungary and even cultural intercourse was barred.[40] The special 'Minority Treaties' provided for certain minimum rights for the minorities; the execution of these provisions was under the ultimate control of the League of Nations. The Hungarian public felt that the League had failed to do its duty in this field. Certain adverse criticism was undoubtedly justified, since the competent organs of the League did not show much interest in this delicate matter, and the procedure had many shortcomings. The Hungarian public did not realize that the very existence of such machinery acted, in many cases, as a restraint upon governments planning oppressive measures against minorities. They saw only the negative side of the League and a spirit of exasperated opposition developed in the country against the whole postwar international order.

During the interwar period the revision of the Trianon Treaty remained an almost inevitable policy of all Hungarian governments. The Hungarian people probably would not have tolerated any government which neglected this program, for all social classes were convinced of the injustices and absurdities of the new peace settlement. The peace treaty was considered the source of all evil. The government authorized the activities of some revisionist associations, since such authorization promised to be a means of controlling the general exasperation and preventing violent outbursts against the Treaty. The aim of these societies was to win world opinion for a peaceful revision of the Peace Treaty by application of Article XIX of the Covenant. Their enthusiastic but rather naive propaganda usually ignored the mentality of foreign countries. The false optimism and emotional exaggerations caused by the Rothermere campaign are the best examples of this mood, so favorable to self-deception.[41]

The Hungarian public enthusiastically received the news in April, 1927, that Bethlen had signed in Rome a treaty of friendship and arbitration with Italy. Although the text followed the usual pattern of treaties of the same nature, it was considered as a break in Hungary's isolated diplomatic position. The Italian orientation of Hungary's foreign policy was further favored by the fact that in the next year Mussolini openly sponsored the Hungarian revisionist case.[42]

From this time on friendship for Italy remained a characteristic feature of Hungarian foreign policy. Bethlen visited Italy again in 1930, and expressed his thanks to Mussolini for the support given to Hungary by the Italian Government during the conference on Eastern reparations.[43]

When the world economic crisis reached Hungary in 1931 and shook the economic structure of the country, Bethlen resigned (August, 1931). His successor, Count Gyula Károlyi, continued Bethlen's Italian orientation,[44] and sought to resolve the crisis by introducing into the budget measures of economy. But world developments further aggravated the economic and financial situation of the country, and resulted in the overthrow of his government (September, 1932). With the resignation of Count Károlyi, the period of old-type conservative policy in Hungary came to an end. Germany was on the eve of revolutionary transformations which in turn affected political developments in Hungary and throughout Europe.

Fateful Years.

The new prime minister, General Gyula Gömbös, was an outstanding representative of the strongly pro-Nazi elements in the Hungarian army. These officers despised the liberal traditions of the Hungarian upper class, cherished great admiration for Mussolini and had a profound sympathy towards the rising Nazi power in Germany. Contempt of democracy, worship of totalitarian methods, and propagandistic use of popular slogans characterized their way of thinking. Even though Gömbös was more of a special fellow traveller than a simon pure Nazi, his confused rhetoric prepared the ground for the eventual spread of extremist slogans. His most fateful contribution was the introduction of politics into the army. He appointed army officers to important posts in the state administration and under his protection extremist secret societies were organized. Nazi ideas took the place of real patriotism in many quarters. Although there were many fine patriots among the Hungarian army officers, few of them were appointed to leading positions during these crucial years. Jingo-nationalist elements of the lower middle class were put into key positions and able persons of independent

27

mind were gradually eliminated from the higher positions of public life.

Another officer full of political ambitions was the mentally un-balanced Major Ferenc Szálasi, the later Arrow Cross[45] leader. Gömbös was much above the intellectual standard of Szálasi and most of the pro-Nazi officers and politicians. He could accommodate himself to political realities, and in spite of his German leanings wanted to be an independent master in Hungary. He soon visited Hitler and main-tained intimate relations with him, but several times he protested strongly to Germany against organizing German minorities in Hungary along Nazi lines, and approved closer cooperation with Italy and Austria to check growing German influence. For the same reason Gömbös visited Marshal Pilsudski and sought to strengthen the ties of Hungary's tra-ditional friendship with Poland.

The result of the pro-Italian policy was the signing by Gömbös, Mussolini and Chancellor Engelbert Dollfus of the three Rome Protocols (March 17, 1934) providing for cooperation among Austria, Hungary and Italy. The first protocol dealt with political matters and established the principle of common consultation. In the second protocol Austria and Italy promised to take measures to overcome the difficulties incurred by Hungary when the prices of grains fell. Moreover, the contracting parties agreed to facilitate transit traffic to the Adriatic ports and to set up a permanent committee to formulate concrete proposals for the development of their economic relations. A third protocol provided for some special aspects of Italo-Austrian economic relations.

The ultimate object of Hungarian diplomacy was to establish an economic union with Austria and Italy. It was thought that this would have solved to a large extent the problem of marketing Hungarian agricultural products. Because of German opposition this goal was never achieved. Although the Rome protocols were of momentary help, they did not solve Hungary's economic difficulties.

While Italo-Austrian-Hungarian cooperation was developing, the Little Entente established permanent political and economic organs among Czechoslovakia, Rumania and Yugoslavia. Besides, Greece, Ru-mania, Turkey and Yugoslavia concluded the Balkan Pact, mutually guaranteeing one another's frontiers on the Balkans and accepting the principle of consultation.

These two groups of states, together with those states involved in the Rome protocols, were composed of members with widely divergent political interests, and with mostly competitive rather than comple-mentary economies. None of these groupings possessed inherent strength. The Danubian situation was characterized from 1919 on by the lack of real power in the area. Exaggerated nationalism and economic forces worked at cross purposes within the area, and outside powers—France and Italy—supported the various states and groups of states.

Since the European power situation underwent fundamental transformations in the 1930's, which revitalized the two really great outside forces, Germany and Russia, and which had strong repercussions in the Danubian Valley, it is necessary to glance at some of these changes.

In these fateful years the impotence of the League of Nations in political matters became obvious. The Four-Power Pact initiated by Mussolini and signed by Great Britain, Germany, France and Italy (June 7, 1933) purported to recreate the old Concert of Europe, but this Pact was not ratified by France and Germany. Thus, the active cooperation of the major representatives of Western European civilization never became a reality. Although Hitler's arbitrary actions gradually isolated Germany, his treaty violations never evoked punitive measures.

The semblance of Western European unity was momentarily established by the common declaration of France, Great Britain and Italy in February, 1934, concerning the maintenance of Austrian independence. Four months later, when Chancellor Dollfuss was killed, Mussolini mobilized, and the Italian army moved to the Brenner Pass.

But Hitler's aggressive policy caused the most fateful changes in the relations between Soviet Russia and the Western world. After Hitler's siezure of power, the Kremlin initiated a *rapprochement* with the Western democracies and instructed the foreign Communist parties to cooperate with Social Democrats and other left-wing parties. In September, 1934, the Soviet Union was admitted into the League of Nations; and Litvinov, who skillfully used the jargon of Geneva, became the champion of collective security. Moreover, the Soviet Union renewed diplomatic relations with the United States of America and concluded treaties of mutual assistance with France and Czechoslovakia. Thus, a Communist state, aiming at the destruction of the Western state system, was accepted as a full-fledged leading member of the family of nations.

Germany's repudiation of the military clauses of the Versailles Treaty (March 1935) caused general consternation in the Western democracies, and France demanded a special session of the League to censure Hitler's action. Before this session, the representatives of Great Britain, France and Italy met at Stresa in April, 1935, and under the chairmanship of Mussolini drafted a resolution for the Council which condemned Germany. They agreed on the necessity of an independent Austria, and reaffirmed their determination to resist aggression. At the same time, however, the British delegation made it clear that Britain "would not consider the possibility of sanctions in the event of Treaty violations."

The French delegation professed similar feelings. Thus Mussolini left the conference with the impression that, in case of a showdown with Germany, Italy would not get effective military help from the Western powers. Moreover, he thought that Italy's actions in Africa would not be resisted beyond verbal protestations. This belief of Mussolini, first gained from earlier contacts with Laval, was strengthened by the attitude of the English and French delegations at Stresa.[46]

But the first serious shock administered to Italy's Stresa policy was the British-German naval agreement, concluded in June, 1935. Such a step could have been part of a wise policy and might have had a beneficial effect in the midst of the growing international tension. Italy and France, however, were not informed of the preceding negotiations, although the agreement was clearly a modification of the Versailles Treaty. Thus it could be considered as another treaty violation committed by Germany—this time with British connivance. The resultant weakening of faith in British reliability, both in Italy and France, contributed to the further general deterioration of the political atmosphere in Europe.

The Ethiopian war (October, 1935), and the sanctions that followed, definitely alienated Italy from the Western powers.[47] The first direct political consequence of Italy's changed relations with France and Great Britain was the German occupation of the Rhineland, a move which immensely strengthened Germany's power position in Eastern Europe. Although Hitler, on this occasion, repudiated the freely negotiated Locarno Treaty, France and Great Britain again satisfied themselves with formal protestations. The Council of the League of Nations branded Germany as a treaty breaker but remained passive. French passivity was particularly strange in that France alone could easily have crushed the German army at this time. Her attitude had the worst possible psychological and strategical effect throughout Europe. It set the pattern for a large-scale appeasement in the West, it opened wide the door for German expansion in the East, and it strengthened pro-Nazi political trends, especially in the Danubian countries.

The occupation of the Rhineland was followed by an Austro-German agreement (July 11, 1936), and by a steady Italo-German *rapprochement*. In October, 1936, the Rome-Berlin Axis was created, and a year later Italy adhered to the Anti-Comintern Pact.[48]

This new situation weakened day by day the political value of Italo-Hungarian-Austrian collaboration, since, economically, Germany could offer much more than Italy. The Hungarian public followed these developments with anxiety as pro-Nazi political forces grew in strength.

In October, 1936, Gömbös died. His successor, as head of the government, was Coloman Darányi, a correct civil servant with little political dynamism. He vaguely followed the policy initiated by his predecessor. Under his weak government Nazi seeds began to grow in Hungarian politics. The demagogic agitations of the various Nazi groups, supported by Germany, made good use of the defects of the social system and the economic difficulties of the country. Anti-semitic slogans became the order of the day.[49] In foreign affairs, Nazi propaganda emphasized the inability of the Western powers to bring about a viable political system in the Danube Valley, and promised that Germany would correct the injustices of Trianon. This political game was greatly strengthened by the eastward economic penetration started by the Third Reich.

The deceptive economic diplomacy of Hitlerite Germany was, as a matter of fact, of great momentary help to Hungary and to the other overwhelmingly agricultural Danubian states, which had been unable to sell their products since the crisis of 1931.[50] Germany solved their marketing problems, and this German "help" resulted in a steady increase of the influence exerted by the Third Reich in these countries. It became apparent only later, that because of ingenious clearing agreements, the Danubian states themselves had to finance exports to Germany. This started an inflation and impoverishment which were camouflaged for a short time by a false prosperity. Mouth organs, aspirin, and other similar commodities soon flooded the Danubian markets, and later the Germans generously exported some scrapped armaments.

In economic matters there were only poor alternatives, but in home politics Darányi finally sought to check the spread of Nazism by dissolving the Arrow Cross Party and imprisoning its leader, Major Szálasi. In the meantime, however, he brought the first anti-Jewish bill before Parliament in the spring of 1938.[51] He was led astray by the vain hope that moderate anti-Semitic measures could dam the rising flood of anti-Semitism, swollen by the Extreme Right.

Meanwhile, Hungarian diplomacy developed further cooperation with Italy,[52] and tentatively explored possibilities of *rapprochement* with neighbors. Various Polish endeavors to bring about a reconciliation between Hungary and Rumania failed. Stakes were too great for both countries.

As early as 1926 Hungary made overtures toward Yugoslavia, and Hungaro-Yugoslav relations were, in general, slightly better than those with Rumania and Czechosloviakia. After the assassination of King Alexander in Marseilles on October 9, 1934, this relationship was greatly disturbed. Yugoslavia accused Hungary, before the Council of the League of Nations, of having supported the Croatian underground movement, and several thousand Magyars were expelled by the Yugoslavs.

Constant Hungaro-Yugoslav negotiations in 1935-1937 did not produce any really positive results, but did improve the somewhat strained relations between the two countries.[53]

Hungary considered Czechoslovakia the weakest Little Entente state and as least capable of resisting revisionist aspirations. Official relations were formally correct but reserved. Meanwhile, private feelers were put out concerning the possibilities of a larger settlement. For example, a Smallholder politician, Paul Auer,[54] repeatedly discussed with Beneš, Foreign Minister Kamil Krofta, and Prime Minister Milan Hodža the problems of Hungaro-Czechoslovak reconciliation. Auer suggested to Krofta the formation of a Hungaro-Austrian-Czechoslovak collaboration or possible union. The leaders of Czechoslovakia's foreign policy stiffly rebuffed these overtures. Krofta explained to Auer that Czechoslovakia would not enter such a tripartite union in which the Austrians and Hungarians would vote together and Czechoslovakia be isolated and relegated to a minority position. In vain Auer tried to persuade him that within a tripartite union Hungary and Austria would not follow an anti-Czechoslovakian policy, but that the position of the member states would shift in the various issues according to their individual interests. Krofta retorted that Czechoslovakia was not afraid of the Germans, with whom they had learned to deal in the past centuries.

Hodža had a very friendly conversation with Auer on June 29, 1938, concerning the amelioration of the fate of the Hungarian minorities. He offered to intervene in Bucharest for a more liberal treatment of the Magyar minorities and added that in this spirit one could negotiate even on territorial adjustments in a few years. Auer, amazed, replied that because of the Germans, there were only a few months, at the utmost, in which to settle the differences between Hungary and Czechoslovakia, and to create a close collaboration in the Danubian Valley. "We are not afraid of Germany" replied Hodža.[55]

Beneš was especially irritated by the pro-Habsburg propaganda of the Hungarian legitimists and declared to Auer—who himself was not a legitimist—that he would prefer *Anschluss* to restoration. Moreover, he put the blame on Hungarian revisionism and contended that Hungary could not be satisfied by minor concessions, which would only stimulate revisionist ambitions.

Actually the extreme revisionist claims were harmful to Hungary's cause abroad and played into the hands of the Little Entente. They used them in persuading the West that Hungarian grievances could not be taken seriously. Meanwhile, Hungarian revisionism had become embittered, and blocked sound political developments in many ways.

Under the influence of Nazi successes and propaganda, the revisionist policy cautiously advocated by Bethlen was openly pursued. This emotional state of mind, however, had an objective cause: the situation brought about by Trianon. Irrespective of the impact of Hitlerism, a real democratic evolution would have been very difficult in Hungary without the removal of some of the economic absurdities and political injustices created by the peace settlement. Reconciliation between Hungary and her neighbors thus was hindered by a sort of vicious circle.

Hungarian diplomacy tried to extricate the country from the German grasp by relying on Italy and Poland. In March, 1936, new protocols were signed with Italy and Austria which bound the three states more closely together than had been the case under the original act of 1934. Horthy visited Victor Emmanuel III (November, 1936) and the visit was returned in Budapest (May, 1937). Both occasions were manifestations of Italo-Hungarian friendship. In February, 1938, Horthy paid an official visit to Warsaw in order to emphasize friendship with Poland. The German orientation of Hungarian foreign policy, however, became almost inevitable, due to the general trend of European events. Representatives of the powers of the Rome protocols met for the last time in January, 1938, in Budapest.[56] After the Austrian Anschluss there was no further possibility of Italo-Hungaro-Austrian collaboration. Germany became Hungary's immediate neighbor and acquired an almost monopolistic position in the Hungarian economy.

The Crisis.

In May, 1938, Darányi was succeeded as premier by Béla Imrédy, a former President of the National Bank of Hungary, and noted up to that time for his liberal views and pro-English sympathies. Imrédy was promptly attacked by the Germans and the extreme right as an Anglophile. This probably was true, but under the influence of European political events Imrédy gradually changed his political views.[57] This excellent financial expert proved to be a poor statesman, and in the latter stage of his Prime Ministership, underwent an amazing transformation in the direction of Nazism. In spite of Imrédy's drift toward a German orientation, Foreign Minister Coloman Kánya, an old career diplomat, succeeded in maintaining the relative independence of Hungarian foreign policy.

Imrédy and Kánya visited Rome in the middle of July 1938, and discussed with Mussolini and Ciano the Czechoslovak crisis.[58] Kánya declared that Hungary would never take the initiative in the action against Czechoslovakia but would intervene after the conflict had been begun by Germany. The Duce assured them that a German attack

33

against Czechoslovakia would not cause a European crisis. Italy would give complete support to Germany, and Hungary would not run the risk of attacks on the part of the Little Entente. He also promised to tell the Yugoslavs that Italy approved of an increase in Hungarian power. At Kánya's request the communiqué on the conversation stated that the Rome protocols retained their economic and political force as far as relations between Italy and Hungary were concerned.

Hungary's reluctance to take part in the German military action planned against Czechoslovakia soon became obvious, and this was one of the first serious incidents in German-Hungarian relations. Hitler invited Regent Horthy and leading Hungarian statesmen to the Reich, where they attended the launching of the cruiser, *Prinz Eugen* at Kiel. At first the Western press erroneously pictured this visit as a complete submission of Hungary to Germany. Far from being a submission, the visit coincided with the publication of the communiqué on the Bled Agreement, August 23, 1938. The agreement reached between the Little Entente and Hungary included "the recognition by the three States of the Little Entente of Hungary's equality of rights as regards armament, as well as the mutual renunciation of any recourse to force between Hungary and the States of the Little Entente." The Hungarian delegation on the S. S. Patria at Kiel became the target of German reproaches. Ribbentrop blamed Foreign Minister Kánya, who accompanied Horthy, for the agreement, and pointed out to him that the renunciation of the use of force would not protect Hungary from Yugoslavia, particularly in the event of a Hungarian-Czech crisis. On the contrary, said Ribbentrop, this Hungarian policy would make it more difficult morally for the Yugoslavs to leave their Czech allies in the lurch. All impartial observers would conclude that Hungary was, in effect, renouncing revision. Finally, Ribbentrop asked the Hungarians how they would act if the Fuehrer put into effect his decision to reply, by the use of force, to any new Czech provocation. The Hungarians hedged on two points. They argued that: "Yugoslavia must remain neutral if Hungary were to march northward and, eventually, to the east. Moreover, Hungarian rearmament . . . would require another year or two to complete." [59]

According to the German record, Horthy told Hitler that "Hungary intended to cooperate", but the Hungarian Ministers were skeptical, and remained so even later. Imrédy was most relieved when the Fuehrer stated that, in this particular case, he required nothing of Hungary, and that he himself did not know the precise moment. But Hitler noted that "he who wanted to sit at the table must at least help in the kitchen." [60]

Foreign Minister Kánya, visited Ribbentrop in Berlin two days later.

Ribbentrop called his attention to the jubilation of the Czech, French and British press over the Bled communiqué, and repeated that this event was regarded as a rift in German-Hungarian friendship and as a renunciation of Hungary's revisionist aims. Kánya thereupon amended his statement, made two days before, and explained that Hungary's military strength had in fact improved and that therefore she could take part by October 1, 1938.[61] The German record failed to explain why Kánya changed so radically his views about Hungary's military preparedness.

Such conciliatory Hungarian statements notwithstanding, the Germans clearly recognized Hungary's reluctance to take part in military action against Czechoslovakia. Otto von Erdmannsdorf, the German Minister to Hungary, reported on August 29 that Regent Horthy said to him that the extraordinary situation had arisen whereby he, who for years had desired nothing more ardently than a speedy realization of Hungarian revisionist aims, was now forced to sound a warning note owing to the international political situation. Kánya added that the Hungarians would fight even "if the chances of success were only 60 to 70 percent. But they could not be expected to commit suicide." [62]

The Hungarian public received with enthusiasm the news that the Government refused to commit the country in a common venture with Germany against Czechoslovakia. Imrédy gave an interview, published in the *Daily Telegraph* on September 2, in which he stated that, "The key words of Hungary's foreign policy . . . were peace and justice, and if any conflict broke out in Europe Hungary's aim would be to remain neutral." This article was reproduced in a Hungarian newspaper *Az Est* under headlines pointing to disagreement between Hungary and Germany. This in turn evoked an energetic German protest. The Government suspended the newspaper, and from this time on, the intimidated Imrédy began to show understanding toward Nazi demands and ideas.

In the critical days of September the dissatisfaction of the Nazi leaders with Hungarian passivity became more vocal. Field Marshal Goering invited Döme Sztójay, the Hungarian Minister to Germany, to Karinhall, and explained to him that Hungary was not doing enough in the crisis. He emphasized that the Hungarian press was keeping comparatively quiet. "There was complete calm prevailing in the Hungarian minority districts in Czechoslovakia in contrast to the Sudeten German ones, and the Hungarian Ministers in the various capitals were not making a practice of going to the Foreign Minister twice or three times a day, in contrast to their Czech colleagues. Finally neither the Hungarian Government nor even the leaders of the Hungarian minority had demanded in clear terms the detachment of the Hungarian region from

Czechoslovakia." [63]

After the German intervention Kánya promised a more active Hungarian attitude. The Hungarian memorandum of September 17 pointed out to the British Government that "a more peaceful atmosphere in Central Europe attaches itself to the principle that . . . no discrimination should be made in the treatment and ultimate rights between the various minorities in Czechoslovakia." [64]

The Hungarian Minister to Great Britain, George Barcza, handed Lord Halifax a new memorandum on September 20 and at the same time received the British reply to the insistent Hungarian interventions. The British note purported to be a sedative, and emphasized that the British Government had concentrated all its efforts on the problem of the Sudeten minority in Czechoslovakia "on the solution of which depends the issue of peace or war in Europe." The British government fully appreciated the interest felt by the Hungarian government in the future of the Hungarian minority in Czechoslovakia, but trusted that "they will be careful in the present delicate situation to do nothing to extend the scope of the present crisis, and will be content that their point of view has been placed on the record and will receive consideration in the appropriate moment." [65]

Two days later the British government protested to Warsaw and Budapest against alleged Polish and Hungarian military measures, and expressed the hope that these would not involve Hungary and Poland in actual aggression against Czechoslovakia. The note emphasized that there could be no justification whatsoever for attempting to compel an immediate settlement by direct action instead of through the process of normal negotiation.[66]

When Sir Geoffrey Knox, the British Minister to Hungary, presented this note to Kánya, the latter turned to the claim of the Hungarian minority in Czechoslovakia for equal treatment with the Sudeten Germans. Kánya told Knox that the answer Halifax gave to Barcza in London had been a bitter disappointment to him.

"The Sudeten territories" [said Kánya, as reported by Knox] had lain from time immemorial inside the frontiers of the Kingdom of Bohemia and the Sudeten Germans had in history known the Prussians more often as an enemy than a friend; moreover their case had been backed by threats and military measures. The Magyar minority on the other hand had been an integral part of the Hungarian Kingdom, and their case had been put forward for many years with calm and moderation. Hungary had made it abundantly clear that she sought a solution only by peaceful and lawful means.

Now, if I would allow him to speak with all frankness, it was sadly evident that it was not the moral wish to see justice done that lay behind the concessions we [the British Government] had wrung from Prague to the Sudeten Germans but the threat of overwhelming force." [67]

Obviously the overwhelming force did not exist in the case of the Hungarians, and the evasive British attitude caused disappointment in Hungary. Knox himself admitted in his report addressed to Lord Halifax that the Anglo-French message addressed to President Beneš on September 19 offered more grounds for Kánya's suspicion than he (Knox) had supposed to exist. Knox referred to paragraph two of the Anglo-French message, which envisaged the Sudeten German problem as a case by itself and therefore anticipated direct transfer instead of a plebiscite.[68]

The German and Hungarian positions concerning Czechoslovakia came up once more in a conversation between the Fuehrer, Prime Minister Imrédy, and Foreign Minister Kánya on September 21, 1938. Hitler, first of all, reproached his visitors "for the undecided attitude" in the crisis. He told them that Germany was determined to settle the Czech question even at the risk of a world war, and that neither France nor England would intervene. "It was Hungary's last opportunity to join in, for, if she did not, he would not be in a position to put in a word for Hungarian interests." Hitler demanded that Hungary should make an immediate demand for a plebiscite in the territories she claimed, and that she should not guarantee any proposed new frontiers for Czechoslovakia. He stated that the Czechoslovak problem would be settled by Germany within three weeks.

Imrédy replied that it was thought in Hungary that a settlement would take a year or two. In the meantime, the Hungarian minorities had already demanded a plebiscite and "the Hungarian Government would now take this matter into their own hands. Further, Hungary would immediately put in hand preparations for military actions, but a time limit of 14 days was not long enough to complete them." [69]

Hitler never forgot the "weak" Hungarian attitude demonstrated in the Czechoslovakian crisis. When Count Stephen Csáky, the successor of Kánya, visited him in January 1939, he pointed out that unfortunately the relations between Germany and Hungary were overshadowed by a dark cloud, a fact which could not be ignored by a great power like Germany. He then described the Hungarian attitude before the decisions of September, and pointed out that he had always considered Kánya as an enemy of Germany. At the very moment when he (Hitler) dis-

37

cussed the possibilities of a German-Hungarian collaboration with Horthy, during the latter's visit, Kánya did not hesitate to support the Little Entente against Germany in Bled. This was why the Fuehrer had summoned Imrédy and Sztójay and asked them, in their own interest, to publish Hungary's demands before the world. As events developed, Hungary was about to fall asleep and took only insignificant steps while Poland started to stir. Hitler further explained that Germany did not intend to sacrifice herself for friends who let her down in decisive moments. He stated that if at the right time Hungary had sided with Germany, he could have laughed in Chamberlain's face.[70]

The hesitation of Hungarian statesmen greatly increased Hitler's antipathy to Hungary.[71] Whatever happened in August and September, 1938, the policy of the Western powers gave a free hand to Germany in the Danube Valley, and Hungary's agreement with the Little Entente thereby lost all political significance. And the Munich Conference greatly undermined the forces of resistance to Germany in the Danubian countries.[72] The artificial character of the French alliance system on the Continent was shown by its rapid disintegration. In the crucial moment the Little Entente collapsed; Czechoslovakia was liquidated without a gunshot. The London *Times* noted: "Self-determination, the professed principle of the Treaty of Versailles, has been invoked by Herr Hitler against its written text, and his appeal has been allowed." [73] The Danubian countries found themselves in the sphere of influence of the Third Reich. In spite of certain Hungaro-German parallel interests created by the treaties of Versailles and Trianon, even pro-German Hungarian politicians tried to stave off the Germans. But the aftermath of the Munich settlement automatically bound the Hungarian revisionist cause to that of the Axis.

A Declaration attached to the Munich Agreement of September 1938 provided that "The problems of the Polish and Hungarian minorities in Czechoslovakia, if not settled within three months by agreement between the respective governments, shall form the subject of another meeting of the heads of the Governments of the four Powers here present." On October 1, the Prague government accepted all the demands made in a Polish ultimatum of September 28, and Polish troops subsequently occupied the Teschen district. Hungary, however, desired to solve the frontier problem by direct negotiations and plebiscite.

The Foreign Minister of Czechoslovakia, Kamil Krofta, took the initiative in solving the problem of the Hungarian minority. He handed a note, on October 1, to the Hungarian minister in Prague proposing that a Committee of Czechoslovak and Hungarian experts should be set up to deal with the question.[74] At the same time, the Hungarian minister delivered a note to him, pressing for direct negotiations between the two Governments. The Rumanian and Yugoslav Governments had been advised of the steps taken by the Czechoslovak Government. Both of them informed the German Government that they did not object to the cession to Hungary of areas of Slovakia inhabited by Magyars.[75]

As is well-known, German foreign policy in the post-Munich period favored the liquidation of Czechoslovakia and opposed all attempts at integration in areas east of Germany. The objectives of this policy, as it appears in published documents, is clearly defined. The Supreme Command of the Wehrmacht explained, in a memorandum addressed to the German Foreign Ministry on October 5, 1938, that the creation of a compact bloc of states along Germany's eastern frontier, with lines of communication to southeast Europe, would not be in accordance with German interests. Hence, "for military reasons a common Hungarian-Polish frontier was undesirable." [76]. The German Foreign Ministry prepared a similar memorandum for Hitler on the Slovak and Carpatho-Ukrainian question.[77] The memorandum opposed an autonomous Carpatho-Ukraine oriented toward Hungary, and advocated an independent Slovakia or a Czechoslovak solution for the Slovaks.[78]

In accordance with these general ideas the German Government decided to support Hungarian demands for adjacent Magyar territory and Slovak demands for autonomy within the Czechoslovak state, but rejected plans for a common Hungarian-Polish frontier, supporting Ukrainian national aspirations. German missions abroad were instructed along this line. Nonetheless, the hostile attitude of the German press toward the creation of a common frontier between Poland and Hungary was resented in Budapest, and Kánya explained to the German envoy that with reincorporation of the territory, Hungary would strengthen the Rumanian front against Bolshevism and form a strong bulwark against it on the Carpathian passes.[79]

Polish and Hungarian foreign policy aimed at the reestablishment of the centuries old common frontier on the Carpathian mountains. The British ambassador to Poland, Sir H. Kennard, reported on October 6 that the Polish government favored attainment of this goal by a grant of autonomy to Ruthenia under Hungarian sovereignty. He was informed in the Polish Foreign Ministry that there was a 20 percent Hungarian minority there, and that if the Hungarian districts were detached, including essential railways therein, the rest of Ruthenia could not exist. The Polish press pointed out that in any case Czechoslovakia never had any proper historical or economic claim to Ruthenia. It asserted that the problem of Ruthenia's restitution to Hungary was a Polish problem and involved Poland's military security.[80] In accordance with these ideas, Foreign Minister Joseph Beck attempted to persuade the British ambassador in Warsaw of the reasonableness of the Polish attitude regarding Ruthenia, which he considered to be a no-man's land and Hungarian rather than Czechoslovak. He explained to him that Poland had no territorial claims in Ruthenia, but he felt that no definite stabilization in Central Europe could be hoped for, unless Hungary's aspirations were satisfied.[81]

Meanwhile the United Hungarian Party in Ruthenia demanded the right of self-determination for all inhabitants of Ruthenia, including Hungarians,and asked that the maintenance of order in Hungarian districts be entrusted to the Party. This appeal was addressed to the British, German, Italian, French, Polish and Hungarian Governments as well as to the Czechoslovak Government.[82]

The British and French policies were rather cautious with regard to the importance of Ruthenia, and of a stronger Hungary. Knox reported from Budapest on October 8, 1938, that a Rome-Warsaw Axis could not form a barrier against German penetrations because of the weakness of the central link, Hungary. He expressed the opinion that no opposition to Germany could be made in Danubian Europe north of the Save river. Knox disagreed with the view of the British ambassador to Poland, who held that Slovakia in a Hungarian orbit could be an obstacle to German penetration. Knox thought that German domination of Hungary's indefensible western frontiers remained complete irrespective of strong defenses in the north. On the other hand, he considered Hungary to be a very solid link with all the power of Germany behind her if the Axis was to be a barrier built with the participation of Germany to cut off Russia from Western Europe.[83]

Viscount Halifax, in his instructions sent to the British Embassy in Berlin on October 26, 1938, expressed the opinion that the solution of the Ruthenian question depended to a considerable extent on Germany's policy. According to his evaluation Germany intended to use Czechoslovakia to spread German influence along the frontiers of Poland and Hungary to the Rumanian border. He suggested, specifically, that Ruthenia, in German minds, was a spring-board to the Ukraine and a starting point for fomenting a Ukrainian movement. Halifax was not disposed to attach too much importance to the argument that Poland and Hungary would be able to form a bloc to resist further German expansion if Ruthenia fell to Hungary. But he thought it possible that "a common frontier between them might strengthen Poland and Hungary in their desire to retain sufficient independence to avoid becoming the vassals of Germany." The British Foreign Secretary seemed to appreciate the Rumanian objection both to the aggrandizement of Hun-

gary and to the separation of Rumania from Czechoslovakia. But he
raised the question as to whether the maintenance of the connection
between the three Little Entente States was, at that time, of such great
importance, and whether the separation of a German-controlled Czechoslovakia from Rumania might not compensate the latter for the success
which would be won by Hungary.[84]

While new policies were pondered and decided upon in various quarters of Europe, negotiations between Hungary and Czechoslovakia (October 9-13) had broken off, since Czechoslovakia was prepared to give up
only a fraction of the territory inhabited by Magyars.[85] Since Czechoslovakia had not demobilized, Hungary partially mobilized, pending an
appeal to the four great powers.[86] Darányi visited the Fuehrer for support on October 14. On this occasion Hitler recalled that

> he had given the Hungarians many warnings, both on board ship
> [S. S. Patria at Kiel] and also during the visit of Imrédy and Kánya
> to the Obersalzberg. He had told them plainly enough that he
> would solve the Czechoslovak problem one way or another in Oct-
> tober. Poland had recognized the right moment, taken action, and
> achieved her goal. This problem could only be solved by means of
> negotiation if one were determined to act. Only in this way had
> he (the Führer) obtained all he wanted. M. Kánya however, had
> expressed nothing but doubt, although the Führer had told him that
> France and Britain would not fight. The position now was that, if
> it came to a conflict, Hungary would be completely alone and the
> outcome would be very doubtful. If it came to a conference of the
> Great Powers the outcome would also be doubtful, as no one was
> willing to fight, even if the Great Powers were in agreement, ...
> The decisive factor in any case would not be who was right but
> who had the power. He, the Führer, had told M. Kánya all this
> in detail and he had proofs of the Hungarian Government's actions
> during the crisis which had not particularly impressed him, such as
> the statements made by the Hungarian Ambassador [sic] in London
> and the Bled Agreement during Horthy's visit. Whereas we and
> Poland had prepared ourselves to stake everything we had and had
> also suffered loss of life, Hungary constantly stated that she insisted
> on her rights but did not wish to achieve these by aggressive means.
> The moment had passed. He, the Führer, was glad that for Ger-
> many the matter was settled.[87]

Darányi's visit to Hitler did not bring concrete results, although he
presented himself cap in hand, and offered various gestures such as Hungary's resignation from the League of Nations and adherence to the

Anti-Comintern Pact.[88] But, simultaneously with Darányi's visit, Ribbentrop received the Czechoslovak foreign minister, František K. Chvalkovsky and advised a speedy resumption of the negotiations with Hungary.[89]

After renewed and protracted negotiations and exchanges of notes between Hungary and Czechoslovakia, the Hungarian Government, in a note of October 24, suggested a plebiscite in the areas still under dispute. In the event of Czech disagreement on a plebiscite, the Hungarian note proposed arbitration by Germany and Italy, with the inclusion of Poland for the eastern sector. The government of Prague chose arbitration and proposed the inclusion of Rumania, if the Hungarian proposal to include Poland was accepted. Eventually Ciano and Ribbentrop arbitrated the dispute in Vienna on November 2, 1938.[90] The award was based mainly on ethnographic factors and restored to Hungary 12,103 square kilometers of territory with over one million population. In the course of the arbitral procedure Ribbentrop supported the Slovak, and Ciano the Hungarian case.[91] The overwhelming majority of the people living in the territories reattached to Hungary were Magyars,[92] but the fate of the Slovak and Czech settlements planted in Magyar districts caused further frictions and was settled only by protracted negotiations.[93]

British foreign policy was rather favorable to the settling of the Hungaro-Czechoslovak conflict according to the principles adopted by the Vienna Award. The Earl of Perth, British ambassador to Italy, advised the Czechoslovak foreign minister, Chvalkovsky, on October 7, 1938, to meet immediately Hungarian claims to regions bordering on Hungary where Magyar populations predominated.[94] Sir Nevile Henderson, British ambassador to Germany, in his report of October 18, 1938, envisaged a settlement along the lines subsequently put forward in the Hungarian note addressed to Czechoslovakia on October 24. It seemed essential to him that full justice should be done to legitimate Hungarian claims in order to avoid the criticism of having treated Hungary less well than Germany, solely because the latter was more powerful and dangerous. He even added as a "less worthy consideration" that Prime Minister Imrédy's position would be seriously compromised if Hungary failed to obtain all reasonable justice, and that he could conceivably be replaced by a pro-German who might get greater concessions as a result of German help.[95] The British Government informed the Czechoslovak Minister in London on October 20, 1938, that they saw no objection to the settlement of the Czech-Hungarian question by means of arbitration by Germany and Italy, if the Czechoslovak and Hungarian Governments agreed to settle their differences in this way. Simultaneously Lord Halifax instructed the British ambassador to Italy to inform the Italian Government that "His Majesty's Government are, in principle, in favour of the return to Hungary of those districts in which the population is predominantly Hungarian, subject possibly to certain modifications that may be desirable for economic reasons, e.g., Bratislava." [96]

In the period between the Vienna Award and the total break-up of Czechoslovakia, Hungarian diplomacy continued its efforts for the reincorporation of Ruthenia. Meanwhile, the Prague Parliament hurriedly passed a law in November, 1938, which granted the Ruthenians their own legislative, executive and judicial organs. Defense, finance, foreign affairs and transportation still remained in the hands of the central Czechoslovak Government. Thus the autonomy of Subcarpathian Ruthenia, guaranteed by the Trianon Treaty and vainly demanded by the Ruthenian people for twenty years, was established. This new political status was received with enthusiasm in Ruthenia, and the province became the center of a Ukrainian independence movement aimed at the unification of all Ukrainians living in Soviet Russia and Poland. Germany supported and fostered this trend. The Nazis prepared for future events. Their goals included the detachment of the Ukraine from Soviet Russia and the possible use of Ukrainian ambitions against the Poles. Nazi influence increased in Slovakia and Ruthenia.[97] The German Foreign Ministry sent agents to the Carpatho-Ukraine and the German Security Service financed the study, in Germany, of German state and party institutions by Slovak ministers and other official Slovak personages.[98]

A Hungarian plan to seize the Carpatho-Ukraine with Italian help was opposed and vetoed by Germany in November, 1938.[99] In the following month the provincial government of Monsignor Augustin Voloshin in the Carpatho-Ukraine gave, to a German company, complete prospecting rights for minerals in any part of the country and the right to exploit fully these minerals.[100] The German press showed an extremely friendly attitude toward Carpatho-Ukraine and Ukrainian national ambitions. Ukrainian propaganda was broadcast regularly from Vienna. Despite the fact that defense was under the control of the Central Government, the Voloshin Government organized with German help a semi-military body, called the Ukrainian National Guard *(Sitsch)*. Ukrainian refugees from Poland were incorporated into this organization which fought, with German blessings, against occasional intrusions by Hungarian irregulars. The Government of Voloshin was strongly Ukrainian nationalistic, a tendency which was bolstered by German help and encouragement.[101]

Strengthened by German support, the Voloshin Government eliminated from public life politicians and political parties opposing Ukrainian nationalist tendencies, and suppressed the Hungarian party. On February 12, 1939, elections were held on the basis of a single, unopposed slate of candidates. The "Magyarophile" list was declared invalid by the electoral commission and all elected deputies represented the nationalistic Ukrainian trend.[102] The Hungarian Minister in Berlin informed the German Government in February, 1939, that the Hungarian Government expected serious disturbances to break out in the Carpatho-Ukraine, due to these events. He reminded Berlin that in a situation such as this Hungary might be forced to intervene "for the protection of her own nationals." Berlin advised the Hungarian Government to "keep to the Vienna Award." [103]

Meanwhile British foreign policy began to show some understanding toward Hungarian aspirations. The British parliamentary undersecretary of state for foreign affairs, R. A. Butler, explained on February 17, to the Hungarian envoy, Barcza, that, in his opinion, Great Britain and France had committed a mistake in not supporting the establishment of a common Hungaro-Polish frontier. Czechoslovakia, he said, became a German colony after Munich. Thus, the attachment of Ruthenia to Hungary would have been in accordance with British interests. By the same act German expansion toward the Ukraine and the Rumanian oil fields would have been checked. Butler pointed out that it was difficult for him to understand the political blindness which had overlooked these facts. A few days later Sir Alexander Cadogan, permanent undersectary of state for foreign affairs, stated to Barcza that he had recently studied the Ruthenian problem and had become convinced that the vital interests of the Ruthenian people demanded their reattachment to Hungary; irrespective of such local interests, the interest of the great powers and European peace demanded that the German push to the East should be barred by a common Hungaro-Polish frontier. He recognized that it would have been to the Franco-British interest to attach Ruthenia to Hungary and that this interest still existed. The question, however, was not definitely closed, and at an opportune time Great Britain was willing to give political support to Hungary as well as the economic support necessary to strengthen Hungarian independence against Germany.

Butler and Cadogan apparently intended to stimulate Hungarian resistance against Germany with these goodwill remarks, but they were twenty years late in trying to form a bloc of states capable of resisting the eastward expansion of Germany.

Meanwhile Danubian Europe was heading toward new developments. On March 4, the German Government was still refusing the Hungarian proposal asking that Hungary's first claim to the territory of Carpatho-Ukraine be recognized.[104]   The Poles still hoped to secure a common frontier with Hungary.[105]   The Italian Government did not bolster Polish optimism in this respect.   When Ciano was visiting Warsaw in early March, 1939, he told Beck that he considered the question settled by the Vienna arbitration, and that Italy would do nothing further in the matter.[106]   A few days later the Polish Government informed Prague that Poland, while not pursuing any interests of her own in the Carpatho-Ukraine, would support Hungarian claims in view of Polish-Hungarian friendship.[107]   At the same time Hungary declared, in Prague, that she had no interest in Slovakia and proposed only to purchase Carpatho-Ukraine.[108]

A reversal in the German attitude toward the common Hungarian-Polish frontier then took place.   On the eve of the complete break-up of Czechoslovakia and the creation of an independent Slovakia, Germany probably wanted to give some satisfaction to Hungary and Poland.   On March 13, the Hungarian authorities in Budapest received the green light for the occupation of Carpatho-Ukraine.[109]   Regent Horthy expressed his thanks in an enthusiastic letter to Hitler, in which he announced that a frontier incident would take place on March 16, to be followed by the "big thrust." [110]

But, in view of the declaration of independence by Slovakia on March 14, the Voloshin Government, on the same day declared the Carpatho-Ukraine to be an independent state "under the protection of the German Reich." [111]   The local Diet met the next day, and, in its only session, sanctioned the proclamation of independence and elected Voloshin as president of the republic.   Voloshin asked the German Government to state whether or not the Carpatho-Ukraine had been promised to Hungary. Berlin advised Voloshin not to resist and regretted that Germany was not in a position to assume responsibility for the protectorate.[112]   These political events were overshadowed by military events.   The *Sitsch* first fought the Czech troops and then the invading Hungarian army.[113]   In these critical days the Poles reinforced their troops in the areas facing Ruthenia.   The freshly recruited Hungarian troops completed the occupation of the much coveted region from March 15 to 18.[114]   Rumania sought to intervene at the last moment and attempted to seize the eastern part of Ruthenia where there were villages inhabited by Rumanians, but she was decidedly too late.[115]

Simultaneously with the memorable visit of the Czechoslovak President Emil Hacha to Hitler, German troops invaded Bohemia and Moravia.[116]   On March 16 Hitler proclaimed a German protectorate over these historic Czech lands.[117]   Amidst the general indignation over the

German action, the Western countries observed with tacit satisfaction, and perhaps not without malice, the occupation of Carpatho-Ruthenia by Hungary. The economic and strategic position of Hungary thus improved. The common frontier with Poland, through which 140,000 Poles escaped into Hungary a few months later, was reestablished.[118] At the same time the Rumanian Government asked London for financial support and informed the British Government "that within the next few months Germany would reduce Hungary to vassalage and then proceed to disintegrate Roumania." [119]

During this period a few important changes took place in the Hungarian Government and in domestic politics. Foreign Minister Kánya, repeatedly attacked because of his well-known anti-Nazi attitude, resigned shortly after the Vienna Award. Under his successor, Count Stephen Csáky, the threatening shadow of the Third Reich stretched over Hungary's foreign policy. The Western powers revealed some understanding of Hungary's difficulties, but Soviet Russia severed diplomatic relations when Hungary joined the Anti-Comintern Pact in February, 1939.[120]

Regent Horthy, displeased with the increasingly pro-Nazi trends of the Imrédy cabinet, replaced the prime minister in February, 1939, with Count Paul Teleki. Imrédy's formal resignation occurred under spectacular circumstances. It was discovered, just when he was advocating a strong anti-Semitic policy and proposing the enactment of a second anti-Jewish bill, that he had had a Jewish great-great grandparent.

Teleki dissolved the National-Socialist Party and prohibited the so-called "Hungarist" movement. These measures notwithstanding, the rightist parties gained some ground. Nazi propaganda made good use of German successes and pointed out that some of the injustices of the Trianon Treaty had been corrected only with the consent and help of the Axis powers. In the general elections of May, 1939, held by secret ballot all over the country, a governmental majority was obtained, but the presence of a great number of Nazi-minded deputies and the decrease of deputies belonging to the left-wing opposition was significant. The balance in Parliament had shifted decidedly to the right.

Foreign Minister Csáky displayed great activity and had frequent contacts with the leaders of Italian and German foreign policy. He thought that Hungary could not maintain her independence, and, in case of war, her neutrality without some coordination of her policies with those of the Axis. Teleki and Csáky visited Mussolini and Hitler in April, 1939.[121] In the following month Italo-German cooperation was solidified by the conclusion of the Steel Pact.[122]

During 1938, and 1939, Hungarian statesmen had repeatedly told the

German government that Hungary was not willing to take part in any hostile action against Poland. Teleki desired to make Hungary's position absolutely clear. On July 24, 1939, he addressed identical letters to Hitler and Mussolini in which he confirmed the adherence of Hungary to the Axis, and in a second letter to both Hitler and Mussolini, written on the same day, he stated that "Hungary, for moral reasons, can by no means take part in any military actions directed against Poland." [123] The Italian Foreign Minister, Count Galeazzo Ciano, suspected that the "first letter was written in order to launch the second."[124] This letter caused such a furore in Germany that Csáky had to meet Ribbentrop in Fuschl on August 8, and upon Ribbentrop's insistance Csáky instructed the Hungarian envoys in Berlin and Rome to retract both letters. This, however, did not change Teleki's attitude. He overruled Csáky's retractions and ordered him to return to Budapest.[125]

A few days after this incident, Csáky suddenly arrived in Rome, and submitted to Mussolini the idea of a Hungarian alliance with the Axis in order to save Hungary from a German invasion or a "friendly occupation". For the same reasons the Hungarian Government thought of putting a member of the House of Savoy, possibly the Duke of Aosta, on the throne of Hungary. Csáky sounded out the Italian Government on both these propositions. He described the temper of the times in Hungary by pointing out that "95 percent of the Hungarian people hate the Germans. The Regent himself, speaking of them [the Germans], called them 'buffoons and brigands', and Madame Horthy said that even she would take up arms if they had to fight the Germans." [126] Mussolini and Ciano, baffled at this unexpected outburst, remained diplomatically reserved toward Csáky.

Thus, on the eve of the Second World War, the Hungarian Government made some desperate moves to maintain independence and some freedom of action. The alternatives were poor. And after the conclusion of the Russo-German pact the prospects reached their lowest ebb. The unfortunate Danubian nations were nothing but "puppets of fate" [127] in the hands of unscrupulous and overwhelming outside forces. The Teleki Government faced an international situation in which there were insoluble difficulties for Hungary. Geography, revisionism and the weakness of Western Europe limited the possibilities of Hungarian foreign policy.

IV. THE SECOND WORLD WAR

The Road from Non-belligerency to War.

After the outbreak of the second World War the Hungarian Government issued a proclamation which amounted to a declaration of neutrality. Prime Minister Teleki sought to maintain a non-belligerent status and, in the face of the growing Nazi influence, some measure of independence for Hungary—despite the territorial gains obtained with the help of the Axis powers. This policy was put on trial immediately after the German attack on Poland began.

The German Government asked the Hungarian Government to allow the use of the Kassa-Velejte railroad line for transporting German troops dispatched to attack the retreating forces in Southern Poland from the rear. Budapest informed the Italian Government of the German demand and Mussolini approved of the negative attitude of the Hungarian Government.[1]

On September 9, Foreign Minister Csáky formally rejected Ribbentrop's telephone demand made in the name of the German Government. According to the documents of the Hungarian Foreign Ministry, Csáky firmly told Ribbentrop that the Hungarian Government was "compelled, to its great regret, to request Germany not to use the Hungarian railroad line for the transportation of German troops against Poland." Hungary did not think it "compatible with the honor of the Hungarian nation" to permit such action. The Hungarian attitude remained the same despite a German territorial offer in Galicia. When approached some days later with a similar demand by the Slovak Government which joined Hitler in the aggression against Poland, Count Csáky was even more outspoken, warning the Slovaks that such a move would be an act of aggression against Hungary. In the meantime, as a precautionary measure, the Hungarian authorities ordered the mining of all tunnels and bridges, leading to the Kassa-Velejte railway.[2]

This energetic manifestation of Hungary's decision to maintain a neutral status could not last for long. German-Russian collaboration gradually reduced the possibility of an independent Hungarian policy—made difficult anyway by the unfortunate geographical situation of the country. The situation was aggravated by circumstances developing from the Trianon Treaty, and by the gradual disappearance of Western influence in Eastern Europe. The Western powers ceased to exist as power factors along the Danube, and Trianon Hungary was squeezed between overwhelming German and Russian forces.

48

The Soviet Union renewed diplomatic relations with Hungary in September 1939, and the extreme right in Hungary did not cease to praise the wise cooperative policy of the two greatest powers in Europe, Germany and Soviet Russia.[3] Telegraphic communications and railway connections were established between Hungary and the Soviet Union. Following a Soviet initiative, the Hungarian Government exchanged the now well-known Hungarian Communist leader, Mátyás Rákosi (in an Hungarian jail), for banners taken by the Russian army in 1849, when it intervened on behalf of Austria in crushing the war of independence in Hungary. The anti-Soviet attitude of the Hungarian public, however, manifested itself especially in connection with the Russo-Finnish war. Public manifestations and collections were organized for Finland, and Hungarian volunteers left the country, with the help of the authorities, to fight in Finland against the Red army.

During this period Rumania began to worry about the possibilities of a Soviet attack, and a special emissary of the Rumanian king asked the Italians to "work on the Hungarians," because any Hungarian threat on the Rumanian rear would "oblige the Rumanians to come to an agreement with the Russians." [4] Csáky assured Ciano that "Hungary will not take the initiative in the Balkans and thus spread the fire," [5] but he emphasized Hungary's demand for equality of treatment for Hungarian minorities in case Rumania should cede territory to Russia or Bulgaria without fighting.[6] The Hungarian attitude was expressed even more clearly by Teleki on a visit to Rome in March 1940. Ciano noted that "he [Teleki] will not do anything against Rumania, because he does not want to make himself responsible, even indirectly, for having opened the doors of Europe to Russia . . . Teleki has avoided taking any open position one way or the other but has not hidden his sympathy for the Western Powers and fears an integral German victory like the plague." [7] Later Teleki frankly told Ciano that he hoped "for the defeat of Germany, not a complete defeat—that might provoke violent shocks—but a kind of defeat that would blunt her teeth and claws for a long time." [8]

Shortly thereafter Hungarian hopes for possible Italian help against the Germans were ended. Assuming that Russia would soon move into Bessarabia, Germany intended to occupy the Rumanian oil fields. The German General Staff approached the Hungarian General Staff and requested free passage through Hungary. The price of this permission allegedly would have been Transylvania. The Hungarian Government sent a special messenger to Rome who explained that "For the Hungarians there arises the problem either of letting the Germans pass, or opposing them with force. In either case the Hungarian liberty would come to an end." [9]

49

During these Hungaro-Italian negotiations the Germans began the occupation of Denmark and Norway, and the Italian Ambassador to Germany, Bernardo Attolico, denied the rumor of an attack on Rumania. The Duce advised the Hungarians to "keep calm and moderate, and . . . accede to German requests." Ciano commented: "This was not the answer the Hungarians expected and hoped for. They went so far as to ask whether, in case of military resistance, they could count on Italian help. Mussolini smiled, 'How could this ever be,' he said, 'since I am Hitler's ally and intended to remain so?' "[10]

The spectacular occupation of the smaller Western European states by Germany, and the unexpected collapse of France deeply impressed the Hungarian public. In fact, these events caused general consternation. The government press manifested a dignified reserve and, when Italy declared war on France and Great Britain, Foreign Minister Csáky stated that Hungary would continue her non-belligerent status.

Soviet Russia reacted to the German victories in the West by the incorporation of the Baltic states and Rumanian territories. Following a Russian ultimatum, Rumania evacuated Bessarabia and northern Bukovina and ceded these territories to the Soviet Union. After these events, Hungary and Bulgaria, in Bucharest, demanded the settlement of their territorial issues. In August, 1940, at Craiova, the Rumanian government agreed in principle with Bulgaria concerning the retrocession of South-Dobrudja, but declined to entertain seriously the Hungarian claims.

The Hungarian Government displayed great restraint and did not push the issue of Transylvania until August, 1940, but after the satisfaction of the Russian and Bulgarian demands, the negative Rumanian attitude towards Hungary was difficult to accept. At the 1919 peace settlement Rumania received from Hungary a larger amount of territory than that retained by the Hungarian state, and, according to the Rumanian census, one and a half million Magyars remained in Transylvania. The settlement of the Transylvanian problem was thus of great importance for Hungary. Although direct negotiations were conducted between the two countries in Turnu-Severin (August 16-24) the two delegations could not find a common basis for agreement.

Meanwhile the great powers expressed approval or understanding of the Hungarian thesis. Molotov declared to the Hungarian Envoy, Joseph Kristóffy, on July 7, 1940, that the Soviet government considered the Hungarian claims well-founded and would support them at the peace table. At the time of the negotiations in Turnu-Severin, Molotov again stated to Kristóffy that the Hungarian claims were justified.[11] The Western powers also indicated their understanding of Hungary's attitude. In July, 1940, Rumania renounced the Anglo-French guarantee of Rumania's political independence. Subsequently the permanent undersecretary of the British Foreign Office declared to Barcza, the Hungarian Minister, that the British government fully understood that Hungary was pressing her territorial demands but hoped that these would be realized by peaceful settlement. The Hungarian minister to the United States, John Pelényi, reported that the head of the European division in the Department of State showed an understanding toward Hungary's attitude in the Transylvanian problem and disapproved of the delaying tactics of the Rumanians.

After the failure of the negotiations both Hungary and Rumania mobilized, and Teleki decided to settle the Rumanian issue by force if necessary. However, Hitler resolved to take a direct hand in the affair since a conflict in the southeastern European area would have resulted in serious complications for Germany and, especially, could have hindered the flow of Rumanian oil to Germany. In addition, the possibility of Russian intervention in a Hungarian-Rumanian conflict also existed. Later the German leaders repeatedly pointed out to the Hungarians that Germany had to decide the Hungaro-Rumanian conflict in order to save Rumania from collapse, and Russian intervention.[12] The German and Italian governments invited the representatives of the Hungarian and Rumanian governments to Vienna. The day before the meeting Hitler told Ciano that he was leaving the decision up to him and Ribbentrop. The only thing he had at heart was that "peace be preserved there, and that Rumanian oil continue to flow into his reservoirs."[13]

The Hungarians thought that the Axis Powers would mediate, but were not prepared to submit the issue for arbitration. Ribbentrop assailed the recalcitrant Teleki in Vienna. He accused Hungary of having adopted anti-German policies on more than one occasion.[14] Finally the Hungarian delegation obtained, from Budapest, full power for submitting the issue to Italo-German arbitration. This document was deposited at the German Legation in Budapest only half an hour before the second Vienna Award was delivered on August 30, 1940. Based mainly on ethnographical considerations, the Award restored the northern part of Transylvania to Hungary. At the same time Germany and Italy guaranteed the territorial integrity of Rumania, which still retained the major and economically more important part of Transylvania with a minority of more than a half million Hungarians.[15] There was a general outcry in Rumania against the Award, and at the same time disappointment in Hungary was great. The new frontier created great complications for Hungary from the point of view of communications, and it left under Rumanian control the most important assets and resources of Transylvania, such as the district of Meggyes-Kissármás where mineral oil and natural gas could be obtained.

The Award caused serious friction between Moscow and Berlin. Germany informed the Soviet Union only after the Vienna decision had been delivered, and Molotov claimed that Germany violated the Non-aggression Pact which provided for consultation in questions of common interest to both countries. Molotov declared that the German Government "could not have been in doubt that the Soviet Government was interested in Rumania and Hungary." [16]

Hungary's position nonetheless was made more difficult by the pro-Axis reorientation of Rumania's foreign policy. This had been achieved with amazing speed. Rumania resigned from the League of Nations and from the Balkan Entente, and began to transform the internal structure of the country according to National-Socialist principles. The most dangerous step, however, was the invitation extended by Rumania in early October 1940, to the German "instructor corps". General Friedrich Paulus stated, in his deposition at Nuremberg, that an entire panzer division was transferred to Rumania, manifestly as a training unit but actually for the purpose of preparing the Rumanian Army for war. These troops had to cross Hungary, and some military personnel were also stationed in Hungarian railroad stations "to maintain the lines of communication between Rumania and Germany." [17] Although Teleki restricted the Germans to a few important railroad stations, this was the beginning of the German military penetration into Hungarian territory. Shortly after these events Hungary adhered to the Tripartite Pact (November 20, 1940) concluded on September 27, 1940, in Berlin between Germany, Italy and Japan. This was considered as one of the means for maintaining the relative independence of Hungary in Axis Europe.[18] But the Hungarian Government refused to accept a secret additional protocol which aimed at the implementation of the Pact in the field of newspapers and propaganda. Such a cooperation naturally would have led to the liquidation of all anti-Nazi opposition newspapers in Hungary.[19]

Simultaneously negotiations were conducted with Belgrade. It was hoped that the pact of eternal friendship soon concluded with Yugoslavia (December 12, 1940) would strengthen Hungary's position by leaving open possibilities for the future. But these hopes were shortly destroyed by the course of events. On March 25, 1941, the Yugoslav Government adhered to the Tripartite Pact, and two days later, the Cvetković Government was overthrown by a *coup d'état*. Germany considered this a hostile act, and Hitler promptly demanded Hungarian approval for the passage of his troops as well as active military cooperation against Yugoslavia.[20]

This demand was preceded by direct and confidential parleys between the German and Hungarian general staffs, without the knowledge of the Hungarian Government. General Paulus testified in Nuremberg that he arrived in Budapest on March 30 and had a conference with the Chief of the Hungarian General Staff, General Henry Werth, and with Colonel László, chief of the operational group of the Hungarian General Staff. The conferees discussed deployment of German troops on Hungarian territory and participation of Hungarian troops in the forthcoming attack on Yugoslavia. Paulus noted that these conferences were brief and orderly and achieved the desired results.[21]

Quick understanding between German and Hungarian high army officers was not an accident. The Chief of the German General Staff, General Franz Halder, informed General Werth as early as November 1940—that is, before the conclusion of the pact of eternal friendship between Hungary and Yugoslavia—that in the spring of 1941 "Yugoslavia would have to be compelled, if necessary by force of arms, to adopt a definite position in order to exclude, at a later date, the menace of a Russian attack from the rear. In this preventive war, possibly against Yugoslavia and definitely against Soviet Russia, Hungary would have to participate if only in her own interests." [22]

Werth replied that he agreed with Halder and asked that Germany complete the Hungarian re-armament program. After that a Hungarian armament commission was invited to Berlin, and close contact was maintained between the two general staffs. In March, 1941, Halder urged Werth to mobilize certain army corps in order that Hungary be prepared for war against Yugoslavia and Soviet Russia.[23]

The Hungarian General Staff wholeheartedly supported the German plans, made the necessary preparatory steps, and thus confronted the political authorities of the country with a *fait accompli*. When the decisive moment arrived the Hungarian Government had no choice. Unable to alter the course of events, Teleki committed suicide on April 3, 1941, the eve of the crossing of Hungary's boundary by German troops marching to attack Yugoslavia.[24] Winston Churchill noted in his memoirs that "His suicide was a sacrifice to absolve himself and his people from guilt in the German attack upon Yugoslavia. It clears his name before history. It could not stop the march of the German armies nor the consequences." [25]

With the death of Teleki a new era began. Up to that time the Department of State and the British Foreign Office appreciated the merits of the Hungarian moderate and dilatory policy, particularly during the sad days of the invasion of Poland. This appreciation was repeatedly asserted to the Hungarian ministers in Washington and London. The Ambassador of France in London, M. Charles Corbin, characterized the Hungarian attitude as an *"acrobatie diplomatique digne de toute éloge."*

Teleki's successor was his Foreign Minister, László Bárdossy, a professional diplomat, but a man of scant political experience. Death had prepared the way for his ill-fated career.[26] He had been Hungarian Minister to Rumania at the time of the second Vienna Award. Upon the sudden death of Count Csáky in January, 1941, Bárdossy succeeded him as foreign minister. Although a patriot and originally an anti-Nazi, he followed a pro-German policy. Impressed by the successful pro-Nazi policy of the Rumanian dictator, General Jon Antonescu, he believed that limited cooperation with Germany was the only means for maintaining some independence for Hungary. In the course of this policy he committed grave mistakes and proved especially weak in his dealings with the Hitlerite element in the Hungarian Army.

Germany attacked Yugoslavia on April 6. A death blow was soon administered to the Yugoslav Army in the south by German troops previously massed in Rumania. On April 10, the independence of Croatia was proclaimed in Zagreb. Thereafter, Regent Horthy declared that, since Yugoslavia had ceased to exist, the Hungarian Army would protect the Magyar population living in territories taken from Hungary by Yugoslavia in 1918. Between April 11, and April 14, and without serious fighting, the Hungarian Army occupied part of the former Hungarian territory attached to Yugoslavia by the Trianon Treaty.[27]

Under Bárdossy, Hungary's international position rapidly grew worse. On April 8, 1941, Great Britain severed diplomatic relations with Hungary, since the latter country had become a base of military operations against the Allies. Following the outbreak of the German-Russian war, Bárdossy was induced by the General Staff to declare war on Russia, on June 27, without consulting parliament. The town Kassa (Košice) was bombed allegedly by Soviet planes on the preceding day, and Bárdossy considered this action a *casus belli.*[28] The declaration of war caused violent protests from the opposition parties. At the time the chief of staff of the Hungarian Army, General Werth, suggested that the war against Russia would be just a matter of weeks and Hungary must not be late this time. He had announced the forthcoming attack on the Soviet Union at a secret meeting of Hungarian army corps commanders in May, 1941, and stated that Rumania and Hungary would take an active part on the side of Germany.[29]

The British declaration of war against Hungary (December 6,

1941)[30] and the severance of diplomatic relations with the United States (December 12, 1941) followed by an Axis-enforced declaration of war (not recognized by the United States), were the other important international events during Bárdossy's premiership.

Hungary's entry into war with the English-speaking powers was not without dramatic incidents. When the American Minister to Hungary, Herbert Pell, representing British interests in Hungary, handed over, on November 29, 1941, the above-cited British ultimatum, Bárdossy, according to his own record of the conversation, replied as follows: "Your information comes as a surprise. I never believed it would go that far, nor that England could help the Soviets, only by declaring war on us. . . . There are no Hungarian forces fighting in Russia now. We have withdrawn our forces from the front. The Hungarian Government is not participating in any direct military action. . . . Most of the Hungarians placed their faith in English fairness to judge the present situation. They will feel hurt by such a decision of the British government."

In the course of the ensuing conversation Pell showed a most understanding attitude toward Hungary. Counselor Howard K. Travers stated that the American Legation tried every means to prevent a declaration of war by England on Hungary after the first rumors of such a decision. Minister Pell said that he considered the decision of the English Government as his own defeat.[31]

After Pearl Harbor, Hitler declared in the Reichstag that a state of war existed between Germany and the United States. As a subterfuge the Hungarian Government simply stated its solidarity with the Axis and severed diplomatic relations with the United States. According to the files of the Hungarian Foreign Ministry, in answer to the question of Minister Pell "Does it mean war?", Bárdossy replied with a categorical "No."

The Italian minister and the German *chargé d'affaires* at Budapest called the next day on Bárdossy, urging the Hungarian Government to declare war on the United States.[32]

The Hungarian declaration of war was duly dispatched. This declaration, together with those of the other satellites, was rightly characterized later in a note of the American Government delivered in Budapest by the Legation of Switzerland on April 7, 1942. This note considered the satellite declarations of war as made "under duress, and . . . contrary to the will of the majority of the peoples of the countries in question." Similarly President Roosevelt stated in a message to Congress on June 2, 1942, that although the Governments of Bulgaria, Hungary and Rumania had declared war against the United States, "I realize that the three governments took this action not upon their own initiative or in response to the wishes of their own peoples but as the instruments of Hitler." However, on the recommendation of President Roosevelt, Congress declared on June 5, "that a state of war exists between the Government of Hungary and the Government and the people of the United States." [33]

The reluctance of Hungary and the other satellites to declare war on the United States reflects the fact that the free will of small nations is very limited in a world conflagration.

Bárdossy well described the tragic dilemma of Hungarian statesmen when he told Mussolini's representative in Budapest, Filippo Anfuso, that: "God confronted us with Hitler. If the Germans demand something, I always give a quarter of it. If I refused categorically, they would take everything, which would be worse." [34] Bárdossy expressed the same idea even more strongly before the people's court in 1945 when in his last speech he explained that half of his audience would not have been present for his trial but would have perished on the battlefield had he refused to declare war on Russia in 1941. In that case, said Bárdossy, the German occupation of Hungary would have taken place three years earlier, and a government installed by Hitler would have carried out a total mobilization in Hungary.

From the autumn of 1941 onward the German attitude toward Hungary stiffened. Up to that time Hungarian military help in Soviet Russia had been of token value. Time and again the Nazis pointed out to the Hungarians that the Rumanians, Slovaks, Czechs and Croats were more cooperative toward Germany and that Hungarian unfriendliness might have unpleasant consequences. In January, 1942, Ribbentrop himself came to Hungary to convey Hitler's insistence upon a 100 percent mobilization of all Hungarian resources needed for a speedy termination of the war. He dangled the idea of territorial concessions to Hungary in Transylvania with their magnitude depending on the amount of Hungarian support. This, combined with threats, was the usual German device. Ribbentrop extolled the merits of Antonescu, the Rumanian dictator. He pointed to Rumania's complete participation in the war as a shining example for Hungary to follow.

Bárdossy, still seeking to reduce to a minimum Hungarian participation in the war, refused to yield to German pressure for total mobilization. He argued with Ribbentrop that Hungary could not be expected to send all her military forces abroad, leaving her own frontiers undefended. This had been the main cause of Hungary's First World War catastrophe. Germany's interests, he said, could not be served by an unruly Hungary, in which all production would be seriously curtailed. Ribbentrop expressed regrets about this unexpected reply, intimating that it was likely to lessen Hitler's good will toward Hungary.

Hitler's next move was the dispatching of General Keitel to Budapest with a large military suite. Even so, for the spring offensive in Russia, he could bring about the mobilization of but one-third of Hungary's military forces.[35]

In January, 1942, during the last weeks of Bárdossy's Premiership, tragic events occurred in the territories reattached to Hungary from Yugoslavia. In some regions Tito's partisans were particularly active and repeatedly carried on raids against units of the Hungarian armed forces. The military commanders in the area received orders to take punitive measures against the partisans. Under the pretext of reprisals the Hungarian Army and gendarmerie carried out organized massacres of the Serbian and Jewish population, especially in the triangle of Zsablya and in Ujvidék (Novi Sad). The army instituted a regime of terror and isolated the area, while local civilian authorities were intimidated and blocked from all intervention. The indiscriminate murders were accompanied by extensive looting. The number of victims totaled over three thousand,[36] a large number of whom were thrown into the Danube through holes in the ice.

Shortly after these shameful events, Horthy accepted Bárdossy's resignation (March 10, 1942) because of various disagreements between them. From this time onward Bárdossy took a leading part in extreme rightist movements and became an ardent pro-Nazi.

Hungary's Efforts to Steer a New Course.

Bárdossy's successor, Miklós Kállay, an intimate friend of the Regent, sought to extricate Hungary from the German grasp. This was no easy undertaking, for the country was completely encircled by German satellites and German-occupied territories. Thus outwardly Kállay had to adopt Bárdossy's policies. Changes were made only gradually and with great discretion.

Kállay's cautious anti-Nazi policy also prevailed in regard to the massacres of Ujvidék. The opposition parties demanded that the perpetrators of the crimes be court-martialed. One of the leading Smallholder deputies, Endre Bajcsy-Zsilinsky was particularly insistent. He went to see the Regent personally and presented him and the Government with extensive memoranda on the matter. On December 2, 1942, Bajcsy-Zsilinsky vigorously protested in parliament that the criminals of Ujvidek had not yet been condemned, and demanded that the surviving families of the victims receive annuities and compensation. The government allotted twelve million pengoes yearly for this purpose in the spring of 1943. Kállay ordered an investigation and initiated court martial proceedings against two generals and twenty-five army officers, many of them affiliated with the German Nazi Party. The principal criminals, however, escaped with German assistance into Germany before the completion of the proceedings. The ranking general among them was appointed *Obergruppenführer*. For the indemnification procedure the council of ministers appointed a committee working on the spot, under the chairmanship of the undersecretary of state, Paul Balla. The committee settled 90 percent of the requests for annuities and 25 percent of the indemnification cases. The German occupation of Hungary, however, cut short the completion of this work.

It is not possible to clarify fully the real background and purpose of the massacres. According to a widely circulated rumor these crimes were deliberately planned by the Nazis in order to compromise Hungary's record, and thus to bind her fate more closely to that of Nazi Germany. Whatever may have been the direct connection between Berlin and the organizers of the massacres, it appeared on this and some other important occasions that a few leading officers in the Hungarian army owed greater allegiance to Germany and Hitlerite ideology than to their own fatherland. In view of Hungary's political position it was not possible to eliminate from the army these officers, some of whom were in key positions. Such conditions made Kállay's undertaking very difficult.

Kállay cautiously undertook the hard task of preparing the way for an armistice with the Allied powers, and of freeing Hungary from Nazi domination. This was the beginning of "underground diplomacy." The Foreign Ministry still formally maintained unchanged relations with the Axis, but in the meantime it established contacts with the Western powers. Exponents of Hungary's pro-Allied foreign policy had to be very watchful. The government itself was not without pro-Nazi members. In his efforts to reach an understanding with the Allies, Kállay could place absolute faith in only two members of his government; his minister of the interior, Ferenc Keresztes-Fischer, and his secretary general of the Foreign Ministry, Jenö Ghyczy. To Ghyczy he had turned over the portfolio of that Ministry in July, 1943.

The Ghyczy administration had been inaugurated by the reshuffling of the Foreign Ministry staff and the diplomatic representatives abroad, and by replacing pro-German officials with reliable ones.[37] Kállay's policy was made easier by the turn of international events. The demoralized retreat of the Germans in the second winter of the Russian venture clearly fore-shadowed Germany's defeat. In particular, the Voronezh disaster suffered by the Hungarian Army (January, 1943), caused widespread discontent. This calamitous defeat reduced Hungarian military help to Germany to a badly equipped token force. Anti-Nazi

Hungarian politicians became more vocal. Kállay had no reluctance in stating at a meeting of the foreign affairs committee of Parliament, that Hungary's interest in the war did not go beyond the Russian campaign. Still, much caution was needed. In a statement before Parliament about the future peace negotiations, Kállay named his minister of public instruction, Bálint Hóman, a staunch pro-German, as the head of a prospective peace delegation. In the meantime, the real preparations for peace were made secretly under the leadership of the political division of the Foreign Ministry with the full conviction of the inevitability of a German defeat.[38] Government offices, research institutions, and selected experts were given assignments without being aware of the underlying purpose of the peace preparatory work. With the possible occupation of Hungary by the Germans always in sight, duplicate copies of all documents were sent to the Hungarian legation at Berne.

However, before continuing the examination of Hungary's foreign policy under the Kállay government, it is perhaps desirable to give a picture of the Nazi penetration of Hungarian life and of the main forces and methods of anti-Nazi resistance.

In the midst of the political and ideological chaos prevailing in Europe before the Second World War, unscrupulous Nazi methods were bound to score successes. The state of mind of the Hungarian middle class was, on the whole, somewhat unbalanced and confused, although the majority remained anti-Nazi. Some features of the political situation in Hungary were particularly favorable to the spread of Nazi doctrines, and some sections of the Hungarian middle class became infected by them. For people who disregarded basic human issues, all the abuses of dictatorial systems were completely justified by the conspicuous successes of a policy of accomplished facts, and by the hesitant behavior of democratic countries in the face of German violations of international obligations. The striking rise of German might impressed many people, but especially the army officers.

Under the impact of the unfortunate situation created in the Danubian Valley after the First World War, the Hungarian public welcomed any new trend which promised alleviation of the country's economic difficulties, and reparation of the injustices attributed to the Trianon Treaty. And the Nazis were rather generous with promises. They did not hesitate to practice the old imperial policy of pitting the national aspirations of one Danubian people against those of another. To Hungary they promised the correction of the "injustices of Trianon"; to the neighboring states, defense against "Hungary's exaggerated claims." A substantial part of the ethnic Germans in Hungary became adherents of Nazi principles and organizations. A minority of the Germans courage-

59

ously and under most difficult circumstances opposed Hitlerite ideology. They even organized a "loyalty movement."

Besides economic and nationalistic arguments, a most effective means of spreading Nazi ideology was anti-Jewish propaganda. This was made easy by the fact that Jews in Hungary occupied very advantageous positions in the country's financial and intellectual life. One could hear everywhere, as a result of well-planned Nazi propaganda, that Horthy and the statesmen who resisted Nazi penetration were bribed by the Jews. It was constantly repeated that Western democratic, capitalistic, and Jewish influence were responsible for all the privations and misery of the people and for the corruption in public life, as well. Under constant German pressure two anti-Jewish laws (Act 4, 1939 and Act 15, 1941) were enacted which went much farther than the first anti-Jewish law of 1938, contained strong political discrimination, and also penalized the Jews in economic and social respects. The government hoped by such measures to take some of the wind out of the Nazi sails. But these laws did not menace the physical existence of the Jews and did not apply the inhuman measures practiced in other satellite states—measures that the German Government consistently demanded from Hungary. However, some of the Jews who had been conscripted into the labor service and taken to the Russian front suffered brutal treatment. But the Minister of Interior, Keresztes-Fischer, and Kállay's short-lived Minister of National Defense, Vilmos Nagy, managed to re-establish justice toward the Jews.[39]

It was characteristic of the situation that Jews from neighboring countries endeavored to seek refuge in Hungary. About 70,000 foreign Jews managed to reach Hungary, and with the help of the Hungarian authorities, many of them were able to go to Palestine. A Jewish writer dealing with the fate of Hungarian Jewry and with the annihilation of Jews in adjacent countries, concluded: "While the Germans had practically annihilated Central European Jewry, roughly one million Jews lived in Hungary. They all had to thank the 'protection' afforded them by Regent Horthy and the Kállay Government for their physical existence in what the Nazis called the 'Central European Jewish Island.' "[40]

It was reassuring to see that Nazi methods and principles could not deceive the bulk of the Hungarian people. Even in the worst days of pro-German influence, there were in Hungary forces who openly defied Hitler and worked against Nazi penetration, courageous people of sound political and moral judgment. They despised the momentary advantages offered by a wicked system, and fought for the underlying moral forces which guide—amidst many ups and downs—the course of mankind. To Hungarian common sense the ideas of the Nazis were alien. This fundamental humane trend vindicated itself by moderating the attitude of Hungarian governments even in desperate situations. Parliament was in session throughout the war, as in Finland. This gave an opportunity to the partly muzzled opposition parties—mainly the Small-Landholders (hereafter Smallholders), Democrats, and Social Democrats—to censure Hungarian foreign policy and to protest pro-German policy.[41] The *Journal of Parliament* gives testimony of the courageous attitude of the opposition members of Parliament.

Until the German occupation, over a dozen leftist and anti-Nazi daily papers and periodicals were more or less vocal against pro-Nazi policy. Centers of resistance against Nazi penetration came into being. Churches of all denominations and left-wing parties fought desperately against the spread of Hitlerite ideology. So did prominent Hungarian writers as well as outstanding personalities in Hungarian intellectual life.[42] Justinian Cardinal Serédi defied the Nazis openly in bold speeches. Other Catholic and Protestant clergy followed suit. Especially bold was the Catholic Bishop of Veszprém, William Apor, in defending persecuted Jews.[43] The masses of peasants and workers remained indifferent if not hostile to Nazi ideas. The great number of journalists were fundamentally anti-Nazi, although a small minority produced noisy pro-Nazi propaganda. This latter group of journalists, provided with much money, founded daily and weekly papers and even bought the favorite daily of the Hungarian middle class, the *Magyarság*, formerly a pro-Habsburg, legitimist newspaper.

As the war continued, an ever increasing number of war prisoners and refugees of all sorts found asylum and warm hospitality in Hungary. The treatment of refugees went far beyond the prescriptions of international law. After the defeat of Poland, 140,000 Poles found shelter in Hungary. The majority of these people, with the help of Hungarian authorities and private persons, managed to cross the border of Yugoslavia and to join the Allied colors in the Near East.[44] While the Germans shut down all Polish high schools and cultural associations in Poland, these, in addition to grammar schools, were established in Hungary, and Polish papers were published until March, 1944. No fewer than 14,000 Polish Jews succeeded in procuring so-called "Christian papers" from the Hungarian Ministry of Interior. The Polish emigrants had every facility for communicating with underground organizations in Poland, and the Hungarian diplomatic pouch forwarded their correspondence to London via Lisbon. In charge of affairs concerning Russian war prisoners who escaped from German camps was a Soviet Russian partisan captain, who acted as an official of the Ministry of Interior.

About 1400 French war prisoners managed to escape from German camps into Hungary and enjoyed the same hospitable treatment.[45] Hungarian hospitality provided all comforts. French ex-prisoners were lodged in hotels on the shores of Lake Balaton, the playground of Hungary. They had freedom of movement all over the country. Some of them were even helped to escape to unoccupied France. The Hungarian Government refused to surrender them to the Germans in spite of repeated Nazi protests. They were followed by a number of Dutch, Belgian, British, and American war prisoners who found hiding places with private persons. This happened, even after the German occupation of Hungary, with the connivance of the authorities.

Not only in the treatment of Jews and refugees did Hungary manifest her true feelings. Food in considerable quantities went to German-occupied countries, especially to Greece and Belgium. By means of the International Red Cross gift parcels were forwarded regularly to Polish and French war prisoners in Germany, to the camps in Yugoslavia, and to those unfortunates interned in German-occupied Poland. International Red Cross reports indicate that the most substantial help to occupied territories came from Hungary. Nor did Hungary fail to send generous amounts of food to the Vatican.

The most important results of the Hungarian resistance were attained in economic matters. As statistical data demonstrate, exports to Germany did not approach anything like the volume stipulated.[46] Throughout the war, Hungarian sabotage curtailed deliveries to Germany. Economic resistance here became of the utmost importance. Between 1940 and 1943, Hungarian grain deliveries to Germany did not reach more than one-fourth of the quantities stipulated. This accounts for the fact that, while the value of food imports into Germany totalled $39.7 millions in 1939, this total fell to $21.1 millions in 1941. As a result, in spite of ravenous German demands, Hungarian live-stock increased by eleven percent during the war. At the time of the Russian invasion eighteen million metric quintals of cereals were housed in the public stores of the "Futura".[47] Nor did Hungary comply with the German demand that she mobilize her industries for war. As late as 1943, war industries consumed only twenty percent of the total electric energy of the country, the remaining eighty percent serving to supply other industrial and civilian needs.

This non-cooperative Hungarian attitude provoked angry reproaches from the Germans. Comparisons of Hungary's behavior with that of the more friendly satellites and occupied countries were loud and bitter. As early as 1943, Karl Clodius [48] hinted to Kállay that Hungary's economic sabotage might lead to military occupation, since the Germans could get much more out of the occupied countries. As an example Clodius mentioned the output of Czech industry and agriculture.

The centers of Hungarian resistance to Nazi penetrations were certain high government agencies, notably the Foreign Ministry. There were not many pro-Nazi elements in the Hungarian diplomatic service. It was never a hotbed of Nazism, although there were some who were not averse to a policy of limited cooperation with the Nazis. They thereby hoped to prevent the total exploitation and occupation of the country. Fear of Soviet expansion was another argument for such limited cooperation.

Nevertheless, even during the years of a more cooperative policy, the anti-Nazi forces in Hungary always had a core in the Foreign Ministry. With the help of Hungarian diplomats the conservative forces succeeded in keeping Hungarian politics from complete "nazification". These diplomats, joining hands with elements of similar conviction, were able to show results which, under the circumstances, were gratifying. One result of the moderating influence of Hungarian diplomats was that even pro-German members of the Government had to comply with the policy of minimum concessions or compromise in a given situation. They were handicapped in playing the Nazi game. No wonder that the Germans gave voice to their dissatisfaction.

An example of official resistance was the Hungarian policy toward citizens who enlisted in the SS forces. One of the Nazi devices in the southeastern European countries was to enlist young members of the German minority in the SS forces. In other satellite countries, local authorities made such enlistments easy, but Hungary discouraged this practice by depriving such young men of their Hungarian citizenship. Until the German occupation of Hungary the prime minister and the Foreign Ministry made a strong effort to maintain this policy. This was probably one of the reasons why Goebbels wrote the following entry in his diary: "I have received a report about the fate of the German minorities in Hungary. The Hungarians still dare to commit acts of effrontery toward us that go far beyond what we can stand for. I suppose, however, we must keep quiet for the moment. We are dependent upon them. But everyone of us is yearning for the moment when we can really talk turkey to the Hungarians (*wenn wir einmal Fraktur reden koennen*)." [49]

These few examples of the methods of Nazi penetration in Hungary and the nature of the resistance to it should clarify the main course of political events to which I now return.

The Plight of Satellite Diplomacy.

In the face of the growing assertiveness of Hungarian independence, the Germans whipped up interest in the formation of a Rumanian-Croat-Slovak bloc against Hungary. Hungary's relations with the two German protected puppet states, Tiso's Slovakia and Pavelić's Croatia, were, to put it mildly, unfriendly, and relations with Rumania were even worse, having several times approached the point of a severance of diplomatic relations. Both Hungary and Rumania were manifestly preparing for a private showdown at the end of the general war, if not sooner.

As first secretary of our Bucharest legation, in 1942 I had a special assignment regarding the affairs of the Hungarian minority in southern Transylvania. Thus I witnessed the Antonescu regime apply ruthless discriminatory measures against members of the Hungarian minority group. Thousands of tragic cases accumulated in the files of our legation and consulates. Diplomatic protests had no result whatever. The Rumanian Government on their part complained about the persecution of the Rumanians in northern Transylvania. The whole situation seemed utterly confused and hopeless.

Hitler himself envisaged the war between Hungary and Rumania but desired to postpone it. He explained his views on the matter to Mussolini, recalling how he had stated to the Rumanians and Hungarians that:

> if, at all costs, they wanted to wage war between themselves, he would not hinder them, but they would both lose by it. However, it would be a problem if both countries now withheld petroleum for the war which they wanted to fight between themselves later. It would be the duty of the Foreign Ministers of the Axis to deal with both countries persuasively and calmly so as to prevent an open break.[50]

In order to avoid an open conflict in the Axis camp, Berlin and Rome decided, in the summer of 1942, to appoint an Italo-German commission headed by a German and an Italian plenipotentiary minister (Hencke and Ruggieri) to study the complaints of the Hungarian minority in southern Transylvania and those of the Rumanian minority in northern Transylvania. The commission spent almost two months in Transylvania, investigated hundreds of individual cases, and prepared a long report which recommended several measures to the Hungarian and Rumanian governments aimed at ameliorating the situations of their respective minorities. Moreover, Italo-German military commissions were established in northern and southern Transylvania. These watchdog commissions informed the German and Italian governments of the troubles in Transylvania and tried to improve the situation of the minorities by means of direct intervention with the local authorities.

Such Italo-German conciliatory efforts proved to be superficial palliatives and the Germans supported the Rumanians almost openly. The weakening of Hungary, as recommended by the German General Staff in 1938,[51] remained the constant goal of German foreign policy. This policy was strengthened in Hungarian-Rumanian relations by the fact that Rumania had a strategic key position in the war against Soviet Russia, had carried out a full mobilization, and in general had contributed to the German war efforts incomparably more than Hungary. In addition Hitler disliked the Hungarians, and had a great liking for the Rumanian dictator, Antonescu. As Hitler's interpreter later was to put it, Antonescu was "one of Hitler's closest intimates and was even kept more closely in the picture than Mussolini. He was the only foreigner from whom Hitler ever asked for military advice when he was in difficulties. . . . He made long speeches just like Hitler, usually starting off at the creation of Rumania, and somehow relating everything he said to the hated Hungarians, and the recovery of Transylvania. This hatred of Hungary, too, made him congenial to Hitler, for the Führer despised the Magyars." [52] Antonescu indicated to the Führer his determination to recover northern Transylvania by force of arms and "Hitler took a secret pleasure in Antonescu's outbursts against the Hungarians, and even went so far as to hint that he might perhaps give him a free hand later in his plans of conquest." [53]

Surrounded again by a sort of revived Little Entente, which was protected this time by Germany, the Hungarian Government, on its part, tried again to rely on Italy. This policy was bound to fail because Italy gradually declined to the status of Hitler's vassal and Mussolini decided to fight along with Hitler until the very last. Despite several disappointments the Hungarians tried to win Italy's support because they saw no other alternative.

For these reasons, the Hungarian Government sought time and again to explore tentatively the possibilities of electing an Italian king.[54] The advanced age of the Regent was another reason for such soundings. The Duke of Aosta, cousin of Victor Emmanuel III, and a possible candidate of the Hungarian Government for the throne of St. Stephen, became seriously ill and died in March, 1942. Meanwhile, the son of Regent Horthy, Stephen, was elected deputy Regent. The right of succession was not attached to this position, but Stephen Horthy might have been elected as Regent in case of vacancy. He was notoriously anti-Nazi and his election was strongly opposed by Germany and the rightist Hungarian politicians. Stephen Horthy, however, soon disappeared from the political scene. In August, 1942, the day before he was scheduled to return to Budapest, he was killed in a mysterious airplane accident at the Russian front behind the Hungarian lines. The Hungarians then reverted to the Italian solution and endeavored to strengthen Hungary's independence with the establishment of a personal union with Italy under King Victor Emmanuel. But the Duce reacted adversely to this plan, saying that he had entertained a similar proposition in regard to the Duke of Aosta, "but with him dead, nothing else will be done." [55]

Prime Minister Kállay was anxious to clarify personally the delicate political problems in Rome, and arranged for a trip to Italy in November of 1942. This was postponed by Mussolini because of the collapse of the Libyan front. "In fact, this is not the time to welcome any guest," remarked Ciano.[56] Eventually Kállay visited Rome in early April, 1943. The main object of his visit was to gain Italian support for the policy of resistance to Germany. Kállay explained to Mussolini that the formation of an anti-Hungarian Little Entente was being effected under German auspices, and requested support against it. Mussolini was also informed of the Hungarian determination to send no more soldiers to Germany for the Russian campaign. Kállay told him of Hungary's intention to fight the constantly growing German threat with the aid of the Rome Government. He expounded the idea of creating a bloc in the Balkans to resist Germany. The Duce, however, seemed to have no interest in the Hungarian suggestions.

As a matter of fact, events in Italy soon brought the situation to a conclusion. Italy's exhausted forces were weakened to a point where she was not even able to press her own interests. After the African campaign the English and Americans landed in Sicily in July, 1943. Mussolini was forced to resign, and Marshal Badoglio's government prepared the way for Italy's surrender. The Italian Armistice Treaty, signed on September 3, was published five days later.

The political division of the Hungarian Foreign Ministry, having received news of the Italian armistice in the absence of the prime minister and the foreign minister, immediately set about drafting a government announcement. This stated that the Tripartite Pact ceased to be valid after the collapse of Italy, and Hungary had regained her liberty of action. But Kállay and Ghyczy did not see their way clear to accept this course, for they feared German reprisals. With the Allies so far removed, both thought it premature to expose the country to such a test in the absence of the most elementary technical means necessary for a change of front. To proclaim the termination of the Tripartite Pact would have undoubtedly provoked an immediate German occupation of Hungary, followed by the total extermination of all anti-Nazi elements and the complete mobilization, by a puppet government, of all Hungarian material resources and manpower against the Allies.

As events developed in Italy, the Germans were prepared to press home their demands. The German minister to Hungary, Dietrich von Jagow, informed Ghyczy of Hitler's impending message to Mussolini acknowledging the government constituted by the latter as the only legitimate Italian government. He made it clear that the German Government awaited a statement expressing a similar attitude from the Hungarian Government. The Hungarian Government, however, was reluctant to follow this course, for the Badoglio government appeared to be the sole legal representative of Victor Emmanuel. After repeated German pressure, Ghyczy found a compromise solution. In a letter he merely recognized *de facto* the Mussolini government,[57] an action which infuriated the Germans. In this confused situation the Foreign Ministry could and did consider pro-Badoglio members of the Italian Legation staff as accredited representatives of their country. The situation became more complicated after the establishment of a pro-Mussolini Legation in Budapest. Two Italian Legations fought each other. Still, the diplomatic privileges of the Badoglio diplomats were safeguarded; they were received in the Foreign Ministry, and the Italian Cultural Institute of Budapest was left in the hands of its former administrators. Only after the Germans had ousted Kállay's government was the Institute turned over to Casertano, Mussolini's Minister to Hungary. After the German occupation of Budapest the SS treated the Royal Italian diplomats outrageously, "making the members of the so-called Badoglio Legation run around for hours in the courtyard." [58]

Kállay's general policy was founded on the supposition that British and American forces would reach Hungary's frontiers by the beginning of 1944, possibly at an earlier date. Such a development would have opened the way for Hungary to join the Allies against Germany. Some contacts were made with the Allies in 1942, but official talks did not take place before 1943.

The first feeler was in February, 1943. A Hungarian newspaperman, Andrew Frey, was sent by the Foreign Ministry to establish contact with English and American diplomats in Istanbul. Subsequently an official of the Foreign Ministry László Veress, was dispatched on a special mission to Istanbul, where he informed the British Embassy of Hungary's determination not to resist the Allies (should their forces reach the frontiers of Hungary), but to turn against the Germans. At the same time he transmitted Hungary's request that Czechoslovak, Rumanian, and Yugoslav troops should not take part in the occupation of Hungary.

The British took cognizance of this information and asked that a staff officer be sent to discuss the military aspects of the case. Nevertheless, such a risky step was not undertaken. The Allied forces were still at a great distance from the boundaries of Hungary.

Talks resumed when Dezsö Ujváry was appointed Consul General at Istanbul. Ujváry and Veress told the British Minister plenipotentiary, Sterndale Bennett, on August 17, 1943, that Hungary was ready to accept the Casablanca formula for unconditional surrender, and asked Bennett to inform the other Allied governments of Hungary's decision. Hungary's surrender, of course, was still regarded as practicable only if the military situation made it possible.

President Roosevelt and Premier Churchill allegedly received the news of Hungary's acceptance of the "unconditional surrender" clause at the Quebec Conference, and the Soviet government was informed shortly thereafter. The reply was dispatched to the Hungarian government through Sir Hughe Knatchbull-Hugessen, British ambassador to Turkey. On September 9, 1943, he received Veress aboard a British ship on the sea of Marmora. The British statement, made in the name of the three major Allied Powers, suggested how the Hungarian people could "work their passage home" in the following manner:

(1) The Hungarian Government was to confirm its August 17 declaration about Hungary's capitulation, and the acceptance of the Allied conditions;

(2) The capitulation of Hungary was to be kept secret; to be published by the Allies and by the Hungarian Government at the same time only at a date found mutually suitable. At the express wish of the Hungarian negotiator, it was agreed not to publish it, in any case, before the Allies reached the boundaries of Hungary;

(3) Hungary was to reduce her military cooperation with Germany, step by step, notably by withdrawing her forces from Russia, and by promoting the passage of Allied air forces across Hungary to attack German bases;

(4) Hungary gradually was to stop her economic cooperation with Germany, refusing to carry out her share in German war production;

(5) Hungary was to pledge herself to resist a possible German attempt to occupy Hungary. To further this object, the Hungarian Army Staff was to be reorganized to enable the army to cut loose from the Germans, and to attack them;

(6) Hungary was to surrender all her resources, her transportation system and her air bases to the Allies, at a given date, to pursue the fight against the Germans;

(7) An Allied Military Commission was to land on Hungarian soil, at an opportune date, to prepare the necessary measures for Hungary's surrender;

(8) A regular radio connection was to be established between the Allies and the Hungarian government organs. The Allies were to be kept informed about the German and Hungarian situations. The dispositions and instructions of the Allies concerning Hungary's moves were to be conveyed in this manner.[59]

But it did not prove easy to live up to these conditions, the mere preliminary understandings for an armistice treaty to be concluded when the Allied forces reached the boundaries of Hungary. Hungary was hemmed in and controlled by the Germans. Still some important results were achieved.

Through the Hungarian Minister in Lisbon, Andor Wodianer, and Sir Ronald Campbell, British ambassador to Portugal, Ghyczy confirmed Ujváry's power in the August 17 notification of Hungary's acceptance of the Casablanca formula for unconditional surrender.

Allied flying units, in passage over Hungary, were not fired upon or chased by Hungarian fighter planes. On the contrary, their flights were facilitated by information about air defense. The demand of the German Army High Command (September, 1943) that it should be allowed to garrison western Hungary with five German flying units was firmly refused. The important practical result of this attitude was, that until German troops occupied the country, Hungarian territory was not bombed by the British and Americans.

Secret radio connections had been established between Budapest and the Allies in September, 1943. Veress brought a shortwave transmitter and receiver from Istanbul. This had been placed in the basement of the Budapest police headquarters building. At certain hours of the day regular, direct, short-wave communication, via Istanbul, was maintained with an Allied agency.

The government made repeated efforts to secure the return of all Hungarian troops from Russia. The Chief of Staff of the Hungarian Army went, on three occasions, to German Headquarters, under instructions to arrange for the sending home of Hungarian soldiers from Russia. Hitler did not give a direct answer. He merely said he would not place any more Hungarian soldiers in the front lines. At last, on February 9, 1944, Regent Horthy himself wrote to Hitler, asking for the release of the Hungarian forces. His argument was that the war's approach to Hungary necessitated their presence at home for the defense of their country's frontiers.[60]

After the contacts had been made and maintained in Istanbul, further negotiations were undertaken through the Stockholm,[61] Lisbon, and Berne legations. The Stockholm and Berne legation staffs were reorganized to facilitate strictly confidential parleys. No such changes were necessary in Lisbon.

To reshuffle the Army Staff was more difficult, and the rearrangements in it were much less extensive. A reliable military attaché, however, was sent to Istanbul to get in touch with the Allies.

Talks with the emissaries of the United States took place mainly in Switzerland, and were conducted by the Hungarian Minister to Switzerland, Baron George Bakách-Bessenyey. A glance at the first contacts will perhaps characterize the atmosphere of these conversations.

At the end of August, 1943, I was dispatched as diplomatic courier from Budapest to Geneva where Bakách-Bessenyey had the first secret talks with an American emissary. I carried instructions for Bessenyey in my diplomatic pouch through Germany, and was supposed to return with Bessenyey's report containing the American suggestions.

During my stay in Geneva I contacted several persons in touch with the Western Allies and the governments-in-exile. I discussed with them the world situation and the expected fate of Hungary. One of the best informed persons told me the following: Stalin was no maniac of the Hitler sort. He was too much the shrewd Georgian peasant to be misled into a downright expansionist policy, fraught with so many dangers. Thus, the almost certain Russian occupation of Hungary would be but a temporary measure. Hungary would be allowed to work out an independent political existence of her own after the conclusion of the peace treaty. That did not mean, of course, that Soviet Russia would tolerate an anti-Bolshevist regime in Hungary, of the Horthy type. No doubt, it would be necessary to reform Hungary's antiquated social and political system, and to carry out a radical land reform with the progressive parties of the country, like the Smallholders Party, the Democratic Party and the Social Democrats, supported on a coalition platform by a Communist Party.

I was deeply impressed by this opinion, which was expressed in the most decided manner and shared by other competent persons in contact with Western circles, and relayed the conversations to Bessenyey. I risked mentioning to him the possibly dubious value of our parley with the Americans in case of a Russian occupation of the Danubian area. Bessenyey, instead of arguing, simply referred me to the map of Europe in our Geneva consulate-general. He pointed to the Balkans and the Danube Valley with the remark that the Western powers simply could not afford a Russian domination of this geographically most important area, the gateway to Western Europe, because it would be more dangerous to their safety than a German victory. With these words Bessenyey expressed the general conviction of leading Hungarian statesmen and diplomats.

As was mentioned, during this period the Allied powers pressed the Hungarian Government to withdraw all Hungarian troops from Russia. At the same time Hitler urged Hungary to occupy a substantial part of the Balkan peninsula. The Hungarian Foreign Ministry opposed the acceptance of Hitler's proposal, which was considered as a further involvement in the war. It was Regent Horthy's idea that Hungary should combine the two suggestions coming from the opposite camps. There would be an apparent compliance with Hitler's demands. Hungary would withdraw her troops from Russia, and Hungarian troops would take part in the occupation of the Balkans where they would be in a position to surrender to the advancing Anglo-American armies, and push on against the Germans. Horthy, like most of the Hungarian statesmen, supposed that the Allied offensive in the Balkans would soon take place. When Bessenyey explained Horthy's idea to the American negotiator, the American opposed it most resolutely. His advice was that Hungary should immediately withdraw her troops from Russia, should not take part in the occupation of the Balkans and should turn against the Germans as soon as Italy's imminent surrender was announced. Otherwise, he said, it would be too late to change sides in the war and the Hungarian nation would share the terrible punishment to be imposed on the German people.

Bessenyey's report about the Geneva parleys would have badly compromised both the Kállay government and Regent Horthy if it had fallen into the hands of the Germans. Since the Nazis were not very discriminating in their choice of means, I put several small bottles of benzine and some inflammable material into my pouch containing the reports to facilitate their quick destruction should the Nazis try to acquire them during my two days transit through Germany. At night I slept with the pouch under my head, and a cigarette lighter was always at hand.

I had hardly reached Budapest when the Italian armistice agreement was published.[62] Ghyczy reviewed Hungary's foreign political situation in the Council of Ministers on September 14, 1943. The Council decided to ask Germany for the repatriation of all Hungarian troops from Russia and took a stand against Hungary's participation in any military action on the Balkans.

In Budapest, when I reported the various rumors and hints predicting the Russian occupation of Hungary, the general reaction was exactly like that of Bessenyey. The Italian minister in Budapest, a staunch Fascist, registered ironically the opinion prevailing in Hungary in the following manner: "I hear from all quarters: We are expecting an Anglo-American invasion in the Balkans. The decisive battle will be fought southeast of Budapest, in the plains of Lake Balaton. It will be there that the Magyars will unite themselves with the Allies and will get rid of the Germans and probably even of the Russians. Until then all efforts in any direction would be futile and harmful." [63]

Parleys with Western emissaries continued under the assumption that an Anglo-American landing would take place in the Balkans. Up to the German occupation of Hungary this assumption was not contradicted by the Western negotiators, although they repeatedly advised Hungary to contact Soviet Russia. Thus Hungarian politicians and diplomats were in the dark about the real situation created by the Quebec and Teheran Conferences.

Following Hungaro-American conversations, conducted in Berne, three days before the Germans occupied Hungary, a United States military mission was parachuted to Hungarian soil. It was composed of four members under the command of a colonel, and provided with a special radio set, one of its tasks being to utilize this means to give information directly to the American Army Command. A prominent American diplomat, well acquainted with Hungary, was assigned to take part in the expedition but was unable to arrive in time. According to a preconceived plan, the mission landed in the vicinity of the Yugoslav border. The Hungarian detachment which took them prisoners was told that they had been about to fly to Tito, but having lost their bearings had landed farther to the north than they intended. In Budapest, the head of the intelligence section of the Ministry of Defense, aware of the real purpose of the mission, talked over the gloomy situation with the American flyers, who were soon to become German war prisoners. The sending of a British Army Mission was also contemplated, but failed to materialize because of the German occupation of Hungary.

Throughout these contacts with the English and Americans the Hungarian diplomats and statesmen were under the spell of "wishful thinking." They were loath to believe rumors about an exclusive Russian occupation of Hungary. Despite repeated Western advice, they did not start negotiations with Moscow. Such negotiations seemed futile. Their convictions, however, had some realistic foundation, based on political and strategical considerations. In the war the Western powers, and specifically the United States, had by far the greatest resources and increasing power. Under these conditions the handing over of central Eastern Europe to Soviet Russia in the last period of the war seemed inconceivable. Russian rule in this strategically important area was equivalent with its Bolshevization. Therefore they simply refused to credit rumors that Southeastern Europe could be recognized as an exclusive Russian zone of interest by the Allies.

In this conviction the leading Hungarian statesmen and diplomats were willing to take all risks and were eager to make all possible preparatory steps for an Anglo-American occupation, which was the basis of their policy. On the other hand, for the British and Americans, talks with Hungarian emissaries were only part of the Allied psychological warfare. British and American negotiators, following the course of international events, gradually limited the objectives of the conversations. Finally their interest was mostly concentrated on matters of military intelligence and sabotage. After the Anglo-American decision at Quebec and the Anglo-American-Russian decision at Teheran, the game was up for Hungary, as far as military occupation of the Danubian region was concerned. With no Anglo-American forces to rely upon, Hungary never was given a real opportunity to assist the Western Allies.[64]

In the course of the contacts with the Western powers Hungary obtained little positive encouragement as to its future position in Danubian Europe, but instead was threatened with a variety of unattractive possibilities in case it failed to turn in time against the Germans. It is true that threats remained far behind the realities which actually occurred in Hungary in the postwar period, but these tragic events were not the consequence of Hungary's good or bad behavior. Western negotiators repeatedly demanded that Hungary should begin an all-out resistance against Germany irrespective of consequences to the anti-Nazi elements in the country, but never indicated the possible reward for such suicidal action. The example of Poland was not reassuring and that of the Baltic states even less. Under the circumstances a limited cooperation with the Axis powers seemed to be the only means for the maintenance of Hungary's relative independence for the final show-down.

Another characteristic feature of the parleys was the emphasis laid by Western representatives upon Allied unity. Simultaneously with the advice that Hungary should start negotiations with the Soviet Union, they gave optimistic assurances concerning Soviet Russia's prospective role and intentions in international affairs. For example, it was suggested that Stalin would welcome Count Antal Sigray—a leading legitimist with an American wife—as Hungarian foreign minister. Allied unity seemed to be so perfect that the coming world was pictured as a sincere collaboration between the Western and the Soviet political systems. The dissolution of the Comintern, formal reestablishment of the Orthodox Church, the revival of patriotism in Russia, and other Soviet gestures seemed to support this opinion. There were some hints too that the Soviet Union might develop her internal structure on the lines of the Western democracies. The Atlantic Charter and the noble principles of other wartime agreements, accepted by both East and West, seemed to be the indication of a changed Soviet approach toward international cooperation. It was assumed that the leaders of the Soviet Union understood and accepted the inevitability of the simultaneous existence of Communism and capitalism, and that differing ideological systems could co-exist and peacefully cooperate as they had done so many times in the past. It was even thought that a middle road between Soviet Communism and Western capitalism was possible.

Such ideas, commonly accepted in the western countries, found little credit in Hungary—a country which had already had experience with Communists in 1919. Nonetheless, the fact remained that the Soviet Union was a much praised ally of the great western democracies, and people—fearful of a Russian preponderance in postwar Europe—were inclined to ponder comforting arguments. Another factor was, that in the territories under German occupation, the Communist and non-Communist parties closely collaborated against the Nazi invaders.

The Four Freedoms, together with the principles expressed in the Atlantic Charter and in the United Nations declaration, had a tremendous impact upon all social classes in Hungary. It was supposed that the Western powers, in addition to these general principles, had some concrete plans for the reorganization of Europe in general and the Danubian region in particular. It was obvious that principles alone, without the support of adequate military strength and political determination, could not operate in the vacuum created by the collapse of Hitler's Europe. Few persons, at that time, had a premonition that the fate of Europe was being shaped by extra-Continental forces—perhaps full of good-will but often very far from political realities. However it may have been, the nations living in the critical danger zone had no choice and thus accepted inevitable facts and welcomed ideas which sometimes gave a gleam of hope for a decent future. They felt some misgivings, but had no conception of the scope of the impending catastrophe.

End of Independence.

In the last years of the war, the Germans became increasingly dissatisfied with Hungary's military and economic contributions to the Axis war efforts. Nevertheless, what provoked the most vehement outburst of wrath from the Nazis was the fact that German demands that Hungary persecute the nearly one million Hungarian Jews in the Nazi way, were to no avail. Hungary was the only place in Hitler-dominated

Europe where the Jews had a relatively tolerable life. All other German satellites were willing to adopt and carry out the anti-Jewish Nuremberg rulings as a preliminary condition for German favor. This policy increased in violence as the war proceeded, and became a categorical rule in Hitler's Reichstag address of April 26, 1942.

Hitler's government at first repeatedly approached Döme Sztójay, the Hungarian Minister in Berlin. Later, on October 17, 1942, it sent a sharply-worded note to the Hungarian government enumerating the steps to be taken. Essentially it demanded the marking of Jews with the yellow star badge, their complete exclusion from all economic and cultural life, and their deportation to the east.[65] The Hungarian Government flatly refused to accede to these measures. Martin Luther, assistant Secretary of State in the German Foreign Ministry, expressed to Sztójay his "sincere regret" about the negative answer. He emphasized that the German government was willing to accede to all the wishes of the Hungarian government by designating areas in the east suitable for the settling of the Jews. He strongly disclaimed the rumors broadcast by England and America about the treatment of Jews in Germany, and said they could hardly be substantiated by facts.[66]

In early 1943 the Germans became infuriated with Kállay and, through Horthy, tried to force him from power. Hitler invited the Regent to his headquarters in April 1943. The German leader did not conceal his dissatisfaction over Hungary's small military contribution in Russia and over the general trend of Kállay's policy. He dwelt upon the ill-concealed decline of Hungarian cooperation and mentioned certain facts proving Hungary's determination to approach the English and Americans. The Germans summed up their accusations in a memorandum which particularly emphasized Hungary's firm determination not to commit any act of war against the Western powers, and the small output of Hungarian industry and agriculture. Moreover, the German memorandum accused the Hungarian cabinet of failing to support the war, Prime Minister Kállay of having lost faith in an Axis victory, and Professor Albert Szent-Györgyi, the famous biologist and Nobel prize-winner, of having conducted negotiations in Istanbul with the Western powers and of boasting there that Hungary was protecting 70,000 Jewish refugees. The memorandum then listed a number of threats to force Hungary into a more active participation in the Axis struggle. Hitler and Ribbentrop attacked Horthy with special vehemence because Hungary refused to settle the Jewish question according to the course set by Germany. To Horthy's counter-question as to what he should do with the Jews, now that he had deprived them of almost all possibilities of livelihood—he could not kill them off—the Reich Foreign

Minister declared that "the Jews must either be exterminated or taken to concentration camps. There was no other possibility." [67]

As is evident from the memorandum handed to Horthy, the Germans were not entirely ignorant of the moves and purposes of the Kállay government. Hitler again brought up the German demand that Hungarian forces be sent to the Balkans. Horthy flatly refused, referring to an earlier decision of the Hungarian Government. He reiterated Hungary's determination not to allow troops to go beyond her borders. [68]

After Horthy's return to Hungary the German Government proposed to the Italian Government that the German and Italian envoys in Budapest should cease all their personal contacts with Kállay, who at that time also acted as foreign minister. This scheme, an attempt to overthrow Kállay through boycotting, failed because of the non-cooperative attitude of the Italian Government.

In the following months Hungaro-German relations went from bad to worse. [69] In January, 1944, Luther bluntly told Sztójay that Hitler was not willing to wait until the end of the war for the settlement of the Jewish question. He once more pointed out that the handling of the Jewish question in Hungary was responsible for the chilly atmosphere surrounding German-Hungarian relations.

In late February, 1944, the German Government requested the Hungarian Government's consent to the passage of 100,000 German soldiers, urgently needed to check the Russian offensive. The Hungarian Government first refused passage, saying that this would provoke Allied bombings of the country. Consent was later given, on condition that German troops avoid Budapest. After this answer was received the Germans dropped the matter. On March 15, Horthy received an urgent invitation from Hitler. The German minister in Budapest indicated that Hitler would like to discuss the question of the withdrawal of Hungarian troops from Russia—a wish expressed in Horthy's letter of February 9. [70] The German minister suggested that, since the negotiations would be of a military nature, Horthy should take the minister of defense and the chief of staff with him.

Previously the Hungarian Government had received reliable reports of German troop concentrations along the Hungarian border, and asked the purpose of these. The Germans indignantly rejected the supposition that the troops were intended to be used for the occupation of Hungary, and claimed to be insulted. The troops were, according to the German answer, destined to strengthen the sector of the Russian front held by the Rumanians. But, in spite of the categorical German denial, officials of the Foreign Ministry made preparations to destroy secret documents. Kállay sought to persuade the Regent to postpone the visit for a fortnight. Horthy, however, accepting the advice of those who wanted "to face the danger," declared he was not afraid of Hitler. He left for Germany on March 17, accompanied by the Foreign Minister, the Minister of Defense and the Chief of Staff.

In Klessheim he was told by Hitler, during a violent scene, that Germany could no longer tolerate the repetition of events which had occurred in Italy. Therefore the Kállay government should be dismissed immediately and a new and reliable government must assure, by every means, full military and economic cooperation between Hungary and Germany. The Hungarian press and radio must change their tune, and the Jewish question must be settled. And to enforce these demands, Hitler added, a German military occupation of Hungary was absolutely necessary.[71]

Horthy flatly refused. He announced that in the event of an occupation he would resign. When it appeared that Hitler intended to confront him with a *fait accompli* Horthy left the room and decided to return to Hungary immediately. By various pretexts his departure was prevented. Nor could the delegation get in touch with Budapest by telephone. As an eyewitness described it, "a most convincing fake air-raid was staged, which even included a smoke screen over the castle, as an excuse for preventing Horthy's special train from leaving, and the telephone line to Budapest turned out to be 'badly hit', so that the Regent was cut off from the outside world." [72]

In the meantime Horthy's military suite did everything to convince him of the futility of military resistance. Their main argument was the German threat that Hungary would be occupied by Rumanian, Slovak, and Croatian troops.[73] Moreover, they emphasized that a hostile German occupation would mean the extermination of the Hungarian leading classes, not to speak of the fate of democratic elements, and of Jews, Poles, and other refugees. Horthy was forced to see Hitler again. In the course of another dispute Hitler sent for Field Marshal Keitel and asked about the possibilities of suspension or change in the plan of occupation. Keitel's answer was that the trains already were rolling toward Hungary; the occupation could not be deferred, and the plans could not be changed. Horthy was then assured that the occupation would be of an exclusively military nature and that the occupying force would not interfere with the political life of the country, and would be withdrawn after the appointment of a new government. Influenced by all these considerations, Horthy showed a willingness to remain Regent for the time being. In spite of this agreement, however, his return was again delayed until after the occupation of Budapest. The Nazis did not take chances.

The German war machine started rolling into Hungary on the night of March 18-19, 1944. On the morning of March 19, the capital, the most important airfields, railway junctions, and other places of strategic importance were in the hands of the Germans. The Hungarian Government, concurrently with the military occupation, received false messages from the Hungarian delegation indicating that everything was settled with the Germans and that nothing should be done until the return of the Regent. Ghyczy had arranged, before his departure from Budapest, to communicate Hitler's plans to the Hungarian Government by one of two alternate code messages. But the Germans were too cautious to be fooled by this device and did not transmit the seemingly harmless text, addressed to Mrs. Ghyczy about a social engagement, until the occupation was well under way. It now became clear why Horthy was asked to bring the leaders of the Hungarian Army to Germany. In the absence of the Regent and the minister of defense there was no central military authority to order the Hungarian Army to resist. There were isolated cases of resistance, but these did not substantially change the timetable of occupation. The minister of the interior intended to issue an order of resistance to the police forces, but was dissuaded from this action, the futility of which was obvious. On March 19 when Horthy was allowed to return, he was received before the Royal Palace by a German *Ehrenwache*.

March 19, 1944, was a tragic day in Hungarian history. From this time onward the relatively calm atmosphere of the Hungarian scene changed radically. The Hungarian people began to feel the full impact of war and occupation. Allied bombing started. The looming shadow of the Nazi dictator became a cruel reality. Subsequent protestations and resignations of Hungarian diplomatic representatives in neutral countries were received with sympathy by the free world, but this did not alleviate the fate of the Hungarian people. The German security police arrested members of the Hungarian Parliament. The finest Hungarian patriots were jailed or forced underground. Hitler's promise concerning the exclusively military character of the occupation proved entirely worthless. The Gestapo started its usual work. Persecution and mass deportation of the Jews began.[74]

Kállay himself never resigned formally. Horthy first wanted to appoint a purely administrative, non-representative government composed of officials, but this was not accepted by the Germans. Subsequently Horthy asked for the cessation of arrests, and guarantees of no further intervention in Hungarian home affairs. Receiving only some vague promises, he did not comply with the German demand for the appointment of an Imrédy government but, eventually, appointed Döme Sztójay, a former general and Hungarian Minister to Germany. Sztójay had always fervently advocated a policy of complete submission to the Nazis. The new government dissolved the trade unions and the opposition parties, such as the Smallholders, the Democrats, and the Social Democrats, and, in close collaboration with the Germans, carried out the Nazification of Hungary.

The Regent assumed an ostensibly passive attitude in the first months, later resisting more or less openly the Germans and their Hungarian accomplices. The fact that the Germans did not directly take over the major government agencies left open certain possibilities for the future. The officials of the Foreign Ministry especially tried to check Nazi influence whenever they had the opportunity. Although Szentmiklóssy and Szegedy-Maszák were arrested by the Germans, the traditions of their policies prevailed to a large extent, and were revived, in a different form, by the new secretary general of the Foreign Ministry, Mihály Jungerth-Arnóthy.

Immediately after the occupation the Germans, in cooperation with the puppet Sztójay Government, carried out the anti-Jewish measures rejected by the Kállay Government in 1942. The Jews were first obliged to wear a yellow star, then they were put into ghettos and concentration camps, and finally most of them were deported "to work in Germany." These actions were carried out with amazing speed by the Germans and their chief Hungarian accomplices, László Endre and László Baky, secretaries of state in the Ministry of Interior.[75] One of the German organizers, Dieter Wisliceny, described this process at the Nuremberg trials in the following manner:

> After the entry of the German troops into Hungary, Eichmann went there personally with a large command. By an order signed by the head of the Security Police, I was assigned to Eichmann's command. Eichmann began his activities in Hungary at the end of March, 1944. He contacted members of the then Hungarian Government, especially State Secretaries Endre and von Baky. The first measure adopted by Eichmann in cooperation with these Hungarian Government officials was the concentration of the Hungarian Jews in special places and special localities. These measures were carried out according to zones, beginning in Ruthenia and Transylvania. The action was initiated in mid-April, 1944.
>
> In Ruthenia over 200,000 Jews were affected by these measures. Consequently, impossible food and housing conditions developed in the small towns and rural communities where the Jews were assembled. On the strength of this situation Eichmann suggested to the Hungarians that these Jews be transported to Auschwitz and

79

other camps. He insisted, however, that a request to this effect be submitted to him either by the Hungarian Government or by a member thereof. This request was submitted by State Secretary von Baky. The evacuation was carried out by the Hungarian Police.

Eichmann appointed me liaison officer to Lieutenant Colonel Ferency, entrusted by the Hungarian Minister of the Interior with this operation. The evacuation of Jews from Hungary began in May 1944 and was also carried out zone by zone, first starting in Ruthenia, then in Transylvania, northern Hungary, southern, and western Hungary. Budapest was to be cleared of Jews by the end of June. This evacuation, however, was never carried out, as the Regent, Horthy, would not permit it. This operation affected some 450,000 Jews. . ."[76]

Although the ultimate fate of the deported people was not known at that time, the Pope, the King of Sweden, President Roosevelt, the British Government, and the International Red Cross protested the anti-Jewish measures, particularly the mass deportations. Representatives of neutral powers in Budapest, under the leadership of the Papal Nuncio, Angelo Rotta, made energetic collective protests. The Nuncio personally lodged several protests with Prime Minister Sztójay.

The secretary general of the Foreign Ministry called the attention of the council of ministers to these protests, but the Nazi-minded ministers denied the alleged atrocities. Hungarian Nazis were enraged because of these "unjustified foreign interventions" while innocent civilians were victims of the Allied air attacks in Hungary. Secretary of State Endre in his report to the council of ministers in June, 1944, pictured the deportations in such a euphemistic way that Jungerth-Arnothy remarked sarcastically that he almost regretted not having been born a Jew and thus not having been able "to join these pleasure trips." [77]

Gradually the Regent's position strengthened and in July, he succeeded, by threatening to use force, in hindering the deportation of Jews from Budapest.[78] Protests of Allied and neutral states, interventions of the papal nuncio, and actions of the Catholic episcopate and the Protestant churches were instrumental in stiffening the resistance of the Regent. The neutral legations issued letters of protection, safe-conduct passes, and passports to Hungarian Jews. Eventually an international ghetto was established in Budapest under the protection of the neutral powers. The co-operation of the Hungarian Foreign Ministry greatly facilitated the success of these actions.[79] Throughout this period, a secretary of the Swedish Legation, Raoul Wallenberg, alone saved the lives of several thousand persons.[80]

During these months the Germans gave the Hungarian Government the most emphatic assurances about the fate of the deported Jews, and protested against the "malicious rumors" spread abroad. Germany even claimed from Hungary the food ration of these deported people.[81]

In regard to Hungarian Jews the following general ruling was laid down in Auschwitz: "Children up to the age of 12 or 14, older people over 50, as well as the sick, or people with criminal records (who were transported in specially marked wagons) were taken immediately on their arrival to the gas chambers. The others passed before an SS doctor who, on sight, indicated who was fit for work and who was not. Those unfit were sent to the gas chambers, while the others were distributed in various labor camps." [82]

As Sztójay proved a mere German puppet, Horthy sought to replace him with General Gyula Lakatos, but this action was hindered by a German ultimatum. German protests notwithstanding, Horthy gradually dismissed the most savage pro-Nazi members of Sztójay's administration. The attempt on July 20 to kill Hitler created confusion among German authorities, somewhat increasing Horthy's freedom of action. Eventually he dismissed the sick Sztójay and appointed General Lakatos as prime minister. Contact was established between the government and the underground parties.[83] The problem of an armistice was discussed in the cabinet, and in various top level secret meetings. The Germans, however, received exact information of these intentions, and arrangements were made for Ferenc Szálasi, the Hungarian Arrow-Cross leader, to take over the government at an appropriate time.[84] Meanwhile Szálasi lived in Budapest at German Headquarters.

Historical experience and practical considerations made Hungarian military strategy aim at the establishment of a strong line of defense in the eastern and southern Carpathian mountains.[85] For a variety of reasons such plans were not accepted in time by the Germans. Nazi policy was influenced to a great extent by propaganda considerations and the Nazis were reluctant to give up territories solely for strategic reasons.[86] Moreover, in Rumania the Germans desired to hold the Ploesti oil fields under any circumstances. Eventually Hitler agreed to the establishing of a line of defense in the southern Carpathians, but it was too late. When the Rumanian armistice was proclaimed on August 23, the entire Rumanian Army ceased to fight against the Red Army, and shortly afterwards the German Army in Rumania was practically annihilated. On September 5, the weak and unprepared Hungarian army began an offensive aiming at the occupation and eventual defense of the southern Carpathians in Rumanian Transylvania, but this desperate move did not take military realities into consideration and achieved little success.

In early September, 1944, the Red Army, without much difficulty, occupied the passes of the southern Carpathians. The door to the Hungarian lowlands lay open. The German military attaché in Budapest reported the critical military situation to the Hungarian authorities. The Lakatos government demanded the immediate dispatch of seven German armored divisions for the defense of the Hungarian lowlands, and intimated that otherwise Hungary would ask for an armistice. The Germans promised to fulfill the Hungarian demand. Some armored divisions promptly arrived, but did not go to the battlefront. They remained around Budapest, thus further curtailing Horthy's freedom of action.

On September 8, a Crown Council, upon the proposal of Count Stephen Bethlen, decided that Hungary should ask for an armistice. In the cabinet, however, the opinions were very much divided in the matter. During those days the experts of the Foreign Ministry alternately prepared and destroyed a variety of requests for an armistice. One type was to be addressed to the Allied Powers through the neutral legations functioning in Budapest, the other directly to the commander-in-chief of the Red Army. Because of the unpleasant alternatives, indecision and hesitation prevailed at the last moment in responsible quarters.

The Lakatos government sent out feelers to the Allies, and the invariable reply was that Hungary should ask Moscow for an armistice. This answer notwithstanding, Horthy sent General Stephen Náday by plane to Caserta on September 22, to negotiate an armistice, and suggested that Anglo-American troops should take part in the occupation of Hungary. In Caserta Field Marshal Sir Henry Maitland Wilson, Allied Commander of the Mediterranean theatre, took note of Hungary's determination to conclude an armistice but showed no particular interest in Náday's mission. Náday was told that the merits of the case must be negotiated in Moscow, since Hungary was within the Russian zone of military operations.

A few days later an armistice delegation left for Moscow.[87] Following an arrangement made with the Russian high command, Russian partisans took care of the delegation in Slovakia, which was still under German occupation. Taken by car to the city of Zvolen, the delegates left by plane for Kiev, and arrived in Moscow on October 1. General Kuznetsov received them, and Horthy's letter addressed to Marshal Stalin was delivered to him. The Hungarian delegation signed a preliminary armistice agreement on October 11.

Meanwhile, the Lakatos government made some preparations for the proclamation of the armistice, but the German military preparations in Hungary were more advanced and of greater magnitude. Before the Hungarian delegation was dispatched Hitler had been informed of Horthy's decision to offer surrender to Soviet Russia. He briefed his trouble shooter, Otto Skorzeny, and sent him to Budapest to prepare for the occupation of the Royal Castle Hill and the government buildings.[88] The German secret service knew of the anti-Nazi activities of the Regent's son, Nicholas Horthy, Jr., and a Croat spy was planted among his close collaborators. Thus Skorzeny was informed of young Horthy's meeting on October 15 with emissaries of Tito, who themselves were agents of the German secret service.[89] A trap was prepared and Nicholas Horthy, Jr., was kidnapped by Skorzeny's men after a shooting and struggle in which Horthy, Jr., was wounded and some of his guards killed. On the same day a Crown Council was held and the Regent's armistice proclamation read on the Budapest radio.[90]

This desperate attempt was bound to fail. Several German armoured divisions occupied the outskirts of Budapest. German "Tiger" tanks moved into the capital. The Nazis and their Hungarian accomplices organized everything with German thoroughness. Horthy, wanting to remain chivalrous to the end, informed Hitler's representative in Hungary about the impending armistice before the proclamation was read on the radio. Thus the Nazis had all possible advantages. Besides, as early as October 10, the Germans had kidnapped General Szilárd Bakay, commander of the army corps stationed in Budapest. Bakay was in charge of the organization of the scattered Hungarian military units and had made preparations for the arrest of the pro-German Hungarian generals. After his arrest all serious preparations for a showdown were frustrated. But in spite of these odds, Horthy decided to remain in Budapest rather than join the Hungarian fighting forces at the front and proclaim the armistice from there. Only one plan was carried out concurrently with the armistice proclamation, the release of political prisoners from Hungarian jails.

Shortly after Horthy's proclamation was read over the Budapest radio, the station was taken over by the Nazis and the proclamation countermanded and refuted. Pro-Horthy military commanders were arrested. Nazi-minded officers were in important key positions in the Hungarian Army, and they organized a conspiracy simultaneous with Skorzeny's mission. The attitude of these Hungarian army officers was probably the greatest disappointment in Horthy's life, filled as it was with vicissitudes. The bulk of the Hungarian Army and people did not know about the events until everything was over. After a short fight against the overwhelming German forces, the Lakatos government was deposed and the Arrow Cross gang of Szálasi installed by the Germans. Horthy, forced to resign, was taken prisoner with his family and taken to Germany. With the violent end of the Horthy regime, a chapter of Hungarian history terminated.[91]

It was officially announced that Horthy abdicated of his own free will, placed himself under German protection (it was not stated against whom) and surrendered his rights and powers to Ferenc Szálasi.[92] Although Justinian Cardinal Serédi, in a session of the state council of Hungary, challenged the validity of Horthy's resignation and Szálasi's seizure of power, such legalistic considerations did not change the course of events.[93] Serédi's appeal to free the detained members of Parliament was of no avail. An incomplete Parliament took note of the accomplished facts and under duress accepted Szálasi as leader of the nation.

A new wave of political persecutions began. Leading patriots were arrested, among them Joseph Mindszenty, at that time Bishop of Veszprém. In many places the mob took over. Atrocities and pogroms continued. In October and November, more than 30,000 Jews were deported from Budapest. They had to walk to the German border (almost 200 kilometres) under dreadful conditions. A large proportion of these people died during the death march or later in work camps.[94]

The cruelties were somewhat mitigated by the collective interventions of the neutral powers, notably by the representatives of the Vatican, Sweden, Switzerland, Portugal, and Spain. Protests from the Christian churches continued and the International Red Cross made great efforts. Such actions had some restraining influence on the irresponsible elements in power.[95] Officials of the Foreign Ministry invented rules of international law to convince the Arrow Cross leaders of the validity of neutral protection extended to Hungarian Jews. Daily events brought forward manifestations of both human solidarity and bestiality. Former opposition politicians formed a committee of liberation under the leadership of Endre Bajcsy-Zsilinszky and planned to overthrow the Szálasi regime by force. The plot was betrayed by a planted spy, most of the organizers caught, and the leaders executed.[96]

As the Red Army advanced the Arrow Cross Government moved to western Hungary. The Germans discovered with astonishment the inability of Szálasi, who withdrew to a castle on the Austro-Hungarian frontier to write his lifework à la Hitler's *"Mein Kampf."* Confusion and arbitrariness prevailed throughout the country, while the various factions of the Hungarian pro-Nazi parties quarreled and intrigued among themselves.[97] The Papal Nuncio and the representatives of the neutral powers, like Sweden and Switzerland, refused to follow the

Arrow Cross Government to western Hungary and remained in Budapest.[98]

Meanwhile, as the Red Army steadily approached Budapest, Hungarian patriots lived in a tragic dilemma. Overwhelming outside forces had trapped the Hungarian people between two barbarian worlds. The Hungarian nation was almost entirely engulfed in the flood of invading armies and cast into the Danubian whirlpool.

V. CHAOS: AN INTERLUDE

At the close of hostilities geography proved decisive in the misfortune of Hungary. None of the Axis satellites was in so precarious a position, for Hungary had been situated in the inner circle of the German power sphere. The peripheral location of Italy, Finland, Bulgaria, and Rumania made possible their early surrender. Events in Hungary turned out differently. Hungary did not succeed in changing sides effectively during the war, and eventually was probably in the worst political position among the former Axis satellites. She did not enjoy much sympathy in the West, and was positively disliked by the Russians. Anthony Eden said to President Roosevelt that "he thought Stalin would want to be pretty arbitrary about Hungary" because the Russians did not like the Hungarians.[1]

The Arrow Cross government decided that the entire population of Hungary should be transferred to Germany for the winter. They were supposed to return the next spring when the new German secret weapons would definitely defeat the Russians. This scheme for wholesale evacuation proved to be impracticable, both because of its inherent absurdity and because of general resistance. Nevertheless, as a consequence of forced evacuation, several thousand young men and most of the ranking government officials left the country along with the retreating German troops and the remnants of the Hungarian Army. When news spread about the lootings, rapes, and other atrocities of the invading Soviet Army, the flight became more widespread.

The country was first ravaged by the Germans, then systematically looted by the Russians. The retreating Germans blew up many important bridges and destroyed a substantial part of the transportation and communication system.[2]

Because of all these circumstances, the physical destruction and the vacuum of political power and administrative authority were more extensive in Hungary than in any other satellite state. Public administration completely disintegrated throughout the devastated territories.

The invading Red Army found a ruined country void of administration and political authorities. The old administration was non-existent or not recognized by the occupying army, which with the help of experienced Communist advisers created an entirely new political framework. Eastern Hungary was in Russian hands in the last months of 1944, but the Germans were not driven out of western Hungary until

April, 1945. Although the Red Army completely encircled Budapest on December 25, 1944, the siege of the city lasted until mid February.

In this chaotic world the survival of individuals depended on chance. Perhaps my personal experiences may give a direct and realistic picture of this period. The incidents I am about to relate occurred before and immediately after the Soviet occupation.

After the German occupation the position of officials of the political division of the Foreign Ministry became extremely precarious. Certain leading officials were arrested.[3] Consequently I withdrew into an agency of the Foreign Ministry which represented the Hungarian Government before the Mixed Arbitral Tribunals and the Permanent Court of International Justice. This agency, by a bureaucratic miracle, existed even in the war years. Under cover of this little known office I could continue the peace preparatory work with my most reliable collaborators. When Lakatos was appointed as prime minister, the secretary general of the Foreign Ministry, Jungerth-Arnóthy, officially asked me to continue the peace preparations and to use for this purpose the documents accumulated in the Foreign Ministry since the German occupation. A few days later he told me that the Government intended to appoint me as consul in Zurich where I could continue my work undisturbed by the immediate events in Hungary. He pointed out that under the forthcoming Russian occupation the government agencies might be completely paralyzed, while in Switzerland I could make good use of the material deposited at our Berne Legation. I declined to accept this appointment for a variety of reasons.

From a purely personal point of view it would have been comfortable to observe the apocalyptic events in Europe from a quiet watchpost. But I felt that it would have been a rather cowardly action to run away from the imminent danger and not to share the fate of my countrymen. Moreover, our contacts with the Western powers convinced me of the very slight value of backdoor diplomacy. If Hungary was to survive the holocaust, there must be a government in the country, and it might be more useful to try to influence events at home than to seek the goodwill of foreign powers abroad. It seemed probable at that time that the Allied powers had made certain decisions according to their own well considered interests, and I had no illusions about our capacity to influence the course of events in the last phase of the war. Since 1939, I had advocated the establishment of a government-in-exile, but competent authorities did not approve of this plan. In September, 1944, burdened with our wartime status, we were decidedly late. However, at that time, I did not suspect that the ultimate fate of Hungary was altogether independent of our wartime attitude.

Jungerth-Arnóthy appreciated my reasons and we agreed upon a compromise solution. I was to go to Switzerland as a diplomatic courier as soon as possible, and spend two or three weeks there in order to organize and prepare certain material for publication. The Foreign Ministry asked for the German transit-visa, which I received in early October. I was scheduled to leave Hungary on October 16 with another official of the political division.

The events of October 15 intervened, and shortly afterwards the new government arrested me, together with four of my colleagues from the Foreign Ministry. I was accused of having been in contact with the underground parties and of having taken part in the preparations of the armistice negotiations—actions which were considered treason. We were put in jail and dragged as traitors from various political prisons into a military prison, then to western Hungary to the internment camp of Sopron-Köhida, and finally back to the military prison in Budapest for trial.

After my arrest my apartment—especially my library—was thoroughly searched. Some compromising documents were hidden among the files of a Hungarian case we had before the Permanent Court of International Justice. While three detectives discussed whether or not to go through this huge bundle of files, I called their attention to some more books and files in the next room and suggested that they should inspect everything and divide their time accordingly. They dropped the files, and confronted with the great mass of material became confused. Having seized a few ridiculously irrelevant papers, they decided to return for a detailed search if this was deemed necessary by higher authorities.

My first jail was a huge schoolroom. About fifty people were sitting on the floor like statues. I learned later that most of them were suspected or actual Communists. In front of them was seated a gendarme, playing carelessly with his tommy gun. When I was escorted into the room the gendarme explained that it was only his merciful heart which kept him from shooting the whole undignified collection of worthless dogs. Such were the mild epithets used in his endless harangues. The young gendarme was not, however, without a sense of humor. When he asked a Serbian partisan in the group to tell a story, the latter told an anti-Nazi joke which caused an hilarious outburst. The gendarme laughed with the rest of us and the Serbian was not punished.

I discovered in the crowd two colleagues of mine from the political division of the Foreign Ministry. One of them was nursing head-wounds, the result of tortures inflicted personally by the new chief of the cabinet of the Foreign Ministry during interrogations. We were not allowed to speak to each other even if the distance had allowed it. Anyone who moved or uttered a word to his neighbor was beaten or otherwise punished. Suddenly an air raid began, and we were ordered down into the basement, for, happily for us, the gendarmes prized their own lives. While marching downstairs one of my colleagues managed to get next to me and whispered into my ear the accusations against us, and named the documents they were after. They knew, he said, of our contact with leading members of the Smallholder underground. His words came as a great relief. Relatively speaking, these were minor matters.

During subsequent interrogations it was a great help to know the real goal of the enigmatic questions. I did not deny that I had had contacts with Smallholder politicians and that I had favored an armistice instead of the senseless destruction of Hungary, but I refused to confess that I possessed the document they were looking for.

The detective inspector who led the interrogations was a short fellow with gray hair and sharp looking cold eyes. He acted with the skill of a professional and wanted to deliver something to his new masters. When I continued in my refusal, he suddenly punched me in the face. This was meant to be a *captatio benevolentiae,* because he then emphasized that they have much stronger means to open the mouths of reluctant plotters and reminded me that I had a family against whom they could apply measures. His arrogance only strengthened my determination not to reveal anything to him, whereupon he explained that he had to produce something for the foreign minister, and suggested that I should compose a copy of the document drafted originally by myself. We compromised on that, and during the night I wrote a document which proposed armistice negotiations in a rather cautious way and omitted incriminating passages.

The next day the atmosphere changed. The detective inspector obligingly expressed his conviction that we were gentlemen and that he had always known it. We were conducted to another prison—a former villa in the hills of Buda. In the villa we were put into a small room with two policemen who were told by the detective inspector that they would be shot even if they let us speak to each other. As soon as he left the room the policemen locked the door and asked us politely whether we would like to play cards with them. Our guards were changed every six hours, and with one exception all of them treated us well. We slept on the floor and did not get food every day, although later our relatives were allowed to bring us supplies. Interrogations continued under decent conditions. My wife visited me, and thus I was able to whisper instructions to her concerning which papers to destroy at home.

During the few days in the villa we met some strange people. For a short time two Arrow Cross leaders were imprisoned in our room. One of them was an old man, bleeding about the head and ears. He introduced himself as a professor and the national ideological educator of the Arrow Cross party. He contended that Szálasi was not sincerely pro-German and therefore must be eliminated as a leader. Such doctrines were the cause of his arrest and injuries, but he refused to compromise. The other man, a candidate of the new regime for a diplomatic post abroad, had had a disagreement and fist fight with the new secretary general of the Foreign Ministry over some looted Jewish property, and as a consequence had landed in jail. His fantastic stories about his heroic past greatly amused us.

We were soon separated from the Arrow Cross dignitaries and transported into a gloomy military prison full of high army officers, government officials, and political leaders. All the common criminals had been released to make room for this strange group. Our barbers were alternately a Serbian partisan and a Russian partisan who had been parachuted into Hungary. They visited us twice a week and brought news about the fate of our fellow prisoners and events of the outside world. They were surprisingly well-informed and spoke fairly good Hungarian. During air raids we were not taken to shelters, but the Russian partisans assured us that the Soviet fliers had instructions not to bomb this neighborhood. Almost every day we were escorted for a short walk in the prison yard. During one of these promenades we managed to meet the former head of the information section of the General Staff. He explained with expert knowledge the factors involved in our case and concluded: "Boys, most probably all of us will be shot before long." His matter of fact prediction was something of a shock for us, but gradually we got used to the idea. The daily executions in the prison yard created the necessary atmosphere.

Since Budapest was threatened by encirclement, around November 20 we were suddenly put into buses and taken to western Hungary. One bus took the civilian prisoners, the other the army officers. We had Prime Minister Kállay with us on our bus. Because of his presence we were accompanied by SS guards, in addition to the Hungarian gendarmes and soldiers. During a stop we were able to exchange a few words with General Lajos Veress, commander-in-chief of the Second Hungarian Army. I asked him how, with a whole army under his command, the Germans had been able to arrest him. Veress replied that his own chief of staff had betrayed him to the Germans who had sent a huge armoured unit to escort him to Budapest. He posed the question as to whether we should attack our guards and disarm them. However, the futility of such a plan was obvious. Even if we had succeeded, the problem remained of what to do and where to go. Hungary appeared to be in a state of dissolution, and it was difficult to see any goal that justified fighting against our own countrymen.

Our destination was the concentration camp of Sopron-Köhida, a well-known prison. Our group, however, was soon returned to Budapest, since our indictments had been prepared and the advance of the Red Army temporarily stalled.

A new group of political prisoners filled the military jail in Budapest. The members of the committee of liberation, under the leadership of the Smallholder, Endre Bajcsy-Zsilinszky and General János Kiss, had been arrested and imprisoned. They were tortured for weeks, and their leaders were later sentenced to death and executed. In comparison with this important plot aiming at the overthrow of Szálasi by force, our case became much less interesting—a fact which we welcomed. In the early period of our captivity, the foreign minister asked for daily reports about our hearings. By the end of November we became figures of the past, and were overshadowed by recent plots directed against the Arrow Cross regime. Nonetheless the atmosphere was gloomy. Tortures were commonly used by the Arrow Cross investigators in cases not yet before the military prosecutors. Fortunately, our case was in its last stage and our military prosecutor observed legal formalities and showed understanding toward us. During interrogations he did everything but suggest the best lines for our defense. Yet our position was still not very reassuring, because the court martial consisted of one professional military judge and four Nazi-minded officers selected by the Szálasi regime. Thus our fate depended upon many imponderables and, under martial law, death sentences could be, and actually were, rendered for almost anything. Our counsel sought to reassure us, suggesting that we would not get more than ten to fifteen years at hard labor. In those days this was consolation of a sort. Our only problem was to survive the coming weeks, and we did not think in terms of years.

The fury of the Nazis, as they sensed the inevitableness of their doom, was unrestrained. When being taken to hear our indictment, I saw the corpse of a fellow prisoner, who had been tortured to death, carried by in the corridor. At least sixteen prisoners, many of whom were simple peasants and workers who had deserted from the army, were executed daily. Just below our windows the rifles of the firing squad rattled day and night. Not knowing when our turn might come, we prepared ourselves for the worst. It was reassuring to see the quiet and determined attitude of my fellow prisoners. In the face of death one discovers much strength in the human soul.

We witnessed many human tragedies. The former minister of defense and his wife who was visiting him in the prison committed suicide. A shy-looking young newspaperman made the return trip to Sopron-Köhida with us. He had served in the army and was accused of having drafted an anti-Szálasi poster. Experts could not identify his handwriting, but a witness testified against him. He was court martialed on the day we were transported from Budapest to Sopron-Köhida, but the sentence was not handed down. We discussed his case during our journey, but none of us expected a fatal outcome. When we returned to Budapest he was put into the same prison room with us. The next morning he was escorted to a routine hearing. We never saw him again. A death sentence was imposed and he was executed immediately.

On December 2, 1944, I stood before a court martial, accused of treason. At the trial I stated in my defense that Hungary had been a battlefield for many wars in past centuries and, by our actions, we had only tried to save the country from a repetition of this tragic fate. Moreover, I pointed out that we knew, from a report of the Hungarian Minister to Germany, of Japanese mediation and German peace overtures, and we had attempted similar parleys. Before the trial our military prosecutor encouraged us to emphasize this motive for our action. After a trial lasting five hours, the court martial acquitted us. An additional factor in our acquittal probably was the proximity of the Red Army, for the court was comprised of officers fearful of the approaching Russians. Following our release I feigned colitis and took refuge in a hospital. A few days later the Nazis were again searching for us, with even more serious charges. We were designated as the representatives of the Hungarian diplomats abroad who had denounced the new Hungarian regime and had already been sentenced to death *in absentia*. Each time a door opened I had the feeling that they had come to get me.

After the complete encirclement of the city by the Red Army, I went home to spend the long ordeal of the siege with my family, in the basement of our apartment house. More than a hundred persons were crowded in the small basement with us. The siege lasted seven weeks. Conditions were most precarious; there was no water, gas, or electricity. The house was about 800 feet from the Russian lines, so we lived in the midst of the actual fighting. Human nature is very elastic, and after the first few days of the siege nobody paid much attention when the building was hit by mortar shells or bullets. However, the house was hit twice by thousand pound Russian bombs, but fortunately neither bomb exploded. Other huge bombs exploded about twenty feet from the house, and on these frightful occasions the earth was shaken and the building moved like a ship on a stormy sea. On such occasions we thought that this meant the end of our suffering.

Several times a day I had to climb upstairs to our apartment on the fourth floor to get articles needed for our daily existence. One of my duties was to prepare candles, which offered at least some light in the darkness of the shelter. Remembering the adventures of Robinson Crusoe, I used shoe laces as wicks and collected all the fats and oils I could find. The wind, snow, and bullets whistled through the apartments, long since without doors and window panes. The house was truly a ghostly castle, inhabited by a few scarcely living shadows. Since no one was prepared for such a long siege, food supplies were soon exhausted. Old people, incapable of enduring the hardships, died. It was difficult to dig their graves in the deeply frozen courtyards. Yet the frost was not without its uses. It prevented the development of epidemics—when elementary hygienic rules could not be observed.

People were starving. When horses were killed in the streets, the news spread quickly, and the population of the neighboring houses assailed the frozen bodies with all kinds of knives and axes. We had horse meat twice. This was a delicacy compared with our usual diet of beans, sauerkraut, and potatoes.

At least once a day I had to go to the next street to fetch water from an improvised well. One never knew whether or not he would return from such an expedition, since there was continual fighting in the area. We often found dead and wounded civilians around the well. We knew that Russian occupation was inevitable, and were waiting in the hope that it would bring an end to the Nazi terror and the senseless destruction.

The blatant Nazi propaganda had so often turned out to be untrue that we did not want to believe the widely publicized stories about Russian atrocities. Unfortunately, this time the Nazis told a great amount of truth. The siege was followed by general looting, robbery, and wholesale rape committed by the "liberators." The frightened population regarded the first misdeeds of the invading Russians as the cruel consequences of long and bloody fighting. Later the people became desperate, but were helpless. There was no remedy or protection against Russian action. Yet in the midst of these outrages it was good to see occasional signs of human solidarity. Some Russian soldiers gave bread and candy to starving children.

My first direct contact and "negotiation" with the Russians occurred in a rather peculiar way. One day a Russian captain came to see me and courteously explained that they knew about my resistance to the Nazis and would like to talk over with me the problems of Russian-Hungarian cooperation. Consequently, I had to spend the following two days at Russian Headquarters. The Russian officers, however, were exclusively concerned with the names and whereabouts of former Nazi spies and collaborators. I vainly explained to them that I worked in the political division of the Foreign Ministry, being in charge of the preparation of the Hungarian case for the Peace Conference, and knew nothing about spies. Having first been in jail, and then, for the last few months, in a shelter, I could have no knowledge about the behavior and whereabouts of the suspected persons. But the Russians were convinced that I knew much more and was simply reluctant to tell it. The second day their attitude became more threatening, and finally they handed me a register from the cultural section of the Foreign Ministry, containing a list of students who had received scholarships to carry on studies in foreign countries. I was supposed to disclose the spying assignments of these students. I tried in vain to explain to my interrogators that the students were sent abroad to make certain special studies in such fields as chemistry, modern languages, and so on. But by this time they had grown angry, and excitedly told me that nobody could be sent abroad without a spying assignment and that I should cease talking such nonsense. At this moment I had the same feeling that I had experienced before the Nazi interrogators, who could not believe the simple truth but were rather pleased and impressed by fantastic stories. So I explained that these fellows might, after all, have been spies, but if so, their assignment had been given them by the Ministry of Defense and the Foreign Ministry knew nothing about it. This explanation partially satisfied them and I got away with a promise that I would try to find out the names and whereabouts of Nazi spies and collaborators. Fortunately this Russian Headquarters soon moved away and I was not molested by them again.

A few days later our apartment house received a summons from the Russian military police that all men of military age should appear the next day at 6:00 A.M. with their personal documents. At headquarters they would get a certificate which would assure them free movement in town. The reason for the early hour was to enable everybody to get to his job in time. The procedure, according to the Russians, would not take more than five minutes. The whole thing seemed strange to me and aroused my suspicions. I decided not to go.

In the morning I left the house with the other men, and asked them to give the Russians the message that I had to see the Russian Commandant in Pest that same morning and therefore would have to present my documents another time. Actually I went to see friends living on the bank of the Danube. There I met two girls who were rowing champions. The day before they had found a derelict light boat on the Danube and had hidden it in their own apartment. Although crossing the river was strictly forbidden by the Russians, the girls offered to take me, along with two other persons, to Pest in the boat. This was the only way to cross the river, since all bridges had been blown up by the retreating Germans. At this time of the year, because of the floating ice, it was doubly hazardous. We lifted the boat to our shoulders and headed for the river, but as we approached the river bank we noticed four Russian soldiers, apparently under the command of a civilian.

The latter shouted at me in a fluent but hardly understandable Hungarian: "Who are you?"

"I am an official of the Hungarian Foreign Ministry and was asked by the Russian Commandant in Pest to go to see him," I replied. "These girls will take me over to the other side of the river."

The stranger snarled at me, "Where is the Hungarian Foreign Ministry? Where is such a country as Hungary? All these are of the past. A new world is here, don't you know this?"

"Of course I know very well that a new and better world will be established after the ordeals of war," I answered. "The Atlantic Charter accepted by Stalin, Roosevelt, and Churchill is a guarantee of that."

We continued our strange conversation in this vein, amidst the ruins of a ghost city. In the meantime the girls had disappeared into their house with the boat. When the Russians began to look for them I gave them wrong directions and returned to my friend's house. We waited there for an hour until everything was clear. Then we tried the crossing again. This time there were no Russians in sight, but now we would see whether a boat built for three lightly clad sportsmen could carry five persons in heavy winter clothes. As we stepped in, the boat settled lower and lower in the water, until the icy water reached to within inches of the gunwales. But the boat did not sink, and slowly and precariously we made our way across the Danube to Pest on the further shore.

The old Foreign Ministry in Buda had been completely destroyed, and a new office had been established in Pest. Exactly where it was I did not know, but finally in an old apartment building without doors or window panes, I located the new office. There I met a few colleagues who told me about a new national government at Debrecen. I was amazed to hear the following message from the new foreign minister, János Gyöngyösi: "The officials of the Foreign Ministry should not go to Buda [the part of town where I lived] because they might be deported by the Russians and in this case the Hungarian authorities could not help at all."

Thus my original skeptical outlook soon changed to deep suspicion. Moreover, I understood that experiences with the Russians in Pest were the same as in Buda, if not worse. The popular feeling was well expressed by an inscription scrawled in huge letters on the wall of a public building in Pest: "Hitler is brown; Stalin is red; both are the same gangsters."

On my return later in the day, I had to wait two hours in a snow-storm on the bank of the Danube. Because of the Russian patrols, the girls could not risk the crossing at the agreed time. When I finally arrived at home in Buda in the evening, entirely exhausted, I learned that none of those who had gone to Russian Headquarters in the morning for the five minute interview had returned. We found out later that they were first taken to a concentration camp. Then, three or four months later, those who had survived the starvation ration and other hardships in the camp were sent as prisoners of war to the Soviet Union.[4]

That evening, after the excursion to Pest, I had a high fever. The next morning my wife, accompanied by my father, went to the Russian military police to explain that I was ill and could not report with my documents for a couple of days.

"It does not matter, the MP will go to get him anyhow," was the brusque answer.

After this incident I decided to flee. I did not know that the Russians were not like the Germans. Their method of operation was vastly different. On the street where I lived they made no attempt to get the men who had not gone to headquarters themselves. Whereas we were accustomed to the methods of the uniformly applied German system, Russian procedure was a whimsically changing pattern.

I went to a friend who made arrangements to help me to cross the Danube again by boat the next morning. The same evening, however, three Russians came to the house and told him that, since he spoke Russian, he must go with them the next day as a translator. My friend gave me a huge Red Cross badge, and I was introduced as the president of the Red Cross in Buda. He explained to the Russians that I had promised to go to Pest to get milk for the children and that he must go with me in the morning. The Russians, apparently needing his services, replied cheerfully that all of us would go together in a truck over a Russian military bridge built outside the town. We made an appointment for 9:00 A.M.

The next morning, however, the Russians were not to be found. We searched around for them and at last we found them—dead drunk. It took at least an hour before we succeeded in getting them into the truck. Finally, though the driver was still intoxicated, we miraculously arrived at Pest.

It was dangerous even to walk in the city, since the Russians continued to seize men on the streets. I felt ill and found it necessary to look for a room. By chance I went to see a friend of mine who invited me to stay with him. It was a strange household, but typical of those days. The host could hardly move. He had been shot in the left foot by the Germans while escaping through their lines. His brother-in-law, a very young man, had been shot in the lung. The boy had gone to the garden to fetch some fresh snow, which was used instead of water during the siege, and the German SS troops in the next house shot him simply for sport. A doctor living in the house took care of them. I had a high fever myself, and the doctor discovered that I had pneumonia, but fortunately he was able to procure some medicine.

I stayed in bed for ten days in a rather serious condition. Then, while still convalescing, I tried to hunt for a truck or train to take me to Debrecen, the chief town in northeastern Hungary, to join the new government. I obtained the necessary official papers and recommendations from the only government office in Pest. These papers, however, were of no great value, since the Red Army did not respect documents issued by Hungarian authorities. Trucks were operated by the Communist Party, and the drivers took no interest in official papers. They were willing to take passengers, but only for a huge tip which I was not able to afford. Three times a week there was an overcrowded train to Debrecen. By train the journey of about 120 miles took, at that time, from two to five days. It was necessary to change at least twice. On these occasions the men were often taken by the Russians and put to work for a couple of days. Then they were sometimes seized and taken as prisoners of war.

These prospects were not appealing, but I had to risk the journey since the situation in Pest was intolerable. Personal safety did not exist. Moreover, I was in rather bad shape after the pneumonia. I had lived for months chiefly on beans and potatoes, and was very weak. In Debrecen, where more food was available, I hoped to recover my strength and to be able to send food to my family. Finally, together with a friend, I succeeded in getting on a train. My friend spoke Russian, and, at that time, such ability was a great advantage. Of course the train consisted only of freight cars. Everybody had to stand, and people were pressed together like sardines. The warmth of human bodies made up for the lack of heat. For two days we travelled under these conditions, but after some narrow escapes from being taken prisoner, we eventually reached Debrecen. I had started the journey still weak from pneumonia, and arrived emaciated and completely exhausted.

In Debrecen I contacted Gyöngyösi, the new foreign minister. I told him of the peace preparatory work done under the old regime. In the course of our conversations I reported that the bulk of the material had been deposited with the Hungarian Legation at Berne, while a smaller portion was hidden in Budapest. At this time the Foreign Minister showed little interest in the matter. His lack of interest was, in all probability, due to his mistrust of individuals who served under the old regime. To some extent, however, his apathy may have stemmed from a realization that to continue peace preparatory work in the face of the Russian occupation was futile.

This being the case, I did not make further efforts to see the new leaders of the country, but did my best to regain my physical strength. In April, 1945, I returned to Budapest. This time I travelled under decent conditions on a special government train which took the officials of the central authorities to the capital. I did not begin to go regularly to the Foreign Ministry until the end of May, when I had to assume new responsibilities.[5]

Part II

Diplomacy in the Shadow of the Red Star

VI SOVIET AND WESTERN POLITICS

Armistice Agreement and Allied Control Commission.

The terms of the armistice agreements were almost equally harsh for all former Axis satellite states, but Hungary was probably in the worst political position of them all at the close of hostilities. In point of time she was the last of the Axis satellites to conclude an armistice treaty with the three major Allies.[1] Unlike the armies of Rumania and Bulgaria, the Hungarian Army had not turned against the Germans, a fact which did not improve Hungary's international position in the armistice period. The country was isolated, with neither diplomatic representatives abroad nor friends among the victorious states. Moreover, the Hungarians are not Slavs and have a western political and cultural background and tradition. Thus it was more difficult for them to understand the Russian mind than for the Slav or Orthodox peoples. The Nazis were barbarians but they had a comprehensive system. The Soviet Russians had none and their reactions were incalculable, or at least seemed so to the Hungarians during the initial phase of the armistice period.

The armistice agreement contained clauses of a political, military, economic and financial nature. Hungary declared war on Germany and placed all her resources military and otherwise, at the disposal of the Allied (Soviet) High Command for prosecuting the war. She was reduced to her pre-war frontiers and required to evacuate all Hungarian troops and officials from territories returned to Hungary since 1938. The two Vienna awards were declared to be null and void. Hungary was obliged to release all prisoners of war and persons held in confinement because of their activities in favor of the United Nations, or as a result of discriminatory legislation. All such legislation was to be repealed. Fascist organizations were to be dissolved. Hungary was required to cooperate in the apprehension and trial, as well as the extradition, of persons accused of war crimes. The country was occupied by the Red Army, and until September, 1947, lived under the strict rule of the Allied Control Commission (hereafter ACC)—a fact which greatly reduced Hungarian sovereignty, both in internal and foreign affairs. Hungarian authorities were to carry out the orders and instructions issued by the Soviet High Command or ACC for the purpose of securing the execution of the armistice terms. These terms were interpreted extensively by the same authorities; thus both the Red Army and the ACC

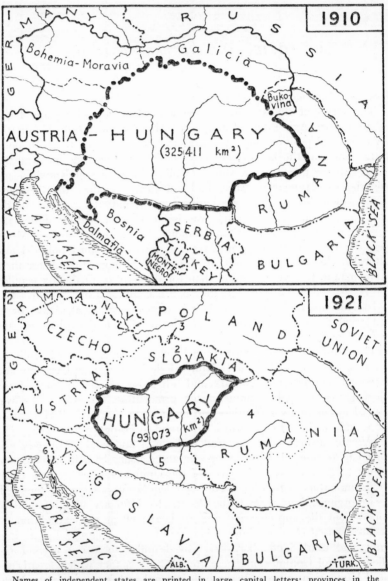

Names of independent states are printed in large capital letters; provinces in the
1910 map are in small capital letters. Seas are in italics.

SIZE OF HUNGARY IN SQUARE KILOMETERS:
1910—325,411 (including Croatia-Slovania)
1920— 92,963 (regained 110 sq. km. by plebiscite of Sopron)
1921— 93,073

1921 MAP: Territory Lost by Hungary After First World War:

1. To Austria	4,020	sq. km.
2. To Czechoslovakia	61,633	sq. km.
3. To Poland	589	sq. km.
4. To Rumania	103,093	sq. km.
5. To Yugoslavia	63,092	sq. km.
6. To Italy	21	sq. km.
TOTAL TERRITORY LOST	232,448	sq. km.

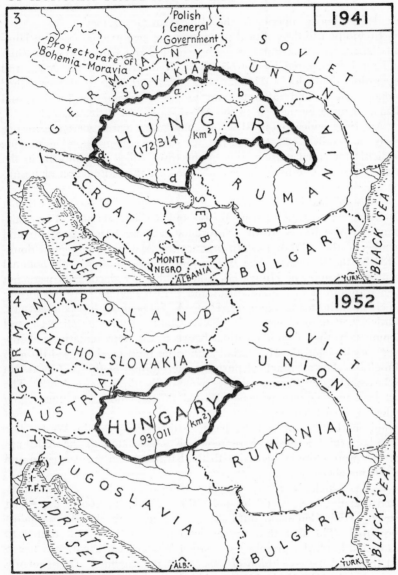

Protectorates listed on the 1941 map are printed in small capital letters
Size of Hungary in 1941: 172,314 Square Kilometers.
1941 MAP: Territory Regained by Hungary between 1938 and 1941:
    a. From Czechoslovakia (1938) .... 12,103 sq. km.
    b. From Czechoslovakia (1939) Ruthenia .... 12,171 sq. km.
    c. From Rumania (1940) .... 43,492 sq. km.
    d. From Yugoslavia (1941) .... 11,475 sq. km.
           TOTAL TERRITORY REGAINED .... 79,241 sq. km.
    (Official publications differ slightly concerning the size of
      the areas regained from Czechoslovakia and Rumania.)
Size of Hungary since 1947: 93,011 square kilometers.
1952 MAP: Hungary lost all areas regained between 1938 and 1941, and had to
cede 62 sq. km. to Czechoslovakia in 1947 (see full arrow). Broken arrow
indicates T.F.T. (Trieste Free Territory).

wielded authority superior to the Hungarian Government.

In addition to the political provisions, the armistice imposed on Hungary great economic burdens. These included payments, commodities and services required by the occupying Red Army and the ACC, and reparation deliveries.[2] Hungary was also required to restore Allied property rights and interests, and to pay compensation for loss and damage caused by the war to the Allied states and their nationals.

American endeavors in Moscow, aiming at a more generous armistice treaty, had failed. Moreover, the Russians were unwilling to provide explicitly for equal participation of the three Allied governments in the work of the ACC during the period following the termination of hostilities against Germany.[3]

As established by the armistice agreement, the ACC was under Soviet Chairmanship, with American, British and Russian sections. The chairman was Marshal Klementy Voroshilov, a close friend of Stalin and member of the politbureau. In practice the ACC was completely dominated by the Russians. The British and Americans were only nominal members. Copies of Hungarian notes and other documents were not even transmitted to the American and British sections. As the former American Minister to Hungary, H. F. A. Schoenfeld, has pointed out: "Orders had been given by the Soviet Chairman of the Allied Control Commission that communication between the representatives of the Western allies and the Hungarian authorities must be channeled through himself." [4] For all practical purposes the business of the ACC was run exclusively by the Russians—in the name of the three major Allies. The fact that the Western powers tolerated this situation, and thus tacitly endorsed Soviet control of the country, discouraged even the most optimistic Hungarians and did harm to the prestige of the West. The Yugoslav and Czechoslovak representatives delegated to the ACC apparently were more influential with the Russians than the American and British members.

It was article 18 of the armistice agreement which expressly provided that the ACC would be under the general direction of the Allied (Soviet) High Command until the conclusion of the hostilities against Germany.[5] The fact that the Soviet chairmanship was restricted to this period implied a promise for a larger Western participation between that time and the conclusion of peace with the satellites. Consequently at Potsdam in July, 1945, the three Allied Governments:

> took note that the Soviet representatives on the Allied Control Commissions in Rumania, Bulgaria and Hungary, have communicated to their United Kingdom and United States colleagues pro-

posals for improving the work on the Control Commissions, now that hostilities in Europe have ceased.

The three Governments agreed that the revision of the procedures of the Allied Control Commissions in these countries would now be undertaken, taking into account the interests and responsibilities of the three Governments which together presented the terms of armistice to the respective countries, and accepting as a basis in respect of all three countries, the Soviet Government's proposals for Hungary as annexed hereto.[6]

After the Potsdam conference President Truman reaffirmed the joint responsibility of the three major powers to establish governments broadly representative of the democratic elements of the population in the liberated and satellite nations of Europe. In particular references to Rumania, Bulgaria and Hungary, he stated that these nations:

> are not to be spheres of influence of any one power. They now are governed by Allied Control Commissions composed of representatives of the three governments which met at Yalta and Berlin. These control commissions, it is true, have not been functioning completely to our satisfaction, but improved procedures were agreed upon at Berlin. Until these states are re-established as members of the international family, they are the joint concern of all of us.[7]

The revised statutes of the ACC accordingly set forth that the United States and British representatives on the ACC should have the right "To receive copies of all communications, reports and other documents which may interest the Governments of the United States and United Kingdom." [8]

In actual practice, however, no change took place. Control Commissions in the Danubian states remained under Russian domination throughout their existence.[9] For example, General V. P. Sviridov, deputy chairman of the ACC in Hungary, ordered the dissolution of certain Catholic youth organizations and demanded the dismissal of some government officials, in July, 1946, without consulting or informing the American and British representatives.[10] The Soviet High Command issued instructions regarding the size, personnel and organization of the Hungarian Army, without consulting Western representatives. The chairman of the ACC refused the American members permission to visit Hungarian Army units, and refused even to permit freedom of movement for the American and British members of the ACC. In short, the Soviet chairman or his deputy consistently acted unilaterally

105

in the name of the ACC, without consultation with, or notice to the American and British representatives. Thus even the semblance of effective participation in the work of the ACC was denied to them. Sometimes the Soviet chairman simply stated that the matter was within the jurisdiction of the Red Army, or that it must be referred to Moscow. This latter position, for example, was taken when the American and British representatives protested, in a plenary session of the ACC, against the conclusion of the Hungarian-Russian economic cooperation agreement, signed in Moscow on August 27, 1945. On this occasion, direct Anglo-American protests were made to the Russian Government without any result." [11]

Because of this practical exclusion of the British and Americans from the business of the ACC, the Hungarians had no forum whatever, to deal with Soviet violations and abuses of the armistice agreement. The vague and ambiguous provisions of the armistice left the door open for manifold interpretations and arbitrary Soviet actions, which reduced Hungarian sovereignty to a minimum.[12] In this period Hungary could not renew diplomatic relations without permission of the ACC. This permission was in some cases delayed, in others refused. Usually, the ACC did not even acknowledge these or any other notes. For instance, the Hungarian Government never received an answer to its several requests concerning the renewal of diplomatic relations with the Vatican. The ACC seldom used the Foreign Ministry as a channel of communication with Hungarian authorities, but intervened directly with various government agencies. The Foreign Ministry was only later informed—if at all—through the Hungarian authorities, of various Soviet demands and interventions. This practice made an integrated Hungarian policy toward the ACC and the Red Army impossible. If the Foreign Ministry gave an unsatisfactory answer to a certain demand, they simply addressed the same demand to the prime minister or another governmental agency. Soviet interventions for the expulsion of the Germans from Hungary was an example of this. Many times such moves were coordinated with communist actions.

All foreign travel required permission from the ACC. This prerogative was exercised in an arbitrary way. It was next to impossible for the average man to obtain a travel permit if the application was not supported by the Communist Party. Later, when travel became somewhat easier, it was accompanied by such administrative malpractices as bribery through a middleman. Even official foreign travel was strictly controlled and arbitrarily authorized. Sometimes the departure of foreign service officers was delayed or hindered because they lacked the exit permit of the ACC. For example, the foreign Minister personally asked several times that I be granted a travel permit to go to Switzerland to bring back the peace preparatory material deposited at our Berne Legation during 1943 and 1944. The Soviet political advisor to the ACC, Georgij M. Pushkin, refused this request each time, stating that such material would not be needed. Eventually we asked the American political mission to help us out in this situation and requested that the American diplomatic courier be authorized to bring the documents from Switzerland to Budapest. This request was turned down as incompatible with the regulations of the United States courier service.

The argument that the Russians, in this exclusion of the Western Allies from the business of the ACC in Hungary, Rumania and Bulgaria, simply followed the precedent set in Italy, is not entirely without foundation.[13] In Italy, the Soviets had only an observer with the ACC and membership on an Advisory Council, which, in fact, did very little. The Italian ACC was a joint Anglo-American agency and the Russians often complained about their exclusion.[14] The situation was the same as in the ex-Axis-satellite states in that one side ran the show and the other merely observed, although the institutions were not quite identical. In substance the role of the ACC was entirely different in Italy from that in the Soviet satellite states. The Western powers did not abuse the provisions of the armistice agreement. Italy had no reason to complain because of the behavior of her liberators. She was not looted or otherwise abused by the Anglo-Americans, but was in fact greatly assisted in her rehabilitation. As early as January, 1945, the political section of the ACC in Italy was abolished, while in the following two years the remaining sections of the Commission fulfilled only an advisory function.[15] In contrast with this situation, in the Soviet satellite states the Allied Control Commissions brought ruthless pressure on the local governments and, in close cooperation with the local Communist parties, engineered the political transformation of these countries.

Western Attitude.

Contacts between the Russians, and the Americans and British in Hungary were, of course, only a small segment of their larger relationships. The wartime policy of the Western powers was based on a misconception about the possibilities of postwar cooperation with Soviet Russia. Very few Western statesmen were familiar with, or attached any importance to, the basic tenets of Communist strategy and tactics as they were clearly explained in the writings of Lenin and Stalin. In 1945 Western wishful thinking still prevailed in East-West relations. The leaders of the Western powers, and particularly President Roosevelt, had

107

great hopes that the Soviet Union could somehow be brought into a democratic world community if treated with patience and magnanimity. That view was also widespread among the American and British people.

Besides these psychological features, there was also the reality of the military and political situation at the end of 1944 and the first part of 1945. At that time the English speaking powers were still fighting the war, with the Russians as allies, and were building, together with them, a new security organization on which the western hopes for future peace and cooperation were based. Moreover, Soviet military intervention against Japan was considered absolutely necessary. At that time, the Western powers were trying to work out ways of dealing with the liberated areas which would respect the rights of the peoples of these areas and also preserve the unity of the great powers. Perhaps the decision of the historians in the years to come may be that it was impossible to achieve these objectives. A few British and American statesmen and diplomats were realistic and skeptical during the whole period of appeasement. Nevertheless, the official leaders of American and British foreign policy thought that under the circumstances, the attempt had to be made.

Prime Minister Churchill's report on the Crimean Conference in the House of Commons (February 27, 1945) reflected the attitude of the Anglo-American leaders:

> The impression I brought back from the Crimea, and from all my other contacts, is that Marshal Stalin and the Soviet leaders wish to live in honourable friendship and equality with the Western democracies. I feel also that their word is their bond. I know of no Government which stands to its obligations, even in its own despite, more solidly than the Russian Soviet Government. I decline absolutely to embark here on a discussion about Russian good faith. It is quite evident that these matters touch the whole future of the world. Somber indeed would be the fortunes of mankind if some awful schism arose between the Western democracies and the Russian Soviet Union, if all the future world organizations were rent asunder, and if new cataclysms of inconceivable violence destroyed all that is left of the treasures and liberties of mankind.

President Roosevelt in his address to Congress on March 1, 1945, stated:

> Never before have the major Allies been more closely united—not only in their war aims but also in their peace aims. And they are

determined to continue to be united, to be united with each other
—and with all peace-loving nations—so that the ideal of lasting
peace will become a reality. . . . I think the Crimean Conference
was a successful effort by the three leading nations to find a common
ground for peace. It spells—and it ought to spell—the end of the
system of unilateral action, exclusive alliances, and spheres of influence, and balances of power, and all the other expedients which
have been tried for centuries and have always failed. We propose to
substitute for all these, a universal organization in which all peace-
loving nations will finally have a chance to join.

President Roosevelt's speech was characteristic of his approach
toward fundamental international problems, but Churchill's words might
have been only an attempt to dispel unwelcome thoughts. After Yalta
Churchill was increasingly concerned about the Soviet attitude in Eu-
rope. This can be verified by his many cables sent across the Atlantic.
Washington even feared that he "might take some precipitate action
that would seriously endanger the unity of the Big Three." [16] So, in
May, 1945, Joseph E. Davies was sent to visit him. During their meeting
Churchill spoke with such bitterness about Soviet methods that Davies
suggested to him that he was "expressing the doctrines which Hitler and
Goebbels had been proclaiming . . . in an effort to break up Allied
Unity." [17] Eventually Davies' appeasement mission was successful.
Amidst postwar difficulties, Great Britain was hardly in a position to
initiate, alone, a "tough" policy toward the Soviet Union, and thus to
antagonize the United States. Churchill declared that he "was willing
to take the risk of a much 'tougher' attitude" but agreed to the "policy
of trying to exhaust all means consistent with self-respect in order to
resolve the difficulties between the Big Three so that unity might be
preserved to achieve a peace after military victory." [18]

In the course of negotiations in Moscow, Teheran and Yalta, the
Soviet Union was not required to give concrete detailed assurances concerning the independence of the central eastern European countries, and
no attempt was made to give a common meaning to the word "democracy." Later, Soviet Russia was not compelled by serious and concentrated diplomatic actions to live up to the principles laid down in the
wartime inter-allied agreements. The belated Western opposition to
Soviet violations of international obligations was not integrated into a
well-planned European strategy, and in the Danubian region had no
influence whatever on the Russian-controlled course of events. The
quick demobilization of the American Army was probably considered as
a green light for Soviet ambitions.

It was characteristic of the general atmosphere of this period that the American military authorities in Germany were not anxious to obtain guarantees from the Russians to assure freedom of communication with Berlin, but they did show deep concern with regard to securing free lines of communication across the British and French zones.[19]   The Western powers made further substantial concessions to the Russians at Potsdam in July, 1945, and at the Moscow Conference in December, 1945.   As Secretary Byrnes later remarked, his actions in Moscow stemmed from the hope "that the Soviet Union and United States had a common purpose." [20]

This concept was expressed even more clearly in one of Byrnes' speeches in which he drew a parallel between the role of Soviet Russia in Eastern Europe and that of the United States in the Americas.   He pointed out that the United States could not and would not deny to other nations the right to develop a good-neighbor policy and stated that:

> Far from opposing, we have sympathized with, for example, the effort of the Soviet Union to draw into closer and more friendly association with her central and eastern European neighbors.   We are fully aware of her special security interests in those countries, and we have recognized those interests in the arrangements made for the occupation and control of the former enemy states.[21]

Such ideas played directly into the hands of Soviet policy makers, whose ambitions in Eastern Europe could be easily satisfied by a Stalinist version of an Eurasiatic Monroe doctrine, streamlined according to Communist theories and practice.[22]

When representatives of the Western powers arrived in Hungary early in 1945, they clearly based their policy upon a belief in Allied unity. Serious gestures of goodwill toward Hungary nevertheless were made, but the Western powers carefully avoided taking a stand on any delicate political issue which might antagonize the Russians.   They were not willing to expose themselves against their powerful ally for the sake of an ex-Axis satellite such as Hungary.   Thus the initial violations of the armistice agreement by Soviet authorities and the abuses of the rights of an occupying power—as for instance, the wholesale lootings, removal of factories, deportation of civilians on a mass scale, and other violations of international law—took place throughout 1945 without a single Western protest.   In the course of the execution of the armistice agreement the Russians offered and enforced their interpretation of "democracy" and "fascism" without being seriously challenged by the West; the representatives of the Western powers showed manifestly that they could not or would not take a stand against the Russians.

A few lower ranking members of the Western missions sometimes made goodwill remarks which were interpreted by the Hungarian public in a wildly optimistic way. In 1945, rumors spread that the western part of Hungary would be occupied by American and British troops, or that the purely Soviet occupation would be followed by a joint Anglo-American-Russian occupation. Of course nothing of the sort happened, and disappointment was great.

Although American and British goodwill toward Hungary was displayed mainly in the form of advice and friendly gestures, some material help was forthcoming from both English-speaking countries. There also were humanitarian gifts needed badly in the impoverished country. One of the first American moves was a considerable gift of medicine to the Hungarian Red Cross. Later, the United States granted loans totaling $30,000,000 for the purchase of surplus property.[23] Moreover UNRRA relief supplies, valued at over four million dollars, were sent to Hungary.[24] However, the Soviet Government repeatedly refused American proposals aiming at tripartite examinations of Hungary's economic plight and at joint assistance by the Yalta powers.[25]

The heads of the American, British, and Soviet diplomatic missions were political advisors to the ACC and were not accredited to the Hungarian Government. An American representative with the personal rank of Minister, H. F. Arthur Schoenfeld, arrived in Budapest in May, 1945. He functioned as the United States representative in Hungary for the general protection of American interests, in addition to and separate from the ACC, and maintained informal contacts with the provisional Hungarian authorities.[26]

Schoenfeld on May 15, explained to Foreign Minister Gyöngyösi that the American Government intended to help in the reconstruction and rehabilitation of Hungary. Moreover, he made it clear that the American authorities did not intend to seize as war booty the property removed forcibly by the Nazis from Hungary into the American zone of Germany, but intended to restore all identifiable displaced property.[27] As for war guilt, he declared that the United States advocated punishment of war criminals but opposed application to any particular nation of the principle of collective responsibility. Gyöngyösi then called Schoenfeld's attention to the persecution of the Hungarians in Slovakia, and stated that the Hungarian Government would ask for the intervention of the ACC. Later, when an exchange of notes took place between the American Mission and the Hungarian Government in connection with the problem of the Hungarians in Czechoslovakia, Schoenfeld expressed the hope to the Foreign Minister that the American attitude would restrain persecution of the Hungarians.[28] He added that the United States had approved the voluntary transfers of population in the belief that the Danubian countries would become ethnically more homogeneous and thereby more cooperative.

On May 26, 1945, the American Minister personally handed Gyöngyösi a note expressing American willingness to receive a non-official Hungarian representative in Washington even before the renewal of diplomatic relations. Establishment of such representation would have made possible the practical protection of Hungarian interests in the United States. This American offer was reiterated in September, 1945, but the Hungarian government—under the protective custody of the ACC—could not accept it because of Soviet opposition.

The first American and British protests in Hungary took place against the seizure of the landed properties of British and American citizens, in contravention of Article 13 of the armistice agreement. The Hungarian Government explained the impossibility of exempting foreigners from the agrarian reform but promised full compensation according to the rules of international law.

The British political representative, Alvary D. F. Gascoigne, repeatedly pointed out to Foreign Minister Gyöngyösi the shortcomings of Hungarian democratic practices, as for example, the lack of freedom of speech or guarantees for personal liberties. Gascoigne particularly objected to the abuses committed by the political police. Foreign Secretary Ernest Bevin, in a speech along these same lines in the House of Commons on August 20, 1945, had characterized the shortcomings of the new regimes established in the Danubian states. In speaking of the situation in Bulgaria, Rumania, and Hungary he observed:

> The Governments which have been set up do not, in our view, represent the majority of the people, and the impression we get from recent developments is that one kind of totalitarianism is being replaced by another. This is not what we understand by that very much overworked word "democracy," which appears to need definition, and the forms of government which have been set up as a result do not impress us as being sufficiently representative to meet the requirements of diplomatic relations.[29]

All these anomalies were recognized by non-Communist Hungarian political leaders and caused serious anxieties to them, but substantial amelioration of the situation was beyond their reach.

The British and American attitude did help to stiffen the opposition of the non-Communist political parties to the single electoral ticket proposed by the Communist Party, and strongly urged by Voroshilov in October, 1945. This Soviet pressure had occurred after the defeat of the joint Socialist-Communist ticket on October 7, in the Budapest municipal elections. The Western representatives counterbalanced the Soviet move by stating that their governments would not regard elections based on a single electoral list as free elections corresponding to the requirement of the Yalta Declaration. The non-Communist political leaders took courage, refused to give away their political prospects, and their successful resistance to Voroshilov's proposals led to the general elections of November 5, 1945, in which the Communist Party obtained only 17 percent of the votes.

Meanwhile, at the first meeting of the Council of Allied Foreign Ministers,[30] opened in London on September 11, 1945, Secretary Byrnes declared that the United States would not sign treaties with the existing unrepresentative governments of Rumania and Bulgaria, but was ready to recognize the government of Hungary on receipt of a pledge of free elections.

An American note delivered to the Hungarian foreign minister on September 22, 1945, indicated the readiness of the United States to establish diplomatic relations and to negotiate a treaty with the provisional Government of Hungary, provided that Government:

> would give full assurances for free and untrammeled elections for a representative government and if, in the meantime, it would provide to the full measure of its responsibilities under the armistice regime for freedom of political expression of democratic parties and right of assembly, such conditions being essential to permit the holding of free elections.

On September 25, a Hungarian reply to the United States stated that "the Provisional National Government of Hungary was in a position to offer the guarantees required by the Government of the United States." On September 29, the Department of State, having received this assurance, indicated American willingness to renew relations with Hungary.[31] This American diplomatic move clearly aimed at strengthening non-Communist elements in the Hungarian coalition.

The Soviet foreign minister, Vyascheslav Molotov, countered the American move by an immediate and unconditional recognition of the Hungarian Government. Voroshilov informed the Hungarian Government, on September 25, that the Soviet Union was ready to establish diplomatic relations with them.

In the course of recognition of the powerless provisional Government of Hungary, a sort of competition took place between the U. S. A. and the U.S.S.R. The Hungarian press had to publish first the establishment of the diplomatic relations with the Soviet Union and only later the earlier American move. Thus the actual sequence was reversed.

Subsequently, the American and Russian missions were changed to legations and the American and Russian diplomatic representatives to the ACC presented their credentials to the Hungarian Government as plenipotentiary ministers.[32] Great Britain, however, conforming to the rules of traditional diplomacy, manifested a more reserved attitude. She was not willing to renew regular diplomatic relations with Hungary, a country technically at war with the Allied powers, and appointed as British political representative to Hungary, the British political advisor to the ACC, A. D. F. Gascoigne.[33]

Renewal of diplomatic relations with Hungary did not strengthen the position of the British and American representatives in the ACC. The Russians ignored them as before. In the course of the postwar period the most astonishing phenomenon to Hungarian eyes was this striking contrast between the attitude of the Western powers and Soviet Russia.

The Yalta Agreement.

In the spring of 1945, the man in the street read on huge posters all over Hungary the Yalta Declaration on Liberated Europe, signed by Marshal Stalin, President Roosevelt and Prime Minister Churchill. The common man considered it as a pledge made *to him* by the leaders of the three major victorious powers.

It is true that in 1944, inter-allied negotiations took place and allegedly agreements were concluded concerning the establishment of *wartime* zones of influence in Danubian Europe.[34] Whatever may have happened in 1944, the Yalta Agreement appeared to be the valid international agreement concerning the fate of Central and Eastern Europe, at least until the conclusion of the peace treaties. At Yalta the Russians had secured important political concessions, especially with regard to Poland and the Far East, but there were also obligations. No matter what conversations took place and what understandings were agreed upon in earlier periods, Yalta, for better or worse, seemed to be a *lex posterior,* overruling previous decisions.

At the Crimean Conference Prime Minister Churchill, Marshal Stalin and President Roosevelt jointly declared their mutual agreement:

> to concert during the temporary period of instability in liberated Europe the policies of their three governments in assisting the peoples liberated from the domination of Nazi Germany and peoples

114

of the former Axis satellite states in Europe to solve by democratic means their pressing political and economic problems.

Moreover, the Yalta declaration stated that the three governments:

> will jointly assist the people in any European liberated state or former Axis satellite state in Europe where in their judgment conditions require (A) to establish conditions of internal peace; (B) to carry out emergency measures for the relief of distressed peoples; (C) to form interim governmental authorities broadly representative of all democratic elements in the population and pledged to the earliest possible establishment through free elections of governments responsive to the will of the people; and (D) to facilitate where necessary the holding of such elections.

Thus the Yalta Agreement was a contract among the three major powers to act together in giving the peoples of the liberated countries the opportunity to have governments of their own choosing. This pledge was repeated again at Potsdam and solemnly announced to the American public by President Truman. True, this common undertaking of the three major powers was not a pledge by the Western powers to the peoples of liberated Europe which the Western powers were obligated to fulfill against Soviet opposition. The average man, however, did not think in terms of legal niceties. It was difficult for him to realize that the Yalta Agreement was a diplomatic instrument among the three major powers, and that all *joint* actions could be and actually were frustrated by Soviet authorities. The picture was all the more confusing since the Soviet Chairman on the ACC acted in the name of Britain and the United States as well as in the name of Soviet Russia.

In view of Soviet Russian encroachments and Communist abuses, some Hungarian politicians thought it appropriate to ask for Western support in connection with the rights pledged at Yalta. On these occasions the Western attitude was most reserved. As the American Minister to Hungary put it, the representatives of the western Allies:

> were frequently sounded out as to how much help they would provide to the non-Communist political groups. When our invariable reply was that American diplomatic practice excluded the possibility of such interference in the internal political affairs of foreign countries, there was bewilderment at what seemed so unrealistic an attitude compared with that of the Russians.[35]

The same American policy was expressed even more directly in the following passage of a letter addressed by Minister Schoenfeld to Joseph

Cardinal Mindszenty, December 27, 1946:

> It is noted that your letters of December 12 and December 16, touching on internal political problems of Hungary, requested the assistance of the United States Government in altering certain conditions which Your Eminence deplores. In this connection you are of course aware of my Government's long standing policy of non-interference in the internal affairs of other nations. This policy has proven over a long period of time and through many trying situations the best guarantee of spontaneous, vigorous and genuine democratic development. It will be clear to Your Eminence that it necessarily precludes action by this Legation which could properly be construed as interference in Hungarian domestic affairs or which lies outside the normal functions of diplomatic missions.[36]

Such diplomatic or other inhibitions did not embarrass the Soviet representatives in Hungary.

Soviet Attitude.

From the very beginning of the Soviet occupation the attitude of the Soviet military and political representatives towards the Western powers was anything but cooperative. The diplomatic representative of Soviet Russia, Georgij Pushkin, came with the Red Army to Debrecen, seat of the provisional Hungarian Government, and there, in cooperation with the Soviet military authorities and the Hungarian Communists, shaped the things to come. Later a few members of the American and British missions arrived, forming the nucleus of the American and British sections of the ACC. They, however, occupied a very isolated position, and did not take part in the actual work of the ACC. It was not suspected at that time that this would remain, in essence, the Western position throughout the armistice period.

In the course of the military occupation of Hungary, it was amazing to hear many simple Russian soldiers freely explain that the Red Army, after defeating the Germans, would expel the British and Americans from the Continent. As early as March, 1945, Soviet propaganda even against Switzerland appeared. At the seat of the new Hungarian Government, in Debrecen, a huge poster depicted the Swiss cow fed by the western Allies and milked by Hitler.

A group of British and Dutch officers who had escaped from German captivity were active in the underground in Hungary during the last years of the war.[37] When the Red Army entered Hungary, some of them reported to the Russians and were promptly interned in the town of

Hatvan. The best-informed men of this group were not released, but later mysteriously disappeared.

Russian and Hungarian Communists looked upon Hungarians educated in western countries with deep suspicion; in fact, anyone possessing any kind of contacts with the West was regarded in the same manner. Even superficial social contacts with western representatives were considered as treacherous behavior. Democratic leaders who returned from concentration camps, and others who had worked underground risking their lives during the war for the Allied cause were simply eliminated from public life, while former Nazis were welcomed into the Communist party. This suspicion of and hostility to any Western "taint" was, from the outset, characteristic of the Russian and Communist attitude.

The chief instruments of Soviet actions were the Red Army and the ACC. In the entire armistice period, part of the Soviet technique in Hungary was to act in the name of the three major Allies while keeping Britain and the United States from effective action. The Russians always barred joint action, invoking either the exclusive rights of an occupying power or the independence of the Hungarian State. The chairman of the ACC was at the same time commandant of the Soviet military forces in Hungary. To evade all Western intervention, Marshal Voroshilov, or his deputy, usually neglected to explain whether he addressed his demands to the Hungarian Government in the name of the ACC or as the commander-in-chief of the occupying forces. To ask for precision on such occasions was considered as an unfriendly act toward the Soviet Union.

In December, 1945, Marshal Voroshilov warned the Hungarian public that the foreign policy of Hungary did not depend entirely on the Hungarians. At the same time, he pointed out that the Hungarians should not count on considerable outside help at a time when the world was in such a state that no nations could count on external aid.[38] Nonetheless, when Western help was offered to Hungary, it was opposed by the Russians. For instance, UNRRA assistance offered to destitute Hungary in March, 1945, was declined by the ACC on the ground of "no necessity," and Soviet opposition to such assistance was continued for some months. Eventually the direct requests of the Hungarian Government and those of various Hungarian private organizations received a favorable response from the UNRRA.[39]

The Russians had a wide choice of means in exerting pressure on Hungarian authorities, for they had practically unlimited power. Personal liberty, the daily bread of the population—in fact, all the necessities of life—depended entirely upon them. Devastated Hungary had to feed an occupying force of several hundred thousand men. Food

117

supplies were seized. Factory equipment was removed at will as war booty. Hungary was compelled to begin reparation deliveries in 1945. Civilians by the thousands, including women from Eastern Hungary, were taken to the Soviet Union as prisoners of war. Public safety did not exist; there was no authority capable of giving protection against the Russians. Even when the period of large-scale deportations came to an end, people were arrested and judged by Soviet military tribunals on fantastic charges, sometimes for merely having carried out the instructions of the Hungarian Government. In such cases, there was no question of legal assistance or of due process of law. The accused simply disappeared.

One of the first important actions of the newly organized Foreign Ministry was intervention with the Soviet authorities on behalf of the civilians taken as prisoners of war. This action began in Debrecen as early as March, 1945, as part of the activities of the newly organized political division of the Foreign Ministry. A few weeks later when the Ministry moved to Budapest, it became necessary to organize a special division for the prisoners of war cases. This division dealt mainly with requests for intervention from the relatives of deported civilians. The magnitude of the problem grew daily. In a few weeks tens of thousands of cases were registered in the files of the Ministry. In all cases routine interventions were made with the Soviet authorities. They paid no attention to any of them.

Probably the largest number of civilians were taken as prisoners of war after the occupation of Budapest. This may have been due to the small number of soldiers captured after the siege. It was suggested that the Soviet High Command, in its reports, overestimated the strength of the Nazi forces in Budapest and after the occupation of the city wanted to increase the number of war prisoners accordingly. Later, however, requests pouring in by the thousands into the Foreign Ministry from all parts of Hungary, made it evident that the same practice was followed all over the country.[40] This procedure was most cruel in East Hungary, where, in communities inhabited by people of German origin, the entire adult population of many villages, men and women alike, were taken into Soviet Russia. In other parts of the country Soviet military practice usually disregarded political affiliation, age, social position, or ethnic origin of captured people. They simply needed a certain number of prisoners, and anybody was good enough to fill their quota.

Besides making routine interventions, the Foreign Ministry asked for the release of those who had worked for the cause of the Allies during the war. After a while the Russians became tired of these requests and said that they could understand an intervention in behalf of

118

100,000 people, but it really did not matter whether a few odd individuals were in Hungary or in the Soviet Union. Only the Communist Party managed, in certain special cases, to liberate a few prisoners
still in Hungary in concentration camps.

When prisoners were taken by train-loads to the Soviet Union, some
prisoners in utter desperation jumped out of the moving trains or otherwise escaped. To make up for the losses the guards often encircled the
next railroad station and picked up the necessary number of persons to
replace the missing men. The train then continued on the journey to
Russia. Thus it was entirely a matter of sheer luck whether or not one
was kidnapped as a war prisoner. Sometimes Jews returning from Nazi
concentration camps were intercepted and rerouted to Russia. A man
living in the neighborhood of a Budapest railroad station left his home
to buy some matches. Four months later his family received their next
news of him from Archangelsk.

From the practical handling of the civil deportation cases it clearly
appeared that the liberty and dignity of the human individual, the
cornerstone of Western civilization, was a non-existent category in the
Soviet Russian mind.

Besides the prisoners of war, some Hungarian politicians were taken
to Russia. This happened without any publicity or accusation of any
sort. They were simply rounded up. This procedure of elimination
was a warning given to all politicians who would not submit entirely to
Soviet dictation. Among the politicians who suffered this fate was Count
Stephen Bethlen, prime minister of Hungary between 1921 and 1931. He
publicly denounced Nazi ideas and anti-Jewish laws. In the Crown
Council he advocated direct armistice negotiations with the Soviet
Union. He countered the objection that the Russians would commit
robberies, rape, loot and so on, with the remark that they would do less
if they came as friends. Despite these facts, Bethlen was arrested, and
deported to the Soviet Union.

A strongly anti-Nazi publicist, Iván Lajos, published a so - called
"Grey Book" in 1939. In it he denounced the German war preparations
and revealed the weaknesses of the German economic system and war
potential. This book—translated into several languages—was later
confiscated under German pressure by the Hungarian Government. The
author himself was taken by the Germans to Mauthausen. Upon his
return after the war he studied Franco-Hungarian relations and became
one of the propagators of the cooperation of the Danubian peoples, and
allegedly advocated the restoration of the Habsburg Monarchy. On one
occasion he informed me, enthusiastically, that he had discussed the
various possibilities of Danubian cooperation with a Soviet captain who

showed much interest in the matter. Shortly thereafter he disappeared.

Count John Esterházy, the leader of the Hungarian party in Slovakia during the Second World War, was the only member of the Slovak Parliament who voted against the Hitlerite anti-Semitic laws and strongly criticized them as not being in accordance with humanitarian principles. Esterházy was arrested in 1945, and a few weeks later was suddenly taken to Soviet Russia together with the other leading personalities of the Hungarian minority in Slovakia. A Slovak people's court sentenced him to death *in absentia*.

The fate and whereabouts of politicians taken to Russia was usually unknown. Count Bethlen and Iván Lajos are believed to have died. Esterházy was returned to Slovakia and his death sentence commuted to life imprisonment.

This method of eliminating political opponents was unknown in countries belonging to Western civilization. In Horthy's Hungary the Communist party was banned, but the Communist agents, if caught, had an open trial and legal assistance, and usually were sentenced to several years for subversive activities. The example of Rákosi and Zoltán Vas are cases in point.

Irrespective of other political considerations, the mass deportation of civilians and selected politicians was but one of the initial means to frighten the population into conformity with Soviet wishes. At first it was difficult to understand the apparently senseless Soviet behavior, which seemed harmful even to the Communist cause. After a while, however, it became obvious that behind these actions there had been an over-all plan. Abuses and atrocities were carried out to frighten the population and to weaken its moral and economic resistance. The Russians did not care for popularity. They wanted servile submission; they preferred to be feared rather than loved. The abuses of the Red Army made the Russians and Communists unpopular, but at the same time created a feeling of helplessness in all social classes. The creation of an atmosphere of fear and of absolute personal insecurity was a necessary precondition for subsequent Soviet political actions supporting the Hungarian Communists. In Hungary, unlike Czechoslovakia, the seizure of power did not take place by one stroke, but was a gradual process. With the help of the Red Army and the ACC in the armistice period, the Communists gradually seized all key positions and created a state apparatus which eventually served their interests alone.

Hungarian Expectations.

Despite all the difficulties with the Russians, a strange optimism was discernible in the Hungarian coalition parties, especially after the Communist defeat in the elections of November 1945.[41] All political parties recognized the impact of Soviet Russia's overwhelming power position in the Danubian area and were well aware of Soviet methods, but nevertheless a spirit of wishful thinking prevailed. Soviet Russia appeared a newcomer in the society of great powers. She was a much-praised ally of the great western democracies. Her harsh manners seemed due to a different tradition and not to ill will. After the armistice period she would, so some Hungarians thought, withdraw into the vastness of Russia and refrain from interfering in the internal affairs of Hungary. Even a few non-Muscovite Communists who pictured the future along lines that today would be considered Titoism, openly discussed such ideas. At that time this way of thinking was not a crime. Moreover, Communist leaders and the Russians openly encouraged it.

Such optimism was not generally shared but was all the more remarkable because events in other countries clearly foreshadowed the things to come in Hungary. In Yugoslavia and in Poland communist-dominated regimes were installed and free elections had not been held. In the two westernmost Danubian countries—Hungary and Czechoslovakia—free elections were permitted and almost genuine coalition governments were established, but in Bulgaria and Rumania other considerations prevailed. In the region of the lower Danube and on the shores of the Black Sea, Soviet Russia had direct strategic interests for which Molotov repeatedly had exposed himself at his last meeting with Hitler and Ribbentrop, in November 1940.[42] This region was part of the road to Istanbul, and there was the Rumanian oil. Thus the Soviet action was immediate and inexorable. Both in Bulgaria and Rumania the non-Communist elements were eliminated from the government by force. Soviet Russia dominated these former Axis satellite countries through the Red Army and the Allied Control Commissions. The puppet regimes and the Soviet authorities refused to consider American and British interventions.[43]

In Hungary the alarming news of Soviet interference and Communist seizure of power in Yugoslavia, Poland, Rumania and Bulgaria was discounted under considerations such as the following: Hungary's geographical and political situation is different; our Communists are different; it can't happen here; we defeated the Communists at free elections, recognized as such by the whole world; we are neither Slavs nor Orthodox; we belong culturally to the West; the Russians fully realize that an Eastern system would be completely foreign to our people; they prefer a free cooperation with the majority of the people instead of the imposition of a minority rule.

Many progressive liberal intellectuals, disgusted with the previous

121

regimes, considered the Communists as one species of the left-wing parties, and hoped that the Hungarian Communists would be the spokesmen for the Hungarian cause in Moscow. Foreign Minister Gyöngyösi followed a policy of strict cooperation with the Soviet Union. His attitude notwithstanding, the Russians frequently intervened in the conduct of Hungary's foreign affairs both in major and minor matters. Contacts with the West were hindered and all propositions of collaboration with neighboring states rebuffed.

The Potsdam Protocol of August 2, 1945, caused a further deterioration of Hungary's position.[44] The undefined category of "German external assets" in territories under Soviet occupation, granted to Soviet Russia as reparations, opened new possibilities for Soviet conquest of the Hungarian economy. In the political field, the Western acceptance of the principle of collective responsibility in connection with the transfer of the German population from Hungary was a blow to Hungary's position, which was based on individual responsibility in the matter of war criminals and traitors.[45] This also contradicted official American policy repeatedly expressed to the Hungarian Government. The Potsdam Protocol did contain some favorable provisions. It looked forward to the early conclusion of a peace treaty and Hungary's admission into the United Nations. These and certain other provisions filled Hungarian politicians with new hope. They thought that after the evacuation of Hungary by the Red Army a real democratic evolution would take place. Their optimism was further bolstered by President Truman's report to the American people after the Potsdam Conference.

The greatest disappointment of Hungarian foreign policy in the armistice period was the attitude of the three major Allies concerning persecution of Hungarians in Czechoslovakia. The leaders of new Hungary planned and eagerly wished to establish friendly relations with Czechoslovakia. Prague did not reciprocate this policy. A Government proclamation announced that Czechoslovakia was going to be transformed into a national state and President Beneš emphasized in his speech of May 9, 1945, that the Czechs and Slovaks did not want to live together in the same state with Germans and Hungarians. Persecution and expulsion of Hungarians began.[46]

The Hungarian Government between April, 1945, and July, 1946, addressed 184 notes to the ACC protesting specific cases of persecutions in Czechoslovakia.[47] The result was neither action nor answer. The United States was the only power which gave some indirect support to Hungary. An American memorandum handed to the Hungarian Government on June 12, 1945, took a stand against collective punishment of ethnic groups, and emphasized that the removal of minorities could take place only in accordance with international agreements, and "in an orderly way." [48]

These principles of American foreign policy were expressed in Prague as well, but neither these nor the Hungarian protests addressed to the ACC influenced the course of Czechoslovak policy. As the persecutions continued, the Hungarian Government repeatedly sent complaints accompanied by extensive memoranda directly to the British, American and Soviet representatives in Budapest and asked for the intervention of the major victorious powers. In a note of September 12, 1945, the Hungarian Government requested to be heard by the Council of Foreign Ministers on the question of the Hungarians in Czechoslovakia, and proposed that an international commission of inquiry, composed of the representatives of France, Great Britain, the Soviet Union and the United States, should investigate and examine the controversial issues between Czechoslovakia and Hungary.[49] In spite of the negative attitude of the victorious powers, the Hungarian Government reiterated its request in another note of November 20, 1945, and asked that the districts of Slovakia inhabited by Hungarians be placed under international control, pending the appointment of the commission of inquiry.[50]

These moves met with no success, and the Government of Prague intimated that an exchange of population was the price for the reconsideration of their anti-Hungarian measures. Negotiations began at Prague in December, 1945. The head of the Czechoslovak delegation, Vladimir Clementis, under-secretary of state in the Czechoslovak Foreign Ministry, proposed that the Czechoslovak Government should have the right to remove, in equal numbers, Hungarians from Czechoslovakia in exchange for the Slovaks in Hungary who spontaneously declared their wish to be transferred. The transfer would take place under the supervision of a Hungaro-Czechoslovak mixed commission. The Hungarians who were not subject to the exchange would also be removed to Hungary and their goods confiscated.[51]

The Hungarian delegation proposed the immediate abolition of all discriminatory anti-Hungarian measures and refused to enter into negotiations about the removal of Hungarians remaining in Czechoslovakia after the population exchange. It expressed the opinion that the transfer of these Hungarians to Hungary could only be effected with the simultaneous cession of the territory on which they lived.[52] Moreover, the Hungarian delegation tried once more to secure Western cooperation in the settlement of the conflict with Czechoslovakia. However, the Hungarian proposal concerning the participation of Western representatives in an international commission to be established for the supervision of the population exchange was opposed not only by Czecho-

123

slovakia, but was later rejected by the British and United States Governments as well.[53] Clementis made it clear that the persecution of Hungarians would be continued until the conclusion of the population exchange agreement and pointed out that Czechoslovakia, enjoying the support of both East and West, would be able to expel all Hungarians, or remove them if necessary, to the Sudeten territories. The Hungarian delegation repeatedly pointed out that Hungary disapproved the population exchange as an action contrary to the principles of democracy and humanity. Nevertheless, the Hungarian Government was prepared, under duress, to accept the transfer. But it stipulated that the rights of the Hungarian population, remaining in Czechoslovakia after the exchange, would have to be guaranteed until the peace settlement. It appeared that the Hungarian and Czechoslovak standpoints were irreducible, and since the delegations could not agree even on the text of a communiqué, the two governments published separate statements.

After the failure of the Prague negotiations, the Russians increased their pressure on the Hungarian Government for the acceptance of the Czechoslovak standpoint with respect to the settlement of the Hungarian question in Slovakia. Pushkin complacently explained to Foreign Minister Gyöngyösi that the clumsy Czechoslovak politicians committed a serious political mistake in not removing the Hungarians from Slovakia at the close of the hostilities. Thus an accomplished fact would have been created which would have solved the chief difficulty between Hungary and Czechoslovakia, and the negotiations between the two countries would have been made a lot easier. Pushkin repeatedly made it clear that Czechoslovakia enjoyed the unqalified support of Soviet Russia because in the past she had proved a reliable friend; Hungary should accept the Czechoslovak thesis and should look for compensation from Rumania, a country which had been in the same boat as Hungary. Such were Pushkin's suggestions.

The present writer and the Czechoslovak experts of the Hungarian Foreign Ministry advised Foreign Minister Gyöngyösi that Hungary should delay negotiations and submit to the peace conference the whole problem of Hungarians in Czechoslovakia, including the population exchange. Gyöngyösi, however, felt that this policy would run against Western advice and would provoke strong Soviet retaliation. All these powers remained unresponsive to Hungarian proposals and complaints concerning the persecution of Hungarians in Czechoslovakia, and the Hungarian Government had no means of defending its suffering kinsmen or to hinder mass expulsions or internal removals to the Sudeten territories. Under these conditions, Gyöngyösi saw no other possibility for the defense of the Hungarians in Slovakia but to go ahead in the direction of the population exchange. Moreover, he was convinced that the population exchange would prove that the Czechoslovak allegations of the existence of several hundred thousand Slovaks in Hungary were absolutely without foundation.[54] Gyöngyösi was afraid that the Czechoslovak Government with its great propaganda facilities might convince the peace conference of the validity of these allegations, and hoped that the results of the population exchange would reveal the real situation and thus strengthen Hungary's position at the peace table.

Negotiations were renewed at Prague, and, in February, 1946, Hungary signed a population exchange agreement with Czechoslovakia—an unequal treaty, containing a series of unilateral benefits to Czechoslovakia.[55] By the conclusion of this treaty, however, the Hungarian Government obtained some pledges from the Czechoslovak Government and thus hoped to assure at least physical survival for the bulk of the Hungarians in Czechoslovakia until the decision of the Peace Conference.[56]

All in all, the failure of Hungarian endeavors to obtain Western cooperation for the preservation of the basic human rights of Hungarians in Czechoslovakia was anything but encouraging for the future. The passive attitude of the Western powers in this affair increased the feeling among Hungarian politicians that the Hungarian nation had been completely abandoned to Soviet Russia and the Slav interests. Even considering the fact that Hungary had lost the war and Czechoslovakia belonged to the United Nations, Western aloofness did not portend much good for Hungary, and caused serious worries for non-Communist Hungarian politicians, who were eager to promote a friendly cooperation of peoples in the Danubian region on the basis of equality.

VII. REORGANIZATION OF HUNGARY

Muscovite Prelude.

Soviet Russia could have established a Communist dictatorship in Hungary right after the occupation of the country by the Red Army. This was probably not deemed opportune because of the various inter-Allied agreements and internal conditions in Hungary—where the Communist Party had no significant popular support. The Muscovite satrap of Hungary, Mátyás Rákosi, recently stated that the Communist Party, in the spring of 1945, was not able to win over the majority of the toiling masses to the aims of a proletarian dictatorship. He added that "the approval and support of the decisive majority of the toilers cannot be substituted even by the liberating intervention of the Soviet Army."[1] Moreover, he explained, the Hungarian Communist Party "was burdened with the cares of ruling a state when it had as yet hardly any organizations." [2]

Instead of attempting to introduce the Soviet system in one sweeping move, the Kremlin decided to establish a coalition regime—a course which corresponded to inter-Allied agreements. On December 5, 1944, a Moscow-trained Hungarian Communist leader, Ernö Gerö, presented a list of the designated cabinet members to the Hungarian armistice delegation in Moscow and to the Hungarian generals who had gone over to the Red Army after the armistice proclamation of Horthy. General Kuznetsov assisted on this occasion. Gerö explained that the plan for a provisional government was formulated and a list prepared with the consent of the United Kingdom and the United States. General Béla Dálnoki Miklós, former commander of the first Hungarian Army, and János Vörös, former chief of staff of the Hungarian Army, accepted the proposed list and the positions offered to them. Miklós was designated prime minister, and Vörös, minister of defense.[3]

The members of the armistice delegation asked for twenty-four hours in which to reply. A few hours later, however, the conference was to be continued. This time Molotov met with the delegation and stated that he was glad that the designated persons had accepted their positions in the cabinet. Count Géza Teleki attempted to decline the portfolio offered him, but was forced by threats to accept.[4]

This prelude in Moscow was closely connected with the activities of Communist agents in Hungary. Moscow-trained Communists, like Gerö

126

and Imre Nagy, previous to the presentation of the cabinet list, were roving throughout eastern Hungary behind the Red Army, selecting members of the cabinet.

There moved with the Soviet Army into devastated Hungary, a group of Hungarian emigrés, members of the 1919 Communist regime of Béla Kun—the so-called Muscovites. They had become Soviet citizens—some of them were members of the invading army—and having been trained in Moscow were entrusted to apply the recipe for world revolutionary conquest as explained in the works of Lenin and Stalin. Some of them played an important role in the international Communist movement and had fulfilled missions as Communist organizers in various foreign countries. Besides their indoctrination, they had been deeply impressed in Russia by the purge of Béla Kun and other Hungarian Communists.[5] Thus their only loyalty had been an absolute obedience to the Kremlin. The fact that they spoke Hungarian, had a Hungarian background, and were informed about conditions in the country greatly facilitated their task. Hungary, politically disintegrated, economically ruined, and occupied by the Red Army, seemed a good case where the teaching of Lenin and Stalin could easily be applied.

The Horthy regime in the 'twenties' and 'thirties' had suppressed the Communist Party, so the Communists could maintain in Hungary only a few underground cells. Between these cells and Moscow, an underground communications system had functioned. The returned emigrés knew that these Communist groups could not possibly form the basis for the realization of their political aims. They did not follow the clumsy and violent policy of the 1919 Hungarian-Communist regime of Béla Kun, which had left such a deep feeling of resentment among the Hungarian people. To win sympathy and popular suport they now advocated a coalition government, praised the principles of democracy, and even preached the necessity of collaborating with the Catholic Church. Communist brigades actually helped to restore destroyed churches. Such actions were greatly publicized. It was emphasized that the Russians wanted only to annihilate Fascism and did not intend to interfere with internal politics. Patriotic slogans were the order of the day. The bourgeois and peasant leaders of the underground parties were publicly extolled by the Communists as progressive and reliable democrats who were entitled to share in the leadership of the country. Thus in this first postwar period in Hungary the Communists acted with extreme caution and cunning. At that time the pattern of their later designs was anticipated by only a few people.

The sapping and undermining of democracy nonetheless had already begun. Communist good faith could not have been questioned publicly in any way. Freedom of speech did not exist. Even after the end of

127

Russian censorship the Communists effectively controlled the press through a system of licenses, allocation of newsprint, and the printers trade-union.

Pattern of Reorganization.

The political reorganization of the country was undertaken by the "Hungarian National Independence Front." This was a coalition established shortly after the German occupation of Hungary by the underground leaders of the Smallholder, Social Democrat, and Communist parties. The Communists organized in this period under the name of the Peace Party. Later, the National Peasant Party, and in December, 1944, the Citizen's Democratic Party, were also admitted into the Hungarian Front. Another important event in underground politics was the agreement of collaboration concluded between the Communist and Social Democratic parties.[6] Point two of the agreement declared the necessity of merging the Communist and Social Democratic parties, in order to form a united revolutionary worker's party. The carrying out of the unification was left for the postwar period. Point eight provided for immediate unification of Hungarian workers through the trade-unions.

In the villages, towns, districts and counties occupied by the Red Army, so-called "national committees" immediately arose, with representatives of the former underground parties and the trade-unions. The committees were formed almost everywhere through the intervention of Communist emissaries, who did their best to select docile fellow travelers from all parties as members. The crippled transportation system was controlled by the Red Army. Joseph Gábor and, a few months later, Ernö Gerö—both Muscovite Communists—became the ministers of commerce and transportation in the provisional government. Freedom of movement was thus assured to Communist agents, who were supported in every respect by the occupying forces and spoke with authority to the terrorized population.

From the very beginning of the new regime, national committees handled all public affairs on the municipal level. In most places the committees were Communist-dominated. The situation was particularly anomalous in the villages where the vast majority of the peasants considered the Smallholder Party their own. The Communist Party had not previously existed in the villages, and the Social Democratic Party had few, if any, members. The Peasant Party had just begun to organize. The peasants soon realized that through the national committees they were being ruled by a new oligarchy of incompetent persons, who were either of dubious reputation or else entirely unknown in the villages.

128

While Budapest and western Hungary were still in German hands, the Muscovite Communists, moving around behind the front in Russian army cars, picked up the available members of the former opposition parties and took them to Debrecen. There these former opposition politicians approved a Communist proposal to convene a provisional national assembly.[7] This seemed to be a sensible course under the circumstances.

In the larger villages and towns the national committees quickly organized meetings which elected representatives by acclamation.[8] The Provisional National Assembly in Debrecen consisted of 230 deputies of whom 72 were Communists, 57 Smallholders, 35 Social Democrats, 19 representatives of trade-unions, and 12 members of the Peasant Party. The rest of the deputies were without apparent party affiliation. Seven Muscovite Communists became members of the Assembly. The elected representatives were transported by Russian army cars to Debrecen where they were lavishly entertained by the Russian High Command.

The Provisional National Assembly declared itself the sole representative of the sovereignty of the Hungarian State. Its speaker fulfilled an important role in the absence of a head of the state. At the first session of the Assembly, December 21, 1944, Ernö Gerö, as a leading Muscovite, emphasized that the policy of the Hungarian Communist Party was "a Hungarian, democratic, and national policy." [9] The following day the Assembly fulfilled its two major tasks by electing a provisional national government and authorizing it to conclude an armistice agreement with the Allied powers.

Under the leadership of Foreign Minister János Gyöngyösi, a new Hungarian delegation traveled to Moscow. Molotov's first question addressed to the second armistice delegation was whether or not they considered themselves a successor of Horthy's armistice delegation. Gyöngyösi replied negatively and stated that the new democratic government of Hungary in no way considered itself as a successor of the Horthy regime. Thereafter Gyöngyösi asked for a reduction of the reparations to be imposed on Hungary in view of the devastated country, a part of which was still under German rule. Molotov suddenly became severe and began to read from a sheet of paper: "Nobody attacked Hungary. Hungary attacked the Soviet Union. . . ." And so he continued to read a long list of accusations against Hungary. The Hungarians had to sign the text of the armistice as it was presented to them.[10]

When the Germans were driven out of Hungary and the Government could move to Budapest in March and April, 1945, the number of deputies in the Provisional National Assembly increased to 495. Together with the Social Democratic and trade-union representatives the

Communists had an absolute majority. Although the Assembly declared itself the only representative of the sovereignty of the Hungarian state, it actually delegated its power to a political committee and to the cabinet. The Government promulgated the most important reforms as decrees, subsequently approved by the Assembly. In the two short sessions of the Assembly, acceptance of the decrees and other proposals took place almost without debate. Ratification of the armistice agreement and of the declaration of war on Germany, agrarian reform, and establishment of a National Supreme Council for the exercise of the powers of the head of state were the most important legislative acts of the Provisional Assembly.

The constant effort of the Kremlin to give an appearance of legality to all its actions appeared clearly in this call for the National Assembly and establishment of a new government. The members of the Government were the same persons designated by Molotov in the name of the three major Allies on December 6, 1944. The Communist policy makers did their best not to irritate popular feelings, in order to gain the approval of the constitutionally minded Hungarian public. A constitutional setting was necessary for the birth of the new regime, to prove it a legitimate child of the Hungarian people.

The exterior appearance of the Provisional National Government was better than expected.[11] Members were carefully selected in order to win the confidence of the public. In the cabinet the Communists and Smallholders each had two portfolios, the Social Democrats three, and the Peasant Party one. Besides these eight party men there were four nonparty men. Prime Minister Dálnoki Miklós had been the commander-in-chief of the first Hungarian Army and he surrendered to the Russians after the armistice proclamation of Regent Horthy. Two ministers, János Vörös and Gábor Faraghó, had also been generals during the Horthy regime. Count Géza Teleki, was a professor of geography and son of the popular late prime minister. Erich Molnár, labeled in Moscow as a Social Democrat, later turned out to be an old member of the Communist Party.

The most important portfolio, the Ministry of Interior, was given to Ferenc Erdei, ostensibly a member of the Peasant Party, but actually owing exclusive allegiance to the Communist Party. Under his cloak and protection the Communists, from the outset, continued to organize the police all over the country. They dismissed as "fascists" the members of the old police force, and only members of the Communist Party could obtain a position of real importance in the new police force, even in the smallest villages. Rákosi stated that "there was one single organization over which our Party demanded full control from the very first moment and refused to accept any coalitionist solution. This was the State Defense Authority," i.e. the political police.[12] The political police were organized practically as a branch of the Communist Party. If anyone objected to this Communist domination of the police, the usual reply was that the Communists had the expert knowledge necessary for purging Nazi collaborators and Fascists. Once the police force was purified, its control was to be transferred, they said, to a non-party organization. This never happened.

The whole political set-up created at Debrecen, and particularly the composition of the new government, demonstrates one of the main principles of Communist politics. It was and has remained a constant pattern to give formal authority to non-Communists, while retaining effective control in the hands of Communists or fellow travelers. In terms of real power the Communists in the new Hungarian Government had the most important positions.

Many times the Communists suggested names of suitable persons for high political positions, claiming that they would be acceptable to the Russians, whose good will, or at least tolerance, was a necessary condition for all governmental activities. A few months after their appointment the very same persons were forced to vanish from the scene under attack by the Communist-dominated press as "reactionary Fascists" working against the interests of the people. For example, as soon as Count Géza Teleki was elected president of the Civic Democratic Party, he became the target of concentrated Communist attacks. This procedure of gradual elimination has remained a constant Communist practice. The fate of politicians hence was most uncertain and unpredictable. Whether someone was a genuine patriot and selected as conservative window dressing or was a fellow traveler apparently made little difference. Nobody could foresee who would be thrown out—when, how or why—of the Communist-run train.

In countries occupied by the Red Army and ruled by Russian-dominated Allied Control Commissions, the freedom of choice in political matters was very limited. The Western powers themselves advised the non-Communist politicians to cooperate with the Communists in a coalition regime.[13] In view of the conditions existing under Soviet occupation which were rapidly becoming worse, it was difficult to draw the line between the various categories of fellow-travellers and politicians intending to serve national interests, and the people who had to cooperate in order to exist.

The Debrecen Government endeavored to function under miserably difficult conditions. Even in matters such as office space, there was great difficulty. All governmental offices were crowded into one small building. The effectiveness of governmental measures depended entirely on the goodwill of the Russians. Some destitute members of the Government even got clothes from the Red Army whose soldiers had "liberated" them from their belongings. The Government truly was not much more than a show window. There were no regular railroad, telegraph, or postal communications. The *Official Bulletin* published in Debrecen could not be distributed beyond the outskirts of the town. Real power lay in the hands of the occupying Soviet forces. In addition, the Communist-dominated local national committees and Communist-organized police actually administered the affairs of the country. Moreover, the Debrecen Government's feeling of deprivation and absolute dependency on the Russians had an important psychological impact even in the later period when the situation somewhat improved. Many non-Communist politicians came to realize that the Russians were all-powerful and that the existence of the new Hungarian state, emerging on the ruins of Axis-Satellite Hungary, depended entirely on Soviet Russia. The passive attitude of the Western powers greatly strengthened this view. It seemed in Debrecen that only a cooperative policy with the Soviet Union could assure the survival of the Hungarian nation after the catastrophe of the war. There was no other alternative but to try to get along with the occupying Soviet authorities, and this seemed no easy task considering the strongly anti-Communist attitude of the Horthy regime. In this situation the Hungarian Communists presented themselves as handy go-betweens. Some people hoped that they would represent Hungarian interests in Moscow.

When the government agencies moved to Budapest, the Russians, the Communist Party, and the various Communist-sponsored organizations already were occupying the best buildings. Since many government buildings were entirely destroyed during the siege, the government departments obtained only badly battered tenement houses. It was characteristic of the situation that the Foreign Ministry had to move into a shabby old apartment house, while the Communist-organized "Democratic Youth Movement" resided in a magnificent palace. This difference in location and equipment expressed the actual power position of the Communist Party and the government—a fact which could not but impress the public mind.

A leading Moscovite, Zoltán Vas, was in charge of supplying Budapest with food. From the country and through the Red Army he could obtain some potatoes, flour, and other victuals. After the ordeals of the siege it seemed to the famine-threatened and thoroughly looted capital as if the Communists were the only good organizers and general benefactors. These transactions, however, had an interesting background.

132

During the war Hungarian authorities sabotaged agrarian exports to Germany. As a result of this policy, Hungarian livestock increased by 11 percent between 1940 and 1943, and at the time of the Russian invasion eighteen million metric quintals of cereals were hoarded in public stores.[14] The Red Army seized this hoard, and also about one-half of the country's livestock. Part of it, however, was given as a loan to the supply agency headed by Zoltán Vas in Budapest. This act the newspapers hailed as the greatest gesture of Russian generosity. But the Hungarian Government was expected to make a return in kind.

The new regimes established screening boards in all branches of the public services, professions, and private firms. The political parties, members of the National Independence Front, and the trade unions sent representatives to the screening boards. The real meaning and the implications of the screening process were not realized by the non-Communist parties and the non-Communist members of the screening boards. As a result, the outcome was unpredictable. In a number of cases the verdicts of the boards were just. But frequently people with a doubtful or worse record were able to keep their positions while others were summarily dismissed. Often petty jealousies or Communist zeal prevailed over the facts. In all fairness one can say that the screening boards were asked to do the impossible. Party politicians were judging people not only for their actions but even for the motives of their actions when, apart from criminal cases, no standards were available. The excitement created by the screening had hardly died down when purges on new pretexts and mass dismissals brought it to a new pitch. This process disintegrated the national and municipal administration, weakened initially by the earlier flight of civil servants to the West.

Before the war Hungary had a non-party civil service. Now the Communists proposed that all important positions be divided among the parties. The non-Communist parties accepted this system, which theoretically would have secured a non-Communist majority in the administration and offered the opportunity to reward their own party men. But at the same time the Communists began to train a well indoctrinated Marxist elite for the various government positions.

It was taken for granted that the coalition parties would participate in organizing the new civil service, and in suggesting appointments for leading positions. But this general acceptance of a coalition type of spoils system[15] led to abuses and opened wide the door for Communist infiltration tactics, gradually assuring important positions to opportunists and to men owing exclusive allegiance to the Communist Party. Communist members of the cabinet, as a matter of course, filled their ministries with Communists. At the same time the Communist Party claimed

133

and obtained key positions in the ministries headed by non-Communist ministers.

The Communists were glad to support the nomination of incompetent non-Communists in the public service. In this troubled period the qualifications of sons, sons-in-law, and, in general, devoted party men were not questioned. The Communists were delighted to see this state of affairs and to support such appointments, because this was the surest way to demoralize the non-Communist forces and to strengthen the Communists' own grip on the country.

The predicament of civil servants who refused to sell themselves to a political party became increasingly difficult. In the first years toleration by the Communists was a necessity. But as soon as the Communists trained a reliable party man for a job, the bourgeois expert was attacked as a reactionary fascist and eliminated.

After a while the Smallholder Party, sensing the Communist tactics, attempted to defend competent officials in the course of various purges and dismissals. Although the Smallholder actions were successful in some cases, they could not change the over-all picture. One by one the Communists seized the key positions in the administration. Non-Communist cabinet members gradually became mere figureheads. The philosophy underlying the spoils system particularly favored the Communist plans; for as soon as a political leader was declared "undemocratic" his group was dealt with accordingly, and there were new vacancies for Communists in the administration.

Agrarian Reform.

In Hungary the large farm and big estate system had continued to exist for a variety of reasons. Since the number of landless laborers and those holding only a few acres amounted to three million, or nearly one-third of the population of the country, an agrarian reform was long overdue, mainly for social reasons. Moreover, in the completely devastated and disorganized country any revival of agricultural production would have been difficult without an agrarian reform. This was the basic program of the Smallholder Party, but the plan proposed by their members in Debrecen was rejected by the Communists. As the first important legislative act of the new regime, a most radical agrarian reform was promulgated on March 15, 1945, under the dictation of Marshal Klementy Voroshilov, Chairman of the ACC.[16] This decree included many provisions with exclusively political objectives. The Communists combined the necessity of an agrarian reform with three major political goals; (a) liquidation of the old land-owning class, (b) winning the support of the landless peasantry, and (c) gaining gradual control of the whole

134

agrarian population. The average holding to be retained by the land-owners was one hundred cadastral yokes (142 acres), but those who owned property over one thousand cadastral yokes (1420 acres) were deprived of all their land.[17] The Communist Minister of Agriculture and the Communist-dominated national committees took care of the prompt and thorough execution of the law. In many places the local commandants of the Russian forces were ready to intervene and expedite matters. The actual execution of the agrarian reform often went beyond, and actually violated, the provisions of the law. The former landowners had no recourse whatsoever. In all, 642,342 persons received land under the agrarian reform.

Experts suspected this agrarian reform to be the first preparatory step toward the introduction of the collectivization of agriculture. The allot-ments, which were too small, and the whole structure and execution of the decree were designed first to get the support of the landless peasantry, and then to prove that small farms privately owned cannot successfully operate in modern agriculture. In 1945, however, the Communist Party was fighting for acceptance by the peasantry. It then claimed that the reform respected private property in land. Anyone who even hinted that this agrarian reform would necessarily be followed by collectiviza-tion was promptly denounced as a reactionary agitator and an enemy of the people.

This cautious policy was followed throughout 1945 and 1946. The official newspaper of the Hungarian Communist Party, *Szabad Nép*, described the final goal of the Communist agrarian policy in these words:

> The time has come for us to present the peasantry with a new economic program, extending for a greater length of time. This will really serve the interest of the peasantry and its aim will be to turn the masses of working peasants into independent and prosperous farmers. The independent smallholder system is the best-suited to the particular Hungarian conditions and to the ideas of the Hungarian peasantry. . . . The land of small and medium peasants will never become the nest of corruption and exploitation. The defense of such property rights is the interest of the Hungarian democracy as well as that of the Communist Party.[18]

In 1946 the Communists were in desperate competition with the Smallholder Party and the views expressed in this article aimed to popu-larize Communist policy.

People's Courts.

The seizure of power by the Communists was facilitated by the people's courts. This was one of the first institutions introduced in all countries after Russian occupation. The activities of these courts contributed considerably to the creation of an atmosphere of fear, intimidation, and insecurity.

Originally the people's courts had been established to pass judgment on Hungarian war criminals.[19] Most of them took refuge in Austria and were extradited by the American occupation authorities to the new Hungarian regime. The people's courts were organized by decree in January, 1945, at all the seats of courts of justice. Members were selected from a list prepared by the political parties who were members of the National Independence Front. Later a decree authorized the Trade Union Council to appoint a sixth member. This was one of the rare occasions when the Democratic Civic Party was mentioned among the members of the National Independence Front. Actually, however, the Democratic Civic Party was usually not given an opportunity to present candidates, and the fifth member was selected from another party. The people's court was presided over by a professional judge. Special people's prosecutors were appointed by the minister of justice to each people's court, while a National Council of People's Courts reviewed the sentences in case of appeal. Its members were appointed by the five political parties from persons who passed the bar examination.

In some countries, like Bulgaria, the People's Courts administered a large scale purge, with little regard for legal formality. In more constitutionally minded countries like Hungary, the formalities were better observed and the number of victims smaller. As of January 1, 1948, the people's courts in Hungary had pronounced death on 295 persons, of whom 138 were executed. Official statistics, of course, do not reveal the number of victims who perished in concentration camps and in the hands of the political police.

Beginning in 1947, the well-known "spy," "conspiracy," "treason," and "sabotage" trials were staged before packed courts. These trials were arranged at first for the elimination of democratic opposition and church leaders, and later for the liquidation of potential leaders of national Communist movements.

In this latter period, especially, the people's courts did not administer law or any sort of objective justice, but rather fulfilled the Communist party instructions labelled as "popular will" or "social interest." Eventually the people's courts came to consider all actual or potential opponents of the Communist dictatorship as "fascist traitors," and dealt with them accordingly.

Trade-Unions and Factory Committees.

In Hungary the number of organized Communist workers was not very significant before 1945. Hence the immediate unification of the workers through the trade-unions was advocated and effected. The Communist Party seized control of the trade-unions immediately after the end of hostilities. The Hungarian trade-union movement in the past had been intimately connected with the Social Democratic Party. Under the German occupation, the trade-unions were dissolved and their leaders arrested. The leader of the Social Democrats, Charles Peyer, who for twenty years had also been secretary-general of the Hungarian Trade Union Council, was interned in the Mauthausen concentration camp. In his absence, Árpád Szakasits, former editor of the Social Democratic Party newspaper assumed leadership of the Party. Szakasits was eager to accept Communist suggestions when he reorganized the party after the Russian liberation. Left-wing Socialists were put into almost all key positions. The moderate and independent elements of the party were considered rightist deviationists, traitors to the unity of the workers. They were not allowed to play any role. When in May, 1945, Peyer returned from the Mauthausen concentration camp, he was offered a diplomatic post as a means of honorable exile. He did not accept this offer but courageously carried on a losing battle. Eventually he was excluded from his own party and finally fled the country with a great many other Socialists. In his absence he was tried and sentenced as a spy and a traitor.

Membership in the thirty-one Social Democratic trade-unions in Hungary had dwindled to about 102,000 in 1944. Twenty new trade-unions were formed in 1945, and the over-all membership in the trade-unions rose to 850,596 that same year and to 1,288,095 in January of 1947. Unions appeared in all branches of the state administration, industry, and business. Practically all laborers and white collar workers had to belong to one of the unions, which soon became an important tool in the hands of the Communist policy-makers.[20] Communists seized all the leading positions in the National Federation of Trade-Unions and in the Trade-Union Council. No genuine elections were held.

A delegate of the trade-unions sat on the screening boards and on the national committees on equal footing with the representatives of the coalition parties. Under these conditions Communists soon had an absolute majority in all agencies established by the coalition parties. The delegates of the trade-unions and of the Social Democratic Party were usually instructed by their pro-Communist central authorities to support the Communist point of view in the name of the unity of workers. Since the attitude of the National Peasant Party was uncertain, the Smallholder representative most of the time remained isolated.

The trade unions obtained other important prerogatives, such as the monopolistic management of the labor exchanges. Moreover, the system of the collective agreements was introduced. Such agreements were negotiated and signed by the National Federation of the Free Trade-Unions on behalf of the employees and by the employer's organization. As for the application and the interpretation of the agreements, disputes in doubtful cases were referred to the National Committee of Wages—another Communist controlled organization. The system of collective agreements compelled the employees, whether manual laborers or white collar workers, to work 48 hours a week. Maximum and minimum wages were fixed among the different categories of the employees. Overtime work and shock-work was rewarded according to special rules. All workers were entitled to a vacation with pay of from six to twenty-five days. A decree introduced the system of the factory committees in all enterprises employing twenty or more persons. These committees were entitled to deal not only with questions relating to working conditions, economic and welfare interests of the employees, and production control but also with disputes between the employer and employees. Through the network of these committees the Communist Party found additional means to strengthen its control over the workers. Such committees were formed even at the universities and exercised control over many scholarly activities.

The trade unions and the factory committees manifestly purported to strengthen the position of the workers in relation to management, but eventually under them freedom was even more limited than before. Gradually they became tools in the hands of the Communist leaders, performing their duties under strict control and discipline. Strikes were forbidden. The Hungarian Communist leader, Mátyás Rákosi, explained, according to H. F. A. Schoenfeld, American Minister to Hungary, that "strikes for the improvement of working conditions or higher wages were not permissible in Hungary; they were a luxury which only the American economy could afford." [21] In this spirit the right of labor to organize freely for the protection of its own interests was entirely suppressed. It was argued on behalf of this policy that since the state belongs to the workers, they would wrong themselves by strikes. This situation is justified by Soviet philosophy, which affirms the right of a small Communist elite to take power in the name of the proletariat.

VIII. HUNGARY A REPUBLIC[1]

Elections and Aftermath.

The elections held in the autumn of 1945 were the turning point in postwar Hungarian politics. The Hungarian electorate had been rather restricted in the past, and until the 1939 elections the secret ballot had been limited to towns. According to the terms of the electoral law of September, 1945, the members of the National Assembly were elected on the basis of general, secret, direct, and equal suffrage. Proportional representation was introduced in the whole country and ten electoral constituencies were formed. The list of candidates in the constituencies were prepared by duly authorized political parties. Each 12,000 votes secured a seat in the assembly. After the seats had been distributed along these lines, the remaining votes were computed on a nation-wide special list.

It was an important and distinctly less democratic feature of the law that only those political parties whose right to participate was recognized by the Central National Committee, could take part in the elections. Thus the coalition parties had a sort of monopoly over the political life of the country.[2]

The new elctoral law lowered the voting age to twenty years and omitted most of the elaborate restrictions of former laws. Those who had taken part in the armed fight against the Germans and Fascists had the right to vote at the age of eighteen. On the other hand, a broadly defined category of pro-Nazis and supporters of similar ideologies were disfranchised. The new law almost doubled the electorate. In 1945, the population of Hungary was 8,943,533 and the electorate was 5,164,-661, i.e., 59.7% of the total population. Legal requirements for suffrage and for election to the Assembly were the same. The National Assembly was authorized to elect twelve more members from among outstanding personalities.

It was a part of the Communist tactics to have the Budapest municipal elections on October 7, a month before the general elections. The Communists felt sure that the working-class districts of the capital and the city proletariat would assure a sweeping victory of the united Communist-Socialist ticket. The Communist mayor of the Capital, Zoltán Vas, did his best to organize Communist propaganda through all modern means of communication like loudspeakers, radio, posters, newspapers, while the other parties were in a much less privileged position. But the outcome of the elections was the first major disappointment of the communist brain trust, for the Smallholders obtained an absolute majority. The results of the Budapest municipal elections were:

	Votes	*Seats*
Smallholder Party	295,197	121
United Socialist-Communist ticket	249,711	103
Civic Democratic Party	22,392	9
National Peasant Party	11,741	5
Hungarian Radical Party	5,013	2
	584,054	240

Feverish Communist activities followed this defeat. They proposed a single electoral ticket for the forthcoming general elections. Voroshilov himself intervened and eventually offered 47.5% of the single electoral list to the Smallholders, who refused. The embittered Socialists also strongly insisted on separate electoral lists because they attributed their defeat in Budapest to the anti-Communist feeling of the population. The resistance of the non-Communist parties was strengthened by the stand of western representatives, who intimated that elections based on a "single" electoral list would not be in harmony with the Yalta agreement.[3]

In view of the general opposition to a single block ticket, Voroshilov peremptorily demanded instead the continuation of the coalition government whatever the results of the elections might be. The non-Communist parties accepted this condition as a better alternative than a single block ticket. The Communists still were optimistic. They enjoyed tremendous practical advantages. Besides the support of the occupying forces, they had newspapers, transportation, and other propaganda facilities in quantities not available to non-Communist parties. In addition, many potential anti-Communist voters had fled before the Red Army into Austria and Germany, and individuals taken as war prisoners had not yet returned at the time of the elections.[4]

It was a great surprise to the Communists and the Russians when, in these general elections held on November 4, 1945, the Communists polled only 17% of the total vote. The Smallholders obtained 57% of the votes cast, and with the help of the residual votes, almost 60% of the seats in the Assembly. The results of the general election were:

	votes		seats
Smallholder Party	2,691,384	57.0%	245
Social Democratic Party	822,666	17.4%	69
Communist Party	801,341	17.0%	70
National Peasant Party	323,571	6.9%	23
Civic Democratic Party	76,331	1.6%	2
Radical Party	5,762	0.1%	–
Total	4,721,055	100.0%	409

The overwhelming Smallholder victory expressed the determination of the Hungarian people not to be bolshevised. Not only the peasants, but most of the anti-Communist elements of the population voted for the Smallholder Party because this seemed to offer the greatest resistance against the bolshevization of the country. The Smallholder Party at that time represented the national unity of the anti-Communist forces.[5] Without proportional representation the Smallholder victory would have been even more sweeping and the number of Communist deputies almost insignificant. According to a Hungarian scholar, "A study of the local results revealed that the Smallholders Party had an absolute majority in 82% of the 3,300 towns and villages of Hungary, and a relative majority in 10 percent. The Communist Party had 74 absolute and 74 relative majorities, while the Social Democratic party had 19 absolute and 44 relative majorities. The National Peasant Party obtained 14 absolute and 30 relative majorities." [6]

The electoral defeat proved that the Communists had not gained overwhelming support from the former agrarian proletariat, which had been their greatest hope. A considerable number of the new landowners, no matter how small their allotment was, had become class-conscious and staunch supporters of private ownership. The idea of Communism did not appeal to them. According to Rákosi the Communist Party gained 24-28 percent of the votes in the poorest agricultural regions in southeastern Hungary, but they won the smallest number of votes in the western agricultural areas.[7]

The Budapest municipal elections and the general elections had world-wide repercussions. Both were considered highly important because the evidence showed the elections to be free and unfettered, and they were officially recognized as such by East and West. The leading Western newspapers featured front-page articles and editorials. The following dispatch of the London correspondent of the *Christian Science Monitor* was most characteristic:

This concrete proof that free elections—as they are understood in the United States and Great Britain—have occurred in at least one Balkan country is heartily welcomed by Anglo-American officials. This election result would indicate that even in areas beyond Anglo-American control—and about which many officials had been privately worrying—the peoples of Europe can be given a chance to choose their own officials honestly and openly. . . . In view of the fact that Hungary is wholly under control of the Red Army and that this quite naturally has been of no small benefit to the Communist Party, some observers had been concerned that it might be difficult to conduct completely free and unhindered elections. The result of the weekend balloting would seem to have disposed of that worry in convincing manner.[8]

After the elections Voroshilov was quick to point out to the Smallholder leaders that "the Soviet Union wished to base its friendship with Hungary on its relations with the Smallholders party."[9] The Smallholders, impressed by their victory, were greatly pleased by this statement. They visualized a new era of constructive Hungarian-Soviet cooperation. The fact of the apparently passive Soviet attitude at the elections encouraged everyone.

The Communists were astonished but not greatly disturbed. They had to change their tactics and Rákosi had to give explanations to Moscow. The elections notwithstanding, the political situation remained favorable to them. The aristocracy and landowning classes had already been liquidated. Land reform had also deprived the Catholic Church of its main economic basis. An inflation on an unprecedented scale increased the general confusion and difficulties. People of the middle class lived in insecurity, and, in order to exist, were gradually selling their belongings. The Communists possessed the key positions, and exercised effective control throughout the country by means of the national committees and the police. Trade-unions and factory committees were in Communist hands. Fifth columns were carefully planted in all parties. The continuance of the coalition government was secured by the pre-election agreement. Thus the Communists hoped to be able to rule the country conveniently behind the screen of a coalition, as was the case in other satellite countries.

After the elections the coalition parties agreed that the minister of interior should be a member of the Smallholder Party. A few days later the Communists explained that the Ministry of Interior must be given to them, because Voroshilov was astonished to hear that in Hungary the situation in this respect would be different from the situation in other countries "friendly to the Soviet Union," and he had therefore vetoed the proposition. The Smallholders yielded. Otherwise they obtained 50 percent of the seats in the cabinet, but, not the real power positions, and they had no majority. The prime minister, one minister of state, seven other members of the cabinet, the speaker of the assembly, and later the President of the Republic were all Smallholders. The Communist and the Socialist Parties each obtained three portfolios, and the Peasant Party one. In addition, the Communist and Socialist Parties each had a deputy premiership.

Simultaneously with the political penetration, the Communists were anxious to seize one by one key positions in the economic life of the country as soon as they had trained experts in sufficient number. This process was greatly facilitated in November, 1945, by the establishment of the Supreme Economic Council, of which a leading Muscovite, Zoltán Vas, became the secretary general. The functions of this council were more important than the activities of the ministries dealing with economic and financial problems. In the most significant questions it had supervisory powers. Zoltán Vas actually became the economic dictator of the country and the ministers concerned had little power, although nominally the prime minister was the chairman of the Supreme Economic Council. Rákosi noted that the Communists "created the Supreme Economic Council, thus gradually acquiring all the economic key positions." [10]

The Republican Constitution.

On January 31, 1946, the new National Assembly by its first legislative act declared Hungary a republic. The new constitution guaranteed to the citizens the natural and inalienable rights of man and to the Hungarian people the right to an organized community life and peaceful cooperation with other peoples; personal freedom; the right to a human life free of oppression, fear and want; freedom of thought and opinion; free exercise of religion; the right of assembly and the right to form associations; the right to property, to personal security, to work, and to dignified human living; the right to free education; and the right to participate in the affairs of the state and municipalities. These rights were regarded especially as the natural and inalienable rights of man. The constitution declared that no citizen could be deprived of these rights without due process of law. The Hungarian state guaranteed these rights, in an equal and uniform way, to all its citizens without discrimination within the order of a democratic state.

The President of the Republic was elected for a four year term by the National Assembly. Every Hungarian citizen who had attained the age of thirty-five and who was eligible for membership in the National

Assembly, was eligible for the office of the President. No one could be elected President of the Republic twice in succession. The President of the Republic represented Hungary in international relations, sent and received envoys, appointed consuls and granted the *exequatur* to foreign consuls. He was authorized, through the ministry, to conclude treaties with foreign powers but the approval of the Assembly was needed if the subject matter of the treaty was within the competence of the legislature. He was entitled to declare war, to announce the existence of a state of war, to conclude peace and to use the armed forces with the previous authorization of the Assembly.

In internal affairs the President had important prerogatives. He exercised the executive power by means of a ministry responsible to the Assembly. He appointed and dismissed the prime minister in accordance with the principle of parliamentary majority and he appointed the cabinet ministers upon the proposal of the prime minister. The prime minister or a competent cabinet minister countersigned all acts of the President.

The President appointed all the judges and the government officials above a certain rank. He could not resign without the consent of the Assembly. In case of the death of the President, or if he was continuously hindered in the exercise of his functions, these were fulfilled by the speaker of the National Assembly until the election of the new President.

The President signed and promulgated within fifteen days the laws enacted by the Assembly. Before promulgation however, he had the right, within fifteen days, to return any law to the Assembly with his recommendations for reconsideration. But he was obliged to promulgate the law within fifteen days if it was sent to him by the Assembly for the second time. The President had the right to adjourn the Assembly, but for no longer than thirty days in any one session. He also had the power to dissolve the Assembly on the recommendation of the government or if two fifths of the members of the Assembly demanded the dissolution.[11]

It appears from these and other provisions that the laws establishing the Hungarian Republic corresponded to the accepted western standards and were in many respects exemplary. However, in March, 1946, another law was promulgated to protect the democratic order of the Republic. This law declared all agitations against the democratic order of the state, and against persons or groups because of their republican convictions, to be criminal activity. In apparent defense of the Republic, the law had very far-reaching provisions. For example, it considered as criminal activity any statements which could be interpreted as contemptuous to the democratic-state order or as harmful to the international prestige of the Republic, whether they be true or false. As the

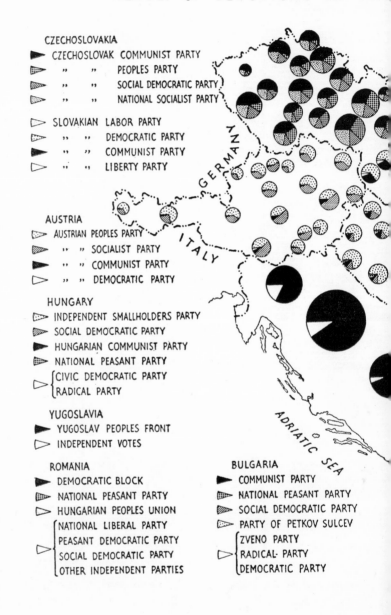

CZECHOSLOVAKIA
- ▶ CZECHOSLOVAK COMMUNIST PARTY
- ▷   ,,   ,,   PEOPLES PARTY
- ▷   ,,   ,,   SOCIAL DEMOCRATIC PARTY
- ▷   ,,   ,,   NATIONAL SOCIALIST PARTY

- ▷ SLOVAKIAN LABOR PARTY
- ▷   ,,   ,,   DEMOCRATIC PARTY
- ▶   ,,   ,,   COMMUNIST PARTY
- ▷   ..   ..   LIBERTY PARTY

AUSTRIA
- ▷ AUSTRIAN PEOPLES PARTY
- ▷   ,,   ,,   SOCIALIST PARTY
- ▶   ,,   ,,   COMMUNIST PARTY
- ▷   ,,   ,,   DEMOCRATIC PARTY

HUNGARY
- ▷ INDEPENDENT SMALLHOLDERS PARTY
- ▷ SOCIAL DEMOCRATIC PARTY
- ▶ HUNGARIAN COMMUNIST PARTY
- ▷ NATIONAL PEASANT PARTY
- ▷ { CIVIC DEMOCRATIC PARTY
  { RADICAL PARTY

YUGOSLAVIA
- ▶ YUGOSLAV PEOPLES FRONT
- ▷ INDEPENDENT VOTES

ROMANIA
- ▶ DEMOCRATIC BLOCK
- ▷ NATIONAL PEASANT PARTY
- ▷ HUNGARIAN PEOPLES UNION
- ▷ { NATIONAL LIBERAL PARTY
  { PEASANT DEMOCRATIC PARTY
  { SOCIAL DEMOCRATIC PARTY
  { OTHER INDEPENDENT PARTIES

BULGARIA
- ▶ COMMUNIST PARTY
- ▷ NATIONAL PEASANT PARTY
- ▷ SOCIAL DEMOCRATIC PARTY
- ▷ PARTY OF PETKOV SULCEV
- ▷ { ZVENO PARTY
  { RADICAL PARTY
  { DEMOCRATIC PARTY

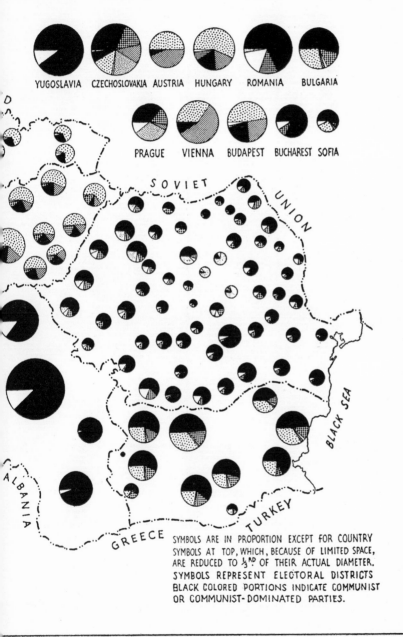

YUGOSLAVIA CZECHOSLOVAKIA AUSTRIA HUNGARY ROMANIA BULGARIA

PRAGUE VIENNA BUDAPEST BUCHAREST SOFIA

SOVIET UNION

BLACK SEA

ALBANIA

GREECE

TURKEY

SYMBOLS ARE IN PROPORTION EXCEPT FOR COUNTRY
SYMBOLS AT TOP, WHICH, BECAUSE OF LIMITED SPACE,
ARE REDUCED TO ⅓ᴿᴰ OF THEIR ACTUAL DIAMETER.
SYMBOLS REPRESENT ELECTORAL DISTRICTS
BLACK COLORED PORTIONS INDICATE COMMUNIST
OR COMMUNIST-DOMINATED PARTIES.

democratic-state order gradually became identified with Communist dictatorship, the extremely broad provisions of the law could be used, and actually were used, against anyone who refused to accept this identification or criticized the activities of the Government. The political police and the people's court, interpreted this law according to the directives received from the Communist Party. Moreover, the National Assembly periodically authorized the government to govern by decrees to assure the economic order, the balance of the budget, and the regular course of the administration.[12]

By such actions, the National Assembly strengthened the executive and relinquished its own prerogatives. This attitude was largely the consequence of the conditions prevailing in the country but, oddly enough, it helped to consolidate Communist positions and influence in the executive and judiciary in the period when the National Assembly was dominated by a Smallholder majority.

Party Politics.

Clever Communist policy asserted itself in the field of party politics even more than in Parliament. The most skillful tactical step in undermining the Smallholder position was the formation, in March, 1946, of a left-wing bloc by the Communists, Socialist, Peasant Party,[13] and the Trade-Union Council. Thus the Communists isolated the Smallholders within the framework of the coalition, assumed the offensive and began to address ultimatums to them in the name of the progressive Hungarian people. Politicians opposing the demands of the leftist bloc were denounced as "fascists" and "enemies of the people." A revolutionary atmosphere of increasing tenseness was created, making a normal functioning of parliament impossible.

Mass meetings and other Communist-organized demonstrations of the workers, synchronized with Russian political and economic demands, pressed the government towards a leftist policy. These demonstrations were not spontaneous actions. Most of the participants, especially the workers, were compelled to take part in them. Some of them received money or were promised positions. Those who were unwilling to picket under Communist leadership were declared "reactionary," and a variety of threats was used against them and their families. Lynching and mob trials were instigated throughout the country by the Communist Party.

Gradually the Smallholder Party was maneuvered into a self-liquidating process which began in March, 1946, with the expulsion of twenty-one deputies, attacked by the Communists as "reactionaries." This was a compromise measure, since the Communists had originally demanded the expulsion of eighty deputies. Simultaneously with Communist actions

147

strong Soviet pressure was exerted on the Hungarian Government. In the coming months this action was followed by the adoption of various Russian and Communist-dictated political and economic measures.[14] But the Smallholders still hoped to keep a parliamentary majority. The ousted Smallholder deputies remained members of Parliament and certainly did not strengthen Communist voting power there. But the fate of Hungary was not decided in the Hungarian Parliament. Almost simultaneously with these concessions and perhaps as a reaction to them, the Smallholders initiated a more energetic policy against Communist abuses. Under the leadership of Béla Kovács, the Secretary General of the Smallholder Party, they began a political offensive, and in June, 1946, they handed the Communist Party a list enumerating their political demands. The most important among them were: proportional representation in the administration in general and in the political police in particular; municipal elections in the fall of 1946; abolition of the people's courts and reestablishment of the jury system; abolition of the internments; and passage of an act by the Assembly concerning the Trade Unions and another act concerning the representation of peasant interests.

In the course of numerous inter-party negotiations the Communists accepted, in principle, some of the Smallholders demands, such as their demand for municipal elections and a more adequate proportional representation in the administration and in the political police, upon condition that the Smallholders first liquidate all "reactionary" elements in their own party. The Communists wanted to determine who was "reactionary" according to their own changing doctrine and then compel the Smallholders to exclude them from political life.

The only practical result of the negotiations was the gradual release of a substantial number of persons from the internment camps and the reinstatement of a few dismissed civil servants.

In speeches and articles, Béla Kovács and some other Smallholder leaders openly challenged the Communist Party and advocated the fulfillment of the Smallholder demands.[15] The Communists reacted violently. In reference to the Smallholder demands and accusations, the *Szabad Nép,* official newspaper of the Communist Party, declared:

> It is a great exaggeration to state that the Communist party "took over" the police. . . . It is true that the share of the Smallholder Party in the leading positions of the Police is nowhere proportional to the results of the elections. There are mainly historical reasons for this. After the liberation, nobody was willing to undertake the reorganization of the police, except the Communists: that

is why there is a Communist "preponderance" in the police. . . .
But let us speak of the "proportional representation." Indeed, the
Smallholder Party is inadequately represented in the top police
positions. Is it possible and is it desirable to change this? It is.
. . . But while the Smallholder Party lives in concubinage with reactionaries, the matter of proportional representation will not be
carried one step further. . . . Everything for the real democratic
Smallholders, nothing for the reactionaries hidden under the skin
of Smallholders. All pleasantry must stop in connection with the
police force of a democracy. . . . According to Béla Kovács and his
group, the Communists are preparing to seize power. We have
always said and we still say that this is nonsense. The very fact that
the democratic elements in the Smallholder Party take this absurdity
seriously, shows how much they are under the influence of reactionary gossip. Béla Kovács talks about Communist danger in
the state apparatus perhaps to distract attention from the real
danger, namely that of the spreading gentry under the wings of the
Smallholder Party.[16]

Despite all the serious difficulties with the Russians and Communists,
a strange optimism prevailed in all the coalition parties, especially after
the elections of November, 1945. The Communist defeat in the free
elections created, for Hungary, an exceptional position in Russian-
occupied Danubian Europe.[17] Under the circumstances this was almost
a miracle, and some people thought that general developments along
democratic lines would follow. It is an important fact, which one cannot
overlook, that the non-Communist parties in the coalition were progressive on social, economic, and cultural questions and the Communists, at
the outset, adapted their tactics to the general mood of the country.[18]
The coalition parties, during the Horthy regime, were all in opposition,
and they cooperated to some extent with the Communists during the
German occupation. As throughout Nazi-oppressed Europe, so in Hungary, the common fight against the Nazi foe developed into a marriage
of convenience if not into a sort of *camaraderie* between the Communist
and non-Communist politicians. The mere fact that Hungary survived
and avoided complete annihilation at the end of a disastrous war seemed
a promise of a better future, and the leading politicians of the new
regime seemed determined to make the most of a desperate situation.
This task called for courage and an optimistic outlook, especially in
regard to the possibilities of cooperation with the Russians and Communists. The Western powers, as early as 1943-44, gave encouraging advice
to Hungarians as to the possibility of such cooperation.[19] In the postwar

149

period—in view of the passive Western attitude—there were no alternatives.

Above all there was a great common task before the parties: the rebuilding and rehabilitation of the devastated country. In that respect the Communists displayed zeal and energy. According to Rákosi's words, the Communist Party "not only advocated the amalgamation of national democratic forces, and appeared not only as the staunchest persecutor of fascists, Hitlerite elements, but at the same time was foremost in healing war wounds, in cleaning up the debris, in starting reconstruction." Non-Communist leaders hence "thought it natural that the Communist Party should be more radical than other parties, but expected it would work shoulder to shoulder with the others in reviving the country." [20]

The fact that Communists in Hungary behaved differently in 1944-45 than in 1919, was a part of their most deceiving tactics. Largely because of apparent Communist moderation during the prelude of the postwar Hungarian drama, the opinion of some of the foreign observers was equally optimistic. For instance, Oscar Jászi rejected the suggestion that "what is taking place in Hungary is simply a repetition of what has occurred in the Baltic states, in Bulgaria, Rumania and Jugoslavia." [21] He characterized the Hungarian situation in the following manner:

> The old demagogy of the first Bolshevik revolution was completely absent; Communism had become respectable and gentlemanly. Even the criticism of certain Governmental measures by the Roman Catholic hierarchy was listened to with respect, and when Archbishop Mindszenty attacked the expropriation of the estates as a "product of hatred," the rejoinder was moderate and tactful. Though the large ecclesiastical estates were dismembered like the others, liberal grants-in-aid were provided for the maintenance of the lower clergy, the Churches and parochial buildings. Generally speaking, there is not much talk about Communism in Hungary today; the leitmotiv is democracy with intensely patriotic overtones.[22]

It took some time to realize that this was not the case. The Communists hated left-wing politicians or Socialists of independent views even more than they did the former Nazis.[23] A number of former Nazis were welcomed into the Communist Party and became its obedient tools.

Gradually it became clear that in decisive questions the Communists did nothing but carry out the orders of Moscow and that the Communist Party was, in reality, a disguised third branch of the Soviet administration represented in Hungary outwardly by the Soviet Army and

Soviet officials. Not having popular support, the Hungarian Communist Party could rely only upon the Russians. Under these conditions genuine cooperation between the Communist and non-Communist parties never really took place. Political expediency at all times guided the Communist attitude. They sought control. This was the aim and driving force of all Communist actions. Economic and social reforms played a secondary and merely tactical role in relation to this chief goal. In pursuing this objective the Communists sometimes changed their policies quite suddenly and without any apparent motive or reason. Always, however, they invoked the "will of the people." This "will," they cleverly manipulated through the Communist-dominated press and through Communist-organized mass demonstrations.

In addition to Russian support, the Moscow-educated Communists had two other advantages. One was a concrete program—the blueprint of a revolutionary conquest laid down in Lenin's and Stalin's works and applied to the Hungarian situation. The other was their freedom, in moral and political ethics, from any restraints in carrying out their well-premeditated plans. The Communists did not feel any obligation to keep promises given to non-Communists, but were outraged if others did not strictly abide by agreements or act according to expectations.

Their task became somewhat easier in Hungary due to the fact that the non-Communist politicians of the coalition had previously always been in opposition and had no experience in the "business of the state." The Communists were cautious enough to eliminate gradually all skilled non-Communist politicians from public life, and were rather proud of their "know how" in political matters.[24] This political "know-how," however, could not have asserted itself for any length of time without Soviet political support and the presence of the Red Army.[25] In all phases of Hungarian politics, energetic Soviet intervention helped the Hungarian Communist Party. If the Hungarian Government was not responsive enough to suggestions, there quickly followed threats, ultimatums, and the use of sheer force. The methods by which the transformation of Hungary's political structure has been manipulated were repeatedly admitted and even described by leading Communists. Joseph Révai pointed out retrospectively:

> We were a minority in Parliament and in the government, but at the same time we represented the leading force. We had decisive control over the police forces. Our force, the force of our Party and the working class, was multiplied by the fact that the Soviet Union and the Soviet army were always there to support us with their assistance.[26]

151

Rákosi later said more explicitly that it was "the imperishable merits and the support of the Soviet Union that tipped the scales" and helped to establish the Hungarian People's Democracy. He mentioned that the presence of the Soviet Army in Hungary precluded any attempt at armed rebellion, and protected the country "from imperialistic intervention." Moreover, the Soviet Union shielded Hungary "from diplomatic interference of the great Western Powers," and assisted "in the building up and consolidation" of Hungary's foreign relations. The preamble of the new Constitution of the Hungarian People's Republic openly admitted the fact that the assistance of Soviet Russia has been the deciding factor in the postwar transformation of Hungary's political structure.[27]

Notwithstanding many difficulties and odds, political life in postwar Hungary was rich in potential democratic leadership. A correspondent of the *London Times* noted that a visitor in Hungary "will be surprised by the vigorous intellectual activity displayed both in print and in conversation. In comparison with the mental sterility and haunting fear prevalent in the Balkans, Hungary seems an oasis of culture and liberty." [28]

The great issues, however, were settled by external and not by internal forces. Hungarian democracy would have developed on sound lines and would have restricted Communist influence to due proportions —if a free political evolution could have taken place. The decisive factors in Hungary were not the shrewd Communist leaders but the occupying Soviet Army, Soviet leadership in the Allied Control Commission, the proximity of the Soviet Union, and the lack of western assertiveness.

Postwar Conditions and Reparations.

It would be impossible to appraise Hungary's enormous difficulties in the armistice period without considering what the Soviet occupation was doing to Hungary's economy. Without such understanding, no one can comprehend why political and diplomatic questions were settled as they were.

One of the fundamental difficulties in the armistice period was the fact that Soviet Russia was exploiting Hungary. Soviet methods for this purpose were efficient, far more than the German devices, and it was imperative that endeavors be made to stop the various forms of exploitation. The most pressing task of the provisional government was to provide for the physical survival of the people. This situation provided the Russians with their most effective means for applying pressure. Soviet interference in economic matters was frequently connected with major political goals.

The armistice agreement compelled Hungary to furnish goods, facilities and services for the occupying army. The Soviet Union took the old principle of *la guerre doit nourrir la guerre* seriously, and the Red Army lived off the land. Besides carrying the legal burden of the armistice obligations,[1] Hungary suffered through illegal seizure and large scale looting. The notion of "war booty" was interpreted most extensively. Valuable machines, and in numerous instances whole plants, were dismantled and removed to the Soviet Union. Grains and other victuals were seized in huge quantities. Almost one-half of the livestock was taken out of the country. Safe deposit boxes were forced open and their contents removed. Whether the property was private or public did not make any difference. Private homes, public warehouses, stores, government agencies, and banks all received the same treatment. Legations of neutral powers, such as Switzerland, Sweden, or Turkey were not spared.

Obviously these large scale lootings could not have taken place over a period of several months unless approved by the Soviet High Command. When Hungarian political leaders complained to the highest Soviet authorities—Voroshilov, Pushkin, or Susmanovich[2]—the usual answer was that the looters were deserters from the Red Army and that the Soviet authorities would be happy if the Hungarian authorities assisted in capturing them. After such an answer, Count Géza Teleki asked

Susmanovich about the number of these deserters. The Russian replied that there were, in Hungary, about 150,000-160,000 deserters. Actually masses of looters in Soviet uniform could not have operated without some organization and tolerance on the part of the Soviet High Command. There were no Hungarian armed units, and any forceful action against the so-called deserters would have been considered as a treacherous attack against the Red Army. If a private individual complained to the Soviet authorities about the looting of the Red Army, his complaints were rejected and called slander because "soldiers of the Red Army would not commit robbery." Thus if anyone mentioned that he had been looted, he hurriedly added, "of course, by Finnish whale hunters disguised in Soviet uniforms." The propaganda of Goebbels did much less harm to Communism than the behaviour of the Red Army.

The looting violated the pertinent customary and contractual rules of international law, which determine "war booty" and prescribe that an occupying power is responsible for the population living on territories under its control. But the rules of international law were a poor consolation to a people at the mercy of a ruthless occupying power.[3]

The armistice agreement authorized the Red Army to issue currency to be redeemed by the Hungarian Government. In addition, the Soviet High Command was entitled to demand payments from the Hungarian Government to cover the expenses of the occupation. But the Debrecen government had no money or any other means to meet these and other financial obligations.

The Soviet High Command gave the provisional Hungarian Government, as a loan, part of the stock of bank notes which had been seized by the Red Army in the various institutions and banks in Hungary.[4] As the bank note printing equipment had been removed to Germany, the government quickly procured new equipment of necessity. This became the main source of revenue for the new government. From this time onward, the problem of securing the necessary money for the governmental organization and for the occupation costs was mainly a problem of obtaining paper supplies in sufficient quantity. In the troubled postwar months the authorities found it impossible to proceed with the assesment or collection of taxes. In any case, there would have been few solvent taxpayers. Almost everybody had been looted and economic activity was only very slowly reviving. The state revenue covered about 10 percent of the expenditures between July 1, 1945, and June 30, 1946. It was necessary to rehabilitate quickly at least part of the industrial plants for the fulfillment of reparation obligations. This necessitated investment, and the plants produced little for the home market. Because of a chain of these and other related circumstances, Hungary experienced a record inflation which might be considered unique in economic history.[5] On April 1, 1945 the value of one dollar on the black market was 250 pengös; on December 31, 1945, 265,000 pengös; on May 31, 1946, 52,000,000,000 pengös; and in the last days preceding the stabilization, 4,600,000 quadrillion pengös.[6] This enormous inflation completely disintegrated the Hungarian economic system. The average monthly salary of the government officials varied between one and three dollars in the highest categories and between one dollar and fractions of a cent in the lower categories.

The stabilization was carried out with the help of the gold reserves of the Hungarian National Bank, returned to the Hungarian government by the American authorities. This gold reserve, taken into Germany by officials of the Hungarian National Bank in late 1944, rendered a great service to the country. Had it remained in Hungary, the Red Army would have seized it as war booty, according to its consistent practice.[7] On August 1, 1946 the forint became the new monetary unit. One forint was equivalent to 400,000 quadrillion pengös (30 zeros).

Meanwhile, Hungary had to begin reparation payments in 1945 under desperate economic conditions. Article 12 of the armistice agreement obliged the country to pay two hundred million dollars to Soviet Russia and one hundred million dollars to Yugoslavia and Czechoslovakia—over a period of six years, and in commodities.[8] The first economic agreement between the USSR and the provisional Hungarian Government pertained to the fulfillment of this obligation. This agreement on the delivery of goods by Hungary was signed in June, 1945, under Soviet threats, and provided for deliveries of industrial equipment, vessels, grain, livestock, and other articles, to be made in equal installments annually during the period from January 20, 1945, through January 20, 1951.[9] The value of the goods to be delivered as reparations was to be determined according to 1938 prices in American dollars, with 15 percent added for industrial goods and 10 percent for other goods. In fact the prices fixed by the Soviet Union were arbitrary, and the actual cost of producing or purchasing the goods to be delivered as reparations was greatly in excess of the original amount. The Soviet dictated bilateral agreement actually defined the prices of the commodities and the conditions of delivery in such a way that it doubled and in some cases tripled the original amount of reparations. Moreover, in case of late deliveries, five percent interest per month was to be paid in goods. The bulk of the goods to be delivered were industrial products —a particularly difficult obligation for postwar Hungary. It was a great hardship to see vital branches of the badly damaged and slowly reviving Hungarian industry, in this crucial postwar period, working for the fulfillment of reparation demands instead of reconstruction.[10] Thus, in June, 1948, Soviet Russia could easily cut the remaining reparations payments in half and grant some other concessions,[11] and still receive more than was provided for in the armistice agreement and the peace treaty.

The armistice agreement, as well as some provisions of the Potsdam Protocol—both signed by the three major victorious powers—was interpreted by the Soviet Union with disastrous consequences for Hungary. The country was isolated. In 1945 Hungary had no trade relations with Western countries, and received practically no economic support from the West; thus at this most critical period she was left at the mercy of Soviet Russia.

Economic Cooperation Agreement.

A further major step on the road to the economic conquest of Hungary was the Hungarian-Soviet economic cooperation agreement, the enactment of which has an interesting background.

The Communist Minister of Commerce and Transportation, Gerö, and the Social Democratic Minister of Industry, Antal Bán, were sent to Moscow in August, 1945, to conclude a short term trade agreement, which they signed on August 27. This agreement provided for a bilateral exchange of goods for the period from September, 1945, to December 31, 1946, to the value of about $30 million. It also provided for Hungarian factories to spin thread from Soviet raw cotton and produce fabrics for the USSR. This was the first example of the so-called "hire-work" contracts.[12] The same day, Gerö and Bán, without proper authorization of the Government, signed another agreement of great importance, concerning general economic cooperation between Hungary and the Soviet Union. The latter agreement, which was to run for five years, had as its announced purpose, the facilitating of Soviet-Hungarian economic relations and the development of Hungary's economy by joint Soviet-Hungarian commercial organizations. This was patterned after the joint Soviet-Rumanian companies set up earlier in the same year following the economic cooperation agreement between the Soviet Union and Rumania, signed on May 8, 1945.

The provisional Hungarian Government was at first reluctant to ratify the economic cooperation agreement asserting that such important commitments could not be accepted until the conclusion of the peace treaty. Pressed to discuss it, the council of ministers later accepted the agreement. Its members who opposed ratification were assured that Marshal Voroshilov negotiated in the matter with the Hungarian Government as chairman of the ACC.[13] Subsequently American and British protests took place, but these Allied notes, couched in very mild terms,[14] were addressed to the powerless Hungarian Government. The armistice agreement put Hungary under the control of the ACC, in which both protesting Western powers were members. In view of the fact that the chairman of the ACC put pressure on the Hungarian Government, an effective British and American intervention could have taken place only in the ACC or in Moscow. The Western powers vainly protested in both places.[15] The provisional Hungarian Government, under Soviet military occupation and the tutelage of the ACC, and undermined from within by the Communist Party, simply could not be expected to resist effectively Soviet pressure for any length of time.

In the case of the economic cooperation agreement, the delaying maneuvers of a few Hungarian non-Communist political leaders were successful. The ratification did not take place under the provisional Government. The political committee of the National Assembly did not recommend the economic cooperation agreement to the National High Council for ratification until December 20, 1945, taking cognizance of the statement that this agreement would not prevent Hungary in any way from concluding any agreements whatsoever with other states.

On the same day the National High Council ratified the agreement and the Foreign Ministry informed the Soviet and American envoys and the British political representative in Budapest of this action.[16]

Proposals for Inter-Allied Assistance.

In view of the rapidly deteriorating Hungarian economy, the Hungarian minister of finance soon submitted to the Soviet economic advisor of the ACC, a report on the Hungarian economic and financial situation. This report concluded with the following statement:

> The only way that we can see out of our serious financial and economic difficulties is a plan of reconstruction, to be carried out with the assistance of the Allied Powers, the objective of which would be to raise production to a substantially higher level than at present, and restore equilibrium in the country's economic and financial affairs.
>
> Since, however, we cannot work out a plan of reconstruction until it is known what support we may count upon from the Allied Powers, there is an urgent necessity that the Allied Powers should send a commission which, with the cooperation of the Hungarian Government, would examine the economic and financial situation of the country and the methods by which assistance could be given. We should expect from the work of the commission a statement of what measures and what foreign assistance is necessary, in the

157

present economic state of the country, with its present burdens and requirements, in order that the country may recover economically and be able to meet the triple obligation arising from reparations, other obligations under the Armistice Agreement and pre-war foreign debts.[17]

But the Soviet chairman of the ACC refused to accept or even consider this report. Previously, in October, 1945, Marshal Voroshilov had almost ordered the imprisonment of Arthur Kárász, President of the Hungarian National Bank, because in a memorandum Kárász had proposed that Hungary should join the International Bank for Reconstruction and Development and the International Monetary Fund.[18]

The Soviet Government also showed the same negative attitude towards American proposals made in accordance with the provisions of the Yalta Declaration on Liberated Europe. An official American communiqué aptly summed up the history of these American endeavors:

> Since December, 1945, the United States Government has taken the initiative in proposing that the Soviet Union, Great Britain, and the United States consider means whereby the three powers, as contemplated in the Crimea Declaration, could assist Hungary to rebuild its shattered economy. These proposals, however, have been rejected by the Soviet Government.
>
> In a meeting of the Allied Control Commission in Budapest in December, 1945, the United States Representative recommended the establishment of a subcommittee of the Control Commission to consider questions of Hungarian industry, finance, and economics. This approach was unavailing.
>
> Subsequently, in a note to the Soviet Government on March 2, 1946, this Government again raised the issue by reviewing the grave economic plight of Hungary, by calling attention to the over-burdening of that country with reparations, requisitions, and the costs of maintaining large occupation forces, and by requesting the Soviet Government to instruct its Representatives in Hungary to concert at an early date with the United States and British Representatives there in devising a program which would bring to an end the process of disintegration in Hungary and at the same time provide a framework within which the rehabilitation of the country and its reintegration with the general European economy might be accomplished.
>
> In a reply dated April 21, A. Y. Vyshinski, the Soviet Deputy Foreign Minister, rejected the United States proposal on the ground

that the working out of an economic rehabilitation plan for Hungary fell within the competence of the Hungarian Government.[19]

Vyshinsky's reply was typical of the constant Soviet policy followed in Hungary. Joint action was always barred by the Russians, who invoked either the exclusive rights of an occupying power or the independence of the Hungarian state.

An American note of July 23, 1946, delivered to the Soviet Government,[20] again requested—but without any results—that instructions be sent to the Soviet representative in Hungary to concert with the American and British representatives there with regards to halting the economic disintegration. This note pointed out that half of the current output of Hungarian manufacturing industry which was operating at only one-third of the pre-war level, was absorbed by reparations and other requirements of the occupying power. In the case of heavy industry— coal, iron, metal, and machine production—reparations alone absorbed between 80 and 90 percent of the current output. Moreover, the note gave detailed data concerning the economic burden placed upon Hungary by the Soviet occupation forces and the war damage to the Hungarian manufacturing industry. As to the $300,000,000 reparations, the note stated that at the time of the conclusion of the Armistice with Hungary, the U. S. Government believed:

> that with careful management, Hungary might have been able to pay $300,000,000 in reparations. It did not foresee that Hungary's production capacity and national income would be cut to half or less in the space of a few months, and that the reparations payable by Hungary in 1945, for example, would equal 24 per cent of the national income. Likewise it did not foresee that Hungary would be required to surrender large quantities of goods and services over and above its reparations obligations.

Concerning the Soviet accusation that any outside economic help would mean interference in Hungary's domestic affairs, the American note retorted:

> The United States, in proposing tripartite discussion of an economic program for Hungary, had in mind the discussion of aid and assistance which the three powers could give to Hungary, once the economic obligations of that country were carefully defined and scheduled so as to permit their discharge without depriving the people of Hungary of their means of livelihood. The United States

has no desire to impose a plan for Hungary's economy, but does desire to lend assistance to Hungary through a concert of policies such as was envisaged in the declaration made by the three powers at the Crimea Conference.[21]

The Soviet Government, in a reply,[22] nonetheless disputed the facts regarding the economic situation in Hungary as explained in the American note, and at the same time again rejected the proposal of the United States for a tripartite investigation and a plan aiming at the economic restoration of Hungary. The Soviet note reiterated the usual Soviet argument that "the working of such a plan belongs exclusively to the competence of the Hungarian Government."

The American position was expressed once more in a note of September 21, 1946. The note reaffirmed the facts presented in the previous American communications addressed to the Soviet Government concerning the economic situation in Hungary, and stated regretfully that because of the non-cooperative attitude of Soviet Russia it would be impossible to obtain agreement as to the exact situation existing in Hungary, and as to the causes of that situation. Accordingly, the United States Government considered "that no useful purpose will be served by further assertions and denials." As a conclusion to the exchange of views between the two governments, the American note again referred to the joint undertaking entered into by the three major victorious powers at Yalta, and pointed out that "the Soviet Government not only has refused to implement the undertaking freely assumed by it at the Crimea Conference, but moreover has failed to indicate its reasons for so refusing." [23]

So much for the agreements at Yalta. The Soviets had flouted them openly and often. But there were other Allied agreements made at Potsdam in the summer of 1945. And the Russians soon managed to break these too.

Potsdam Agreement and Soviet-Hungarian Joint Companies.

According to Part III of the Potsdam Protocol, reparation claims of the USSR were to be met mainly by removals from the eastern zone of occupation in Germany, as well as by German foreign assets in Bulgaria, Finland, Hungary, Rumania and Eastern Austria. But the arbitrary Soviet interpretation of the phrase "German foreign assets" had a disastrous result throughout Eastern Europe. The Soviet Union considered as German assets, not only German war investments and other German properties, but even all properties and rights seized by the Germans during the Nazi occupation. This interpretation violated the general principles of law and the specific rules of international law. In addition, it contradicted the declaration of London issued on January 5, 1943, by eighteen Allied Powers, including Soviet Russia, regarding forced transfers in enemy controlled territories.[24] This abusive interpretation was of particular importance in reference to Austria and the considerable Austrian properties in Hungary. In the definition of "German assets" the Russians included even property which was taken under duress from the Austrians or Jews by the Germans after the *Anschluss*.[25]

Thus after Potsdam, Soviet Russia, as successor of Germany, claimed to be the owner of a considerable part of the Hungarian economy. Instead of removing the former "German foreign assets" to the Soviet Union or running them as exclusive Soviet enterprises, the Soviet government offered to hand them over to the jointly owned companies, to be established under the economic cooperation agreement. This Soviet offer was used as one of the arguments for the ratification of the economic cooperation agreement between Hungary and the Soviet Union. It was stated that otherwise the Soviet Government would simply ship to the Soviet Union all former "German assets" that were movable. Some of these assets were vital to Hungarian economy.

Hungary had no really effective means of defense against the abusive interpretation given to the expression "German foreign assets," and used by the Russians to "snowball" through all sections of Hungarian economy. If the Russians, as successors of Germany, claimed to have interest in an enterprise, and this enterprise in the course of regular commercial relationships had claims on other enterprises, the Russians claimed to have interests in all these enterprises—which eventually embraced the whole economic system of Hungary. The Russians moreover declared themselves to have acquired only the net assets and credits without any debts or liabilities whatsoever. All liabilities were thoughtfully left to the non-Soviet part-owners and creditors. This Soviet interpretation of the Potsdam agreement was later strengthened by the peace treaty.[26]

At the end of the war Germany owed over one billion marks and about two billion pengős to Hungary.[27] Russia promptly demanded from Hungary two hundred million dollars as equivalent of certain German claims in Hungary, whereas the aforementioned Hungarian claims against Germany were considered null and void. After protracted negotiations the Russians announced themselves willing to settle their Potsdam claims for a lump sum of $45 million, plus certain concessions and privileges for the Soviet controlled enterprises in Hungary.[28]

Thus the combination of the Potsdam Protocol and the economic cooperation agreements assured a practically free hand to Soviet Russia in the conquest of the Hungarian economic system. Under these circumstances Hungary agreed to establish joint companies with theoretically equal Soviet-Hungarian participation but actually under exclusive Soviet control. The general manager in charge of the operations of each company invariably was a Soviet citizen. The Hungarian chairman was a mere front. Through these joint companies the Soviet Union has, since 1946, controlled Hungarian aviation, river transportation, crude oil and petroleum refining industries, the bauxite industry, and other connected industries and enterprises.[29] These companies were granted exemption from income taxes and enjoy other important privileges. In addition to the joint-stock corporations, exclusively or overwhelmingly Soviet-owned enterprises were created by the dozens with the help of the former German interest in the various industrial, commercial and financial companies. These Soviet enterprises enjoyed privileges almost tantamount to extraterritorial rights, and operated under the supervision of the Soviet Bank in Hungary.[30]

Thus in the armistice period Soviet control over Hungarian economy was gradually established by a variety of means: looting (labelled sometimes as "war booty"), reparations, German assets, creation of joint companies, and Soviet enterprises and trade agreements. The calculated use of trade agreements diverted Hungarian goods from their usual markets and decreased the volume of commerce with the West. Moscow determined, arbitrarily, the prices of both raw materials and finished products in these relationships. At the conclusion of peace, the Hungarian economy was well prepared for further Sovietization and integration toward Moscow.

X.—THE PEACE PREPARATORY WORK (1945-1946)

Frustrated Beginnings.

Preparations of a defeated country for a peace treaty are never easy. But they were particularly difficult for those countries occupied successively by the German and the Soviet Army. The people of free nations—understandably enough—may be unable to appreciate the nature and intricacies of problems for which such countries had to find solutions. The Department of State, in a voluminous text, has published much of the data concerning the peace preparatory work in Washington during the Second World War.[1] Similar work, however, was of an entirely different character in the satellites.

In Hungary foreign politics were begun from scratch and the Foreign Ministry was organized anew. Foreign Minister Gyöngyösi, an old member of the Smallholders Party, was previously editor of an opposition newspaper in the country. He signed the armistice agreement in Moscow and in the Debrecen period of the new regime thought that post-war Hungary first of all had to win the confidence of the Soviet Union and her Allies, and that then things might turn for the better. He particularly hoped that the Red Army would evacuate the country and that the Soviet Union would eventually become a huge market for Hungarian industrial products, thus making possible the much needed expansion of Hungarian industry and the opening of new opportunities for the surplus agrarian population.

At the outset Gyöngyösi showed little interest in diplomacy in general or in preparation for the peace conference in particular.[2] Within a short time, however, he changed his views. As soon as the Foreign Ministry moved from Debrecen to Budapest, Gyöngyösi gradually realized the utter impossibility of initiating any serious activity in foreign affairs without specialists. The newly appointed officials of the Foreign Ministry belonged to various political parties and had neither knowledge nor experience of foreign affairs. Thus the Foreign Minister had to rely increasingly on officials of the Horthy regime. His initial suspicion was somewhat mitigated, since most of these officials were active anti-Nazis and went through the screening procedure without much difficulty. Encouraged by this trend, some of the younger Hungarian diplomats became optimistic, and prepared various projects for the establishment of an up-to-date foreign service.

At the end of May, 1945, I was asked by the Foreign Minister to

163

organize and supervise a division of the Ministry the function of which would be to prepare the Hungarian case for the peace conference. I undertook this work in a devastated and occupied country under the most difficult political and technical circumstances.

The Foreign Ministry began its work in one of the stripped tenement houses of Budapest. The peace treaty division occupied all of three rooms. Since the former building of the Ministry and all its contents had been destroyed during the siege, it was necessary to begin work without files and documents. Office equipment was not available at all for a while and even desks and chairs presented a problem, not to mention such technical items as typewriters. Furthermore, there was no transportation, and undernourished officials had to walk several miles from their homes. As late as autumn 1945, officials on their way home in the evening were occasionally robbed by Soviet soldiers. Fuel was scarce. For example, during the winter of 1945-46, many civil servants worked in offices without windows and without heat. To add to their hardships, their entirely insufficient salaries made it necessary to fight against inflation for their own physical survival.

However serious the technical difficulties were, they appeared unsubstantial in view of the general political conditions resulting from the Soviet occupation, the armistice agreement and domination by the Communist Party. Hungary was not a sovereign state. Foreign affairs were under the control of the Russian-dominated ACC. Civil administration was gradually reorganized by the political parties; however, this not only opened the way to many incompetent political appointees, but offered key positions to the Communists. Since the Foreign Ministry was headed by a Smallholder, the Communists secured important positions which they claimed under the system of the coalition government. In every division of the Foreign Ministry there was a Communist who reported to the party regularly. In addition, the chief of cabinet of the Minister, as well as the deputy head and later the head of the political division, were Communists. Through these key men the Communist Party knew everything that happened in the sphere of foreign affairs, and the Soviet authorities were consulted about all issues of importance. Thus they could intervene at an appropriate time and exert decisive influence. The system of controls was even further developed. The NKVD and later, the Hungarian political police, summoned some non-Communist officials and forced them to report regularly on affairs and personnel.

As soon as Hungary renewed diplomatic relations with foreign countries, many officials who had served under the Horthy regime were sent abroad. This consequently opened new fields of opportunity for the Communists, and decreased the number of competent officials in Budapest.

When I began the peace preparative work anew, my first question addressed to the Foreign Minister was: "What are the peace aims of the Government?" I asked this question repeatedly in the following months, but never received an explicit answer. Gyöngyösi only explained those political difficulties of the coalition regime which hindered an agreement on our peace aims. Under such circumstances I concentrated on searching for and collecting the necessary material and data, and prepared a variety of alternative proposals. On the one hand, the wartime era of cautious double-talk ceased—at least to the degree that we were able to obtain technical cooperation from all governmental agencies, without false excuses. But, on the other hand, we now had to face new difficulties of greater magnitude.

In June, 1945, I organized the peace treaty division in the Foreign Ministry and an interdepartmental committee which held weekly meetings in the Hungarian National Bank building. These meetings were held under my chairmanship until May, 1946, with the participation of the National Bank, the Ministries, certain scholarly agencies, and experts in various other fields. For important problems sub-committees were appointed, and they in turn reported to the general committee. The object of this work was a detailed investigation which embraced the economic, cultural, and financial development of Hungary from 1919 until the end of the Second World War. Then we examined the existing conditions and drew conclusions. The committee members included the country's foremost specialists in many fields. I openly stated that I would not want to have political appointees on the committee, and for a time it was possible to maintain this policy. I did not object to party membership as such, but I found it impossible to do constructive work with delegates whose only merit and qualification was membership in a party.[3] Despite the non-political character of this committee, some experts, in view of the precarious conditions of the country, were not infrequently reluctant to express their opinions with frankness.

Besides the general inter-departmental committee, several specialized committees and coordinating agencies were set up. For example, one prepared nationality and territorial problems, and another supervised the financial and economic findings of the interdepartmental committee. This latter group consisted of the foremost economic experts in Hungary.[4] Besides its supervisory work it considered several variations for the establishment of a Danubian Federation. I invited this committee for weekly meetings over a period of about three months, and found the lively debates therein about the possible impact of the various federative solutions on Hungary's industry and agriculture very useful. The final report of this committee proposed that the Government reveal Hungary's economic plight at the peace conference and ask for substantial reduction of our reparation payments and for the inclusion of properties confiscated and removed by the Red Army in any such payments. But the foreign minister considered these and similar proposals so utterly futile that he did not even attempt to present them to the council of ministers. He thought that such a disclosure might even endanger the safety of the authors of the report. As to the various federative projects, we were never in a position to use the voluminous material collected on this subject.

Eventually the personnel associated with peace preparations consisted of several hundred government officials and experts, and therefore their efforts required a high degree of coordination. After nearly a year of work and mutual consultations, each ministry summed up its findings in a final report based on numerous preparatory memoranda. But, in early 1946, the Communist party discovered the potential importance of this work and delayed its conclusion in certain ministries. Thereafter, Communist delegates appeared in the general committee and consistently sabotaged its work.

In addition to the official interdepartmental committees, a special private group under the direction of Count Géza Teleki investigated certain fundamental aspects of the Hungarian case. This scholarly work was performed by a small group of reliable experts who labored in an atmosphere of comparative freedom. In early 1946, the results of their work were presented in several volumes to certain Western statesmen and experts. One copy of it was transmitted to President Truman.

The most difficult problem, the disagreement among the coalition parties concerning peace aims, remained throughout the peace preparatory period. The extreme differences made it impossible to find common principles acceptable to all parties. Although the Government avoided taking a stand in the matter, I had to look for some expedient in order somehow to proceed in the muddled political situation.

As soon as I began my work I attempted to get around the lack of governmental aims by asking for an advisory delegate for political problems from each coalition party. The delegates were duly appointed and we pledged our mutual good will and readiness for cooperation. I stated that I would always be glad to give any information to the political parties through them, but, for my own enlightenment, asked for concrete formulation of their political stand with regard to peace aims. Since I did not receive any specific proposal from the parties, I interpreted this passive attitude to mean that I could proceed with the peace preparatory work, and did not ask them any more questions. Consequently my position was made somewhat easier, though this situation did not change the basic political difficulties.

Besides the lack of positive peace aims, a further major obstacle arose from the fact that the coalition government considered the members of the war governments, including that of Kállay, as war criminals. Rákosi ironically remarked to me, "Mr. Envoy, you may soon greet your former boss, Kállay, here in Budapest when he stands before the people's court." The Foreign Minister warned me at the outset that the coalition parties would strongly protest against all arguments tending to exonerate the former governments and political leaders. This general punitive attitude toward the past was not, however, entirely of Hungarian origin. In the postwar period the Horthy regime was unpopular in both East and West. In the eyes of the victorious powers Hungary was the junior member of the axis and, with her revisionist claims, one of the chief troublemakers in European politics. Nobody gave a second thought to the causes of Hungarian revisionism. Hungary's reluctant participation in the war and her endeavors toward an early armistice were not considered at all. Unlike the other Axis satellites, Hungary did not change sides effectively during the hostilities, and the fact that Hungarian troops fought with the Germans until the very last became an especial reproach to Hungary. Thus the new Hungarian regime only reflected the general opinion of the victorious nations in punishing some members of former governments. As things stood it would have been difficult to adopt a different attitude. These actions were not within the exclusive jurisdiction of the Hungarian Government. The armistice agreement compelled Hungary to "co-operate in the apprehension and trial, . . . of persons accused of war crimes," and the Russians were greatly dissatisfied with the "lax" Hungarian attitude in the matter. The ACC gave the Russians the legal channel for intervention. The notion of "war criminals" was interpreted very broadly in Nuremberg and elsewhere. Legal and moral principles, let alone political wisdom, were not the most important considerations throughout Europe at the close of hostilities.

Even under such political conditions it was necessary to find ways to tell at least part of the truth. In view of the imposed limitations, the only alternative was to explain that a large majority of the Hungarian people actually resisted Nazism vigorously and that even the "reactionary pro-German" governments resisted under the pressure of popular feeling. On December 28, 1945, in a memorandum addressed to Prime Minister Tildy, I summarized my opinion concerning the extent of our war responsibility in the following manner:

My opinion concerning our responsibility for the war is that we have to present every possible argument which is apt to reduce such charges or at least explain reasons for our conduct during the war. Since the personality of the state remains the same in international relations, irrespective of a change of regimes, our international responsibility is not affected by internal changes. Therefore, we should not assume responsibility for the Hungarian nation above that which is absolutely necessary. To do so would be contrary to the best interests of the people.[5]

Even for the Communists it was difficult to reject openly this reasoning. Although the left-wing elements of the coalition disliked and criticized the use of such arguments, they did not veto them at the outset. Thus it was possible to develop these ideas in pamphlets and books. The aim of these publications was to emphasize that even during the period in which an alliance existed between the German and Hungarian Governments the great masses of Hungarian people were opposed to Nazi ideas and policies. The pamphlets and books moreover contained data concerning the fate of Allied war prisoners and political refugees in Hungary. They also dealt with information concerning the Jewish problem in Hungary, sabotage and resistance to Germany, economic help given to territories under German occupation, and explained some results of the democratization of the country.[6]

Besides the basic political difficulties, there were many other difficulties which constantly disturbed the peace preparatory work. A good illustration is the Soviet interpretation of the armistice agreement concerning the destruction of Fascist literature.

In fulfilling the terms of the armistice agreement, the Hungarian Government appointed a commission to establish a list of Fascist books. The commission was dominated by Communists and determined the Fascist character of the publications according to Communist wishes. All individuals, libraries, and public institutions were obliged to surrender the books on the list for destruction. Only two libraries were exempt, in order to preserve Fascist literature in closed rooms for the exclusive use of authorized persons. Since the Foreign Ministry and certain other government agencies did not receive such exemption, I attempted to persuade the Communists that it was practically impossible to explain Nazi expansionism or fifth column activity if the relevant Nazi literature was not available. My explanations were not accepted, and all alleged Fascist books in the Foreign Ministry or belonging to the scholarly institutions associated with us were destroyed.

Moreover, the Soviet commission controlling the destruction of Fascist books gave only a limited consideration to the list established by the

Hungarian commission. For example, in some libraries they declared as Fascist, and thus to be destroyed, German economic and statistical periodicals dating from the last decades of the nineteenth century. In the catalogue of the Library of the National Museum the Soviet Commission was looking first of all for the word "Horthy" and asked for all the books catalogued under similar headings. Thus they destroyed all the books on "horticulture," some of them published in the seventeenth century, claiming that all such works spread propaganda for Horthy. In this case the Minister of Public Instruction, Teleki, personally intervened without result. Intervention in such cases was considered pro-Fascist action not only by Soviet authorities but even by Western-educated Hungarian Communist leaders.

Hungarian proposals for the peace settlement.

Some politicians, particularly in the right wing of the Smallholders Party, strongly emphasized the necessity of foreign propaganda in view of the coming peace conference. These politicians did not realize that as long as the coalition government did not have peace aims, there was not much to publicize. It was obvious that the Hungarian Government could not freely inform foreign countries about our fundamental troubles and especially of our difficulties with the Soviet authorities. In view of Hungary's diplomatic isolation and especially because of the meager finances at the disposal of the Foreign Ministry, any propaganda initiated by us could easily boomerang. The wartime solidarity between the Soviet Union and the Western powers still had its impact in Danubian Europe. The western Allies made it clearly understood that they were not disposed to antagonize the Soviet Union on Hungary's account.

Furthermore, Moscow could prevent all official Hungarian activities in foreign countries through the ACC.

In order to circumvent the difficulties and break down our isolated position, I began to draft peace preparatory notes. In the course of this procedure the most difficult questions were: To whom could the notes be addressed? What could be said? And how far could we go without arousing the Soviet and Communist wrath?

The first note was addressed to the Soviet Government on July 4, 1945. The Foreign Minister did not wish to assume full responsibility for the note and thus presented the draft to the cabinet. The council of ministers modified and considerably toned down the note, which was signed by the Prime Minister, who was in turn to present it to Marshal Voroshilov. Several days later the Foreign Minister discovered by chance that the Prime Minister had signed but had not delivered the note. In these times the presentation of complaints to the Russians was not an

169

enviable task. It was apt to result in unpleasant repercussions. Finally the Foreign Minister took courage and handed the note to Pushkin.[7]

This note contained propositions dealing with the economic difficulties of the country, the persecution of the Hungarians in Czechoslovakia and the new territorial settlement to be established by the peace treaty. Among other things, the note complained that the industry of the country was disrupted because the Red Army had confiscated raw materials, machines, tools, and manufactured products. The note requested that these materials either be restored or that they be regarded as reparation deliveries, because under international law they could not be considered war booty.[8] Moreover, it was requested that confiscatory actions by the Red Army should be categorically forbidden in the future.[9] The second part of the note described the anti-Hungarian measures in Czechoslovakia, comparing them with Nazi methods. The note asked for Soviet intervention to halt these discriminatory measures and persecutions. Concerning the new territorial settlement, the note proposed the adoption of the principle of nationality and plebiscites.

Realizing the absolute ineffectiveness of our interventions with the ACC or the Soviet Government and the complications caused by discussions in the council of ministers, I proposed not to submit the peace preparatory notes to the council of ministers but to deliver them directly to the representatives of the three major powers, and afterwards to send a copy to the coalition parties. As a result of the lesson learned from the first peace preparatory note, the Foreign Minister accepted this plan. Hereafter all peace preparatory notes were sent directly to the American, British, and Soviet representatives in Budapest, and subsequently copies were forwarded to the coalition parties. Consequently the Communists were confronted with a *fait accompli* and could cause trouble only after the notes had been delivered.

This procedure was in contradiction to the rule laid down by Voroshilov, according to which the Hungarian Government was supposed to channel all foreign contacts through the ACC. Until autumn 1945, no foreign representative was accredited to the Hungarian Government. The representatives of neutral powers were expelled by the Soviet occupation authorities, and delegations of the victorious nations were attached to the ACC. Notwithstanding this situation, the peace preparatory notes ignored the ACC and were addressed directly to the British, Soviet, and United States representatives in Budapest even before renewal of diplomatic relations with Hungary.[10]

Though the new procedure made possible direct delivery of notes to the British and Americans, the Western nations did not show much interest in our proposals. Moreover, the Communist domination of the coalition government, the Soviet occupation, and the general insecurity of our international position contributed greatly to the difficulty of drafting the notes. The Foreign Minister refused to accept responsibility for texts which differed greatly in their content from the general political ideas of the coalition parties. The parties themselves, however, did not have the same conception of foreign affairs. The Communist Party, as the major and in many respects determining factor in the coalition government, declared emphatically that winning the confidence of the Soviet Union by liquidating all reactionary elements and features of Hungarian politics and by thorough execution of the armistice agreement were the only steps necessary for a favorable peace treaty. They claimed other preparations were unimportant.

The Hungarian peace aims were presented for the first time to the representatives of the three major powers in a note of August 14, 1945.[11] This note advocated the establishment of a close economic cooperation among the Danubian nations, and an increased industrialization of Hungary to be carried out in the course of the economic reconstruction of the Danubian region. Moreover, it proposed the establishment of an inter-Danubian cultural commission for the promotion of friendly cooperation among the Danubian peoples. As for the territorial settlement to be undertaken by the peace conference, the Hungarian Government suggested that if boundaries lost their significance, the ideal state of affairs would be in the process of appearing. Failing this, the process of international cooperation would best be served if the boundaries were determined in conformity with the freely expressed wishes of the population concerned. This would bring about the political stability necessary for economic cooperation. Finally, the note emphasized the necessity of providing for the protection of the national minorities by means of some international machinery of the United Nations.[12]

Although ideas concerning political integration of the Danubian nations were more or less hidden between the lines, the Communist Party subsequently objected to the general principles expressed in the note. Rákosi pointed out that projects for a full-fledged cooperation of the Danubian nations were premature. These countries, he argued, must first become truly democratic, and afterwards they would cooperate automatically. Simultaneously with Communist objections, Pushkin presented strong Soviet criticisms. The Western powers did not react at all.

In this situation the Hungarian peace aims could not be developed in further detail. Instead I prepared notes dealing with seemingly technical problems to which the Communists could not easily object. These were, for instance, regulation of problems connected with citizenship, Hungarian water routes giving access to the sea, problems dealing with insuring the overland route to the sea, and improvements of water power in the Carpathian basin.

A note of October 31, 1945,[13] dealing with the citizenship question explained that as a consequence of the provisions of the Trianon Treaty, thousands of inhabitants of prewar Hungary, who had never left the country, had been deprived of their citizenship without any opportunity of acquiring citizenship in any of the successor states. The origin of this situation was the complicated and frequently contradictory provisions of the Treaty of Trianon, which enabled certain states to deny citizenship to the members of an undesirable minority. Consequently, these peoples were left in the neighboring countries without the enjoyment of the rights connected with citizenship, and were greatly handicapped in their economic and other activities. In reference to this situation, the note proposed the measures which were to be incorporated into the peace treaty in order to prevent such an anomaly.

The note dated November 12, 1945,[14] dealt primarily with an extensive elaboration of landlocked Hungary's problem of insuring free access to the sea. In this connection, the note suggested numerous improvements in the Danubian Convention. The second part of the note was devoted to the Carpathian Basin water-ways and suggested solutions which would have resulted in a development similar to the T.V.A. This note particularly insisted on the maintenance of the international character of the Danube. It urged the revival and strengthening of international control over the river, with continued participation of non-riparian states in an effectively functioning commission, and advocated freedom of navigation in the Danubian valley. This aspect of the note was referred to by Cavendish W. Cannon, head of the American delegation at the Danubian Conference in Belgrade, in the following statement:

> It is interesting to note that the postwar government of Hungary, on November 12, 1945, addressed a note to the United States, British, and Soviet Governments, giving its views on the Danube question. It called attention to the great importance to Hungary of a regime which guarantees full freedom of navigation. It suggested that the pre-war system of international navigation be reconstituted with provisions for changes required by new conditions. The Hungarian Government did not envisage elimination of non-riparian representation, for it suggested consolidation into one Commission of the Danube. Both Commissions, as the Conference is aware, had non-riparian representation. There have been changes since 1946 but we believe the long-term economic interest of Hungary remain the same.[15]

Such then, were some of the subjects—and some of the difficulties—involved in bringing a final peace to the stricken Hungarian nation. Surely the task was difficult, and to some of us at that time it was beginning to seem almost impossible.

Deadlock and last efforts in the peace preparations.

In the second half of 1945, Soviet pressure for the expulsion of all Germans from Hungary and the persecution of Hungarians in Czechoslovakia were the most acute issues of Hungary's foreign policy. Both were somewhat outside of the preparations for the peace conference and belonged within the competence of the political division of the Foreign Ministry. I was not informed of all the steps taken. Nevertheless, I intervened whenever I could relate these issues to the peace preparations.[16]

The defeat of the Communists and the victory of the Smallholder Party in the Budapest municipal elections in October and at the general elections in November, 1945, caused a spell of short-lived optimism even in foreign affairs. Nevertheless, the over-all picture did not change substantially, and the new coalition government created under the premiership of Zoltán Tildy (November 15, 1945), proved to be no stronger than the Dálnoki Miklós government.

The Soviet consolidation of the Communist-dominated puppet governments in Rumania and Bulgaria, in violation of the Yalta agreement, as well as various manifestations of Soviet policy in Hungary, forecast a gloomy future for the new Hungarian regime. This was especially conspicuous in connection with such actions as the Soviet endorsement of the persecution of Hungarians in Czechoslovakia, the Soviet abuses violating the armistice agreement, and in general the extreme exploitation which characterized the Soviet Union's treatment of Hungary.

It was clear to every sensible individual that Russian influence would increase after the war and that under the impact of the new political balance in Europe, Hungary's political, social and economic structure would undergo important changes. Nevertheless, Russian abuses, methods, and general intolerance caused great bewilderment and consternation.

Despite all the difficulties, the preparations for the peace conference and a stand for the interest of the Hungarian people appeared to be both a political necessity and a matter of national honor. Continuation of the peace preparatory work, however, became almost impossible because the new government—despite some consolidation of Hungary's internal and international affairs—could not decide on peace aims. The government did not take a stand on any fundamental question of foreign affairs. Despite my repeated proposals, it did not designate delegates and experts for the peace conference. It was an anomalous situation that while the Hungarian peace aims were expressed to the major victorious powers in our note of August 14, 1945, the very same principles were not endorsed explicitly and could not be discussed by the coalition parties. In answer to my pressing proposals, the Foreign Minister informed me that the disagreement on peace aims might easily blow up the coalition, and that such a situation might open the door for developments similar to those in Rumania and Bulgaria.

Another difficulty was that the Foreign Ministry remained at the mercy of party politics. When I criticized this situation, the Foreign Minister in turn complained to me that he was not able to resist Communist wishes in connection with the appointment of their party men in the foreign service, because of the precedents created by the Smallholder and Social-Democratic Parties.

Reflecting on these circumstances, I first orally informed Prime Minister Tildy in December, 1945, that the peace preparatory work had reached a deadlock. Then, on December 28, I presented to him an exhaustive memorandum. The memorandum described the history, progress and actual state of peace preparations, analyzed the main problems, and very frankly discussed some of the outstanding political difficulties. As was already mentioned, I explained my views concerning Hungary's war responsibility and dealt at some length with a decree concerning the expulsion of the Germans from Hungary, issued on December 22, 1945. I thought it necessary to emphasize the danger of accepting the doctrine of collective responsibility in regard to a group of Hungarian citizens. The memorandum pointed out, moreover, that it was not sufficient to make decisions concerning our peace aims and the arguments to be used, but that it would be necessary to concentrate our efforts upon carrying out the accepted policies. In this connection I referred to the lack of governmental experience on the part of the coalition parties, a lack of experience especially conspicuous in the handling of foreign affairs. In this framework I developed my objections to the disintegration of Hungarian foreign policy under the coalition regime, and especially to the scandalous abuses in the field of party political appointments in the foreign service. The conclusion summed up the most urgent agenda.[17]

For a short time this memorandum caused consternation in high governmental circles. As a result, I received promises from the Prime Minister and from the Foreign Minister that they would take steps to eliminate the difficulties. They also authorized me to prepare new peace preparatory notes which, however, had to be in line with the general views of the Government in foreign affairs. Nevertheless, the difficulties did not cease. Friendly pledges could not change the fact that the coalition parties could not agree on principles to follow in foreign affairs—particularly as to our aims at the peace conference.

Concerning our peace aims, Prime Minister Tildy eventually called an inter-party conference in mid-January, 1946, which I attended as an expert from the Foreign Ministry. This conference was dominated and frustrated by the dynamism and dialectics of the Communist leader Rákosi. His obvious goal was to prevent the conference from arriving at any concrete decisions. Szakasits, the representative of the Social Democratic Party, supported him with enthusiasm.

The issue which occasioned the longest debate involved the decree of December 22, 1945, concerning the deportation of the Germans from Hungary. I pointed out again that this decree was a fundamental mistake from the point of view of our peace preparations and national interests, and asked for its revision.[18] In my opposition to the indiscriminate expulsion of the Germans, I was supported only by the Smallholder under-secretary of state, István Balogh. The other Smallholder representatives and the Social Democrats sided with Rákosi. In regard to other issues connected with our preparations for the peace conference, the representatives of the Smallholder Party (Tildy, Gyöngyösi, and Balogh) remained passive. The representative of the Peasant Party, Imre Kovács, firmly stated that we must take a stand for the claims vitally effecting the nation. Otherwise, he explained, the Peasant Party would be obliged to reconsider its participation in the coalition Government. This was a strong statement, but all participants suspected that the Peasant Party was infiltrated by Communists and in case of a showdown would not follow Kovács. Eventually the inter-party conference terminated without having made any substantial decisions.

In addition to the territorial and nationality questions, it was necessary to decide upon the economic problems to be presented to the peace conference, as well as the manner of their presentation. In this respect Soviet and Communist interventions again frustrated all progress. Pushkin considered Hungarian territorial and political grievances and claims as remainders of the Horthy regime, and did not take them seriously. He urged the "democratization" of Hungary and the acceptance of the Czechoslovak demands as to the fate of the Hungarians in Czechoslovakia. He suggested, confidentially, as it was already mentioned, that Hungary should rather stress territorial claims against Rumania which, as a former satellite, was in the same category as Hungary. Marshal Voroshilov also intimated to Prime Minister Tildy that Hungary might obtain some territorial compensation from Rumania if she behaved well and accepted the Czechoslovakian proposals concerning the settlement of the Hungarian question in Czechoslovakia.[19]

Pushkin was somewhat more concerned that the Hungarian Government might reveal to the Western public its economic plight, and especially the Soviet methods for exploiting devastated Hungary. The following incident was characteristic of this situation: When Pushkin discovered that the Hungarian Government was compiling statistical data on war damages by means of detailed questionnaires, to be answered by all inhabitants of Hungary, immediate cessation of this work and the destruction of the data compiled were energetically demanded. Pushkin asserted that the ACC had not authorized this action by the Hungarian Government. He charged that the questionnaires clearly indicated that the goal of this work was to establish statistics concerning damage caused by the Red Army. In due course, the Foreign Ministry transmitted this Soviet protest to the Ministry of Finance. Later, an elaborate reply to Pushkin explained that the war was caused by German aggression and that therefore we intended to attribute all war damages to the Germans. Nevertheless, since the questionnaires covered different periods of time during which the damages occurred, those caused by the Germans and the Red Army were easily distinguished. The balance was decidedly unfavorable to the Soviet Army.

In harmony with Soviet policy, the Communist party made efforts to sabotage preparations of economic questions for the peace conference. A typical example of this was the attitude of Communist ministers, who for weeks in the council of ministers hindered nomination of the chief economic delegate to the peace conference. I initiated the appointment of Arthur Kárász, director and former president of the National Bank of Hungary. Time and again Gyöngyösi brought up the matter in the council of ministers but the Communist ministers always asked for more time to consider the problem. Finally, some weeks later, when Kárász was about to leave the country on an official mission, the council of ministers agreed to his appointment. Upon his return, six weeks later, he prepared a memorandum, revealing the economic situation of the country and proposing that we should ask for a reduction of our reparation payments. When this memorandum was read in the peace preparatory subcommittee of the Parliament's Committee on Foreign Affairs, the Communists reacted violently. Chief Communist delegate, Joseph Révai, launched a sharp attack against it and concluded: "Because of this memorandum a head must fall," adding obligingly, "of course, only politically." The political decapitation of Kárász took place promptly. Upon an ultimatum of General Sviridov, he was dismissed as chief economic delegate and as Director of the National Bank.[20]

176

In view of our impotence, I found it expedient to request the three major powers, in a note dated January 25, 1946, to appoint a committee of experts to investigate problems connected with the Hungarian peace settlement.[21] The memorandum attached to this note pointed out some of the mistakes and errors which were made at the peace conference after the First World War, and suggested that the organizational weakness of the conference partly explained why the Treaty of Trianon accepted exaggerated claims against Hungary.[22]

In a note dated February 1, 1946,[23] it was possible to insert some passages describing the anti-nazi conduct of the Hungarian people during the war and also to make statements on Hungary's war responsibilities in the sense I indicated in my memorandum addressed to Tildy.[24]

Furthermore, this note pointed out that the Hungarian problem after a Second World War must not find an isolated solution. A proper solution would rather consider the common interests of all Danubian peoples in the course of an institutional reorganization of the Danubian Basin. The note emphasized that the settlement of Southeast European problems did not present "insurmountable difficulties," and remarked that

> similar conditions of life brought about by geographic factors, the influence which for centuries one nation had been exercising over the other, the effects of intermarriage and more especially the co-operation of the long period preceding the epoch of exaggerated nationalism had long ago produced forms of life which bore a certain resemblance to each other. The small states are in fact separated from each other only by differences of language and an exaggerated and improper interpretation of their historical traditions, and the chauvinist propaganda to which the former gave rise. Large sections of the population, above all the working classes and the peasants who struggle against the same social evils, have no difficulty in understanding each other. *The first step towards the furthering of mutual prosperity through peaceful cooperation would be an honest and institutional attempt to uproot the nationalism which, for the last century, has been fostering the growth of differences.*

After such general explanations, the note concluded that the settlement of Southeast European problems must be based on the three following principles:

1. The harmonization of questions of territory and nationality.
2. The establishment of economic and cultural cooperation.

3. The elimination of the factors which give rise to political and social discord between countries.

Not until May, 1946, were we able to present a note to the three major powers which put forth more detailed propositions. Between February and May several incidents characteristic of our situation took place.

In early February, 1946, the Social Democratic Party delegate to the peace preparations work, Sándor Szalai, called on me in my office. He informed me in the name of his party that the peace preparatory work under my direction had become partly useless and partly harmful. He accused me of nationalism, and suggested that the Foreign Ministry try to find a practical solution by removing the Hungarian minority from Czechoslovakia, thus assuring amicable relations with our northern neighbor. I rejected his ideas and replied that the peace preparatory work was not my personal enterprise, and that if there were such essential political objections, these should be reported to the Foreign Minister and Prime Minister. Simultaneously with the move of the Social Democratic Party, the Hungarian Communist Party and the Soviet Minister, Pushkin, also expressed dissatisfaction with the peace preparatory notes. Pushkin pointed out to Gyöngyösi that our notes had the character of policies followed under the Horthy regime and actually could have been sent by the Horthy regime. A few days later the Social Democratic press launched a campaign against the Foreign Minister.[25]

Under the impact of these attacks, Gyöngyösi refused to sign a note which he had previously approved, and which dealt with territorial and ethnographic questions and particularly with the problems of Transylvania. He called an inter-party conference in the Foreign Ministry and submitted the text of the note to the representatives of the coalition parties.

At this inter-party meeting, the delegates of the Communist party, supported by Vilmos Böhm, delegate of the Social Democratic Party, refused to accept the general ideas and terms of the proposed note. The Communists themselves did not offer any specific suggestions. They stated only that the note contained veiled revisionist tendencies against Rumania, that Hungary should by no means weaken "Groza's democracy," and that before a definite stand could be taken Soviet support must be sought. Our actions, they said, must be governed by Soviet advice. The inter-party meeting eventually accepted this suggestion, and advised the Foreign Minister to find out more about Soviet intentions as to the peace settlement. I could not make it known there that it was Voroshilov and Pushkin who had privately suggested that Hungary should raise territorial claims against Rumania.

The draft note rejected by the inter-party meeting developed the idea that the Hungarian nation should be given a territory corresponding to the proportion of the Hungarian population in Danubian Europe. It was re-emphasized that the conditions brought about by the Trianon Treaty had contributed greatly to the dissatisfaction of the Hungarian nation and had naturally developed the revisionist and irredentist movements. As to the future, the note again proposed the setting up by the victorious powers of an expert committee whose duty it would be to examine the nationality and territorial problems. The Hungarian Government declared at the same time that it was willing to accept a plebiscite regarding the fate of any territories affected by a new settlement. The Communists and Socialists especially objected to the following passage of the note dealing with Transylvania:

> For the present, the Hungarian Government only wishes to point out that the territorial resettlement affects Hungary most closely where the question of Transylvania is concerned. With the satisfactory solution of the problem of Transylvania—by settling equitably the political and economic claims of Hungary and Rumania —this territory could form a connecting link, rather than a dividing line between the two states. In any case, the solution must be such that any division of the mountainous region of Transylvania lying between the areas of the original settlement of these two neighboring nations—both of which have populations of about the same size, 11-12 million Hungarians, 13-14 million Rumanians, of whom the greater part inhabit the Great Plain—should be affected in such a manner that it should complete most advantageously the economic systems of both countries, and that, from a national point of view, it should also create a state of equilibrium.

After the inter-party meeting the peace preparatory work came to a complete stand-still. The Smallholder Party did eventually prepare a memorandum concerning peace aims, but the party leaders did not want to force a showdown with the Communists since this would have caused the breakdown of the Coalition Government. The Smallholders wanted to avoid this. They played for time. Their leaders hoped that after the peace treaty the Red Army would leave the country, and a truly democratic government could then be established.

Meanwhile, the technical part of the peace preparatory work was nearing completion. All important problems which could have been dealt with at the peace conference were first worked out in detail by

179

competent experts and then synthesized. There were hundreds of memorandums and other material classified into a comprehensive system. Due to the lack of peace aims on the part of the Government and the constant breakdown of cooperative efforts between the parties, we could not use the material for any specific purpose.

In this situation, I felt that my duties had been fulfilled and that I could do nothing more. On March 13, 1946, I asked the Foreign Minister for my release as the head of the division for peace preparation, and suggested that the division be dissolved. I explained that the division had accomplished its mission and that the necessary political decisions must be made by the Government. Since my request went unheeded, I sent an official letter to Prime Minister Ferenc Nagy, informing him of the deadlock of the peace preparation, and expressing my disagreement with the Government's dilatory policy. I stated that under the circumstances I could do no more useful work, and requested that the Government release me from my assignment.

Shortly after dispatching this letter to the Prime Minister, the Foreign Minister informed me, very confidentially, that perhaps the situation was not entirely hopeless. He told me that leading members of the Hungarian Government, following an invitation of the Soviet Government, would shortly visit Moscow. He asked me to prepare material for the delegation and asked me to accompany them as their political advisor. Next day the embarrassed Foreign Minister regretfully informed me that Pushkin had removed my name as well as the name of the economic advisor[26] from the list, stating that this conference would negotiate issues of great political importance and that therefore only leading politicians were needed, and experts were unwanted. Under the circumstances, this was scarcely bad news for me.

I found it amusing that the delegate of the Social Democratic Party to the peace preparations, called on me again and excitedly asked for maps and materials concerning our territorial claims against Rumania. This was the same man, Szalai, who a few weeks before had characterized the entire peace preparatory work as partly useless and partly dangerous. He now explained enthusiastically that this material would be needed by the Social Democratic Party leader, Szakasits, in Moscow. He also indicated that the chances of regaining territories from Rumania were good, and that this would strengthen Hungarian democracy.

Faced with dissatisfied public opinion and strong Smallholder pressure, the Government decided to ask for Soviet support concerning the settlement of the problem of Transylvania. The Communist Party, apparently receiving the green light from Moscow, reversed its attitude towards national aspirations and suddenly became the champion of

Hungarian territorial claims against Rumania—an attitude which previously was branded by them as Fascist and reactionary.

As the armistice agreement declared the Vienna award of August 30, 1940,[27] to be null and void, the Government was looking for a solution of the Transylvanian problem along new lines. The revival of the ethnographic arguments which were the basis of the Vienna award was considered unwise, and was rejected at the outset. Although there were prepared a variety of projects for solution, I would have preferred a rather general than specific demand until we ascertained what support we could get from the great powers. I was overruled, and the Foreign Minister decided to accept a plan worked out by a member of the Paul Teleki Institute for Political Science. This plan envisaged the return of 22,000 sq. kilometers to Hungary with roughly 1,600,000 inhabitants. According to the 1930 Rumanian census, this territory was inhabited by 865,620 Rumanians and 495,106 Hungarians. In the 1941 census the proportion of the Hungarians was somewhat higher, but this difference did not change the basic disproportion. Meanwhile, over one million Hungarians would have remained under Rumanian domination. The idea was to counter-balance the number of the Hungarian and Rumanian minorities in Hungary and in Rumania. It was assumed that these conditions would have resulted in better treatment for minorities in both countries.

A meeting held under the chairmanship of the President of the Republic on the eve of the departure for Moscow endorsed this plan, but decided that the delegation should also present an alternate solution aiming at only the border districts with a clear Hungarian majority. Following the meeting, I was ordered to prepare the alternate plan that night. In a few hours, experts in the Teleki Institute worked out another plan which proposed the return to Hungary of 11,800 sq. kilometers and 967,000 peoples. According to the Rumanian figures of 1930 the Hungarians had a slight majority (442,000 as compared to 421,000 Rumanians) in this territory. Ethnographically, the second plan looked better, but it would have caused economic difficulties to the local inhabitants both in Rumania and in Hungary. In any case, I thought it unwise to put forward two proposals in Moscow. This course was obviously a wrong approach, psychologically, and apt to weaken our position. I vainly opposed this method of procedure.

The delegation returned from Moscow full of optimism. They had been extremely well received. Soviet hospitality knew no bounds. They were lavishly entertained. On April 11, 1946, Molotov and Stalin devoted many hours to discussions with the members of the Hungarian delegation. The atmosphere seemed most friendly. In addition there

were some positive results. The period for the fulfillment of the reparation liabilities was extended from six to eight years. The Soviet demand
for $15,000,000 for the restoration of Hungarian railroads was can-
celled,[28] and the delegation believed that they had received a Soviet
pledge for the support of Hungarian territorial claims against Rumania.

Gyöngyösi explained to the leading officials of the Foreign Ministry
how the discussion concerning Transylvania developed. According to
him, Stalin, after listening to the Hungarian explanations, turned to
Molotov and asked him if there was a basis for such aspirations. Molotov
correctly replied that Article 19 of the Rumanian armistice agreement
left the way open for Hungary's territorial claims regarding Transylvania.[29] Stalin nodded and said that the Hungarians thus seemed to
be really entitled to raise claims. The next day, Dekanozov, head of the
Southeastern European division in the Soviet Foreign Ministry, strongly
advised the Hungarian Foreign Minister that, before raising territorial
claims, direct negotiations should be attempted with the Rumanian
Government. Later Molotov repeated this advice. No one from the
delegation asked Stalin or Molotov if the Hungarian claims would be
supported by them. Nevertheless, the atmosphere of the conversations
was so friendly and the attitude of Stalin so benevolent that the delegation took Soviet support for granted. In reality, both before and after
the Moscow visit of the Hungarian delegation Molotov opposed most
resolutely in the Council of Foreign Ministers an American proposal
favoring a slight modification in the Transylvanian boundary line in
favor of Hungary.[30]

Following the Moscow visit the members of the delegation delivered
optimistic speeches. One of the leading Hungarian Communist authorities in foreign affairs, József Révai, delivered such an irridentist speech
that it would have been envied even by the oldtime League for Revision
of the Horthy regime. Révai demanded, among other things, that the
important cities of Arad, Szatmár, and Nagybánya should be returned
to Hungary. Moreover, he asserted that the Communists in the emigration between the two World Wars were the true representatives of Hungary's national aspirations but that their efforts were annihilated by the
suicidal pro-Nazi and anti-Soviet policy of the Horthy regime. A few
months before that speech he had wanted every "reactionary" who asked
for territory from Groza's Rumania to be brought before the people's
court. "We cannot weaken Groza's democracy," he said at that time.

This reversal of Communist policy concerning Hungary's territorial
claims gave a basis for optimistic speculation. Later it became evident
that the motive behind the change in Communist tactics was the hope
of winning the support of Hungarian public opinion. The change of

tactics did not alter their final goal. The Communists apparently did not want to burden the Party by opposing national aspirations, but preferred to ride a popular bandwagon.

In accordance with Moscow's advice, a high official of the Foreign Ministry, Pál Sebestyén, was sent to Bucharest to initiate negotiations. The Rumanian Prime Minister, Petru Groza, and the Foreign Minister, Gheorghe Tatarescu, gave him a courteous reception, but refused to discuss Hungarian territorial claims. For this reason Sebestyén returned home immediately, and a note was presented to the representatives of the major victorious powers on April 27.[31] This note was based on the above mentioned project prepared in the Paul Teleki Institute and handed over in Moscow as the "major" solution of the Transylvanian question. The Hungarian Government requested the return of 22,000 sq. kilometers to Hungary, that is, 20 percent of the total area of 104,000 sq. kilometers transferred to Rumania by the Treaty of Trianon.

But the optimism which followed the visit to Moscow rapidly vanished, and uneasiness developed. One of the reasons for this change was the conduct of Rumanian statesmen with regard to Hungarian overtures. The shrewd Tatarescu would not have refused negotiations with Sebestyén, had the Rumanian Government lacked assurance of full Soviet support. Groza and Tatarescu hinted as much to Sebestyén.

The coalition parties became more and more disappointed when it appeared that the members of the Government delegation to Moscow could not support with facts, the optimism they expressed in public speeches. The warm reception and the small concessions gained at Moscow had not warranted such optimism. Even the economic concessions gained were of relatively small value.

Because of dissatisfaction and reproaches from many quarters and because of the general depression of public opinion caused by the inactivity of the Government in foreign affairs, the Foreign Minister decided to send me to Paris, where at that time the Council of Foreign Ministers was in session preparing the drafts for the peace treaties. Pushkin once more refused to grant me permission to travel abroad, saying that I would not be needed in Paris. Gyöngyösi—under attack at that time even in the Smallholder Party—remained adamant. He told Pushkin that if he was not allowed to send a high official of the Foreign Ministry to Paris to make contacts and preparations for the peace conference, he would no longer consider himself as foreign minister and would act accordingly. Pushkin, not wanting to make a political issue of this trifle, suggested that I be appointed as counselor to the Hungarian Legation in Paris. He explained that such an appointment would enable him to grant me the necessary permit to leave the country. The

183

Foreign Minister accepted this proposal, and on May 9, 1946, I left for Paris by plane. Shortly before my departure, news arrived that the Council of Foreign Ministers, at a meeting held on May 7, had decided to accept the Trianon boundaries between Hungary and Rumania as final.

A few days before I left for Paris the President of the Republic, Zoltán Tildy, asked me through a confidential go-between whether I would be willing to lead the Hungarian peace delegation as foreign minister. He informed me that a group of Transylvanian politicians discussed with Tildy problems connected with the future peace settlement. In the course of these conversations they had criticized the manifest weaknesses of Hungarian foreign policy, and Tildy himself expressed his concern because of the general discontent with Gyöngyösi. He was considered as pro-Soviet even in his own party. Inasmuch as national unity was of the utmost importance before the peace conference, they agreed with Tildy that I, as a non-party man, should take over the portfolio for the period of the peace conference. I replied that I was a government official and as such I would do my best as administrative leader of the Hungarian peace delegation, but I would not consider accepting the portfolio of the foreign office under Soviet occupation. I added that probably a few things could have been done differently in the past, but that it was questionable whether the Russians would have tolerated a more assertive Hungarian foreign policy. The Western powers did not mean business in Danubian Europe. No Hungarian foreign minister could have changed the existing political situation. It is difficult to play cards if you do not have a partner and your opponents hold all the aces. Moreover, the Smallholder Party played for time and wanted to avoid a showdown. Thus no one could have followed a foreign policy substantially different from that of Gyöngyösi. The only question was whether someone was willing or not to play a political role under such circumstances. I did not feel suited for this and, moreover, thought that I could do more useful work in my administrative capacity.

Before my departure I agreed with Gyöngyösi that I should act in Paris as the secretary general of the Hungarian peace delegation. In Paris I received, to my great surprise, a communication from him announcing my appointment as chief political delegate of Hungary. I refused to accept this latter position, and remained in Paris for six months as secretary-general of the Hungarian peace delegation, and at the same time, as minister-counsellor to the Hungarian Legation, as desired by Pushkin.

Burial of Hopes.

During my activities in Paris I witnessed the burial of many of our hopes. We were not optimistic after the experiences of the postwar period, but still had some hope in the final peace settlement. All these hopes and any optimism that remained evaporated in the course of the Paris Conference. The peace negotiations did not deal with basic problems of the Danubian nations. The issues were not treated on their merits. A few delegations, chiefly the Australian, raised issues of fundamental importance, but such endeavors were out of context in the helpless atmosphere of the Conference. The non-cooperative Soviet attitude stirred up crises and deadlocks in the Council of Foreign Ministers which prepared the first and final draft of the peace treaties,[32] and at the Conference of Paris itself which only had advisory powers. As Philip E. Mosely pointed out, "in a negotiation of this kind, the most reluctant government determines the maximum rate of progress."[33] In the bewildering atmosphere even minor Soviet concessions brought general relief. Under these conditions, the fundamental problems were avoided, and the participants limited the issues and the range of discussions as much as possible. Hungarian and other proposals for the reorganization of the Danubian states on a cooperative basis were not even considered. Some Western delegations thought that all integrations in the Soviet sphere of influence were undesirable, because these eventually would serve Moscow's interests.

It should be noted at this juncture that before the Conference of Paris, in May, 1946, a Hungarian Government delegation under the leadership of Prime Minister Ferenc Nagy visited Washington and London and asked for American and British support. This appeal to the West, a unique action among the states occupied by the Red Army, made perfectly clear that the coalition Government of Hungary was not under an exclusively Soviet orientation but did want to maintain close relations with the Western powers as well. Sympathy and understanding for Hungary were increasing in the West, but under the existing political realities it was difficult to give a helping hand to Hungary at the peace negotiation.

The United States delegation showed much understanding toward Hungary, but their goodwill was limited by the actual power situation in Danubian Europe and by Hungary's position at the peace conference.[34] Eventually Hungarian endeavors for a territorial revision in Transylvania were obliterated by the Conference of Paris. Czechoslovakia asked for five and obtained three Hungarian villages opposite Bratislava. Otherwise the Trianon frontiers were reestablished.

Soviet Russia's grasp on the Hungarian economy strengthened. The

185

United States Delegation did submit to the Conference a proposal to reduce the total amount of reparations to be paid by Hungary from $300 million to $200 million, but the Conference rejected this proposal.[35]

The greatest direct threat to Hungary at the Peace Conference was a Czechoslovak proposal, openly sponsored by the Soviet Union, to insert in the peace treaty a provision authorizing expulsion of 200,000 Hungarians from Czechoslovakia. The peace delegation of defeated Hungary—a state in the Soviet orbit—asked for Western political support, and with energetic American, and some British help, defeated the Czechoslovak proposal. Avoidance of this catastrophe for the Hungarians, however, did not in essence change the general situation along the banks of the Danube.

In the course of Western postwar planning, probably one of the greatest political mistakes was committed at Potsdam and at the Moscow Conference in December, 1945, when Austria, the westernmost Danubian country, was left out of the projected peace settlement, and the conclusion of the Italian peace treaty was connected with those of Bulgaria, Rumania, Hungary and Finland. This procedure was all the more anomalous and illogical since as far back as October, 1943, the foreign ministers of Great Britain, the United States and the Soviet Union had, in Moscow, issued a declaration on Austria in which they recognized that Austria was the first free country to fall a victim of Hitlerite aggression, and in which they stated their desire to see a free and independent Austria reestablished. Stalin himself had proposed the restoration of Austria as an independent state in December, 1941, in the course of his first conversation with Eden.[36]

Austria, however, was not included in the peace settlement and remained an occupied country. In the situation thus created, the Western powers, in order to consolidate Italy's international position, concluded and ratified the peace treaties with the Danubian states. The regained sovereignty, however, was of little value in these Communist-dominated countries. The independence of Hungary and Rumania remained all the more fictitious because the peace treaties authorized the Soviet Union to keep in both these countries armed forces for the maintenance of the lines of communication of the Soviet Army in Austria. At the same time, with the dissolution of the Allied Control Commissions in Bulgaria, Hungary and Rumania, even the nominal Western influence came to an end in the Danubian region. Thus, the policy of the Western powers almost automatically had the effect of a boomerang as far as Western expectations and interests were concerned in central Eastern Europe.

True, the peace treaties obliged the defeated states to take all measures necessary to secure to all persons under their jurisdictions, "without distinction as to race, sex, language or religion, the enjoyment of human rights and of the fundamental freedoms including freedom of expression, of press and publication, of religious worship, of political opinion and of public meeting." [37]   But an international control for the enforcement of these rights, or an adequate machinery for the settlement of disputes concerning the execution and interpretation of the Peace Treaties, was not established.   An Australian proposal aiming at the creation of a European Court of Human Rights was rejected.[38]   The British, United States, and French delegations proposed that any dispute concerning the execution or interpretation of the peace treaties which could not be settled by direct negotiations, might be referred at the request of any party to the dispute, to the International Court of Justice.[39]   This proposition, strongly opposed by the Soviet delegation, was accepted at the Conference by a vote of 15 to 6.   The Council of Foreign Ministers, however, under Soviet pressure, eliminated all reference to the International Court of Justice from the final draft.

The system for the solution of disputes inserted into the peace treaties did not prove to be satisfactory in the face of the obstructive tactics of the Soviet Union in the Communist dominated countries.[40]   When Great Britain and the United States charged Bulgaria, Hungary and Rumania with having violated their obligations under the respective Peace Treaty provisions requiring them to secure to all persons under their jurisdiction the enjoyment of human rights and the fundamental freedoms, they simply refused to recognize the existence of a dispute.   Moreover, the Danubian countries denounced the English and American notes as illegitimate interferences in their domestic affairs, and stated that they had fully complied with the human rights provisions of the peace treaties.   Subsequent proceedings before the General Assembly of the United Nations and the International Court of Justice were fruitless.[41]

As a result of these developments the Danubian countries became the captive states of the Soviet Union.[42]   The Peace Treaties facilitated the consolidation of the Soviet power position established *de facto* at the close of hostilities in Eastern Europe.   Incorporation of Czechoslovakia in the Soviet sphere, and the exclusion of the Western powers from the Danube by the Soviet-dictated Danubian convention, were only further consequences of the peace settlement.   Simultaneously with the process of isolating the Danubian countries from the West, a ruthless Communist minority seized all power positions and has been following a policy of political, economic and cultural integration with the Soviet Union.   A new chapter of history along the Danube began.

In central Eastern Europe we have been witnessing in these last few years the emergence of a new world in which normal rules established for free internal developments and for orderly international intercourse do not operate. Nations have been subjected to Soviet domination which, through forceful methods of social engineering, and especially through the indoctrination of the youth, aims at the total transformation of peoples who belonged, until now, to the Western world.

Hungary has become part of a process in the course of which the most cherished values of Western civilization are gradually being exterminated. Despite this ruthless procedure, results of bolshevization and Russification have so far been limited and superficial. One cannot change the spirit of a people and wipe out traditions of centuries overnight. The passive resistance of the Hungarian people has remained general. The time factor, however, is all important because the spirit of the resistance can not be maintained for an indefinite period.

NOTES TO PART ONE

I—STRUGGLE ALONG THE DANUBE

¹ These are the Polish lowland narrow between the Northern Carpathians and the Baltic Sea, and the Door of Focsani between the Eastern Carpathians and the Danube Delta. The possession of the Carpathian Basin is a necessity for an eastern power which wants to control the northern lowland route toward the Atlantic and the outlets to the Mediterranean (Adriatic and Agean seas and the Straits). For Russia—Czarist or Soviet—it is also the European key-area for the control of the eastern Mediterranean Sea and thus of the Suez Canal route. A western embracement of the Middle East is only possible through the control of the Carpathian Basin and the Balkan Peninsula together. See map on p. 4.

² See for details, H. St. L. B. Moss, *The Birth of the Middle Ages 395-814* (Oxford, 1935), pp. 38-56. Bálint Homan, *Geschichte des Ungarischen Mittelalters,* I. Band (Berlin, 1940), pp. 17-27. Ferdinand Lot, *Les Invasions Germaniques: La Pénétration Mutuelle du Monde Barbare et du Monde Romain* (Paris, 1945).

³ Cf. A. Rónai, *Biographie des Frontières Politiques du Centre-Est Européen* (Budapest, 1936). The map on p. 35, showing the durability of the frontiers in Eastern Central Europe from 1000 to 1920, is of particular interest. However, this unparalleled and almost perfect geographic and hydrographic unity did not prove to be an unmixed blessing to Hungary. The natural frontiers helped to develop an extreme local patriotism in the country in the sense of: *Extra Hungariam non est vita, si est vita, non est ita,* and in certain periods of history, an unconcern for wider horizons. In addition, the protection offered by the boundaries induced many peoples living outside the Carpathians, to seek shelter in Hungary. This fact contributed considerably to the increase of the various nationalities in the country.

For the sources of the various periods of Hungarian history, see the bibliographical article of Stephen Borsody, "Modern Hungarian Historiography," *The Journal of Modern History,* XXIX (1952), 398-405.

⁴ The recent study of Oscar Halecki emphasized the unusual rapidity with which the Magyars integrated themselves into the Christian European community and absorbed Western culture. Moreover, he rightly pointed out the consequences of the establishment of the Hungarian state for the whole later course of Slavic and Central European history. Oscar Halecki, *Borderlands of Western Civilization. A History of East Central Europe* (New York, 1952), pp. 30-32.

The Holy Crown has been throughout history the supreme symbol of the Hungarian Kingdom. Cf. Patrick Kelleher, *The Holy Crown of Hungary,* Papers and Monographs of the American Academy in Rome (Rome, 1951). Mathild Uhlirz, *Die Krone des heiligen Stephan, des ersten Königs von Ungarn,* Veröffentlichungen des Instituts für Österreichische Geschichtsforschung (Graz, 1951).

⁵ For information concerning the various Hungarian wars and alliances with Constantinople and their interplay in general European politics, see Homan, *op. cit.,* pp. 379-403.

⁶ In 1241 there occurred the first great catastrophe in Hungarian history when the country was overrun and devastated by the Mongol armies of Genghis Khan. It was the first time, after the establishment of Hungary, that a major foreign army crossed the Carpathian mountains. Subsequently the Russian army in 1849 and the Red Army in 1944 followed suit.

⁷ Cf. Emil Reich, "Hungary and the Slavonic Kingdoms," *Cambridge Modern History,* Vol. I (New York, 1902), pp. 329-346. Christopher Dawson, *Understanding Europe* (New York, 1952), pp. 86-87.

⁸ Because of the Turkish danger threatening the Christian world on the banks of the Danube, Pope Calixtus III, on June 29, 1456, ordered prayers in every Christian land, and the tolling of bells between noon and vespers. Cf. Ludwig Pastor, *The History of the Popes* (London, 1891), Vol. II, p. 400.

⁹ The Rumanians in Transylvania claim to be descendants of the Dacians, of Trajan's soldiers and Roman settlers. Hungarian scholars say that the Rumanians migrated into Transylvania sporadically after the twelfth century but in great masses only in the seventeenth and eighteenth centuries. The historians of the two nations collected a mass of evidence to prove the correctness of their respective theories. However it may have been, it seems utterly irrelevant today whether the Hungarians or Rumanians were the first settlers in Transylvania. For the two opposite views see Louis Tamas, *Romans et Roumains dans l'histoire de la Dacie Traiane* (Budapest, 1936); G. Bratianu, *Une énigme et un miracle historique—le peuple roumain* (Bucharest, 1937); R. W. Seton-Watson, *A History of the Roumanians* (Cambridge, 1934); Eugene Horváth, *Transylvania and the History of the Rumanians, A Reply to Professor R. W. Seton-Watson* (Budapest, 1935).

¹⁰ Transylvania sometimes played a significant role in international relations. Stephen Báthory, prince of Transylvania (1572-1581) was elected king of Poland in 1575 and defeated the Russian monarch, Ivan the Terrible, who had endeavored to expand toward the West. Several of the Transylvanian princes, chiefly Gabriel Bethlen (1613-1629) and George Rákóczi (1630-1648) maintained close relations and often negotiated alliances with Western European Protestant powers and with France, in order to strengthen their position against the Habsburgs.

Religious tolerance became an official policy of the princes in Transylvania in a period when religious persecution was at its peak in western Europe. The Transylvanian Diet of 1564 proclaimed freedom of religion. In 1571 four religions were recognized: Catholicism, Lutheranism, Calvinism and Unitarianism (*receptae religiones*). The peace treaty of Vienna concluded in 1606 between the Emperor Rudolph II and Stephen Bocskay, prince of Transylvania, went beyond the principle of *"cuius regio, eius religio"* and guaranteed religious freedom for individuals.

Though conditions in Transylvania were far from ideal, they were incomparably better than those beyond the Carpathians. This was the main reason for the constant influx of Rumanians. In the second half of the seventeenth century Transylvania itself was ravaged by Turkish and Tartar hordes. Thus she gradually withered away from the European scene as a power factor. In 1691, the *Diploma Leopoldinum* declared Transylvania a Habsburg province. For the History of Transylvania, see, Ladislaus Makkai, *Histoire de Transylvanie,* (Paris 1946). Cf. C. A. Macartney, *Hungary and her Successors* (London, 1937), pp. 254-270.

¹¹ Rákóczi was a descendant of one of the ruling princes of Transylvania. The Hungarian Diet elected him "ruling prince" and Louis XIV gave him some support during the war of Spanish Succession. In order to win international recognition the Diet proclaimed the dethronement of the House of Habsburg and Rákóczi's troops occupied almost the whole of Hungary. When, however, the Austrian army was released from the West, the long insurrection (1703-1711) was defeated. Rákóczi's commander-in-chief concluded peace with the Emperor, who promised the ancient constitutional rights and religious freedom to Hungary. Rákóczi and a group of his followers died in exile. For details, see, Ladislas

I—STRUGGLE ALONG THE DANUBE

Baron Hengelmüller, *Hungary's Fight for National Existence, 1703-1711* (London, 1913).

[12] Under King Mathias Hunyadi, at the end of the fifteenth century Hungary possessed a population of approximately five million, of which 75 to 80 percent were Magyars. A census in 1720, after the expulsion of the Turks, revealed three and one half million persons in Hungary proper, of which only about 55 percent were Magyars. As a result of colonization, the proportion of the Magyars further decreased in the eighteenth century. For the changes in Hungary's population see *The Hungarian Peace Negotiations*, published by the Royal Hungarian Ministry of Foreign Affairs, Vol. I (Budapest, 1921), pp. 43-53.

[13] An English scholar suggested that the central tragedy of the year 1848 was the fact that "the Magyars, unquestionably the torchbearers of constitutional liberty in all the Danubian countries, become at the same time advocates of racial uniformity and assimilation in its extreme form, and try to apply to the other races of the country, which still form a decided majority of the population, the very methods which they resent so intensely when applied by the Germans to themselves." R. W. Seton-Watson, "The Era of Reform in Hungary," *The Slavonic and East European Review*, XI, American Series, II (1942-1943), 166.

[14] In July, 1849, shortly before the final defeat, the Hungarian Parliament in a belated effort to reconcile the nationalities passed a very liberal nationality act.

[15] Austrian protests notwithstanding, President Taylor stated in his special message to Congress on March 28, 1850: "My purpose . . . was to have acknowledged the independence of Hungary had she succeeded in establishing a government *de facto* on a basis sufficiently permanent in its character to have justified me in doing so, according to the usages and settled principles of this Government; and although she is now fallen, and many of her gallant patriots are in exile or in chains, I am free still to declare that had she been successful in the maintenance of such a government as we could have recognized, we should have been the first to welcome her into the family of nations." John Bassett Moore, *A Digest of International law*, Vol. I (Washington, 1906), p. 113. Cf. Leslie C. Tihany, "America's Interest in Hungarian Struggle for Independence," *United States Department of State Documents and State Papers*, I (1948), 323-339.

[16] Cf. Alfred Francis Pribram, *Austria-Hungary and Great Britain*, (London, 1951), pp. 41-42. Charles Sproxton, *Palmerston and the Hungarian Revolution* (Cambridge, 1919).

[17] There is a considerable literature devoted to Kossuth's stay and activities in the United States. For example, *Report of the Special Committee of the City of New York for the Reception of Governor Louis Kossuth* (New York, 1852). Ph. Skinner, *The Welcome of Kossuth* (Philadelphia, 1852). *Kossuth in New England* (Boston, 1852). F. M. Newman, *Select Speeches of Kossuth* (New York, 1854). Denis Jánossy, "Kossuth and the Presidential Election, 1852," *Hungarian Quarterly*, VII (1941), 105-111. Stephen Gál, "Kossuth, America and the Danubian Confederation," *Hungarian Quarterly*, VI (1940), 417-433. Dénes Jánossy published three volumes in Hungarian on the Kossuth emigration in Great Britain and the United States (Budapest, 1940-1948).

[18] Louis Kossuth, *Memories of My Exile* (New York, 1880). Kossuth also negotiated with various Slav and Rumanian emigré groups on the possibilities of cooperation among Danubian peoples and published a plan for a Danubian federation. Cf. Robert A. Kann, *The Multinational Empire; Nationalism and National Reform in the Habsburg Monarchy, 1898-1918*, Vol. II (New York, 1950), pp. 108-114 and the literature quoted there.

[19] The Polish nation has been in this respect a momentous exception and

Pan-Slavism never became a popular movement among them. One part of Poland lived under Russian rule after the partitions. The Poles knew from experience the meaning of the Russian liberation and protection. In Austria the Poles belonged to the category of the most satisfied nationalities and held high positions in the Austrian administration until the very last. Cf. H. W. V. Temperley, *A History of the Peace Conference of Paris*, Vol. IV (London, 1921), pp. 58-69.

20 Cf., Hans Kohn, *Pan-Slavism* (University of Notre Dame Press, 1953).

21 The compromise meant the recognition of Hungary's constitutional rights by the Habsburgs after a struggle which lasted over three centuries. Its conclusion was preceded by long negotiations in the course of which the chief Hungarian negotiator, Francis Deák, claimed that Hungary had remained an independent country since 1526 and that between Austria and Hungary there was established a union only in the person of the monarch. The compromise was embodied in Hungary in statute 12 of the year 1867: "The relations of Hungary to Austria." For its English text see, Geoffrey Drage, *Austria-Hungary* (London, 1908), pp. 753-766. Cf. Louis Eisenmann, *Le Compromis Austro-Hongrois de 1867* (Paris, 1904).

22 C. A. Macartney, *Op. cit.*, pp 20-21. Cf. Arthur J. May, *The Hapsburg Monarchy 1867-1914* (Harvard University Press, 1951), p. 83.

23 The process of Magyarization began in the first part of the nineteenth century with the increasing use of the Magyar language. It was most successful in the towns. These usually had large German and some Jewish populations. The way of life of the Magyar society had a great attractive force and, especially until the 1880's, Magyarization was to a considerable extent a spontaneous development. The children of the Czech and German officials transferred to Hungary during the period of oppression (1849-1867) frequently became the most chauvinistic Magyars. In the subsequent period of forced Magyarization the Rumanians and Serbians resisted much more effectively than the Germans, Slovaks or Ruthenians because their Orthodox churches enjoyed considerable autonomy and these remained cultural and political centers. Cf. Macartney, *op. cit.*, pp. 32-34.

24 Nevertheless, it is necessary to note that in the same period of time, the nationality policy of other states was harsher than that of Hungary. It is enough to refer to the treatment of the Poles in Germany and the Ukranians in Russia. Undoubtedly, in Hungary, in addition to the policy of Magyarization, administrative abuses occurred which formed a suitable subject of propaganda and were greatly publicized, particularly in France and England. But the legislation of the country did not jeopardize anybody's economic existence because of his nationality. For instance, the Rumanians in Transylvania in the decades preceding World War I, bought up in an organized way large properties from Hungarians. For such transactions money was lent not only by Rumanian but also by Hungarian and German banks. The elaborate legislative and administrative measures of discrimination in economic matters, practiced by the successor states between the world wars against national minorities, was unknown in historic Hungary.

II—CONSEQUENCES OF THE FIRST WORLD WAR

1 According to an American student of international affairs, the sudden disappearance of Austria-Hungary "has been characterized as the most important purely political occurrence since the fall of the Western Roman Empire in 476 A.D." Raymond Leslie Buell, *Europe: A History of Ten Years* (New York, 1928), p. 296.

II—CONSEQUENCES OF THE FIRST WORLD WAR

[2] According to the famous Czech historian, Frantisek Palaczky, it would have been necessary to create the Habsburg Monarchy, had it not existed. Other outstanding Slav and Rumanian statesmen also believed that the polyglot Empire was a necessity to its own people and to Europe. Eduard Benes stated in one of his books that he did not believe in the dismemberment of Austria. He argued that the historic and economic bonds between the Austrian nations are too powerful to make such a dismemberment possible. And he predicted that the national struggles would play an important role in Austria for a long time but that they would not be the same as they used to be in the preceding half century. Eduard Benes, *Le problème Autrichien et la question Tchèque* (Paris, 1908), p. 307.

A Rumanian patriot, Aurel C. Popovici, the Austro-Rumanian champion of ethnic federalism, correctly pointed out the international aspect of the Austrian problem: "Rumania, based on her urge for self-preservation, has a great interest in the existence of a mighty Austria. This interest excludes *a priori* any dream, any thought of an annexation of Austrian territories inhabited by Rumanians. Such annexation would be possible only in the case of an Austrian debacle, and such a debacle with mathematical certainty would in the course of a few decades lead to the ruin of Rumania, her destruction in the Russian sea." *Die Vereinigten Staaten von Gross-Oesterreich* (Leipzig, 1906), p. 418. English translation in Robert A. Kann, *op. cit.*, Vol. I, pp. 314-315.

[3] Winston S. Churchill, *The Gathering Storm*, (Boston, 1948), p. 10.

[4] *New York Times*, October 3, 1950.

[5] Oscar Jaszi, *The Dissolution of the Habsburg Monarchy* (Chicago, 1929). Cf. Macartney, *National States and National Minorities* (Oxford University Press, 1934). R. W. Seton-Watson, *Racial Problems in Hungary* (London, 1908). R. W. Seton-Watson, *Southern Slav Question and the Habsburg Monarchy* (London, 1911). Ferenc Eckhardt, *A Short History of the Hungarian People* (London, 1931). Jules Szekfü, *Etat et Nation* (Paris, 1945). A. J. P. Taylor, *The Habsburg Monarchy 1809-1918* (London, 1948). Dominic G. Kosáry, *A History of Hungary* (Cleveland, 1941). Oscar Halecki, *op. cit.* For the general aspects of modern nationalism, see, Carlton J. H. Hayes, *Essays on Nationalism* (New York, 1926); *The Historical Evolution of Modern Nationalism* (New York, 1931). Hans Kohn, *The Idea of Nationalism* (New York, 1944). Alfred Cobban, *National Self-Determination*, Revised edition (Chicago, 1947).

[6] The case of Austria-Hungary has been ably presented by Archduke Otto, the eldest son of Emperor-King Charles, the last Austro-Hungarian ruler. "Danubian Reconstruction," *Foreign Affairs*, 20 (1941-42), 243-252.

[7] Count Ottokar Czernin, writing under the impact of the events in 1918, was rather pessimistic and thought that "Austria-Hungary's watch had run down" in any event. "We could have fought against Germany with the Entente on Austro-Hungarian soil, and would doubtless have hastened Germany's collapse; but the wounds which Austria-Hungary would have received in the fray would not have been less serious than those from which she is now suffering; she would have perished in the fight against Germany, as she has as good as perished in her fight allied with Germany." *In the World War* (New York, 1920), pp. 36-37.

[8] See *Oesterreich-Ungarns letzter Krieg 1914-1918,* published by the Austrian Bundesministerium für Heereswesen, editor-in-chief Edmund Glaise-Horstenau, 7 vols. (Vienna, 1931-1938).

[9] The Austrian Minister to Great Britain between the world wars made the following statement concerning the foreign service: "Although its personnel consisted of Germans, Hungarians, Poles, Ruthenians, Rumanians, Czechs, Croats, Italians and Serbs from the different parts of the Monarchy, the service was inspired by a single-minded patriotism, and I remember no single case in which

an official ever put the interests of his own nationality before those of the Monarchy." Sir George Franckenstein, *Diplomat of Destiny* (New York, 1940), p. 25.

[10] In the early stages of the First World War, the Entente Powers did not plan the destruction of Austria-Hungary. With respect to President Wilson, Colonel House noted that "In common with the leading statesmen of western Europe he believed that the political union of Austro-Hungarian peoples was a necessity." Charles Seymour, *The Intimate Papers of Colonel House*, Vol. III (Boston, 1928) pp. 335-336. When President Wilson, in his address of December 4, 1917, proposed to Congress a declaration of war on the Habsburg Monarchy, he emphasized that "We do not wish in any way to impair or to rearrange the Austro-Hungarian Empire. It is no affair of ours what they do with their own life, either industrially or politically. We do not purpose or desire to dictate to them in any way. We only desire to see that their affairs are left in their own hands, in all matters, great or small." *Foreign Relations 1917*, pp. XI-XII. According to point ten of President Wilson's Fourteen Points, "The peoples of Austria-Hungary, whose place among the nations we wish to see safeguarded and assured, should be accorded the freest opportunity of autonomous development." At almost the same time, on January 5, 1918, Prime Minister Lloyd George stated that the British were not fighting to destroy Austria-Hungary and that a break-up of that Empire was no part of their war aims.

Notwithstanding these various declarations of principle, the specific promises made in the course of the war to Italy, to Rumania, and later to the other nationalities could not have been fulfilled without the destruction of the Monarchy. Moreover, in the last months of the war the propaganda and diplomatic activity of the Entente powers underwent a fundamental change with regard to the fate of Austria-Hungary. Clemenceau's revelations in April, 1918, concerning Emperor Charles' peace overtures had a decisive impact on the course of events. Some Western statesmen possibly fell under the spell of the wartime propaganda encouraged and supported by themselves, at first perhaps only for military expediency. In this process, Czech political leaders in the western countries played a leading role and the creation of Czechoslovakia was the most decisive blow to the Monarchy. For details see, Eduard Benes, *My War Memoirs*, (Boston, 1922). E. Benes, *Détruisez l' Autriche-Hongrie* (Paris, 1916), published in English the following year. T. G. Masaryk, *The Making of a State* (London, 1927). Henry Wickham Steed, *Through Thirty Years 1892-1922* (Garden City, 1925). R. W. Seton-Watson, *Masaryk in England* (Cambridge, 1943). *War Memoirs of Robert Lansing* (Indianapolis, 1935). Charles Pergler, *America in the Struggle for Czechoslovak Independence* (Philadelphia, 1926). Count Stephen Burian, *Austria in Dissolution* (London, 1925). Heinrich Lammasch, *Europas elfte Stunde* (München, 1919). Mitchell Pirie Briggs, *George D. Herron and the European Settlement* (Stanford, 1932). A. J. P. Taylor, *op. cit.* Victor S. Mametey, "The United States and the Dissolution of Austria-Hungary," *Journal of Central European Affairs*, X (1950), 256-270.

[11] The recent allegation made by Stefan Osusky, one of the founders of Czechoslovakia, that Emperor Charles' irresolution and procrastination caused the downfall of the Monarchy is unsubstantiated by facts and is contrary to the events, especially as explained by Masaryk and Benes who, since 1915, had been doing successful spade work for the destruction of the Monarchy. Cf. *Freedom and Union* (May 1949), pp. 22-23. Regardless of what Emperor Charles might have offered to the nationalities in 1918, the positions in Paris, London, Rome and Washington were definitively taken against the survival of the Monarchy.

[12] For details see, Oscar Jászi, *Revolution and Counter-Revolution in Hungary* (London, 1924). Count Michel Károlyi, *Fighting the World; the Struggle for Peace* (New York, 1925). Gusztáv Gratz, *A forradalmak kora 1918-1920* (Budapest, 1935).

[13] For a description of these events, see, C. A. Macartney, *op. cit.,* pp. 275-279, 364-370, 390-395.

[14] A. J. P. Taylor, *op. cit.,* 250.

[15] Albert Kaas, *Bolshevism in Hungary* (London, 1931). F. Borkenau, *World Communism* (New York, 1939), pp. 108-133. In Soviet Russia itself the establishment of the Hungarian Soviet Republic was considered an event of the greatest importance. Even the cautious Lenin asserted in his speech of April 17 that "the Hungarian Revolution plays a larger role in history than the Russian revolution." Quoted by David T. Cattell, "The Hungarian Revolution of 1919 and the Reorganization of the Comintern in 1920," *Journal of Central European Affairs,* XI (1951), 27-38.

[16] Herbert Hoover gave a colorful description of these events in the following: "Hungary in the year 1919 presented a sort of unending, formless procession of tragedies, with occasional comic relief. Across our reconstruction stage there marched liberalism, revolution, socialism, communism, imperialism, terror, wanton executions, murder, suicide, falling ministries, invading armies, looted hospitals, conspirators, soldiers, kings and queens—all with a constant background of starving women and children. . . . The relief organization contributed something to their spiritual recovery. But had there not been a magnificent toughness in the Magyar spirit, the race would have collapsed." *The Memoirs of Herbert Hoover 1874-1920* (New York, 1952), p. 397.

[17] Sarah Wambaugh, *Plebiscites Since the World War,* Vol. I, (Washington, 1933), pp. 163-205. H. W. V. Temperley, *A History of the Peace Conference of Paris,* Vol. IV, (London, 1921), pp. 368-381.

[18] "As regards the question of plebiscites the Allied Powers consider them needless, when they perceived with certainty that this consultation, if surrounded with complete guarantees of sincerity, would not give results substantially different from those at which they had arrived after a minute study of the ethnographic conditions and national aspirations." H. W. V. Temperley, *op cit.,* Vol. IV, p. 422. Concerning the Hungarian peace treaty negotiations see, Francis Deák, *Hungary at the Paris Peace Conference* (New York, 1942).

[19] Winston Churchill, *The World Crisis—The Aftermath* (New York, 1929), pp. 231-232.

[20] At this time the United States had 92,000,000 inhabitants.

[21] Frederick Hertz, *The Economic Problem of the Danubian States* (London, 1947), pp. 24, 38, 49.

[22] *Daily Telegraph,* April 18, 1950. In connection with the centenary of Thomas Masaryk's birth an exchange of opinion took place on the break-up of the Austro-Hungarian Empire in April 14, 17, 18, 19, 27 and June 1, 1950 issues of the *Telegraph.*

With regard to the establishment of Czechoslovakia, Samuel Hazzard Cross of Harvard, gave in retrospect the following description of events:

"It is worth remarking that in 1914 Bohemian ambitions had not extended beyond vague hopes of eventual autonomy within a federalized monarchy, while the utopia of independence was conceived mainly in the minds of emigré leaders like Professor Masaryk and Dr. Benes. It was not until 1917 that the domestic Bohemian attitude became definitely revolutionary, and Slovak sympathy was not finally secured until May, 1918, through the celebrated Treaty of Pittsburgh, which guaranteed the Slovaks a degree of autonomy which they never attained until just before the Czechoslovak Republic was dismembered by Hitler. As a matter of fact, the relations between Czechs and Slovaks were never so dove-like as Bohemian statesmen would have had us suppose and at the Armistice, Czech troops had simply marched in and occupied the Slovak section of Hungary." *Slavic Civilization Through the Ages* (Harvard University Press, 1948), p. 182.

[23] In the light of statistics, his conclusion was that "all the efforts to foster, by an extreme protectionism, either the rapid increase of agricultural production or that of industrial output had only a very limited success. Increases of production were smaller than the progress under the former conditions of free trade within the Austro-Hungarian Customs Union." Hertz, *op. cit.*, p. 220.

[24] See article 222 of the Peace Treaty of St. Germain, and articles 205, 207 and 208 of the Peace Treaty of Trianon.

[25] Hugh Seton-Watson has published the best general description of these events. See *Eastern Europe between the Wars 1918-1941* (Cambridge, 1945) and *The East European Revolution* (New York, 1951). Cf. C. A. Macartney, *Hungary and her Successors* (London, 1937).

[26] The internal development of two newly created states, Czechoslovakia and Yugoslavia was described by a British historian in the following way: "Czechoslovakia and Yugoslavia, despite their national theory, reproduced the national complications of Austria-Hungary. Constitutional Austria had contained eight nationalities; Czechoslovakia contained seven. Great Hungary had contained seven nationalities; Yugoslavia contained nine. Czechoslovakia became a unitary state, in which the Czechs were 'the people of the state', as the Germans had been in constitutional Austria. Yugoslavia had a period of sham federalism; then it too became a unitary state, which the Serbs claimed as their national state, after the model of the Magyars in Hungary. . . .
"The Czechs could outplay the Slovaks; they could not satisfy them. Masaryk had hoped that the Czechs and the Slovaks would come together as the English and the Scotch had done; the Slovaks turned out to be the Irish. In the same way, the Serbs could master the Croats; they could not satisfy, nor even, being less skillful politicians, outplay them." A. J. P. Taylor, *op. cit.*, pp. 254-255.

[27] In his report of November 1, 1938, Newton, the British Minister to Prague, characterized Czechoslovak democracy in the following way: "There can be little doubt that the democratic system as it has developed in this country during the past twenty years has not been a wholly unmixed blessing, even for the Czechs by whom and for whom it was elaborated. Under it quick and clear decisions were difficult to come by, and party considerations were only too often given pride of place over national. Moreover, it is hardly an exaggeration to say that all public appointments even down to that of crossing sweeper depended upon possession of the necessary party ticket so that each party became almost a State within the State. Today there is a natural tendency to say goodbye to all that, and one of the constant themes in the press is that public life and social services must be cleansed of patronage and the misuse of political influence. Criticism is heard not only of the quality but of the quantity of officials in the civil service. It is said, for example, that there are more officials in the Ministry for Foreign Affairs in Prague than there were in the Ballplatz of Imperial Vienna." *British Documents*, Third Series, Vol. III, Doc. 245.

[28] The situation resulting from the peace settlement has been well characterized by the late Professor Cross of Harvard. He writes: "If there is any lesson to be learned from the experience of the last thirty years, it is that setting up a series of economically weak national states solely on the basis of romantic ideals and strategic aims is no guarantee of peace. To bolster up their weak budgets or to favor local industry, such states erect tariff barriers which prevent the normal flow of commerce and exchange on which their very life depends. If their territories contain linguistic minorities, the latter are discriminated

against in business and politics until they seek support from the nearest larger state to which they are akin, and eventually provide that state with a natural pretext for intervention. In order to counterbalance their more powerful neighbors or checkmate some adjacent state with good diplomatic connections, these little states unite in ententes and alliances which become the pawns of international politics, and give statesmen of these minor organisms a chance to assume positions of influence for which they are not qualified by experience or vision." Samuel Hazzard Cross, *op. cit.*, p. 183.

III—*HUNGARY BETWEEN THE WORLD WARS*

[1] Rumania concluded a separate peace with the Central Powers in January, 1918 and re-entered the war in the following November.

[2] The loot of Hungary and the general behaviour of the Rumanian army was described in detail by the American member of the Inter-Allied Mission to Hungary. See Maj. Gen. Harry Hill Bandholtz, *An Undiplomatic Diary* (New York, 1933), pp. 18, 50, 92-93. Herbert Hoover explained that the Rumanian army occupied Budapest on August 5, 1919, in defiance of direct orders of the 'Big Four', and "then began a regime equally horrible with Bela Kun's. The Roumanian army looted the city in good old medieval style. They even took supplies from the children's hospitals. Many children died. They looted art galleries, private houses, banks, railway rolling stock, machinery, farm animals— in fact, everything movable which Bela Kun had collected." *Op. cit.*, pp. 400-401.

[3] Francesco Nitti, *The Wreck of Europe* (Indianapolis, 1922), pp. 170-171.

[4] For the peace negotiations the best general sources are: D. H. Miller, *My Diary at the Conference of Paris*, Vol. XXI (New York, 1924). Harold W. V. Temperley, *A History of the Peace Conference at Paris*, Vol. I-VI (London, 1920-24). *Foreign Relations, The Paris Peace Conference*, Vol. I-XIII (Washington, 1942-1947). The foremost study of the diplomatic history of the Treaty of Trianon is Francis Deák's work: *Hungary at the Paris Conference* (New York, 1942), which is based mainly on original documents and deals with all the pertinent material. The Hungarian Foreign Ministry published the official Hungarian material in The *Hungarian Peace Negotiations*, Vol. I-III and maps (Budapest, 1920-22). C. A. Macartney condensed comprehensive material in his standard work: *Hungary and Her Successors The Treaty of Trianon and Its Consequences* (London, 1937).

[5] Harold Nicolson, *Peacemaking* (London, 1933), p. 117. Cf. Harold Temperley, "How the Hungarian Frontiers Were Drawn," *Foreign Affairs*, 6 (1928), 432-433, and *A History of the Peace Conference* at Paris, Vol. I, p. 258.

[6] Nicolson mentioned as an example that the Committee on Rumanian claims thought only in terms of Transylvania, and the Committee on Czech claims concentrated upon the southern frontiers of Slovakia. "It was only too late that it was realized that these two entirely separate Committees had between them imposed upon Hungary a loss of territory and population which, when combined, was very serious indeed. Had the work been concentrated in the hands of a Hungarian Committee, not only would a wider area of frontier have been open for the give and take of discussion, but it would have been seen that the total cessions imposed placed more Magyars under alien rule than was consonant with the doctrine of Self-Determination." *Op. cit.*, pp. 127-128. Nicolson's observations were not influenced by any sympathy toward Hungary. He repeatedly explained in his various writings that he disliked the Magyars. When the Red

Army advanced on Budapest he was pleased and detected in himself "stirrings of positive delight." *Spectator,* November 10, 1944.

[7] Cf. Deák, *op. cit.,* pp. 27-29.

[8] *Ibid.,* pp. 15-23.

[9] D. Lloyd George, *Memoirs of the Peace Conference* (New Haven, 1939), p. 266.

[10] In the words of an English scholar, "One point after another was conceded; and in the end Roumania was given an area in which the Roumanians formed only 55 per cent of the total population. The Slovaks in Slovakia were 60 per cent, the Ruthenes in Ruthenia 56 per cent, the Serbs in the Voivodina only 28 per cent, or 33 per cent counting all the Yugoslavs together; while the Magyar-speaking persons in each area formed close on one-third of all the inhabitants; over one million in the territory assigned to Czechoslovakia, over 1,650,000 in that given to Roumania, 450,000 in Yugoslavia's portion." C. A. Macartney, *op. cit.,* p. 4. True, these figures were based on the census of 1910 and some aspects of this census were contested. But the overall picture remained the same even according to the censuses carried out by the succession states themselves. For the situation arising from the 1930 censuses, see below, footnote 14.

[11] This observation of Benes was noted by the editor of the *Journal de Genève,* William Martin, *Les Hommes d'Etat pendant la guerre* (Paris, 1929), p. 316. In any case this is an overstatement because not all demands of Benes were fulfilled. For example, a corridor between Yugoslavia and Czechoslovakia was not established.

[12] According to the 1910 census, Hungary proper possessed a population of over 18,000,000 persons, of whom 54.5 percent declared Magyar to be their mother tongue. Including Croetia-Slovania the total population was over 20,000,000 of whom 48.1 percent spoke Magyar as their mother tongue.

[13] In reality the Hungarian peace delegation was confronted with a *fait accompli.* According to Temperley no event affected the frontiers of Hungary more decisively than the Béla Kun regime which, Temperley considered partly a socialist experiment, partly a Hungarian protest against the advance of the Czech and Rumanian army. "Béla Kun finally sent forces to attack both Czechoslovaks and Rumanians, and it was this action that forced the Big Four to come to a decision. . . . And the *finis Hungariae . . .* was decreed on June 13, 1919." Harold Temperley, "How the Hungarian Frontiers Were Drawn," *Foreign Affairs,* 6 (1928), pp. 434-435.

[14] The result of the 1930 censuses disclosed that: with 10.8 million Magyars in Europe, the new Hungary had a population of 8.7 millions on an area of 93,000 square kilometers; with 13.8 million Rumanians in Europe, the new Rumania had a population of 18.1 millions and an area of 295,000 square kilometers; with 11.9 million Serbs, Croats and Slovenes in Europe, the new Yugoslavia had a population of 13.9 millions and an area of 249,000 square kilometers; with 10.2 million Czechs and Slovaks in Europe, the new Czechoslovakia had a population of 14.7 millions and an area of 140,000 square kilometers. This means that the Czechs and Slovaks were able to unite 96.6% of the Czechs and Slovaks living in Europe in their own country, but despite this, these groups made up only 66.2% of the total population of the country. The Rumanians assembled 96% of their own people within their own frontiers but this group was only 72% of the total population. The Yugoslavs had 93% of their own nationals within their country, but they were only 79.8% of the total population of Yugoslavia. In contrast to this, at this time only 74% of the Magyars lived in their own country but they made up 92% of the total population of Hungary.

[15] See the report on Hungary by A. C. Coolidge. Quoted by Deák, *op. cit.*, pp. 16-18.

[16] Nicholas Horthy was the last commander-in-chief of the Austro-Hungarian navy. After the military collapse of the Monarchy, he handed over the fleet to the Yugoslav National Council according to the order of King-Emperor Charles. Subsequently he became minister of war in the counter-revolutionary government of Szeged and entered Budapest in November, 1919 at the head of the national forces as the commander-in-chief. While this book was already in the process of publication, Horthy published his memoirs. Nikolaus von Horthy, *Ein Leben für Ungarn* (Bonn, 1952).

[17] The pertinent documents were published by the Hungarian Foreign Ministry, *HFR.*, Vol. I-II. The intricate Franco-Hungarian negotiations, complicated by many side issues, were described by Deák, *op. cit.*, pp. 253-338. Cf. "The Political Diary of the Hungarian Peace Delegation," *HFR*, Vol. I, pp. 898-911.

[18] The English translation of the Hungarian and French memoranda were published by Deák, *op cit.*, pp. 264-268.

[19] Deák, *op. cit.*, p. 289.

[20] "True to the spirit by which they were inspired in tracing the frontiers fixed by the Treaty, the Allied and Associated Powers have nevertheless considered the case of the frontiers thus traced not corresponding precisely with the ethnical or economic requirements. An inquest held on the spot may, perhaps, make apparent the necessity of a displacement of the limits provided by the Treaty in certain parts. Such an inquest could not be actually pursued without indefinitely retarding the conclusion of a peace desired by the whole of Europe. But when the Delimitation Commission will have commenced activity, should they find that the provisions of the Treaty in some spot, as is stated above, create an injustice which it would be to general interest to efface it shall be allowable to them to address a report on this subject to the Council of the League of Nations. In this case the Allied and Associated Powers accept that the Council of the League may, under the same circumstances, at the request of one of the parties concerned, offer their services for an amicable rectification of the original demarcation at the passages where a modification has been judged desirable by a Delimitation Commission. The Allied and Associated Powers are confident that this proceeding will furnish a convenient method for correcting all injustice in the demarcation of the frontiers against which objections not unfounded can be raised." Deák, *op. cit.*, pp. 552-553.

[21] See pp. 23-24.

[22] For the pertinent conversations between Hungarian and Polish statesmen and diplomats, see, *HFR*, Vol. I, Docs. 51, 383, 441, 555, 689, 739, 891, and 892. Prince Sapieha himself favored a transversal block (Finland-Baltic States-Poland-Hungaria-Rumania). This plan apparently was endorsed by the Baltic States, (Doc. 771), while some leading officials in the Polish Foreign Ministry advocated the necessity of a new Central Europe to be constituted of Poland, Czechoslovakia, Yugoslavia, Rumania, Hungary, Greece and Bulgaria (Doc. 739).

[23] *Ibid*, Doc. 106.

[24] War material from Hungary to Poland was transported through Rumania under Polish supervision. Czechoslovakia invoked her neutrality and refused to permit transportation. *Ibid.*, Docs. 379, 432, 437, 417, 497, and 553. It belongs to the strange occurrences of this period that in December 1920 the Conference of Ambassadors protested against the furnishing of war materials to Poland by the Csepel factory. Cf. *Ibid.*, Doc. 893 and *HFR*, Vol. II, Docs. 7 and 12.

25 *HFR,* Vol. I, Docs. 438, 445, and 496.

26 *Ibid.,* Docs. 536, 555, and 565.

27 *Ibid.,* Docs. 554, 595, 621, 665, and 712. For other aspects of the negotiations concerning Hungary's military assistance to Poland, see, Docs. 126, 383, 509, 510, 518, 526, 528, 536, 538, 543, 580, 594. For the reasons of the Czechoslovak attitude, see, F. J. Vondracek, *The Foreign Policy of Czechoslovakia 1918-1935* (New York, 1937), pp. 155-156.

28 "A Frenchman of very great standing and authority sent word to the Emperor that the chances of a restoration in Hungary were becoming worse by postponement; that at the moment the Powers would protest against his return but that their protests would not alter a *fait accompli."* Baron Charles von Werkman, *The Tragedy of Charles of Habsburg* (London, 1924), pp. 130-131. Cf. Horthy, *op. cit.,* pp. 141-145.

29 Diplomatic steps taken in Budapest by the great powers and Hungary's neighbors were described in a document by the Secretary General of the Foreign Ministry, Coloman Kánya, *HFR.,* Vol. II, pp. 354-357. The Italian *chargé d'affaires* informed Regent Horthy on March 28 that "the prevention of the return of the Habsburgs was a cardinal principle of Italian policy and that his Government would take action in accordance with that principle." The French High Commissioner, Fouchet, explained in a letter that the Conference of Ambassadors on February 16, 1921, renewed its original resolution of February 4, 1920 against the restoration of the Habsburg dynasty.

30 The Little Entente was later consolidated by military conventions and several other treaties, and especially by the establishment of a Permanent Council in 1933. See, John O. Crane, *The Little Entente* (New York, 1931); Deák, *op. cit.,* pp. 320-323.

31 *HFR,* Vol. II, pp. 225, 231 and 233-241. Cf. Deák, *op. cit.,* p. 342.

32 In the course of the negotiations Benes stated that if a neutral agency, such as a League of Nations Commission, found that 300,000 Slovaks in Hungary enjoyed the same minority rights as the Magyar minority in Czechoslovakia, he would be willing to regard these 300,000 Slovaks as having been turned over to Slovakia even though they remained in Hungary, and to return to Hungary territory containing an equal number of Magyar population. *HFR,* Vol. II, pp. 237-238.

33 He made this statement to Joseph Szent-Iványi, a Hungarian member of the Czechoslovak Parliament, on April 29, 1921. *HFR,* Vol. II, p. 393. Cf. below, footnote 35.

34 Notes of Count Bánffy, on the negotiations were published in *HFR,* Vol. II, pp. 559-564.

35 President Masaryk's various statements made from 1921 to 1935 favoring frontier revision with Hungary were quoted in *Hungary and the Conference of Paris,* Vol. IV, pp. 162-169. Cf., p. 32.

36 The 'Venice Protocol' was signed on October 13, 1921 and the plebiscite took place on December 14 and 15. For details see: Sarah Wambaugh, *op. cit.,* Vol. I, pp. 271-297; C. A. Macartney, *op cit.,* pp. 41-72.

37 The ancestors of both Bethlen and Teleki were leading Transylvanian statesmen. Bethlen had the same family roots as Gabriel Bethlen, the ruling prince of Transylvania in the seventeenth century. Paul Teleki in 1909, as an unknown geographer, won the Jomard Prize of the French Academy with his Atlas on the Northwestern Pacific Islands entitled "Atlas zur Geschichte der

Kartographie der Japanischen Inseln." From 1921 until 1938 Teleki concentrated on many scholarly and international activities. He was professor of geography at the University of Budapest and was a member of the Committee appointed by the Council of the League of Nations in the Turkish-Iraqi boundary (Mosul) affair. In 1938 he was appointed a member of the European Council of the Carnegie Endowment.

[38] For Hungary's problems in this period see, Count Stephen Bethlen, "Hungary in the New Europe," *Foreign Affairs*, 3 (1925), 445-458. For Bethlen's view on Trianon Hungary's international situation, see Appendix, Document I.

[39] Cf. C. Révy and N. Czeglédy, *Policy of Hungarian Public Culture* (Budapest, 1946). G. C. Paikert, "Hungarian Foreign Policy in International Relations, 1919-1944," *American Slavic and East European Review*, XI (1952), 42-65.

[40] For a description and evaluation of these measures, see, C. A. Macartney, *op. cit.*

[41] In 1927 the *British Daily Mail* and its owner, Lord Rothermere, launched an ardent campaign for revision of the Trianon Treaty. This campaign excited much enthusiasm and was falsely interpreted in Hungary as a British move for revision of Hungary's frontiers. In fact, the leading political factors in Great Britain remained uninterested in the Hungarian complaints. Concerning the Hungarian revisionist thesis, see Sir Robert Donald, *The Tragedy of Trianon* (London, 1934); *Justice for Hungary* by Count Albert Apponyi and others (London, 1928); Count Stephen Bethlen, *The Treaty of Trianon and European Peace* (London, 1934). Cf. R. W. Seton-Watson, *Treaty of Trianon and European Peace* (London, 1934). E. H. Carr, *International Relations between the Two World Wars* (London, 1948) pp. 10-11. C. A. Macartney, *op. cit.*

[42] In his famous speech before the Senate on June 5, 1928, Mussolini stated that "the territorial provisions of the Treaty of Trianon have cut too deeply into the flesh and it may be added that for a thousand years Hungary has performed an historic mission of importance in the Danubian Basin. The Hungarian people, with their fervent patriotism, their consciousness of their power, their persevering work in time of peace, deserve a better fate. Not only from the point of view of universal equality, but also in the interest of Italy, it may well be that this better fate of Hungary should find its realization." For the full text of the speech, see Muriel Currey, *Italian Foreign Policy 1918-1932* (London, 1933), pp. 234-255. After the delivery of this speech, Mussolini was generally considered as the champion of the Peace Treaty Revision. Actually he advocated this idea in more general terms as early as 1921. Cf. Maxwell H. A. Macartney and Paul Cremona, *Italy's Foreign and Colonial Policy 1914-1937.* (London, 1938), pp. 123, 215-220.

[43] In 1929-1930 the Hague and Paris conferences finally settled Hungary's reparations liability and some other outstanding issues between Hungary and her neighbors, like the so-called "optant question." Since Italy was a major member of the winning team in the first World War, her support at international negotiations was important to Hungary.

[44] Count Károlyi in his speech to the Hungarian Parliament on assuming office stated that "we used to feel during our period of isolation that Hungary was in a prison. The doors of that prison were opened by the friendship of Italy, which is of inestimable value to us. This remains unchanged, and everything shows that it will increase in the future." Cf. Muriel Currey, *op. cit.*, p. 312.

[45] Hungarian version of Nazism.

[46] Winston Churchill, *The Gathering Storm* (Boston, 1948), pp. 132-133.

[47] Hungary and Austria, in line with the Rome protocols, refused to vote for, and to participate in the sanctions.

[48] Cf. Elizabeth Wiskemann, *The Rome-Berlin Axis* (New York, 1949). G. M. Gathorne-Hardy, *A Short History of International Affairs 1920-1939* (London, 1950). E. H. Carr, *op. cit.* Dwight E. Lee, *Ten Years The World on the Way to War* (Boston, 1942). Maurice Baumont, *La Faillite de la paix* (Paris, 1946). J.-B. Duroselle, *Histoire diplomatique de 1919 à nos jours* (Paris, 1953).

[49] Cf. pp. 60-63.

[50] J. Einzig, *Bloodless Invasion, German Economic Penetration Into the Danubian States and the Balkans* (London, 1938). E. Wiskemann, *Prologue to War* (New York, 1940). A Basch, *The Danube Basin and the German Economic Sphere* (New York, 1943). J. Jócsik, *German Economic Influences in the Danube Valley* (Budapest, 1946).

[51] The first anti-Semitic special measure in Hungary was a bill passed in 1921, restricting the admission of Jewish students by the universities to a proportion corresponding to the percentage of Jews in the country. This restriction was later liberally applied, but the anti-Jewish demonstrations of students were recurring yearly phenomena.

[52] For the intimate contacts of Italian and Hungarian statesmen and diplomats see, *Ciano's Diplomatic Papers* (London, 1948) and Galeazzo Ciano, *1937-1938 Diario* (Rocca S. Casciano, 1948).

[53] For Hungary's relations with her neighbors in 1936, see, *Ciano's Diplomatic Papers,* pp. 65-67.

[54] Auer was the chairman of the *Comité Permanent pour le Rapprochement Economique des Pays Danubiens* in which Austria, Czechoslovakia, Hungary, Rumania and Yugoslavia were represented with outstanding statesmen. The Committee was founded on February 12, 1932, and held sessions in Budapest, Basel and Vienna. Auer was appointed Hungarian Minister to France in early 1946.

[55] Cf. Paul von Auer, "Das Neue Mitteleuropa," *New Commonwealth Quarterly,* IV, (1938), 267. Cf. István Borsody, *Magyar-Szlovák kiegyezés* (Budapest, 1945), pp. 75-76.

[56] Galeazzo Ciano, *1937-1938 Diario* (Rocca S. Casciano, 1948), pp. 94-97.

[57] It is interesting to note that Sir Nevile Henderson, British Ambassador to Germany, considered Imrédy in his report of October 18, 1938, as "not specifically friendly to Germany," and recommended that justice be done to legitimate Hungarian claims, partly because Imrédy might be removed and replaced by a pro-German. *British Documents,* Third Series, Vol. III, Doc. 215. See footnote 69 on p. 203 and pp. 35, 37, 42.

[58] *Ciano's Diplomatic Papers,* pp. 227-229.

[59] *DGFP,* Series D, Vol. II, Doc. 383.

[60] *Ibid.,* Doc. 383. Horthy remarked to Mrs. Weizsäcker at Kiel that "We must see to it that we do not get involved in a new war." *Memoirs of Ernst von Weizsäcker* (Chicago, 1951), p. 138. Horthy stated in his memoirs that he and the other members of the Hungarian delegation refused a military cooperation with Germany. See *op. cit.,* p. 200. This statement is supported by the later attitude of Hitler. Cf. pp. 37-38 and 41.

[61] *DGFP,* Series D. Vol. II, Doc. 390. For a detailed account of Hungary's negotiations with the Little Entente and Germany, in 1937-1938, see *Survey of*

International Affairs 1938, published by the Royal Institute of International Affairs (London, 1951), Vol. II, pp. 288-298.

[62] *DGFP,* Series D, Vol. II, Doc. 402.

[63] *Ibid.,* Doc. 506.

[64] *British Documents,* Third Series, Vol. III, Annex to Doc. No. 7.

[65] *Ibid.,* Doc. 15. For further exchange of notes between the British and Hungarian governments on the same subject see, *Ibid.,* Docs. 29, 44, and 52.

[66] *British Documents,* Third Series, Vol. II, Doc. 1024.

[67] *British Documents,* Third Series, Vol. III, Doc. 37. Cf. *DGFP,* Vol. IV, Doc. 47.

[68] *British Documents,* Third Series, Vol. II, Doc. 937.

[69] *DGFP,* Series D, II, Doc. 554. During his previous visit to Germany Imrédy told Ribbentrop on August 26, 1938, that in his opinion "France would hasten to assist Czechoslovakia in the event of a German attack, as France had pledged her honor to do this." *Ibid.,* Doc. 395.

[70] *La Politique Allemande (1937-1943), Documents Secrets du Ministère des Affairs Etrangères de l'Allemagne traduit du Russe* (Hongrie, Edition Paul Dupont, 1946), pp. 74-76.

[71] Hitler's dislike of Hungary was well known and has been proved by many documents. He indicated his feelings frankly to the Rumanian Foreign Minister, G. Gafencu, on April 19, 1939. "They say that I want to restore the grandeur of Hungary. Why should I be so ill advised? A greater Hungary might be embarrassing for the Reich. Besides, the Hungarians have always shown us utter ingratitude. They have no regard or sympathy for the German minorities. As for me, I am only interested in my Germans. I said so frankly to Count Csaky. . . . And I have said so without equivocation to the Regent Horthy and to Imredy: the German minorities in Rumania and Yugoslavia do not want to return to Hungary; they are better treated in their new fatherland. And what the German minorities do not want, the Reich does not want either." G. Gafencu, *Last Days of Europe, A Diplomatic Journey in 1939* (Yale University Press, 1948), pp. 68-69. Cf. the German documents published by the Soviet government in 1946, the pertinent passages of *Goebbels Diaries* (New York, 1948), and Erich Kordt, *Wahn und Wirklichkeit, Die Auszenpolitik des Dritten Reiches* (Stuttgart, 1947), pp. 112-113, 308, 386. Cf. p. 65.

[72] For details see, Graham Hutton, *Survey After Munich* (Boston, 1939); R. W. Seton-Watson, *Munich and the Dictators* (London, 1944). F. Borkenau, *The New German Empire* (New York, 1939); John W. Wheeler-Bennett, *Munich Prologue to Tragedy* (New York, 1948); L. B. Namier, *Diplomatic Prelude 1938-1939* (London, 1948); and the pertinent volumes of the German, British and Italian documents.

[73] *Times,* September 28, 1938.

[74] *British Documents,* Third Series, III, Doc. 113.

[75] *DGFP,* D, Vol. II, Docs. 609 and 660 and Vol. IV, Doc. 9.

[76] *DGFP,* D, IV, Doc. 39.

[77] The German document called the easternmost province of Czechoslovakia "Carpatho-Ukraine", the official name of which was "Subcarpathian Ruthenia." The local authorities in early 1939, used the name "Carpatho-Ukraine." When the province was reattached to Hungary in March 1939, its name became "Subcarpathian Territory" and after the cession to the Soviet Union in 1945 it was renamed "Transcarpathian Region." Cf. A. Stefan, "Carpatho-Ukraine—the Forgotten Land. Variation in Name." *Carpathian Star* (New York), II, May, 1952.

[78] The memorandum of October 7, 1938, argued as follows: "An independent Carpatho-Ukrainian State without support from outside is at present hardly viable. The advantage of this solution, however, would be that a nucleus for a greater Ukraine in the future would be created here. The many million Ukrainians in Poland, the Soviet Union, and Rumania would be given a motherland and thus become national minorities.

"In any case autonomy for the Carpatho-Ukraine under the slogan of self-determination should be demanded, and on this there are hardly any differences of opinion. Orientation of the autonomous Ukraine to Hungary is to be definitely rejected. This solution is desired by Hungary as well as by Poland. A common Polish-Hungarian frontier would thereby be created, which would facilitate the formation of an anti-German bloc. From a military point of view the Supreme Command of the Wehrmacht is also opposed to this common Polish-Hungarian frontier."

The memorandum concluded:

" 1. For Slovakia: Alternatives-independent Slovakia or Czechoslovak solution. Both presuppose orientation toward Germany. For the outside world, a slogan of "right of self-determination," which leaves open the possibility of a plebiscite in Slovakia.
2. For Carpatho-Ukraine: Alternatives-support for an independent but scarcely viable Carpatho-Ukraine and orientation toward Slovakia or Czecho-Slovakia. For the outside world the slogan also to be "right of self-determination" with the possibility of a plebiscite when the time comes.
3. From this results a rejection of the Hungarian or Polish solution for Slovakia as well as for Carpatho-Ukraine. In rejecting the demands of both those powers we would have a good slogan in the phrase "self-determination." For the outside world no anti-Hungarian or anti-Polish slogans are to be issued.
4. Steps can be taken to influence leading persons in Slovakia and Carpatho-Ukraine in favor of our solution. Preparations for this are already on foot."

DGFP, D, IV, Doc. 45.

[79] *Ibid.,* Doc. 57.

[80] *British Documents,* Third Series, III, Doc. 142.

[81] *Ibid.,* Doc. 232.

[82] *Ibid.,* Doc. 144.

[83] *Ibid.,* Doc. 168.

[84] *Ibid.,* Doc. 226.

[85] For the details of the negotiations see, *Ibid.,* Docs. 182, 185, 196, 197, 201, 207.

[86] *DGFP,* D, IV, Doc. 60.

[87] *Ibid.,* Doc. 62.

[88] Hungary adhered to the Anti-Comintern Pact on January 13, 1939, and resigned from the League of Nations on April 11, 1939.

[89] *DGFP,* D, Vol. IV, Doc. 63.

[90] *Ibid.,* Docs. 60-69 and 99 contain a wealth of material elucidating the background of the first Vienna Award. For the original texts of the Hungarian-Czechoslovak notes and other related documents see, *La Documentation Internationale Politique, Juridique et Economique* (Paris, 1939). For the Czech point of view see, Hubert Ripka, *Munich: Before and After* (London, 1939), pp. 498-509, and Eduard Táborsky, *The Czechoslovak Cause* (London, 1944), pp. 21-29.

[91] Galeazzo Ciano, *1937-1938 Diario,* pp. 283-285.

[92] The British Minister in Budapest, Knox, thought that both the Hungarian census of 1910 and the Czechoslovak census of 1930 had a political basis. He submitted to the British Government the following population data of the returned area believed to be approximately accurate: Hungarians, 830,000; Slovaks, 140,000; Germans, 20,000; Ruthenes, Poles, Roumanians and others, 40,000.

Knox estimated that at least 30,000 Czechs and Slovaks and a considerable number of Jews fled the returned areas. *British Documents,* Third Series, Vol. III, Enclosure in Doc. No. 270.

[93] The agrarian reform was used in Czechoslovakia to denationalize the Magyar districts of Slovakia. The Government of Prague brought Czech and Slovak settlers into purely Magyar areas to the detriment of the local peasants, who received only small allotments or nothing at all. A substantial part of the Slav settlers left their lands before the entry of the Hungarian army, but a few unfortunate incidents occurred. The problems of the Czech and Slovak settlers were settled by international agreements concluded with the German Government in the case of the Czech settlers and with the Slovak Government with regard to the Slovak settlers. See Appendix, Document 2.

[94] *British Documents,* Third Series, Vol. III, Doc. 163.

[95] *Ibid.,* Doc. 215.

[96] *Ibid.,* Doc. 227. For the full text see Appendix, Document 3.

[97] *DGFP,* D, IV, Doc. 109.

[98] *DGFP,* IV, Doc. 141.

[99] *DGFP,* IV, Docs. 127-134, 139-140. Cf. *British Documents,* Third Series, III, Docs. 268, 272, 278.

[100] *DGFP,* IV, Doc. 146.

[101] For a Ukrainian nationalist presentation of these events, see, A. Stefan, "From Carpatho-Ruthenia to Carpatho Ukraine," *Carpathian Star* (New York) I, October, November, December, 1951; January, 1952. For the Czech point of view see, Hubert Ripka, *op. cit.,* pp. 260-266.

[102] Cf. S. Stefan, *loc. cit.,* January, 1952.

[103] *DGFP,* Vol. IV, Doc. 165.

[104] *Ibid.,* Doc. 179.

[105] *British Documents,* Third Series, IV, Doc. 83.

[106] *Ibid.,* Doc. 192.

[107] *DGFP,* D, IV, Doc. 181.

[108] *DGFP,* D, IV, Doc. 182.

[109] *Ibid.,* Doc. 198. Cf. *British Documents,* Third Series, IV, No. 305.

[110] *DGFP,* D. IV, Doc. 199.

[111] *Ibid.,* Doc. 210, 236.

[112] *Ibid.,* Docs. 235, 237.

[113] Cf. *New York Times,* March 16, 1939.

[114] *DGFP,* D, IV, Docs. 214, 215, 217, 218, 222, 230.

[115] *Ibid.,* Docs. 240 and 243. Cf. *British Documents,* Third Series, IV, No. 294.

[116] *Ibid.,* Doc. 228.

[117] *Ibid.,* Doc. 246.

[118] Carpatho-Ruthenia had a territory of 12,171 square kilometers and a population of 700,000, the majority of which was Ruthenian. According to the 1930 Czechoslovak census, the number of the Hungarian minority was 121,000. For the strategic importance of Ruthenia in Eastern Europe, see Arnold Toynbee

and Frank T. Ashton-Gwatkin, *The World in March 1939* (London, 1952), p. 234.

[119] *British Documents,* Third Series, IV, Doc. 298.

[120] Hungary established diplomatic relations with the Soviet Union in 1934.

[121] The Duce had summarized the situation thusly: "(1) Italy and Germany desire some years of peace and are doing all they can to preserve it. (2) Hungary is carrying on and will carry on the policy of the Axis. (3) No one wants the dismemberment of Yugoslavia, but everyone is working toward the maintenance of the *status quo.* If, however, any dismemberment should come about, Italian interests in Croatia are paramount. (4) As to the Slovak problem, Hungary will adopt a watchful attitude and will do nothing contrary to German wishes." *The Ciano Diaries 1939-1943,* edited by Hugh Gibson (New York, 1946), April 20, 1939.

[122] For its English text, see, Elizabeth Wiskeman, *The Rome-Berlin Axis,* pp. 350-352. Cf. Mario Toscano, *Le origini del Patto d'Acciaio* (Firenze, 1948).

[123] *La Politique Allemande, (1937-1943),* Documents Secrets du Ministère des Affaires Etrangères de l'Allemagne, Traduit du Russe (Hongrie, Edition Paul Dupont Paris, 1946), p. 90.

[124] *The Ciano Diaries 1939-1943,* edited by Hugh Gibson (New York, 1946) July 24, 1939. Cf. *The Von Hassel Diaries* (New York, 1947), p. 53.

[125] The files concerning this affair are among the unpublished Hungarian documents.

[126] *The Ciano Diaries 1939-1943,* August 18, 1939.

[127] Winston Churchill, *The World Crisis—The Aftermath* (New York, 1929), p. 332.

IV—THE SECOND WORLD WAR

[1] Ciano's notes in his diaries describe the situation in some detail. "The Hungarians do not wish to yield to the demand. They are aware that this is a prelude to an actual occupation of the country. And they are right. On my return from Salzburg I indicated to the Duce that the Germans were using the same language to the Hungarians that they used six months previously to Poland: *querelles D'Allemands.* I accompanied Villani [Baron Frederick Villani, Minister of Hungary to Italy] to the Duce. Villani is extremely anti-German. He talked clearly. He spoke of the menace that would weigh upon the world, including Italy, if Germany won the war. In Vienna they are already singing a song which says, 'What we have we shall hold onto tightly, and tomorrow we shall go to Trieste.' Hatred against Italy is always alive in the German mind, even though the Axis had for a time lulled this hatred to sleep. The Duce was shaken. He advised the Hungarians to turn down the German demand as courteously as they can." *The Ciano Diaries 1939-1943,* September 9, 1939.

[2] When Villani reported to Ciano that the Hungarian Government had denied the right of passage to German forces, Ciano noted: "I believe that this refusal will not be forgotten by the Germans and that at some time or other the Hungarians will have to pay for it." *Ibid.,* September 11, 1939. Later in the month he summarized his information about Hungary: "In spite of the state of alarm there is a good deal of calm and as much decision to fight in case the Germans should want to invade the country. Teleki calls Hitler a gangster . . ." *Ibid.,* September 25, 1939.

IV—THE SECOND WORLD WAR

Horthy shared Teleki's views. Ulrich von Hassel noted in his diaries that Horthy most openly expressed his absolute rejection of Hitler and his methods and that Hitler had tried to treat Horthy à la Schuschnigg and Hacha, but that his attempt had misfired. *The Von Hassel Diaries* (New York, 1947), p. 86. "Bekanntlich zeigte Hitler nie besondere Vorliebe für Ungarn. Er hatte Ungarn seine "schlappe Haltung" 1938 und die Verweigerung des Durchtransportes von Truppen während des polnischen Feldzuges schwer verübelt." Erich Kordt, *op. cit.*, p. 308.

³ One of the leading Hungarian pro-Nazi newspapers announced in huge headlines that "Stalin is divorcing his Jewish wife."

⁴ *The Ciano Diaries,* December 23, 1939.

⁵ *Ibid.,* January 6-7, 1940.

⁶ Csáky requested Ciano to inform the Rumanians of the following: "If Russia attacks Rumania and Rumania resists sword in hand, Hungary will adopt an attitude of benevolent neutrality towards Rumania. On the other hand, Hungary would immediately intervene should one of the three following cases arise: (1) the massacre of the minorities; (2) Bolshevik revolution in Rumania; (3) Cession by Rumania of national territory to Russia and Bulgaria without fighting. Csáky added that even in that case nothing will be done without previous consultation and agreement with Italy." *Ciano's Diplomatic Papers,* p. 331.

⁷ *The Ciano Diaries,* March 25, 1940.

⁸ *Ibid.,* March 28, 1940.

⁹ *Ibid.,* April 8, 1940.

¹⁰ *Ibid.,* April 9, 1940.

¹¹ Before the occupation of Bessarabia and Northern Bukovina, Molotov assured the German Government that the Soviet Union "simply wished to pursue its own interests and had no intention of encouraging other states (Hungary, Bulgaria) to make demands on Rumania." *Nazi-Soviet Relations* (Washington, 1948), p. 160.

¹² According to Hungarian documents, Hitler made statements in this regard to Sztójay on February 1, 1941, and to Bárdossy on March 21, 1941. Hitler told Bárdossy that the Rumanians asked for a quick German intervention because of the preparations of the Red Army to cross the Danube. Cf. P. Groza, *In Umbra Celulei* (Bucuresti, 1945), p. 276.

¹³ *The Ciano Diaries,* August 28, 1940.

¹⁴ *Ibid.,* August 29, 1940.

¹⁵ An area of 43,492 square kilometers with a population of 2,600,000 was reattached to Hungary. According to the Hungarian censuses of 1910 and 1941, the number of Hungarians exceeded the Rumanians in this territory, while the Rumanian census of 1930 indicated a slight Rumanian majority.

Following the delivery of the award, Csáky and Ribbentrop signed a treaty assuring special rights to the German minority in Hungary. With the conclusion of this treaty the problem of the German citizens of Hungary ceased to be exclusively within the domestic jurisdiction of the Hungarian state. For the text of the treaty see, Matthias Annabring, "Das ungarländische Deutschtum," Südost-Stimmen, II (March, 1952), 13-14. For Teleki's attitude in the crisis see, Richard V. Burks, "Two Teleki Letters", *Journal of Central European Affairs,* 7 (1947), pp. 68-70. It should be noted, however, that Burks' evaluation of Teleki's motives is not quite correct.

¹⁶ Molotov considered the Italo-German guarantee to Rumania, with respect to her national territory, as a justification for the supposition that this action was directed against the U.S.S.R. For the pertinent exchange of notes see, *Nazi-Soviet Relations 1939-1941* (Washington, 1948), pp. 178-194.

[17] It should be noted that, at the present time, Soviet Russia keeps an army in Hungary to assure the lines of communications with Russian troops stationed in Austria. This, however, was authorized by Article 22 of the peace treaty of February 10, 1947.

[18] The Government was violently attacked by the opposition in both houses of parliament because of this step. Count Stephen Bethlen and Tibor Eckhardt strongly criticized this move. The Hungarian Minister to Washington, John Pelényi, resigned in protest.

[19] Cf. A. Ullein-Revíczky, *Guerre Allemande Paix Russe: le Drame Hongrois,* (Neuchatel, 1947), pp. 71-73.

[20] Hitler had summoned the Hungarian Minister to Germany on the day following the night of the putsch and had offered Hungary "the most enticing pieces of Yugoslav territory." He even dangled Fiume—which incidentally was Italian territory—before the Hungarians. *The Von Hassel Diaries,* p. 183.

[21] *Trial of the Major War Criminals Before the International Military Tribunal,* Vol. VII (Nuremberg, 1947), p. 257.

[22] *Ibid.,* p. 331.

[23] *Ibid.,* pp. 331-333.

[24] One of the best English experts on Danubian Europe summed up Teleki's activities in the following way: "Teleki had the terrible task of steering Hungary through the first two years of the Second World War. Although Central Europe was now completely dominated by Germany, and although Hungary had received two pieces of territory from her neighbors as a German present, Teleki fought stubbornly to retain some measure of independence for his country. His efforts compare favourably with those of Roumania in the same period. When resistance was no longer possible and his own Regent and General Staff betrayed him, Teleki took the classical way out." Hugh Seton-Watson, *Eastern Europe Between the Wars 1918-1941* (Cambridge, 1945), p. 196. It is necessary to note that Horthy did not betray Teleki but that he himself was betrayed by the Chief of the Hungarian General Staff. It is another question that, under the circumstances, Horthy tolerated such betrayals.

[25] Winston S. Churchill, *The Grand Alliance* (Boston, 1950), p. 168. Cf. Richard V. Burks, *loc. cit.,* pp. 71-73.

[26] After the war the American authorities extradited Bárdossy to the new Hungarian regime. He was sentenced to death by the people's court in Budapest and was executed.

[27] Hungarian troops occupied the Bácska, the triangle of Baranya and two small territories along the river Mura. The size of these areas was 11,475 square kilometers, with a mixed population of about one million. More than one third, the largest segment of the population, was Hungarian, and the rest Serbs, Germans, Croats, Rumanians, and other nationalities.

[28] For details see, A. Ullein-Revíczky, *op. cit.,* pp. 101-107. Kassa actually was bombed by German planes. Cf. Erich Kordt, *Wahn und Wirkklichkeit* (Stuttgart, 1948), p. 308. An officer of the Hungarian Air Force, Ádám Krudy, stated in a report to the prime minister that German planes bombed Kassa, but he was silenced by Bárdossy. Cf. Horthy, *op. cit.,* pp. 235-237.

[29] *Trial of the Major War Criminals before the International Military Tribunal,* Vol. VII (Nuremberg, 1947), p. 335.

[30] The British note was handed to Bárdossy on November 29, 1941, by the American Minister to Hungary. It read as follows: "The Hungarian Government has for many months been pursuing aggressive military operations on the territory of the Union of Soviet Socialist Republics, ally of Great Britain, in closest collaboration with Germany, thus participating in the general European war and making substantial contribution to the German war effort. In these circumstances His Majesty's Government in the United Kingdom finds it neces-

sary to inform the Hungarian Government that unless by December five the Hungarian Government has ceased military operations and has withdrawn from all active participation in hostilities, His Majesty's Government will have no choice but to declare the existence of a state of war between the two countries."

[31] Bárdossy's record of his conversation with Pell and Travers is among the unpublished files of the Hungarian Foreign Ministry.

The British ultimatum was delivered to Finland, Hungary and Rumania as a result of Stalin's repeated and pressing appeal. Prime Minister Churchill tried in vain to convince Stalin that the declaration of war against these countries would not be beneficial to the Allied cause. Churchill explained to Stalin in his telegram of November 4, 1941, that these countries "have been overpowered by Hitler and used as a cat's-paw, but if fortune turns against that ruffian they might easily come back to our side. A British declaration of war would only freeze them all and make it look as if Hitler were the head of a grand European alliance solid against us." Winston S. Churchill, *The Grand Alliance* (Boston, 1950), pp. 528, 533.

[32] Bárdossy's instructions sent to the Hungarian Ministers in Berlin and Rome on December 11 and 12, show how he tried to avoid an involvement in war with the United States. See Appendix, Documents 4 and 5.

[33] Cordell Hull, *op. cit.,* Vol. II, pp. 1114, 1175-1176. Cf. *Documents on American Foreign Relations,* Vol. IV (1942), pp. 123-124.

[34] Filippo Anfuso, *Du Palais de Venise au Lac de Garde* (Paris, 1949), p. 221.

[35] For Hungary's military participation in the second world war, see Jenö Czebe and Tibor Pethö, *Magyarország a második világháboruban* (Budapest, 1946).

[36] This was the figure established by the investigating inter-ministerial committee appointed by the Kállay government in 1943. Serbian sources greatly exaggerated the number of the victims. Although the local population had nothing to do with the massacres, Tito's partisans, in 1944-45, tortured, murdered and deported innocent Hungarians by thousands. In some villages the Hungarian population was completely wiped out and the victims greatly outnumbered those of Ujvidék and Zsablya.

[37] The most important of these were Andor Szentmiklóssy and Aladár Szegedy-Maszák. The former took Ghyczy's old place as secretary general of the Foreign Office, while Szegedy-Maszák had charge of the political division. Under the German occupation both of them were imprisoned by the Gestapo. Szentmiklóssy met a cruel death at Dachau in February, 1945. Szegedy-Maszák was liberated there by American troops. He became Hungarian Minister to the United States in January, 1946, and resigned in June, 1947.

[38] The present writer was in charge of this work in this division. The framework of the peace preparations was outlined in a memorandum drafted by Szegedy-Maszák in the spring of 1943 and approved by a small committee appointed by Prime Minister Kállay. The most prominent members of this body were Count Stephen Bethlen and the Minister of Interior, Ferenc Keresztes Fischer.

[39] Vilmos Nagy was minister of national defense from September, 1942 until June, 1943. He became the target of extreme rightist attacks and his liberal attitude was strongly objected to by Germany. Kállay probably wanted to appease Hitler in dismissing Nagy, while continuing his orientation toward the Western powers. In an interesting volume, published under the title *Fatal Years* in Hungarian, Nagy recorded his experiences displaying some bitterness toward

Horthy and Kállay. *Végzetes Esztendők 1938-1945* (Budapest, 1947). Mussolini's envoy to Hungary, in his memoirs, described how the Axis Powers obtained Nagy's dismissal from Kállay. F. Anfuso, *op. cit.*, pp. 241-242.

[40] Eugene Levai, *Black Book on the Martyrdom of Hungarian Jewry* (Zurich and Vienna, 1948), p. 73.

[41] The leader of the Small-Landholder Party, Tibor Eckhardt, left Hungary in 1941 for the United States. He was deprived of his citizenship by the Bárdossy government. The Smallholders Party submitted a memorandum to Prime Minister, Kállay, in July, 1943, which violently attacked cooperation with Germany, demanded the withdrawal of all Hungarian troops from Russia and the reestablishment of Hungary's neutral and independent status, if necessary by fighting against the German army. The author of this memorandum, Endre Bajcsi-Zsilinszky, later organized a plot against the Szálasi regime and was executed in December, 1944. See pp. 84, 91. On the other hand, the right wing of the government party demanded of Kállay the liquidation of the left wing opposition parties and newspapers and pursuance of an absolutely pro-German policy. They suggested that a German defeat would be followed by Bolshevization of Central Europe and did not think that the Western powers could or would hinder such developments. For the text of the rightist memorandum, see, Ullein-Reviczky, *op. cit.*, pp. 157-164.

[42] "It is a strange fact that Hungary, where Reaction and Terror were introduced earlier, and where the people had fewer rights and liberties, retained longer than any other Eastern European State remnants of Liberalism. Even after the outbreak of war with Russia, newspapers such as the Liberal *Magyar Nemzet* published articles criticizing the New Order; the Liberal leader Rassay and the Social Democrats attacked the government in Parliament; and members of the former "March Front" openly discussed the formation of a Popular Front. One of these intellectuals even wrote an article declaring that Hungary in 1941 needed political liberty and national independence, and that these could be obtained only by a revolution of peasants and workers. . . . All of this is of little importance to the war effort of the United Nations, but it shows that the rulers of Hungary, who have reduced to the minimum their contribution to the Axis, are not 'Quislings' in the same sense as Antonescu, Pavelić or even Boris." Hugh Seton-Watson, *op. cit.*, p. 197. Cf. J. F. Montgomery, *Hungary the Unwilling Satellite* (New York, 1947).

[43] He was murdered by Soviet soldiers in March, 1945, while defending women who sought refuge from the Red Army in the episcopal residence.

[44] One of the leaders of the pro-Polish organization was Monsignor Béla Varga, chairman of the National Assembly in 1946-1947, now in exile in the United States and President of the Hungarian National Council. Cf. *Les Réfugiés Polonais en Hongrie pendant la Guerre* (Budapest, 1946). Cf. *Ecclesia* (Roma), September 1, 1943.

[45] Cf. *Refuge en Hongrie 1941-1945* (Paris, 1946), published by the escaped French war prisoners.

[46] Cf. *Hungarian Economic Resistance Against German Penetration* (Budapest, 1946). This booklet describes the principal means and results of economic resistance.

[47] For the postwar fate of this hoard, see pp. 132-133.

[48] German economic envoy for southeastern Europe.

[49] *The Goebbels Diaries 1942-1943* (Washington, 1948), Louis P. Lochner, ed. and trans., entry of March 5, 1942.

[50] Memorandum of the conversation between the Fuehrer and the Duce, with Ribbentrop and Ciano also present, at Klessheim near Salzburg, April 29, 1942. *Bulletin*, XV (1946), 59.

IV—THE SECOND WORLD WAR

[51] See p. 39.

[52] Paul Schmidt, *Hitler's Interpreter* (New York, 1951), pp. 205-206. Cf. note 71, on p. 203.

[53] *Ibid.*, p. 244. As to Hitler's encouragements given to Antonescu concerning the ultimate fate of Transylvania, see *Trial of the Major War Criminals* Vol. VII (Nuremberg, 1947), p. 322.

[54] Cf. p. 47.

[55] *Ciano Diaries*, August 25, 26, 27, 29, 1942. Mussolini considered the plan as part of an anti-German conspiracy which would have caused a crisis in Italo-German relations. For the details of the affair see, F. Anfuso, *op. cit.*, pp. 230-231.

[56] *Ciano Diaries*, November 5, 1942.

[57] The article of the *New York Times*, September 30, 1943 is not accurate in this respect.

[58] *The Von Hassel Diaries*, p. 346.

[59] The account of these negotiations, published in the city edition of the *New York Times* on February 5, 1945, by C. L. Sulzberger, is erroneous in some of its points. Mr. Sulzberger states that: "An Armistice between the Hungarian Government's envoys and the United Nations was secretly signed on a motor-boat in the Bosporus at midnight of September 9, 1943. The British Ambassador to Turkey, Sir Hughe Knatchbull-Hugessen, acted as the Allied Plenipotentiary and an official of the Budapest Foreign Office was sent especially on a clandestine mission to conclude this armistice." The truth is that in this period of the war the military situation did not make possible the conclusion of an armistice treaty with Hungary.

[60] For Hitler's reaction, see p. 76.

[61] The negotiations conducted at Stockholm are described by the former Hungarian Minister to Sweden, A. Ullein-Reviczky, *op. cit.*

[62] For the Hungarian reaction to it, see pp.66-67.

[63] F. Anfuso, *op. cit.*, p. 240.

[64] For the Rumanian armistice negotiations, see, Alexander Cretzianu, "Rumanian Armistice Negotiations: Cairo, 1944," *Journal of Central European Affairs*, 11 (1951), 243-258. F. C. Nano, "The First Soviet Double Cross", *Ibid.*, 12 (1952), 236-258.

[65] The passage of the note relevant here ran as follows:

"Die königlich ungarische Regierung wird zweck baldiger und vollständiger Lösung der Judenfrage in Europa gebeten auch ihrerseits in Ungarn entsprechende Massnahmen baldmöglichst in die Wege zu leiten. Die bisherigen Ansätze in dieser Richtung werden deutscherseits begrüsst. Sie sind allerdings noch weit davon entfernt, mit der Entwicklung in Deutschland und anderen Staaten Europas Schritt zu halten. Alle Umstände sprechen dafür diese Frage noch während des Krieges zu einem endgültigen Abschluss zu bringen. Es handelt sich dabei nicht um ein deutsches, sondern um ein gesamteuropäisches Interesse. . . ."

"Nach deutscher Auffassung wären daher folgende Massnahmen in Ungarn zweckmässigerweise zu ergreifen:

1) Die Juden auf dem Wege fortschreitender Gesetzgebung unterschiedslos aus dem kulturellen und wirschaftlichen Leben auszuschalten.

2) Durch sofortige Kennzeichnung aller Juden die entsprechenden Regierungsmassnahmen zu erleichtern und dem Volk die Möglichkeit zu klarer Distanzierung zu verschaffen.

3) Die Aussiedlung und den Abtransport nach dem Osten vorzubereiten."

[66] According to Sztójay's report, Luther added details about the settling of the Jews in other countries. He warmly praised Slovakia, where the last of the Jews were being deported. He referred to the considerable number of Jews deported from Rumania. He extolled the severe measures taken by Bulgaria, as, for instance, the compulsory wearing of the yellow star badge. Almost no Jews were left in Yugoslavia. Only difficulties in transportation prevented Croatia from completely executing their deportation laws. The Laval government of unoccupied France was anxious to secure German help for the deportation of the Jews. According to Luther, they were just being extradited across the demarcation line.

[67] *Trial of the Major War Criminals,* Vol. X (Nuremberg, 1947), p. 135. For the details of Hitler's and Ribbentrop's threats in the Jewish question, see Lévai, *op. cit.,* pp. 31-36. He published the full report of the Hungarian Minister to Germany on the discussions with Ribbentrop.

[68] The April 18, 1943, entry in the *Goebbels Diaries* summarized Horthy's visit in the following way: "Horthy's visit on the Obersalzberg has come to an end. On the first day it was conducted in a very heated atmosphere. The Fuehrer minced no words and especially pointed out to Horthy how wrong were his policies both in general and especially with reference to the conduct of the war and the question of the Jews. The Fuehrer was very outspoken. He charged the Hungarians with having tried to contact the enemy via Spain and Portugal. Horthy denied this but that did not help him very much.

"On the second day the conversations were more normal. A communiqué was drafted similar to the one on Antonescu's visit. On the insistence of the Hungarians, however, the passage about our fight against the western plutocracies was eliminated. I suppose the Hungarians believe that in the house of a man who has been hanged one should not talk about rope!" (p. 335.)

In the following period the *Goebbels Diaries* reflect the growing German anger against Hungary: "Horthy heard very little in the way of pleasant things from the Fuehrer. But he does not seem to have taken this very much to heart, for he has so far fulfilled none of the promises he made on the Obersalzberg." (May 7, 1943, p. 352.)

[69] Goebbels noted in his diaries that: "The Jewish question is being solved least satisfactorily by the Hungarians. The Hungarian state is permeated with Jews, and the Fuehrer did not succeed during his talk with Horthy in convincing the latter of the necessity of more stringent measures. Horthy himself, of course, is badly tangled up with the Jews through his family, and will continue to resist every effort to tackle the Jewish problem aggressively. He gave a number of humanitarian counterarguments which of course don't apply at all to this situation. You just cannot talk humanitarianism when dealing with Jews. Jews must be defeated. The Fuehrer made every effort to win Horthy over to his standpoint but succeeded only partially." (May 8, 1943, p. 357.)

[70] Cf. p. 69.

[71] A few days before Horthy's visit, Nazi experts prepared a memorandum containing alternatives for absorption of Hungary. See Appendix, Document 6.

[72] Paul Schmidt, *op. cit.,* p. 271. For a description of these events, see Horthy, *op. cit.,* pp. 262-268.

[73] Hitler mentioned this possibility to Prime Minister Teleki in July, 1940, and intended to apply such harsh measures against Hungary in 1944. Cf. Walter Hagen, *Die Geheime Front* (Linz-Wien, 1950), pp. 344-348. Hagen's book contains a comprehensive, but in many ways inaccurate chapter on the anti-German Hungarian actions and the German counter-measures. The author himself was a member of the German secret service.

[74] For the extermination of Hungarian Jewry by the Nazis and for the various rescue actions, see Levai, *op. cit.*, pp. 77-475. Levai collected and published in four volumes material concerning the fate of Hungarian Jewry. These volumes were published in Hungarian (Budapest, 1946): *Black Book on the Sufferings of Hungarian Jews; Grey Book on the Rescue Actions for Hungarian Jews; White Book on the International Rescue Actions; History of the Ghetto of Budapest.* Two publications in Hungarian review the activities of the Catholic and Protestant churches. In the matter see, Albert Bereczky, *A magyar protestantizmus a zsidóüldözés ellen*: *Hungarian Protestantism against the Persecution of Jews* (Budapest, 1945); Antal Meszlényi, *A magyar katolikus egyház és az emberi jogok védelme: The Hungarian Catholic Church and the Protection of Human Rights* (Budapest, 1947). For the underground activities of former opposition politicians under the German occupation, see, Imre Kovács, *D'une occupation à l'autre* (Paris, 1949), pp. 1-83.

[75] The rank of the secretary of state in the Hungarian state organization corresponded to the British under-secretary of state.

[76] *Trial of the Major War Criminals before the International Tribunal*, Vol. IV (Nuremberg, 1947), p. 367.

[77] Lévai, *op. cit.*, pp. 235-240.

[78] More than 3000 gendarmes were brought to Budapest to deport the Jews. The Regent however, secretly concentrated reliable troops around Budapest, and, on July 8, the gendarmes were ordered to leave the capital.

[79] For details, see, Lévai, *op. cit.*, pp. 197-246.

[80] This tireless and courageous diplomat mysteriously disappeared a few months later during Russian occupation while attempting to return to Sweden. Cf. Jenö Lévai, *Raoul Wallenberg, hjälten i Budapest; autentisk skildring av Kungl. Svenska beskickningens i Budapest räddningsaktion 1944-1945* (Stockholm, 1948). In November, 1952, King Gustav Adolf awarded Wallenberg a high decoration for his humanitarian work in Budapest. Allegedly he is still alive in a Russian labor camp. Cf. Judith Listowel, "Diplomats Behind Bars", *East Europe and Soviet Russia*, VIII (November 20, 1952), pp. 7-10.

[81] In reality: "During July, 1944, Hungarian Jews were being liquidated at the rate of 12,000 daily; and as the crematoria could not deal with such numbers, many bodies were thrown into large pits and covered with quicklime." *Trial of the Major War Criminals*, Vol. III (Nuremberg, 1947), p. 567.

[82] *Ibid.*, pp. 502-503.

[83] Cf. Imra Kovács, *op. cit.*, pp. 38-52.

[84] Cf. Hagen, *op. cit.*, p. 370.

[85] After the occupation of Hungary the Germans demanded that the entire Hungarian Army should attack the Red Army under German leadership. The commander-in-chief of the first Hungarian Army, General Stephen Náday, objected to this plan and proposed that the Hungarian Army should establish a firm line of defense in the eastern Carpathians. Náday was removed and the Hungarian Army was ordered to attack the Red Army beyond the Carpathians south of the Dneister river. Cf. Czebe and Pethö, *op. cit.*, pp. 44-45 Erich Kordt noted: "Man hatte es deutscherseits versäumt, rechtzeitig die Karpatenpässe zu besetzen, was selbst nach dem Abfall Rumäniens noch möglich gewesen wäre." *Op. cit.*, p. 387.

For the operations of the Red Army, see W. E. D. Allen and Paul Muratoff, *The Russian Campaigns of 1944-45* (London, 1946). John A. Lukacs, "Political Expediency and Soviet Russian Military Operations," *Journal of Central European Affairs*, VIII (1949), 390-411.

[86] Cf. Hagen, *op. cit.*, p. 368.

[87] The members of the delegation were General Gábor Faraghó, supervisor of the Hungarian *gendarmery;* Count Géza Teleki, professor of geography and son of the late Count Paul Teleki; and Domokos Szentiványi, a high official of the Foreign Ministry. The delegation crossed the Hungarian frontiers to Slovakia on September 28, 1944.

[88] Otto Skorzeny, *Secret Missions* (New York, 1951), p. 193.

[89] Hagen, *op. cit.*, pp. 372-373.

[90] The text of the proclamation has been published by J. F. Montgomery, *op. cit.*, pp. 236-238.

[91] Skorzeny in his book described the occupation of the Royal Castle Hill and his other activities in these days. *Op. cit.*, pp. 193-218. His story is inaccurate in some of its major points. Cf. Regent Horthy's statement in the *Figaro,* June 13, 1950. For another German version of these events, see Rudolf Rahn, *Ruheloses Leben* (Düsseldorf, 1949), pp. 262-273.

[92] A poster announced to the Hungarian army: "Miklós Horthy hireling of the Jews, traitor and former Regent of Hungary, has broken the oath he has taken to the nation and you. From the moment of his treachery he is no longer your Commander-in-Chief. As he broke his oath, he must be arrested. . . . As from today Ferenc Szálasi is the responsible leader of Hungary. From this moment on your oath is binding to him as the saviour of the nation. . ."

[93] *Important Declarations of Dr. Justinian Cardinal Serédi* (Budapest, 1946), pp. 5-11.

[94] For some details, see Wisliceny's deposition at Nuremberg. *Trials of the Major War Criminals,* Vol. IV (Nuremberg, 1947), pp. 369-370. Cf. Lévai, *op. cit.*, pp. 371-379.

[95] Lévai published the texts of the notes of the neutral powers and described the various actions and their results. *Op. cit.*, pp. 354-361. According to his calculations 124,000 Jews survived the ordeal in Budapest and 105,453 perished. From the provinces all the Jews were deported and thus the total loss of Jewish lives in Hungary reached the figure of 618,000. *Op. cit.*, pp. 469-474.

[96] Cf. Imre Kovács, *op. cit.*, pp. 68-83.

[97] Hagen, *op. cit.*, p. 380.

[98] Cf. Antal Meszlényi, *op. cit.*, p. 30.

V— CHAOS: AN INTERLUDE

[1] This conversation between Eden and Roosevelt took place in Washington on March 14, 1943. Robert E. Sherwood, *Roosevelt and Hopkins* (New York, 1948), p. 711.

[2] For the evaluations of war damages see, *Economic Rehabilitation in Hungary,* Operational Analysis Papers, No. 47. UNRRA European Regional Office (London, 1947), pp. 8, 37-46. For the losses of agricultural machinery and livestock, see *Agriculture and Food in Hungary.* Operational Analysis Paper, No. 33. (London, 1947), pp. 11-12.

[3] See p. 79 and note 37 on p. 209.

[4] Cf. pp. 118-119.

[5] See chapter X.

NOTES TO PART TWO

VI—SOVIET AND WESTERN POLITICS

[1] As related above, the provisional armistice agreement signed by the representatives of Regent Horthy in Moscow on October 11, 1944, was invalidated by the subsequent Nazi *putsch,* and seizure of power. Thus a second Hungarian armistice delegation appointed by the provisional National Assembly, made the trip to Moscow and signed the definitive armistice agreement on January 20, 1945. See p. 129. For the list of the provisional Hungarian Government, see Appendix, Document 7, and for the text of the armistice agreement, Appendix, Document 8.

[2] See below, Chapter IX.

[3] In reference to the negotiations concerning the nature and functions of the Allied Control Commissions for the Axis satellites, Cordell Hull explained: "We felt that the Control Councils should act under instructions of the Soviet High Command only during the military period, which would come to an end with the termination of hostilities against Germany. Between that time and the conclusion of peace with the satellites, we felt that the three Allied Governments should have equal participation in the work of the commissions, and that their representatives should be able to report directly to their respective Governments." *The Memoirs of Cordell Hull,* Vol. II (New York, 1949), p. 1461. Cf. Edward R. Stettinius, Jr., *Roosevelt and the Russians* (New York, 1949), pp. 43, 65, 87.

[4] H. F. A. Schoenfeld, "Soviet Imperialism in Hungary," *Foreign Affairs* 26 (1948), 555.

[5] Article 18 is identical in the Bulgarian and Hungarian armistice agreements. The corresponding article of the earlier concluded Rumanian armistice agreement revealed Soviet intentions more clearly, for it simply stated that an Allied Control Commission "will undertake until the conclusion of peace the regulation of and control over the execution of the present terms under the general direction and orders of the Allied (Soviet) High Command, acting on behalf of the Allied Powers." As a result of American diplomatic efforts in Moscow, paragraph 2 was added to article 18 in the Bulgarian and Hungarian armistice agreements and it restricted Soviet chairmanship to the period of hostilities against Germany.

[6] There then followed a reference to "Annex I", the rather vague text of a letter transmitted on July 12, 1945, to the representatives of the U.S. and U.K. Governments on the ACC in Hungary. For its text, see Appendix, Document 9.

[7] *New York Times,* August 10, 1945.

[8] Art. 6. c. *Bulletin,* XVI (1947), 1161.

[9] For material concerning some aspects of the relations between the American and Russian members of the ACC in Hungary, see Hal Lehrman, *Russia's Europe* (New York, 1947), pp. 192-195.

[10] For details, see Ferenc Nagy, *The Struggle Behind the Iron Curtain* (New York, 1948), pp. 240-244.

[11] See p. 157. Cf. *Background Information on the Soviet Union in International Relations. Report of the Committee on Foreign Affairs pursuant to H.*ɟ *Res.* 206, 81st Congress, 2d Session (Washington, 1950).

[12] I complained once to a Soviet diplomat about the vague terms of the

armistice agreement. During the ensuing conversation he explained to me that the first Russian draft was about 60 pages long and a very precise document. The competent section of the Soviet foreign office was instructed to reduce the text several times until it reached its present size, but the short version still had to include the content of the first draft. Thus the ambiguous text of the armistice agreement might not have been an accidental circumstance, but part of a premeditated plan.

[13] The ACC for Italy was established in November, 1943, and was abolished on January 31, 1947. *Bulletin*, XI (1944), 137-138 and *Bulletin*, XVI, (1947), 1258.

[14] Molotov, for example, complained about this situation at Potsdam. See James F. Byrnes, *Speaking Frankly* (New York, 1947), p. 74.

[15] John C. Campbell, *The United States in World Affairs 1945-1947* (New York, 1947, 1947), pp. 52-54. For further details, see *United States and Italy 1936-1946, Documentary Record* (Washington, 1946).

[16] William D. Leahy, *I Was There* (New York, 1950), pp. 369-370.

[17] *Ibid.,* pp. 378-379.

[18] *Ibid.,* p. 380. Cf. William Hillman, *Mr. President* (New York, 1952), pp. 114-116.

[19] Philip E. Mosely "The Occupation of Germany—New Light on How the Zones Were Drawn," *Foreign Affairs,* 28 (1950), 604.

[20] James F. Byrnes, *op. cit.,* p. 255. Byrnes' actions in Moscow were severely criticized by Sumner Welles, *Seven Decisions That Shaped History* (New York, 1951), p. 209.

[21] Speech delivered before the Herald Tribune Forum in New York, on October 31, 1945. *Bulletin,* XIII (1945), 710.

[22] Rákosi quoted passages from Byrnes's speech in his radio address to the Hungarian electorate on the eve of the general elections held on November 4, 1945. Cf. note 4 on p. 221.

[23] *Bulletin,* XV (1946), 638 and *Bulletin,* XVI (1947), 341. Of the total credit authorized for Hungary by the Surplus Property Administration, over $15,000,000 had not been utilized when the U. S. Government suspended the execution of the surplus property credit agreement on June 2, 1947, after the Communist seizure of power in Hungary. *Bulletin,* XVI (1947), 1166.

[24] George Woodbridge, *The History of the United Nations Relief and Rehabilitations Administration,* Vol. III (New York, 1950), p. 368. *Economic Rehabilitation in Hungary,* Operational Analysis Papers, No. 47, UNRRA European Office (London, 1947), p. 1. Under this program medical aid and emergency supplies of food and clothing have been furnished to priority groups.

[25] See Chapter IX, pp. 158-160.

[26] *Bulletin,* XII (1945), 127, 968.

[27] This American promise was several times reiterated and kept. Cf. p. 155. In connection with the release of Robert Vogeler, the American Government promised to facilitate the delivery of the remaining Hungarian goods in the U. S. zone of Germany, in accordance with Article 30 in the peace treaty. *Bulletin,* XXIV (1951), 723.

[28] *Hungary and the Conference of Paris,* Vol. II (Budapest, 1947), pp. 4-9. Cf., pp. 122-123 and Appendix, Document 12.

[29] *Parliamentary Debates,* Vol. 413 (London, 1945), p. 291.

[30] The Council of Foreign Ministers was established by the Potsdam Protocol to do the necessary preparatory work for the peace settlements. The Council was composed of the foreign ministers of the United Kingdom, the Union of Soviet Socialist Republics, China, France, and the United States.

[31] *Bulletin,* XIII (1945), 478.

[32] On December 14, 1945, the Senate confirmed the nomination of H. F. A. Schoenfeld as American Minister to Hungary, and on January 26, 1946, the American Mission at Budapest was raised to a Legation. *Bulletin,* XIV (1946), 352 and *Bulletin,* XIII (1945), 1023.

[33] In reference to Bulgaria and Rumania, Eden explained to Molotov at Potsdam that "formal recognition was constitutionally impossible for Britain until peace was concluded." Byrnes, *op. cit.,* p. 74.

[34] "When Prime Minister Churchill and Foreign Secretary Eden went to Moscow in October, 1944, to see Stalin and Molotov, they extended the arrangement still further, even reducing to percentage the relative degree of influence which Britain and Russia individually should have in specified Balkan countries. Cables from our Embassies in Moscow and Ankara mentioned that Russia would have a 75/25 or 80/20 predominance in Bulgaria, Hungary, and Rumania, while Britain and Russia would share influence in Yugoslavia 50/50. Later the Russians took it for granted that by the agreement of June, 1944, Britain and the United States had assigned them a certain portion of the Balkans including Rumania and Bulgaria, as their sphere of influence. This assumption had its untoward effect at the Yalta Conference in February, 1945." Cordell Hull, *op. cit.,* Vol. II, p. 1458. Cf. Sumner Welles, *Where Are We Heading* (New York, 1946), p. 151.

[35] H. F. A. Schoenfeld, *loc. cit.,* p. 558.

[36] A photograph of this letter was published in the Yellow Book of the Hungarian Government: *Documents on the Mindszenty Case* (Budapest, 1949), p. 54. There are probably many forgeries in this volume but this particular letter was not disavowed.

[37] Field-Marshal H. R. Alexander, Supreme Allied Commander in the Mediterranean Theatre, later awarded a certificate to certain Hungarians "as a token of gratitude for and appreciation of the help given to the Sailors, Soldiers and Airmen of the British Commonwealth of Nations, which enabled them to escape from, or evade capture by the enemy. 1939-1945. H. R. Alexander."

[38] *Népszava,* December 11, 1945.

[39] George Woodbridge, *op. cit.,* Vol. III, pp. 360-368.

[40] The *White Book* published by the PW Service of Hungarian Veterans concerning the problem of Hungarian prisoners of war (Bad Worishofen, Germany, 1950) estimates that 295,000 civilians were deported by the Red Army from Hungary to Soviet Russia.

[41] Most of the Western observers professed similar optimistic views about the prospects of democratic developments in Hungary. For example, the *London Times,* in an article (December 18, 1945) on "Unrecognized Rumania," compared the Rumanian situation with that of Hungary and highly praised the wisely cooperative and realistic policy of the Smallholders party. In reference to the Hungarian situation the article concluded that "the prospects of democratic development, based on loyal cooperation between the main parties, remain fair." In the same sense, Oscar Jászi, "The Choices in Hungary," *Foreign Affairs,* 24 (1946), 454. Cf. pp. 150, 152. See also Appendix, Doc. 15.

[42] *Nazi-Soviet Relations 1939-1941* (Department of State, 1948), pp. 217-254.

[43] For details, see Vernon Van Dyke, *American Support of Free Institutions in Eastern Europe,* Yale Institute of International Studies, Memorandum 28 (1948). Elizabeth Parker, *Truce in the Balkans* (London, 1948). William B. King and Frank O'Brien, *The Balkans Frontier of Two Worlds* (New York, 1947). Robert Bishop and E. S. Grayfield, *Russia Astride the Balkans* (New York, 1948). R. H. Markham, *Rumania under the Soviet Yoke* (Boston, 1949). *Suppression of Human Rights in Rumania,* published by the Rumanian National Committee (Washington, 1949). Hugh Seton Watson, *The East European Revolution* (New York, 1951). Mark Ethridge and C. E. Black, "Negotiations on the Balkans, 1945-1947" published in the volume *Negotiating with the Russians,* edited by Raymond Dennett and Joseph E. Johnson (World Peace Foundation, 1951), pp. 171-206. R. R. Betts (ed.), *Central and South East Europe, 1945-1948* (London, 1950).

[44] The Russians did not make a secret of their intentions in connection with the Yalta pledges and the fate of the Eastern European countries. "A freely elected government in any of these countries would be anti-Soviet, and that we cannot allow," declared Marshal Stalin at Potsdam, according to a member of the American delegation. Philip E. Mosely, *Face to Face with Russia,* Foreign Policy Association, Headline Series, No. 70 (1948), p. 23.

[45] For the pertinent notes of the Hungarian Foreign Ministry, see Appendix Documents 10 and 11. Cf. Stephen Kertesz, "The Expulsion of the Germans from Hungary: A Study in Postwar Diplomacy", *Review of Politics,* 15 (1953), 179-208.

[46] The Hungarians were deprived of their citizenship, of all political rights and of their most elementary human rights, by a series of legal measures, administrative steps and even by officially tolerated actions of private groups and individuals. They were put into concentration camps by the hundreds and their material existence was made impossible. The agrarian reform discriminated against Hungarians. The state dismissed its Hungarian officials, stopped payment of pensions to retired Hungarian officials, disabled men, and war-widows, and obliged private concerns to do likewise. A Hungarian was not allowed to employ or to be employed. Private property was confiscated in many cases and all kinds of licenses withdrawn. Hungarian cultural and welfare institutions were dissolved and all activities of this kind prohibited. Hungarian schools were closed and private education banned for Hungarian children. The ownership of radios by Hungarians and the publication and sale of Hungarian printed materials was also banned. The use of the Hungarian language on the streets of some cities as well as its use in postal communication and in religious services was forbidden. In fact, the Hungarians were placed almost entirely outside the law.

It was characteristic of postwar Czechoslovakia that a constitutional law, passed by the provisional National Assembly on April 11, 1946, declared that: "Only Czechoslovak citizens of Czech, Slovak or other Slav race possess the suffrage. (Clause 3). Only Czechoslovak citizens of Czech, Slovak or other Slav race may be elected." (Clause 4.) This is almost a classic instance of a nation adopting the very weapon with which it was formerly oppressed. However, not even the Nazis discriminated against the Czechs in such extreme forms. For the list of discriminatory laws and decrees, see *Hungary at the Conference of Paris,* Vol. II (Budapest, 1947), pp. 150-152; Vol. IV, pp. 176-186.

[47] For the list of these notes, see *Hungary and the Conference of Paris,* Vol. II, pp. 155-163.

[48] For the text of the American memorandum, see Appendix, Document 12.

[49] *Hungary and the Conference of Paris,* Vol. II, pp. 13-14.

[50] *Ibid.,* pp. 15-29.

[51] The Hungarians in Czechoslovakia outnumbered the Slovaks in Hungary

at least seven to one. Thus, even after a total exchange of Slovaks for Hungarians there would have remained more than half a million Hungarians in Slovakia. Slovaks in Hungary were the descendants of the group transferred from Northern Hungary to the Hungarian Lowlands in the eighteenth century. Cf. pp. 6-7.

[52] At Prague the present writer summed up, in a draft protocol, the positions of the two delegations. For the material of these negotiations see *ibid.*, pp. 30-49.

[53] The Hungarian Government informed the American British and Soviet Governments of the Prague negotiations. For the text of these notes, see *ibid.*, pp. 50-53. The Soviet Union did not reply to the Hungarian notes at all. The American and British replies to the various Hungarian memorandums, requests, and proposals arrived in February and March, 1946. These replies were negative and reiterated in unequivocal terms the previous verbal refusals. For the text of the American and British notes, see Appendix, Documents 13 and 14.

[54] Hugh Seton-Watson stated that: "Fantastic figures were current in Slovakia. The Slovak communists showed themselves wilder chauvinists than the Slovak nationalists, even than the fascists of Tiso." He added that he personally heard from the mouth of Husak, the communist chairman of the Board of Commissioners that "there were 400,000 Slovaks in Hungary, and that 400,000 Hungarians could therefore be expelled." *The East European Revolution* (New York, 1951), p. 344. The myth of the 400,000 Slovaks in Hungary was definitively exploded when as a result of the population exhange, about 60,000 Slovaks voluntarily transferred from Hungary to Czechoslovakia. At this time the conditions of life were incomparably better in Czechoslovakia than in Hungary.

[55] For the population exchange agreement and connected documents see, *Hungary and the Conference of Paris,* Vol. II, pp. 69-91.

[56] In a protocol annexed to the agreement the two governments recognized that the problem of the Hungarians in Czechoslovakia still demanded a solution and reaffirmed their determination to settle this problem by way of mutual agreement. The Czechoslovak Government pledged, while awaiting the conclusion of the agreement: "to keep in force the suspension of the expulsions and removals of the Hungarians, with the exception of the measures based on the legal dispositions concerning compulsory labor, as well as of the measures of confiscation of their property, provided however that this suspension shall be applied only with regard to persons who have committed no offences against the Czechoslovak Republic.

"As concerns public employees, the Czechoslovak Government shall grant them such social assistance as is necessary to assure them the minimum needed for the maintenance of their existence. . . . " *Ibid.,* pp. 76-77.

VII—REORGANIZATION OF HUNGARY

[1] *The Way of Our People's Democracy,* Rákosi's speech delivered at the Academy of the Hungarian Workers (Communist) Party on February 29, 1952. The text quoted is from the English translation published by the National Committee For a Free Europe (New York, 1952), p. 8. In this speech Rákosi described the methods by which the transformation of Hungary's political structure has been brought about.

[2] *Ibid.,* p. 11.

[3] For the complete list of cabinet members, see Appendix, Document 7.

[4] The two meetings took place within a few hours. Gerö presented the list to the Hungarians on December 5, 1944 at 7:30 P.M. and Molotov received them on December 6 at 2:30 A.M. Between the two meetings the Hungarians

were taken to a long movie. Thus they could not discuss among themselves Gerö's proposals. It is a common Soviet practice to tire people out before negotiations and not to leave them any time for serious preparations or thinking.

[5] Gerö and Joseph Révai, allegedly were Trotskyites. Thus later they had to be "more Stalinist than Stalin" in order to survive.

[6] Gyula Kállay, *A Magyar Függetlenségi Mozgalom, 1936-45* (Budapest, 1948), p. 242. The text of this agreement was prepared by Lászlo Rajk, central secretary of the Hungarian Communist Party. Rajk became minister of interior in 1946, foreign minister in 1948, and was hanged in October, 1949, as a traitor. Árpád Szakasits signed the agreement in the name of the Social Democrats on October 10, 1944, but he denied the existence of such an agreement even before the Social Democratic Party. The agreement was made public by Rákosi on August 15, 1947.

[7] The history of the Debrecen period of the new regime has been published in Hungarian by Jób Paál and Antal Radó, *A Debreceni Feltámadás—Resurrection of Debrecen* (Debrecen, 1947). The book is highly laudatory about everything that happened in Debrecen. Otherwise it could not have been published in post-war Hungary.

[8] Altogether thirty eight towns and villages, representing 1,381,000 people in the Russian liberated areas, took part in these "elections," whereas about three and a half million people lived on this same territory. Regular elections could not have taken place in those days. Paál and Radó, *op. cit.*, p. 160.

[9] Paál and Radó, *op cit.*, p. 180.

[10] For the text of the armistice agreement see Appendix, Document 8.

[11] See Appendix Document 7.

[12] *Loc cit.*, p. 34.

[13] The pattern for such cooperation was set in the Moscow declaration of November 1, 1943, regarding Italy. The three major Allies stated that "It is essential that the Italian Government should be made more democratic by the introduction of representatives of those sections of the Italian people who have always opposed Fascism."

[14] *La Hongrie et La Conference de Paris,* Vol. I, pp. 52, 84.

[15] It will be remembered that the phrase "spoils system" as used in the United States referred to the practice of political parties filling substantially all public offices, even those of the lowest rank, with their own supporters. In more recent times in the United States the increasing strength of the civil service system has considerably lessened the scope of the application of the "spoils system." Here, the term refers to a modified application of the "spoils system" by a government formed by a coalition of parties.

[16] For the ACC, see pp. 103-107.

[17] Rákosi explained in retrospect: "In the process of carrying out the land reform we used the tactics of trying to divide the enemy, or, if possible, to neutralize him. Therefore, we drew the line of land distribution at 200 acres which did not involve the majority of the kulaks; this enabled us to carry out the land reform quickly and smoothly." *Loc. cit.*, p. 13. Cf. Leland Stowe, "Hungary's Agrarian Revolution," *Foreign Affairs,* 24 (1946-47), 490-502. Alexander Eckstein, *"Land* Reform and the Transformation of Agriculture in Hungary," *Journal of Farm Economics* XXXI (1949), 456-468. L. D. Schweng, "Recent Agricultural Developments in Eastern Europe", *Journal of Farm Economics,* XXXIII (1951), 40-54. *Agriculture and Food in Hungary,* UNRRA European Regional Office, Operational Analysis Paper No. 33 (London, 1947), pp. 12-16.

[18] *Szabad Nép,* September 8, 1946.

[19] Even in western European countries, such as France, cases of war criminals were judged by special tribunals.

[20] The infiltration of trade unions is, everywhere, the first step in Communist conquests. Lenin strongly advised the Communists to enter even "reactionary" trade unions in order to conquer them from within. See Lenin's "Left-Wing Communism; An Infantile Disorder" (April 27, 1920), reprinted in *The Strategy and Tactics of World Communism, Supplement I,* (Washington, 1948), pp. 34-42. The Communist International declared, moreover, that "It is the bounden duty of every communist to belong to a trade union, even a most reactionary one, provided it is a mass organization." The Italian and French situations are eloquent examples of the manner in which Communists penetrate and use trade unions in free countries. John Williamson, the national labor secretary of the Communist Party, developed the argumentation of American Communists in a letter published in the *New York Times,* October 4, 1949.

[21] H. F. A. Schoenfeld, "Soviet Imperialism in Hungary," 26, *Foreign Affairs,* (1947-48), 560.

VIII—*HUNGARY A REPUBLIC*

[1] For the transformations of Hungarian society and institutions in recent years, see Loránd D. Schweng, *Political Social and Economic Developments in Postwar Hungary* (Washington, 1950), published by the National Planning Association in mimeographed form. This comprehensive work contains by far the best evaluations and the most reliable information concerning the changing Hungarian scene.

[2] The authorization of the ACC was also necessary for the creation of a political party.

[3] Cf. pp. 112-113.

[4] On the eve of the elections Rákosi delivered a radio speech in which he quoted passages from Secretary Byrnes' address before the *Herald Tribune* Forum on October 31, 1945, to prove that the English-speaking powers abandoned Central and Eastern Europe to the Soviet Union. Mátyás Rákosi, *A magyar demokráciáért* (Budapest, 1947), p. 163. Cf. p. 110.

[5] Rákosi evaluated the result of the elections in the following: "The Smallholders' Party, as became clear in the weeks preceding the elections, won the majority of the peasant votes; it was backed by the bulk of the urban petit-bourgeois, and almost without exception, by the masses composed of fascists, capitalists, great landowners, and reactionaries. It is noteworthy that in Budapest, where it had no serious organization prior to the liberation, it won 50 percent of the votes." *Loc. cit.,* p. 17.

[6] Loránd D. Schweng, *op. cit.,* p. 64.

[7] Rákosi bitterly remarked that "the majority of the new smallholders in the Trans-Danubian area did not vote for us but for other parties. We believed that since we helped them to get land, their majority would side with us. The 1945 elections taught us a lesson, *i. e.* that we could not make the new Trans-Danubian landholders understand that they had to thank first of all our Party for their land, and that they could keep it only if they supported us." *Loc. cit.,* p. 18.

[8] *Christian Science Monitor,* October 9, 1945. Cf. *New York Herald*

Tribune, November 6, 1946. *Journal de Genève,* November 9, 1945. One of the Soviet purposes in allowing free elections in Hungary might have been to divert attention from Communist seizure of power in Bulgaria and Rumania— countries strategically more important to the Soviet Union than Hungary. However, this strategy backfired to some extent in Austria and Berlin, where people, encouraged by the election results in Hungary, voted overwhelmingly anti-Communist.

[9] Ferenc Nagy, *op. cit.,* p. 154.

[10] *Loc. cit.,* p. 18. In another passage of his speech Rákosi described Communist tactics in financial and economic fields. "In stating our demands, we carefully weighed the probable effects of them, and wherever possible proceeded cautiously, step-by-step, so as to make it hard for the enemy to muster and mobilize all his strength against us. We gradually increased our demands in every possible field, using provisional forms. In the banking line, for instance, we insisted at first only on state control over the banks, and only later on the nationalization of the three major banks. We proceeded in a similar way with industry, first demanding state control over the mines, then expanding our demands to the control of large machine manufacturing factories and smelting industry, and ending by their nationalization. Thus we achieved the nationalization of industry by dividing the process into four or five stages during the span of several years." *Loc. cit.,* p. 13.

[11] For the English translation of the important provisions of the Republican Constitution of Hungary, see Andrew Gyorgy, *Governments of Danubian Europe* (New York, 1911), pp. 298-300.

[12] This practice was to some extent the consequence of the lack of means of transportation and communication throughout the country. Many Smallholder deputies had to remain at home to till their own land, and their movement was greatly handicapped by the lack of transportation. The available vehicles were under Communist direction and were used mainly by the Red Army.

[13] The history of the National Peasant Party is characteristic of the political evolution in Hungary. The party was founded in June, 1939, by a peasant writer, Imre Kovács, as a more radical party than the Smallholders. During the war years it worked underground and comprised only a few scattered groups without parliamentary representation. Radical peasant writers—the so-called village explorers—and a group of progressive intellectuals formed the core of the party. Some members were secretly Communists. After the war these secret Communists, with the help of radical slogans and friendly interventions of the Communist Party, gradually seized control in the party. Progressive intellectuals lost all power positions. Gradually the Peasant Party became a mere front, and the Communists used it to expedite the disintegration of the tottering Hungarian political system. Imre Kovács resigned as secretary general when the Peasant Party joined the leftist block, later resigned from the Party and finally fled the country.

[14] Rákosi summed up the result of Communist actions in the following: "At the beginning of March, 1946, the Left-Wing Bloc stressed its demands by staging a demonstration of the Budapest workers. Under the menacing effect of the impressive, disciplined meeting, numbering over 400,000 participants [this is a gross exaggeration] the Smallholders' Party was obliged to meet the demands. It had to oust 21 of its most incriminated members, it was compelled to agree that the new farmers could not be evicted from their newly acquired landholdings, that after the mines also the oil wells and bauxite mines be nationalized, that the banks be put under State control, that the Csepel Weiss Manfred factory, the Ganz factory, and the Ozd Iron Smelting Works come under State management, and that representatives of the trade unions be included in the committees entrusted with the task of purging reactionary elements from the State machine.

. . . The expansion of nationalization, and the fact that the banks and the important heavy industry plants had been placed under State control and State management showed the direction in which we would be able to gear our further development. . . . The Smallholders' Party was constantly compelled to expell or remove single individuals or groups of its discredited members. This gradual, day-by-day 'slicing' off of the reaction lurking within the Smallholders' Party was then nicknamed 'salami tactics'." *Loc. cit.,* pp. 20, 21. For the Russian pressure, see Ferenc Nagy, *op. cit.,* pp. 193-196.

[15] See, for example the speech of Prime Minister Nagy at Bicske. *Kis Ujság,* August 13, 1946.

[16] *Szabad Nép,* November 21, 1946.

[17] For the election results of the Danubian countries, see map on p. 145.

[18] Cf. Oscar Jaszi, "The Choices in Hungary," *Foreign Affairs,* 24 (1946), 462. Jaszi points out that "the Small Landholders' Party is not reactionary, not even conservative; it is a progressive party in favor of social and cultural reforms."

[19] Cf., pp. 72-74.

[20] Ferenc Nagy, *op. cit.,* p. 72. Cf. Rákosi, *loc. cit.,* p. 12.

[21] Oscar Jászi, *loc. cit.,* p. 454.

[22] *Ibid.,* pp. 457-58.

[23] Rákosi even in his recent speech attacked Socialist leadership. "Our competitor in winning over the industrial workers was the Social Democratic Party. The majority of its leaders consisted of Horthy's police agents, or British spies, and after the liberation they entered into the services of the imperialists, just as the Smallholders' Party leaders. Naturally, these leaders would have preferred to see Hungary occupied by American or British troops. Their majority hated the Soviet Union and in the beginning maintained close ties with the Labor Party, serving the interests of British imperialists, and tried to carry out its instructions and follow its advice; later it was guided more and more by the American imperialists. At the same time, however, the great majority of the Social Democratic workers and peasants—of which there were considerable numbers in the Plains of Hungary—sympathized with the liberating Soviet Union, approved of the union of workers, of the unity front with the Communists, and demanded a fight against the imperialists, the remnants of the Fascists and the capitalistic reaction. In the face of this the majority of the Social Democratic Party leaders, as well as the leaders of the Smallholders' Party, played a double game. To the masses they pretended to be members of the Independence Front, the democratic coalition, but in secret, on the sly, however, they aimed from the very first day to deprive the Communists of power, and to reduce their influence on the toiling masses to the minimum." *Loc. cit.,* p. 14.

[24] H. F. A. Schoenfeld, the formed American Minister to Hungary, observed in this respect: "Rákosi told me in one of our early conversations, that he and his Communist colleagues who had been trained in Moscow had a great advantage over the somewhat nondescript aggregation of non-Communist political leaders in Hungary. He said that he and his associates had been part of the working mechanism of government in the Soviet Union. This he claimed gave them an understanding of practical problems of government which other Hungarian leaders emerging on the political scene could not match, and made them the only effective leaders available to the Hungarian people. There was some truth in Rákosi's statement. The Communist leaders were energetic and able men; and it was apparent that they intended to fill the administrative vacuum, with or without the backing of the electorate." H. F. A. Schoenfeld, *loc, cit.,* p. 558.

[25] Cf. Rákosi, *loc. cit.,* pp. 9-10.

[26] Joseph Révai, "On the Character of Our People's Democracy." The

original article appeared in the *Társadalmi Szemle* (Budapest, March-April, 1949). An English translation of the article was published in *Foreign Affairs,* 28 (1949), 143-152.

[27] The new constitution entered into force on August 20, 1949, and its preamble set forth: "The armed forces of the great Soviet Union liberated our country from the yoke of the German fascists, crushed the power of the great landowners and capitalists who were ever hostile to the people, and opened the road of democratic progress to our working people . . . the Hungarian working class, in alliance with the working peasantry and with the generous assistance of the Soviet Union, rebuilt our war-ravaged country. Led by the experiences of the socialist revolution of 1919 and supported by the Soviet Union, our people began to lay down the foundations of socialism and now our country is advancing towards socialism along the road of a people's democracy."—*Constitution of the Hungarian People's Republic* (Budapest, 1949). Cf. Rákosi, *loc cit.,* pp. 9-10.

[28] *London Times,* October 31, 1946. For excerpts of the article, see Annex, Document 15.

IX—SOVIET RUSSIA AND HUNGARY'S ECONOMY

[1] See Article 11 of the armistice agreement. Cf. Appendix, Document 8.

[2] Colonel Susmanovich was a sort of political watchdog over the Soviet occupying forces in Hungary. He allegedly reported directly to the Politbureau.

[3] The provisions of the Hague Convention on the Laws and Customs of War on Land seemed a sad joke. Article 43 of the Convention set forth: "The authority of the legitimate power having in fact passed into the hands of the occupant, the latter shall take all the measures in his power to restore and ensure, as far as possible, public order and safety, while respecting, unless absolutely prevented, the laws in force in the country." Cf. pp. 116-120.

[4] For the food loan given by the Red Army to Budapest, see p. 133.

[5] See Arturo Karasz, "La Stabilizzazione in Ungheria nel 1946," *Rivista di Studi Politici Internazionali,* XV (1948, No. 2), 1-22.

[6] One month before stabilization the bank note circulation had reached the figure of 6,277 trillion pengös.

[7] The restitution of the gold of the National Bank and other looted Hungarian property located in the American zone of Germany was the greatest outside help Hungary had received since the war.

[8] By a special agreement between the Yugoslav and Czechoslovak Governments, Yugoslavia was to receive 70 million and Czechoslovakia 30 million of this sum. However, in September, 1948, the Hungarian Government ceased all reparations deliveries and refused to answer the Yugoslav government's notes of protest. *New York Times,* September 28, 1949.

[9] In 1946, the period of the payment was extended to eight years. Cf. p. 182.

[10] Hungary's reparations and other postwar burdens, and the general economic situation were described in a memorandum prepared by the Hungarian National Bank on November 24, 1945. See Appendix, Document 16. Cf. George Kemény, *Economic Planning in Hungary 1947-1949* (London, 1952), pp. 1-5.

At the peace conference the United States' delegation proposed reducing the total amount of reparations to be paid by Hungary to $200 million. The proposal explained that the economic burdens laid upon Hungary by the various provisions of the armistice and the treaty of peace were beyond the capacity of Hungary to pay. It estimated these burdens to be 35 percent of Hungary's national income, even before any allowance was made for the reduction in Hungary's postwar economic potential. *Selected Documents,* p. 1153. This American amendment was rejected and the peace treaty reiterated the reparations provisions of the armistice agreement.

[11] For detail see Margaret Dewar, *Soviet Trade with Eastern Europe 1945-1949* (London, 1951), pp. 62-72. At the time of these concessions the political power in Hungary was entirely in Communist hands.

[12] The development of trade relations between Hungary and the Soviet Union is treated by Margaret Dewar, *op. cit.,* pp. 58-62.

[13] For the protocol of the council of ministers on October 12, 1945, see Appendix, Document 17.

[14] The texts of these notes are in the Appendix, Documents 18 and 19.

[15] In the ACC the Soviet representative dismissed the American and British protests by declaring that the matter was not within the jurisdiction of the ACC. Cf. p. 106. The Western powers also sent notes directly to Moscow, protesting against the conclusion of economic collaboration agreements with the former Axis satellites during the armistice period. All these steps apparently had no effect whatever.

[16] The Hungarian note addressed to the American and British Missions is in the Appendix, Document 20.

[17] Quoted from the American note of July 23, 1946, addressed to the Soviet Government, *Bulletin,* XV (1946), 231.

[18] Arthur Karasz and others, "Europe's Eastern Frontier," *Common Cause,* IV (1950), 135.

[19] *Bulletin,* XV (1946), 229.

[20] *Ibid.,* pp. 229-232.

[21] *Ibid.,* p. 231.

[22] The full text of the note was published in the *New York Times,* August 2, 1946, and in the *Bulletin,* XV (1946), 263-265.

[23] *Bulletin,* XV (1946), 638-639.

[24] *Bulletin,* VIII (1943), 21-22.

[25] See the pertinent American statement at the Moscow meeting of the Council of Foreign Ministers, on April 3, 1947, *Bulletin,* XVI (1947), 653, and the American note delivered to the Soviet Government on July 29, 1947, *Bulletin,* XVII (1947), 298. Cf. James R. Byrnes, *op. cit.,* p. 162-163.

[26] In the peace treaty the Hungarian government was obligated to waive, "on its own behalf and on behalf of Hungarian nationals all claims against Germany and German nationals outstanding on May 8, 1945, except those arising out of contracts and other obligations entered into, and rights acquired, before September 1, 1939." (Article 30 sec. 4). According to the Soviet interpretation, this provision prevented the achievement of balance between claims and debts in former Axis-satellite and German relationships. The German claims automatically became Soviet claims and remained valid, whereas the counterclaims of the satellite governments and citizens were annulled.

The Italian assets in Hungary also shared the fate of the German assets. According to article 74, sec. 2 of the peace treaty with Italy, Italian assets in

Rumania, Bulgaria and Hungary formed part of the reparations to be paid by Italy to the Soviet Union. However, Italian assets in Hungary were much less significant than the German.

27 It is next to impossible to give the exact dollar equivalent of this amount because of the changing rates. Various calculations might be equally right or wrong.

28 Soviet-Hungarian joint stock companies were exempted even before from all export and import duties, and had many other important privileges.

29 The most important joint companies are: Maszovlet (Hungarian-Soviet Civil Aviation Co.), Meszhart (Hungarian-Soviet River Transportation Co.), Maszovol (Hungarian-Soviet Crude Oil Co.), Molaj (Hungarian-Soviet Petroleum Refining Co.), and Maszobal (Hungarian-Soviet Bauxite Aluminum Co.).

30 *The Final Report on Foreign Aid of the House Select Committee of Foreign Aid* describes the organization of the joint-stock corporations and in general the Soviet economic policy in Eastern Europe. (Washington, 1948), pp. 353-427. For an excellent review of some cases pertinent to the Soviet exploitation process, see Howard G. Hilton, "Hungary: A Case History of Soviet Economic Imperialism," *Bulletin,* XXV (1951), 323-327.

X—THE PEACE PREPARATORY WORK (1945-1946)

1 *Postwar Foreign Policy Preparation 1939-1945* (Washington, 1949).

2 For my first contacts with him, see pp. 97-98.

3 On this subject see my memorandum addressed to Prime Minister Tildy, Appendix, Document 22.

4 The members of the committee were: Gusztáv Gratz, former foreign minister; Lipót Baranyay, and Arthur Kárász, both former presidents of the Hungarian National Bank; Izsó Ferenczi, former secretary of state in the Ministry of Commerce; István Vásárhelyi, secretary of state in the Ministry of Finance; Loránd D. Schweng, special economic adviser, former secretary of state in the Ministry of Finance; and József Judik, head of the research division of the National Bank.

5 Cf. Appendix, Document 22.

6 For a short version of these data and argumentation, see, *La Hongrie et la Conférence de Paris,* Vol. I, pp. 63-107.

7 For its text see, *La Hongrie et la Conférence de Paris,* Vol. I, pp. 1-6.

8 Article 53 of the Hague Convention on the Laws and Customs of War on Land provided that, "An army of occupation can only take possession of cash, funds, and realizable securities which are strictly the property of the State, depots of arms, means of transport, stores and supplies, and, generally all movable property belonging to the state which may be used for the operations of the war."

9 The armistice division of the Foreign Ministry in May, June and July, 1945, repeatedly sent notes with similar contents to the ACC. The note of May 25 enumerated 28 factories which were dismantled and removed but were not included in the reparations deliveries. Other notes completed the list and described in detail the various confiscatory actions and other abuses of the Red Army and asked for restitution and remedies. The ACC refused to negotiate on such matters and Hungary was even made responsible to foreign countries for confiscations and damages caused by the Red Army. For example, a British note of November

19, 1945, in reply to a memorandum of the Hungarian Foreign Ministry, stated that "all loss or damage to British rights, interests and property in Hungary, *regardless of cause*, is to be reinstated under the terms of Article 13 of the Armistice." (Italics mine).

[10] For the process of the renewal of diplomatic relations, see pp. 113-114.

[11] *La Hongrie et La Conférence de Paris*, Vol. I, pp. 7-14.

[12] For excerpts from the note, see Appendix, Document 21.

[13] *La Hongrie et la Conférence de Paris*, Vol. I, pp. 15-20.

[14] *Ibid.*, pp. 21-36.

[15] The Hungarian representative, foreign minister of the, by then, completely Communist-dominated Hungarian Government, did not reply other than by his hundred percent support of the Soviet position, which in fact denied that freedom of navigation for which the Hungarian Government had dared to raise its voice three years before. This statement was made on August 13, 1948. *Bulletin*, XIX (1948), 283.

[16] These aspects of postwar Hungarian foreign policy will be developed in other publications.

[17] For the pertinent passages of the memorandum see Appendix, **Document** 22.

[18] I developed the arguments used in the memorandum addressed to Tildy. Cf. Appendix, Document 22, and Stephen Kertesz, "The Expulsion of the Germans from Hungary", *Review of Politics*, 15 (1953), 179-208.

[19] Cf. pp. 122-125.

[20] General Sviridov demanded that the President and managing director of the National Bank and Arthur Kárász be removed and prosecuted because of alleged mismanagement of the ruble fund in the National Bank. The charges were absolutely false and the Hungarian Government resisted for some time. Eventually the three leading officials were dismissed but not prosecuted. Cf. Ferenc Nagy, *op. cit.*, pp. 238-239.

[21] *La Hongrie et la Conférence de Paris*, Vol. I, pp. 40-50.

[22] Cf. pp. 18-20.

[23] *La Hongrie et la Conférence de Paris*, Vol I, pp. 51-55.

[24] A later memorandum dealt in detail with Hungary's responsibility in the Second World War. Another memorandum explained the development of the Jewish question in Hungary. Both memorandums were handed to the powers participating in the Paris Conference. *Ibid.*, pp. 72-107.

[25] See, *Népszava*, February 24, March 3, 10, and 17, 1946.

[26] The economic advisor was Eugene Rácz who at that time was a non-party man. Later when he was appointed minister of finance, he entered the Smallholders Party.

[27] Cf. p. 51 and Appendix, Document 8, Art. 19.

[28] Actually Hungarian manpower and Hungarian experts were used for this work performed under the direction of the Red Army. Some of the railroad lines for which Hungary was required to pay were situated in the neighboring countries. Cf. Ferenc Nagy, *op. cit.*, p. 208.

[29] Article 19 of the Rumanian armistice agreement set forth: "The Allied Governments regard the decision of the Vienna Award regarding Transylvania as null and void and are agreed that Transylvania (or the greater part thereof) should be returned to Rumania, subject to confirmation at the peace settlement, and the Soviet Government agrees that Soviet forces shall take part for this

purpose in joint military operations with Rumania against Germany and Hungary."

[30] John C. Campbell, "The European Territorial Settlement," *Foreign Affairs*, 26 (1947), 211-213. Philip E. Mosely, "Soviet Exploitation of National Conflicts in Eastern Europe," *The Soviet Union* (Notre Dame, Indiana), p. 75.

[31] *La Hongrie et la Conférence de Paris*, Vol. I, pp. 108-111.

[32] The Soviet draft treaties for the Danubian ex-Axis Satellite countries put forward in the session of the Deputy Foreign Ministers during March, 1946, were briefer even than the armistice agreements themselves. They contained no mention of frontiers, with the one exception of the restoration of Northern Transylvania to Rumania. John C. Campbell, *The United States in World Affairs 1945-1947* (New York, 1947), p. 115.

[33] Mosely, as an eyewitness, stated that: "In the work of the Council of Foreign Ministers the search for a basis of settlement could begin only after the Soviet delegation had become convinced that further delay was no longer working to the advantage of Soviet interests." Philip E. Mosely, "Peace Making 1946," *International Organization*, I (1947), 31. Cf. Harold Nicolson, "Peacemaking in Paris: Success, Failure or Farce?", *Foreign Affairs*, 25 (1947), 190-203.

[34] "In general, the United States sought fair terms for Hungary, but it did not want to place itself in the position of Hungary's champion against Allied nations. American relations with Czechoslovakia had to be considered. Furthermore, Hungary's record as a junior partner of the Axis, both before and during the war, hardly entitled her to over-sympathetic treatment at the peace settlement. That was the main reason why the Hungarians, despite the validity of many of the arguments they presented, found so few friends at Paris, even among the democratic nations outside the Soviet bloc." John C. Campbell, "The European Territorial Settlement," *Foreign Affairs*, 26 (1947-48), 214.

[35] *Selected Documents,* pp. 1123, 1153, 1194-1195. For the full text of the declaration of the American Delegate, William L. Thorp, see, *Bulletin*, XV (1946), 746-748.

[36] Winston Churchill, *The Grand Alliance* (Boston, 1950), p. 628.

[37] Art. 2, par. I, Hungarian Treaty. The same provisions are embodied in Art. 2, Bulgarian Treaty; Art. 6, Finnish Treaty; Art. 15, Italian Treaty; Art. 3, par. 1, Rumanian Treaty. These provisions are due to American initiative and were accepted as a better alternative to the minority protection system adopted at the peace settlement after the first World War. Cf. Stephen Kertesz, "Human Rights in the Peace Treaties," *Law and Contemporary Problems*, 14 (1949), 627-646.

In a memorandum addressed to the Council of Foreign Ministers, the Hungarian Government pointed out the importance of reviving and strengthening provisions for the international protection of minority rights. Later the Hungarian peace delegation submitted an elaborate draft treaty for the protection of minority rights, with the system of mixed commissions and tribunals to enforce them under the supervision of the United Nations. Cf. *La Hongrie et La Conférence de Paris*, Vol. I, pp. 135-171.

[38] The Australian proposal intended that "a new Part should be included in the Treaty providing for the establishment of a European Court of Human Rights with jurisdiction to hear and determine all disputes concerning the rights of citizenship and enjoyment of human rights and fundamental freedoms provided for in the treaty. The Australian case for this proposal rested on the belief that the general declarations contained in the treaty in support of human rights and fundamental freedoms were not sufficient, standing alone, to guarantee the inalienable rights of the individual and that behind them it was essential that

some sufficient sanction and means of enforcement should be established. It was proposed that the Court of Human Rights should have the status parallel to that of the International Court of Justice and that the Court would have the additional obligation of making reports to the Economic and Social Council of the United Nations on its working in relation to the rights within its jurisdiction It was contemplated that the jurisdiction of the proposed tribunal should be voluntarily accepted by States as an essential means of international supervision of the rights of individuals and as necessary method of giving force and effect to obligations accepted in general terms." *Selected Documents,* pp. 444-445.

39 *Selected Documents,* p. 608.

40 Cf. Martin Domke, "Settlement-of-Disputes Provisions in Axis Satellite Peace Treaties," *American Journal of International Law,* 41 (1947), 911-920.

41 Cf. Yuen-Li Liang, "Observance in Bulgaria, Hungary and Rumania of Human Rights and Fundamental Freedoms: Request for an Advisory Opinion on Certain Questions," *American Journal of International Law,* 44 (1950), 100-117. Kenneth S. Carlston, "Interpretation of Peace Treaties with Bulgaria, and Rumania, Advisory Opinions of the International Court of Justice," *American Journal of International Law,* 44 (1950), 728-737.

42 Another publication of the author will deal in more detail with the Paris Peace Conference and with developments of the Hungarian situation since 1946.

APPENDIX

LIST OF DOCUMENTS*

1. Count Stephen Bethlen's view on Hungary's international situation in 1926.
2. Memorandum concerning the case of the Czech and Slovak settlers in Southern Slovakia.
3. British standpoint of October 26, 1938, concerning the settlement of the Hungaro-Czechoslovak question by an Italo-German arbitration.
4. Cipher instructions sent by the Hungarian Foreign Minister, László Bárdossy, to the Hungarian Minister to Germany, Döme Sztójay, on December 11, 1941, concerning Hungary's solidarity with the Axis Powers.
5. Cipher instructions sent by the Hungarian Foreign Minister, László Bárdossy, to the Hungarian Minister to Germany, Döme Sztójay, on December 12, 1941, concerning the state of war with the United States.
6. Nazi Proposal concerning various alternatives for the Absorption of Hungary, March 11, 1944.
7. The list of the members of the Provisional National Government elected by the Provisional National Assembly on December 22, 1944.
8. The Hungarian Armistice Agreement signed in Moscow on January 20, 1945.
9. Text of a Soviet letter transmitted on July 12, 1945, to the representatives of the United States and United Kingdom Governments on the Allied Control Commission in Hungary. (Annex I to the Potsdam Protocol of August 2, 1945.)
10. Note of the Hungarian Government to the British, Soviet and United States Governments concerning the expulsion of the Germans from Hungary, December 1, 1945.
11. Note Verbale of the Hungarian Foreign Ministry to the British and United States Governments concerning the expulsion of the Germans from Hungary, December 15, 1945.
12. Memorandum of the United States Mission in Budapest concerning the transfer of the national minorities in Czechoslovakia, June 12, 1945.
13. Reply of the United States Government to various Hungarian proposals concerning the problems of the Hungarians in Czechoslovakia, February 9, 1946.
14. Reply of the British Government to the various Hungarian proposals concerning the problems of the Hungarians in Czechoslovakia, March 19, 1946.
15. "The Spirit of Hungary. Leaders' efforts to establish democratic state." *London Times,* October 31, 1946.
16. Memorandum of the Hungarian National Bank on Hungary's Reparations, November 24, 1945, prepared for the confidential information of the British and United States Missions in Budapest.
17. Excerpts from the minutes of the meeting of the Hungarian Council of Ministers, October 12, 1945, dealing with the ratification of the Economic Cooperation Agreement signed by Hungary and the Soviet Union.
18. United States Memorandum addressed to the Hungarian Government, October 31, 1945, concerning the Soviet-Hungarian Economic Cooperation Agreement.

230

DOCUMENTS

19. British Note Verbale addressed to the Hungarian Government, November 19, 1945, concerning the Soviet-Hungarian Economic Cooperation Agreement.
20. Note Verbale addressed by the Hungarian Ministry for Foreign Affairs to the Political Mission of the United States of America on December 20, 1945, concerning the Soviet-Hungarian Economic Cooperation Agreement.
21. Excerpts from the Hungarian Note of August 14, 1945, addressed to the British, United States and Soviet Governments on the peace aims of Hungary.
22. Excerpts from the memorandum addressed by Stephen Kertész to Prime Minister Zoltán Tildy on December 28, 1945, concerning the Hungarian peace preparations.
23. Population-breakdown of Hungary according to mother tongue from 1910 to 1941.

---

*Documents 2, 4, 5, 10, 11, 18, 19, 20, 21, 22 are unpublished documents from the files of the Hungarian Foreign Ministry. For the French text of Documents 10 and 21, see *La Hongrie et la Conférence de Paris*, Tome Ier (Budapest, 1947), pp. 37-39 and 7-14. I obtained Documents 16 and 17 through the courtesy of Count Géza Teleki.

DOCUMENT 1

COUNT STEPHEN BETHLEN'S VIEW ON HUNGARY'S INTERNATIONAL SITUATION IN 1926.[1]

Today, we may not clearly realize that the small states formed from the territory of the late Monarchy may become eventually vassals of either Russia or Germany. As a result of the great struggle, not only the Monarchy has been cut to pieces, but also the Russian Empire has been torn by a violent revolution for a decade. Thus, fate has provided us with a breathing spell for the beginning of a new life. But how long is this state of affairs going to persist? There can be no doubt at all for a thinking man that the great Russian nation is going to become a factor in world politics sooner or later, and that the great German nation will also recuperate from its defeat. We, Hungarians, do not want to become a vassal of the Russians, and want to maintain our independence of the Germans, as we have done for a thousand years, in spite of all the historical and cultural bonds between us. We want to remain Hungarians and live our independent national life.

---

[1] Extract from the Memorial Speech of Count Stephen Bethlen on Count Stephen Tisza, delivered on April 22, 1926. *Gróf Bethlen István beszédei és írásai* (Budapest, 1933), Vol. II, p. 120.

DOCUMENT 2

MEMORANDUM CONCERNING THE CASE OF CZECH AND SLOVAK SETTLERS IN SOUTHERN SLOVAKIA.

This memorandum was prepared under the supervision of a leading official of the Hungarian Foreign Ministry, Paul Sebestyén, in August 1946 for the information of members of the Hungarian Peace Delegation. He represented the Hungarian Government in the negotiations conducted with Czech, Slovak and German representatives concerning the case of Czech and Slovak settlers in territories returned to Hungary.

The Czechoslovakian Government used the land reform to Slavonize the Magyar areas of Southern Slovakia. The local Magyar peasants received none or, at most, very few allotments from the large estates which were divided in the Magyar districts, because these lands were allotted to Slovak and Czech settlers brought into the Magyar districts from distant regions for this purpose. Of the 170,000 hectares distributed under the agrarian reform, in the contiguous purely Magyar districts, 130,000 were allotted to Slovak and Czech settlers. For example, on the purely Magyar Danubian Island, Csallóköz, only 6,617 hectares were allotted to the local Magyar population, while 31,673 hectares were allotted to Slovak and Czech settlers brought there from remote districts. Though these settlers formed only four percent of the population of Csallóköz they received eighteen percent of the land. Several thousand Slav families, numbering about 30,000 people, settled in the Magyar districts. This situation, understandably resulted in tension between the local Magyar population and the newly arrived settlers, because the Magyars were, of course, grieved by the fact that land, which had been cultivated by their ancestors as serfs for centuries, had now been allotted to foreign settlers.

After the Vienna award, November 2, 1938, nearly all of the Czech settlers, and part of the Slovaks voluntarily left their lands before the entry of Hungarian troops. Only at one place did an armed clash take place between Hungarian soldiers and Czech settlers. This occurred at Köbölkut, in the district of Párkány. Twenty nine Czech and two Slovak settlers lived there. The Czechs were former members of the Czech Legion in the First World War, and had been rearmed on the occasion of the Czechoslovakian mobilization in the fall of 1938. A few of these Czech legionnaires had remained after their families had left. They possessed a machine-gun with which they opened fire on the entering Hungarian army; the latter reciprocated and three settlers were killed.

The problem of the Czech and Slovak settlers was settled by three international agreements arrived at between the Hungarian Government and the German Government with regard to the Czech settlers, and with the Slovak Government in the case of the Slovak settlers.

Under the provisions of the Agreement signed on October 16, 1940, Hungary agreed to pay 135 million Czech crowns to the Government of the Protectorate as compensation for 20,816 hectares and its appurtenances. Of this amount, ninety million Czech crowns were actually paid in cash at the time of the conclusion of the agreement, while the rest was paid in pre-arranged installments as long as the war events permitted.

Prior to this agreement, another one had been concluded between the Hungarian and German Governments on May 29, 1940, dealing with the property rights and treatment of the Czech and Moravian people who returned or wanted to return to the Protectorate. Under this agreement they were entitled to take with them their cash, securities, savings-bank books, personal jewelry and that of their families, furniture, all objects of personal use, tools, machines, agricultural inventory, live stock, merchandise, crops, etc. No customs or other duties had to be paid on these goods, and the Hungarian Government guaranteed the personal security and property of the returners and their assistants or representatives. The Hungarian Government also supplied the necessary wagons for the transportation of these items and set a time limit of six months for the completion of the task.

In order to facilitate the contacts of Czech individuals with the Hungarian authorities, a mixed Commission was formed under the previously mentioned agreement. The Commission resided in Budapest. This Commission also helped the departing Czech settlers and remaining holders of land to assert their rights under the mentioned two agreements. This Commission, consisting of three delegates from each government, functioned until September, 1944.

The agreement concluded between the Hungarian and Slovak Governments on August 2, 1941, settled the claims of the Slovak settlers. The substance of the Agreement was that the Hungarian Government paid 110 millions of Slovak crowns to the Slovak settlers, who returned to Slovakia, as compensation for their 18,000 hectares of land with its appurtenances. In addition the Hungarian Government undertook the settlement of the mortgage debt on those lands in the amount of forty seven million Slovak crowns.

The Hungarian Government guaranteed those Slovak settlers who did not leave the country free possession of their houses and about 11.5 hectares of land, and compensation for land exceeding this area.

DOCUMENT 3

BRITISH STANDPOINT OF OCTOBER 26, 1938, CONCERNING THE SETTLEMENT OF THE HUNGARO-CZECHOSLOVAK QUESTION BY ITALO-GERMAN ARBITRATION.

Document No. 227[1]

Viscount Halifax to the Earl of Perth (Rome)

No. 476 Telegraphic (C 12924/2319/12)

FOREIGN OFFICE, October 26, 1938. 9:20 P.M.

Berlin telegram No. 632.1

Czechoslovak Minister informed me this morning on instructions that his Government regarded as quite unacceptable the Hungarian demand for plebiscites in the disputed districts on the basis of the 1910 census. On the other hand, the Czechoslovak Government would be in favour of arbitration by Germany and Italy. In response to an enquiry, M. Masaryk later ascertained from Prague that his Government were opposed to Poland being included among the arbitrators and thought that if Poland were included, Roumania should be included also. M. Masaryk said that the Czechoslovak Government would have to reply today to the Hungarian demand, and before doing so wished to have the views of His Majesty's Government on their attitude.

In reply the Czechoslovak Minister was informed this afternoon that His Majesty's Government saw no objection to the settlement of the Czech-Hungarian question by means of arbitration by Germany and Italy, if the Czechoslovak and Hungarian Governments agreed to settle their differences in this way. It was added that if the two parties to the dispute preferred to refer the matter to the four Munich Powers, His Majesty's Government would be ready to join in any discussions.

If the views of the Italian Ambassador, reported in Berlin telegram under reference, represent those of his Government, it seems that the Italian Government would prefer that Great Britain and France, as signatories of the Munich Agreement, should participate in any arbitration. If this is indeed the attitude of the Italian Government, it is no doubt occasioned by their desire to obtain support against Germany, who is believed to oppose the acquisition of Ruthenia

---

[1] *British Documents,* Third Series, Vol. III, pp. 202-203.

by Hungary. Herr von Ribbentrop may of course settle the whole question when he arrives in Rome tomorrow, but it may be of value to the Italian Government to have an indication of our views on this question before the German Minister for Foreign Affairs arrives.

I should therefore be glad if you would seek an early interview with the Italian Minister for Foreign Affairs and inform him that while it is difficult for us to adjudicate between the line claimed by the Hungarians and that offered by the Czechs, and to decide whether or not the 1910 census offers a fair basis, His Majesty's Government are, in principle, in favour of the return to Hungary of those districts in which the population is predominantly Hungarian, subject possibly to certain modifications that may be desirable for economic reasons, e. g., Bratislava. The holding of plebiscites in those regions where the races are so ethnographically entangled and where there is a difference of opinion regarding the figures to be taken as a basis for the voting would, however, in the view of His Majesty's Government be extremely difficult, especially at such short notice as the Hungarian Government propose (before November 30).

His Majesty's Government would, therefore, be happy to see the Czechs and Hungarians agree to settle their differences by reference to arbitration by the Italian and German Governments. If, however, it were deemed preferable or necessary that the questions in dispute between the Czechoslovak and Hungarian Governments should be referred to the four Munich Powers, His Majesty's Government would be ready to take their part in trying to bring about an agreed settlement.

An expression of the views of His Majesty's Government on the above lines might, I feel, be welcome to Signor Mussolini as an indication that they are anxious to co-operate with him in the discussion of European questions. You will, of course, appreciate that His Majesty's Government do not wish to give the impression of trying to profit by any Italo-German disagreement over the future of Ruthenia.

Repeated to Berlin, Warsaw, Prague, Budapest, Bucharest, Belgrade and Paris No. 404.

DOCUMENT 4

CIPHER INSTRUCTIONS SENT BY THE HUNGARIAN FOREIGN MINISTER, LASZLO
BARDOSSY, TO THE HUNGARIAN MINISTER TO GERMANY, DOME SZTOJAY,
ON DECEMBER 11, 1941, CONCERNING HUNGARY'S SOLIDARITY
WITH THE AXIS POWERS.[1]

No. 377
Exung

Berlin

I ask Your Excellency to officially inform the Ministry for Foreign Affairs of the contents of the communication made via telephone.

I emphatically ask Your Excellency to restrict Yourself to the text of the communication and not to enter into its interpretation. Your Excellency should point out the following:

Barely a few hours after the declaration of war between Germany and the United States of America we had ostentatiously stated our solidarity and had

---

[1] The same instructions were sent to the Hungarian Minister to Italy with the omission of the allusion to Weizsäcker and to the Hungarians in the United States.

234

severed diplomatic relations. The Hungarian Government is convinced that we have fulfilled to the maximum what could be expected from us. Without delay we reached the conclusions hinted at by Weizsäcker to you.

If however they want to start a conversation regarding the interpretation of the Government's decision, the following should serve as guidance to Your Excellency's words, expressed as Your private opinion.

Having immediately declared our solidarity and having broken diplomatic relations we have done the maximum that could be expected from us. The Tripartite Pact does not oblige us to do more. The Pact mentioned only political, economic and military assistance. With the declaration of solidarity we gave full political support. Economically we are constantly aiding the Axis to our utmost. There could be no practical question of our military support against the United States.

I ask Your Excellency also to refer to the fact, that the Hungarian Government could not do more, since it would seriously imperil the fate of the nearly one million Hungarians living in the United States.

I emphatically ask your Excellency to maintain the above standpoint *for the time being as your own private opinion.*

In this respect it will be Your Excellency's task to secure acceptance of the above position in case of necessity.

Bárdossy

DOCUMENT 5

CIPHER INSTRUCTIONS SENT BY THE HUNGARIAN FOREIGN MINISTER, LASZLO BARDOSSY, TO THE HUNGARIAN MINISTER TO GERMANY, DOME SZTOJAY, ON DECEMBER 12, 1941, CONCERNING THE STATE OF WAR WITH THE UNITED STATES.[1]

Telephonecipher
Berlin

The Italian Envoy and the German Chargé d'Affaires have informed me this morning of the following:

The Axis Powers concluded from the aggresive acts committed against them that they were obliged to declare the existence of a state of war.

Since it has been established that Germany and Italy are the victims of aggression, in their opinion it is the duty of the states having signed the Tripartite Pact to declare the existence of a state of war. Hungary is among the signatory states. The Axis Powers attach great importance to the fact that this should happen, for reasons of higher political interests and as a demonstration of European solidarity.

I answered as follows:

We have already stated our solidarity with the Axis Powers yesterday. It is our opinion that we have thus fulfilled our obligations emanating from the Pact. In the following I have given the reasons mentioned in paragraph 5 of my cypher No. 337.

The Italian Envoy and the German Chargé d'Affaires in their answer have not contested the legal validity of our standpoint—without having admitted it. They pointed out, that the quick and spontaneous manifestation of our solidarity undoubtedly made a very good impression in Berlin and in Rome. Their in-

---

[1] The same instructions were sent to the Hungarian Minister to Italy.

structions were dated in Berlin and Rome at a time when the attitude of the Hungarian Government could not yet have been considered by their Governments, therefore they will ask their Governments for new instructions. Nonetheless, they emphatically called my attention to the fact that higher political reasons make it necessary that the European states should take a unanimous stand. If we were to maintain our original standpoint, it might easily happen that all the other states which have joined the Tripartite Pact would declare war and Hungary would remain alone with her declaration of solidarity.

I answered that in this case we would reconsider the situation.

I presume that Your Excellency has made communications in accordance with the cypher No. 337. If, in the Ministry for Foreign Affairs, they told Your Excellency that a declaration of war was considered absolutely necessary, I ask You to call on the Foreign Minister again, without awaiting further instructions, and inform him of the following:

The Hungarian government is convinced, that in declaring its solidarity it has fulfilled entirely its obligations emanating from the Tripartite Pact. The "declaration of solidarity", however, really means that in order to document the unity of the signatory parties in accordance with the spirit of the Pact, we are willing to take steps without legal obligations. Therefore, if all signatory powers to the Pact declare war, the Hungarian Government now authorizes the Governments of the Reich and the Kingdom of Italy to interpret our declaration of solidarity in this sense.

In order to avoid misunderstandings, please inform the Minister of Foreign Affairs that when the American Envoy asked me yesterday evening as to whether our decision meant a declaration of war, I answered according to our legal standpoint, that we have spontaneously and immediately declared our solidarity but that this did not mean a declaration of war for the time being. If all states signatory to the Pact declare war, we shall give such interpretation of our declaration of solidarity to the American Envoy in Budapest and to the Government in Washington.

I ask you to act most urgently. Try to find out what is known there of the attitude of the Bulgarian and Rumanian Governments. Report this via telefonecypher at once, so that I can make corrections accordingly to the American Envoy.

Bárdossy

DOCUMENT 6

NAZI PROPOSAL FOR ABSORPTION OF HUNGARY.[1]

[Typewritten draft for a memorandum. It is undated, but one page is written on the back of an unfinished letter dated 11 March, 1944]

(Handwritten corrections made to the original typewritten script by Krallert, Weneck, Kaltenbrunner, Flotte and Urban, are given in brackets with their initials, viz., Kr., W., K., & U., the crossed out phrase being underlined [italics].)

From the point of view of the Reich, an incorporation of the Hungarian

---

[1] *Nazi Conspiracy and Aggression,* Supplement A (Washington, 1947), pp. 908-913.

area as a fundamental part of the old Habsburg sphere of power is in the long run inadmissible.

This aim can be achieved by *force* (by intervention—K.), or as the result of an evolutionary process.

In spite of the extraordinary geopolitical and economic importance of Hungary for the Reich, German foreign policy has made no serious attempt during recent years to gain an influence on developments in Hungary *and to make use of this to attain the goal by means of evolutionary methods* (apart, perhaps, from direct personal endeavors by the Fuehrer to win Horthy over to the dismissal of Kallay and the elimination of the Bethlen influence.—K.)

Those Hungarians who look back, in the field of foreign policy, to a centuries-old tradition as a great power, incline fundamentally towards a conspiratorial policy. The complete lack of German attempts at influence has inevitably trained them to follow that policy of playing off one power against another which has now attained an intolerable character *as the "proofs" have clearly revealed.* (Underlining by W.)

(+) Instead of recognizing therein the necessity of seeking, in the numerous positive forces, bases for a solution which will both secure the total utilization of Hungarian potentialities for the prosecution of the war at the moment, and create for the future the prerequisites for the final aim striven for an attempt at a military solution by force now threatens. This will *by no means lead* (underlining by U.) to the complete fulfillment of the military and economic demands of the Reich in this area, and will, on the contrary, obstruct forever the road to an evolutionary development ((+) the whole paragraph is crossed out and the following substituted: I fear that the road to a future evolutionary development might be blocked by immediate military operations, without achieving for the present the seizure of the military and economic potentialities.—K.).

On the Hungarian side there stands against all this the fear of falling a victim to Bolshevism on the defeat of Germany, which is taken for granted. It is believed that the only way to exercise this danger is by an early adherence to the Anglo-American side. To this is added the deep dislike of the leading upper class towards us as the bearers of a social revolution which will, in the long run, make impossible the continuation of the feudal system of life in Hungary the beneficiary of which is this very upper class.

The consideration that a possible English intervention would have to be met in good time was one of the main reasons for the origination of the plan for a solution by force. (Indecipherable alterations have been made by K. and the whole paragraph has been struck out.)

Against this, I consider—for reasons arising from the geographical situation alone, the probability of an attempt at an invasion to be very slight. (Firstly, because of the geographical situation and then because of an undertaking so unpredictable does not tempt the English who are not minded to take risks.—K.) I believe, on the other hand, that the approach of Bolshevism will in itself soon make even those of the upper class forces which are inimical to us, ready to negotiate, out of despair of the possibility of English aid and out of fear of the even greater Bolshevist danger.

The vitally essential demands of the Reich in this area are now as follows:

(1) Complete exhaustion of all economic and especially agricultural resources in order to safeguard the basis of Germany's and Europe's food supply, in view of the loss of the Ukranian areas.

(2) Employment of all reserves of manpower for carrying on the war and

(3) Complete relaxation of tension, in order to set free the Rumanian troops also, for use on the Eastern front.

The military action will create the following state of affairs, especially in the event of participation by the Rumanians and Slovaks:

(1) A united defense front, such as has never been seen before—from the Communists to the Arrow and Cross party (Pfeilkreuzler).

(2) The impossibility of forming any government; at the most some mercenary persons would be found.

(3) Horthy's immediate resignation.

(4) Military, political and economic chaos. The country—one center of resistance, partisan activity on the greatest possible scale.

(5) And this point carries particularly great weight when the present German military situation is taken into consideration—numerous German divisions will be tied down for an unlimited period.

The desired aims will therefore not be attained. The carrying out of the military action at the time of the cultivation of the land in the spring, in itself decisively damages the prospects for the harvest. Ownership of large estates and the activity of Jewish middlemen, neither of which can be eliminated at short notice, will further lessen results. The partisan activity that can be expected for certain, finally destroys any hope of an increase in productivity.

The Hungarians have for centuries had experience in the organization of national resistance. Even the efforts of the old monarchy, which went on for twenty years, from 1848 to 1867, making use of all means of power, resulted in total failure. On the contrary, they decisively contribute to the creation and intensification of Hungarian national chauvinism. A recruitment of the Hungarian reserves of manpower for the German war effort is out of the question under these circumstances. On the other hand, continuous partisan warfare will ensue in the area occupied by us. As a result of the clash of the two opponents, warfare on a large scale would ensue in Transylvania and would presumably last a long time.

Even assuming the more advantageous case of a final Rumanian victory, the losses the Rumanians would have suffered and the necessity of suppressing northern Transylvania would make the employment of Rumanian troops in the East impossible for some months at least, if not permanently. We would, therefore, not see our present hopes fulfilled, would probably close the road to a later appeasement and final solution and would also evoke far-reaching reactions in the fields of strategy and of foreign politics. The zones of unrest created behind our enemies, with an operational intention, would be closed to form a belt reaching from the Adriatic to the Baltic Sea, if a mutinous Hungary and a Transylvania in a state of war were added to them. Simultaneously, we thereby cut those supply routes, the safe functioning of which is vitally necessary to the southern wing of the Eastern front. If the Soviet intention of cutting, one after another, the supply routes that run parellel to and and outside the Carpathians until the last railway line is cut, succeeds, then the supply lines through the Carpathian basin will alone be the basis for further resistance. But, also, those supply lines into the Balkans which are today the only safe ones and which would be vitally necessary in view *of the possibility of a war against Turkey or a* (of a—K.) *landing in the Balkans* (there—K.) would be endangered.

Almost equally important are presumably the political effects abroad. The German attitude on the Transylvanian question, once again executing a volte face, would entail such a loss of prestige even in friendly foreign countries that *no one could have faith in* (doubts would arise as to—K.) our ability and our will for a New Order in Europe. The effects *must be disastrous* (will be oppressive—K.) even in friendly nations such as Bulgaria, where it would be feared that a possible German agreement with the Serbs or Greeks might one day result again in the loss of Macedonia or Thrace. Thus we would drive the Bulgarians too into the arms of the Anglo-Americans *in the endeavor* (who will endeavor —K.) *to make it possible to retain* (to obtain a guarantee from them (Sewoff) —K.) the territories they have gained, by changing sides in time.

The effects to be expected in Finland, the Baltic States, etc., would be quite similar.

I am therefore convinced that the intended military *coercive measures* (intervention—K.) *will not only not* (will not necessarily—K.) attain *any of the* (the—K.) aims set, will create *new and unforseeable difficulties* (situations that are difficult to get a bird's eye view of—K.) in the fields of strategy and of foreign politics. A successful attempt at a new order on an evolutionary basis *on the other hand* (however—K.), would mean:

(1) An internally consolidated Hungary, friendly to Germany,

(2) Horthy's remaining in his position as a "historical" personality, who would continue to guarantee the functioning of the national institutions.

(3) The Honved and the security units would remain entirely in step and would thus be at the disposal of the Reich's military requirements.

(4) The total economic draining of the Hungarian area is fully guaranteed.

(5) The elimination of all arguments on Rumania's part that she needs troops in Transylvania, makes these troops available for the East, and can postpone the present Transylvanian problem to a later date by clever promises.

(6) Therefore, not only will Hungarian *and* Rumanian troops be gained, but numerous German divisions will be spared.

(7) A distribution of German troops throughout Hungary, which might become necessary for the purpose of security and against a British invasion, can be carried out unhindered, by means of troops in training, in the same way as has been done in Rumania.

These far reaching results can be attained by comparatively simple means.

The point of departure would have to be a personal message from the Fuehrer to Horthy who, as is known, *is* (has been—K.) always *most strongly* (strongly—K.) impressed by the personality of the Fuehrer. The go-between for this message could be a diplomat such as von Papen who is not only known as an honest broker, but who enjoys moreover the personal confidence of Horthy. This message would have to refer to the debit balance of the government (Kallay's—K.) which had been hostile to Germany and express the thought that the full employment of Hungary's potentialities for Germany's and Europe's aims could alone assure Hungary's future existence. The condition and the guarantee for the carrying out of these demands would have to be created by a complete change of regime (in any case with German occupation—K.). Following on this, the Regent will legalize *a new government on the broadest* (a broad —K.) *basis from the right wing of the Government throughout the Party for Hungarian Renewal and the Hungarian National Socialist Party to the Arrow and Cross Party* (Underlining by V.)

The Putsch-like carrying out of this change of government must be organized in such a manner that the entire public *remains unaware of the actual connections, as a result of the authoritative decision of the Regent* and that antagonistic forces do not get a chance to act. *The putting into effect of this plan is guaranteed by the existence of plenty of suitable personalities with whom we have close connections through my collaborators* (underlining by W).

(x) The most important of these men, who could take up leading parts in a new government, are:

Lieutenant-Fieldmarshal of the Reserve Ratz, a respected general who enjoys the confidence of the entire right wing opposition, and who seems certain to be acceptable to the Regent as Prime Minister.

Lieutenant-Fieldmarshal Ruszkay, a highly qualified soldier of pure German descent, who enjoys the very highest respect of the officer class, and who, on taking over the Honved Ministry, would be a certain guarantee that Hungary's military forces would stand unconditionally at the side of the Reich.

The former Prime Minister Imredy, a man of great qualities as an economic leader and financial expert, who meets with very great approval, particularly among the Hungarian intelligentsia.

Major General of the Reserve Baky (deputy—Kr), one of the organizers of the Hungarian gendarmerie, who are generally and quite rightly looked upon as being the surest instrument for peace and order, and who have, at the same time, always been entirely sympathetic to Germany.

A number of popular party leaders of the right wing, as well as acknowledged experts, would also immediately be at our disposal (passage from (x) sidelined by F.).

(+ +) *Conclusion.*

I dare say that such an attempt could, through my collaboration, bring about a government consisting of the above-named people within 3 days. The military undertaking (transports to the Eastern Front) will make its own contribution towards this. The Trojan method remains assured, but so does our good reputation as well.

The discussions taken down on the 13.3 did not even become a "D-day." It rests with the (?) and the "proofs"! (+ +—K.).

DOCUMENT 7

THE PROVISIONAL NATIONAL GOVERNMENT ELECTED BY THE PROVISIONAL NATIONAL ASSEMBLY ON DECEMBER 22, 1944.[1]

Prime Minister: Béla Dálnoki Miklós (non-party man)[2]
Minister of Interior: Dr. Ferenc Erdei (Peasant Party)[3]
Minister of Finance: Dr. István Vásáry (Smallholder Party)
Minister for Foreign Affairs: Dr. János Gyöngyösi (Smallholder Party)
Minister of Religion and Public Instruction: Count Géza Teleki (non-party man)[4]
Minister of National Defense: János Vörös (non-party man)[5]
Minister of Agriculture: Imre Nagy (Communist Party)[6]

---

[1] Foreign Minister Molotov presented the same list to the first Hungarian armistice delegation and to the Hungarian Generals on December 6, 1944.
[2] Former Commander-in-Chief of the First Hungarian Army.
[3] As it turned out later Ferenc Erdei was a crypto-Communist.
[4] Son of the late Prime Minister Count Paul Teleki, Professor of Geography and member of the first Hungarian armistice delegation. For a short period in 1945 President of the Civic Democratic Party.
[5] Chief of the General Staff until October 15, 1944.
[6] Muscovite Communist.

Minister of Trade and Transportation: József Gábor (Communist Party)[7]
Minister of Justice: Dr. Ágoston Valentiny (Social Democratic Party)
Minister of Industry: Ferenc Takács (Social Democratic Party)
Minister of Food Provision: Gábor Faraghó (non-party man)[8]
Minister of Social Welfare: Erik Molnár (presented as Social Democrat
   but professed himself Communist at the first Council of Ministers)

The apparent balance in the Cabinet between the parties was offset by the fact that Communists seized all the effective power positions. The Communist Party organized and controlled the police with the help of the crypto-Communist Minister of Interior. The Minister of Agriculture was a Communist in the critical period of the execution of the agrarian reform. The Communist Minister of Trade and Transportation was in charge of reorganization of the destroyed transportation and communication system. Thus the Communists exercised a tight control over the movement of persons and transportation throughout the country. This situation assured the Communists important advantages, particularly before the elections of 1945. The Communist Minister of Social Welfare could act as public benefactor. In contrast with the Communist advantages, the Smallholders obtained the Ministry of Finance with an empty treasury and many obligations, and the portfolio of the Foreign Ministry. The latter could have been important in Smallholder hands under normal conditions but the Armistice Agreement put foreign affairs under the guardianship of the ACC.

---

[7] József Gábor was replaced in April, 1945 by Ernö Gerö, the strong man of the Hungarian Communist Party. Both were Muscovites.
[8] Supervisor of the Hungarian Gendarmery until October 15, 1944, and a member of the first Hungarian armistice delegation. Previously he was military attaché in Moscow and published a strongly anti-Soviet book. Later in 1945 he entered the Smallholder Party.

DOCUMENT 8[1]

AGREEMENT

CONCERNING AN ARMISTICE BETWEEN THE UNION OF SOVIET SOCIALIST REPUBLICS, THE UNITED KINGDOM OF GREAT BRITAIN AND NORTHERN IRELAND, AND THE UNITED STATES OF AMERICA ON ONE HAND AND HUNGARY ON THE OTHER.

The Provisional National Government of Hungary, recognizing the fact of the defeat of Hungary in the war against the Soviet Union, the United Kingdom, the United States of America, and other United Nations, accepts the armistice terms presented by the Governments of the above-mentioned three powers, acting on behalf of all the United Nations which are in a state of war with Hungary.

On the basis of the foregoing the representative of the Allied (Soviet) High Command, Marshal of the Soviet Union K. E. Voroshilov, duly authorized thereto by the Governments of the Soviet Union, the United Kingdom, and the United States of America, acting on behalf of all the United Nations which are at war with Hungary, on the one hand and the representatives of the Provisional National Government of Hungary, Minister of Foreign Affairs Mister Gyöngyösi Janos, Minister of Defense Colonel General Vörös Janos and State Secretary of the Cabinet of Ministers Mister Balogh Istvan, on the other, holding proper full powers, have signed the following conditions:

---

[1] *Executive Agreement Series 456* (Washington, 1945).

1. (a) Hungary has withdrawn from the war against the Union of Soviet Socialist Republics and other United Nations, including Czechoslovakia, has severed all relations with Germany and has declared war on Germany.

(b) The Government of Hungary undertakes to disarm German armed forces in Hungary and to hand them over as prisoners of war.

The Government of Hungary also undertakes to intern nationals of Germany.

(c) The Government of Hungary undertakes to maintain and make available such land, sea and air forces as may be specified for service under the general direction of the Allied (Soviet) High Command. In this connection Hungary will provide not less than eight infantry divisions with corps troops. These forces must not be used on allied territory except with the prior consent of the allied government concerned.

(d) On the conclusion of hostilities against Germany, the Hungarian armed forces must be demobilized and put on a peace footing under the supervision of the Allied Control Commission. (See Annex to Article I.)

2. Hungary has accepted the obligation to evacuate all Hungarian troops and officials from the territory of Czechoslovakia, Yugoslavia, and Rumania occupied by her within the limits of the frontiers of Hungary existing on December 31, 1937, and also to repeal all legislative and administrative provisions relating to the annexation or incorporation into Hungary of Czechoslovak, Yugoslav and Rumanian territorry.

3. The Government and High Command of Hungary will ensure to the Soviet and other allied forces facilities for free movement on Hungarian territory in any direction if, in the opinion of the Allied (Soviet) High Command, the military situation requires this, the Government and High Command of Hungary giving such movement every possible assistance with their own means of communication and at their own expense on land, on water and in the air. (See Annex to Article 3.)

4. The Government of Hungary will immediately release all allied prisoners of war and internees. Pending further instructions the Government of Hungary will at its own expense provide all allied prisoners of war and internees, displaced persons and refugees, including nationals of Czechoslovakia and Yugoslavia, with adequate food, clothing, medical services, and sanitary and hygienic requirements, and also with means of transportation for the return of any such persons to their own country.

5. The Government of Hungary will immediately release, regardless of citizenship and nationality, all persons held in confinement in connection with their activities in favor of the United Nations or because of their sympathies with the United Nations' cause or for racial or religious reasons, and will repeal all discriminatory legislation and disabilities arising therefrom.

The Government of Hungary will take all necessary measures to ensure that all displaced persons or refugees within the limits of Hungarian territory, including Jews and stateless persons, are accorded at least the same measure of protection and security as its own nationals.

6. The Government of Hungary undertakes to return to the Soviet Union, and also to Czechoslovakia and Yugoslavia and to the other United Nations, by the dates specified by the Allied Control Commission, and in complete good order, all valuables and materials removed during the war to Hungary from United Nations' territory and belonging to state, public or cooperative organizations, enterprises, institutions or individual citizens, such as factory and works equip-

ment, locomotives, rolling stock, tractors, motor vehicles, historic monuments, museum treasures and any other property.

7. The Government and High Command of Hungary undertake to hand over as booty into the hands of the Allied (Soviet) High Command all German war material located on Hungarian territory, including vessels of the fleet of Germany.

8. The Government and High Command of Hungary undertake not to permit, without the authorization of the Allied Control Commission, the export or expropriation of any form of property (including valuables and currency) belonging to Germany or her nationals or to persons resident in German territory or in territories occupied by Germany. They will safeguard such property in the manner specified by the Allied Control Commission.

9. The Government and High Command of Hungary undertake to hand over to the Allied (Soviet) High Command all vessels belonging or having belonged to the United Nations which are located in Hungarian Danubian ports, no matter at whose disposal these vessels may be, for use during the period of the war against Germany by the Allied (Soviet) High Command in the general interests of the Allies, these vessels subsequently to be returned to their owners.

The Government of Hungary will bear full material responsibility for any damage or destruction of the aforementioned property until the moment of its transfer to the Allied (Soviet) High Command.

10. Hungarian merchant vessels, whether in Hungarian or foreign waters, shall be subject to the operational control of the Allied (Soviet) High Command for use in the general interests of the Allies.

11. The Government of Hungary will make regular payments in Hungarian currency and provide commodities (fuel, foodstuffs, et cetera), facilities and services as may be required by the Allied (Soviet) High Command for the fulfillment of its functions as well as for the needs of missions and representatives of the allied states connected with the Allied Control Commission.

The Government of Hungary will also assure, in case of need, the use and regulation of the work of industrial and transport enterprises, means of communication, power stations, enterprises and installations of public utility, stores of fuel and other material, in accordance with instructions issued during the armistice by the Allied (Soviet) High Command or the Allied Control Commission. (See Annex to Article 11.)

12. Losses caused to the Soviet Union, Czechoslovakia and Yugoslavia by military operations and by the occupation by Hungary of the territories of these states will be made good by Hungary to the Soviet Union, Czechoslovakia and Yugoslavia, but taking into consideration that Hungary has not only withdrawn from the war against the United Nations but has declared war against Germany, the parties agree that compensation for the indicated losses will be made by Hungary not in full but only in part; namely, to the amount of 300 million American dollars payable over six years in commodities (machine equipment, river craft, grain, livestock, et cetera), the sum to be paid to the Soviet Union to amount to 200 million American dollars and the sum to be paid to Czechoslovakia and Yugoslavia to amount to 100 million American dollars.

Compensation will be paid by Hungary for loss and damage caused by the war to other allied states and their nationals, the amount of compensation to be fixed at a later date. (See Annex to Article 12.)

13. The Government of Hungary undertakes to restore all legal rights and interests of the United Nations and their nationals on Hungarian territory as they existed before the war and also to return their property in complete good ordeɪ.

14. Hungary will cooperate in the apprehension and trial, as well as the surrender to the governments concerned, of persons accused of war crimes.

15. The Government of Hungary undertakes to dissolve immediately all pro-Hitler or other fascist political, military, para-military and other organizations on Hungarian territory conducting propaganda hostile to the United Nations and not to tolerate the existence of such organizations in future.

16. The publication, introduction and distribution in Hungary of periodical or non-periodical literature, the presentation of theatrical performances or films, the operation of wireless stations, post, telegraph and telephone services will take place in agreement with the Allied (Soviet) High Command. (See Annex to Article 16.)

17. Hungarian civil administration will be restored in the whole area of Hungary separated by not less than 50-100 kilometres (depending upon conditions of terrain) from the front line, Hungarian administrative bodies undertaking to carry out, in the interests of the reestablishment of peace and security, instructions and orders of the Allied (Soviet) High Command or Allied Control Commission issued by them for the purpose of securing the execution of these armistice terms.

18. For the whole period of the armistice there will be established in Hungary an Allied Control Commission which will regulate and supervise the execution of the armistice terms under the chairmanship of the representative of the Allied (Soviet) High Command and with the participation of representatives of the United Kingdom and the United States.

During the period between the coming into force of the armistice and the conclusion of hostilities against Germany, the Allied Control Commission will be under the general direction of the Allied (Soviet) High Command. (See Annex to Article 18.)

19. The Vienna Arbitration Award of November 2, 1938 and the Vienna Award of August 30, 1940 are hereby declared to be null and void.

20. The present terms come into force at the moment of their signing.

Done in Moscow 20 January, 1945, in one copy which will be entrusted to the safekeeping of the Government of the Union of Soviet Socialist Republics, in the Russian, English and Hungarian languages, the Russian and English texts being authentic.

Certified copies of the present agreement, with annexes, will be transmitted by the Government of the Union of Soviet Socialist Republics to each of the other governments on whose behalf the present agreement is being signed.

FOR	FOR
THE GOVERNMENTS OF THE UNION OF SOVIET SOCIALIST REPUBLICS, THE UNITED KINGDOM AND THE UNITED STATES OF AMERICA	THE PROVISIONAL NATIONAL GOVERNMENT OF HUNGARY
	GYONGYOSI JANOS
	VOROS JANOS
	BALOGH ISTVAN
K. VOROSHILOV	
/M. II./	/M. II./

ANNEX TO

"AGREEMENT CONCERNING AN ARMISTICE BETWEEN THE UNION OF SOVIET SOCIALIST REPUBLICS, THE UNITED KINGDOM OF GREAT BRITAIN AND NORTHERN IRELAND, AND THE UNITED

STATES OF AMERICA ON ONE HAND AND HUNGARY ON THE OTHER," SIGNED IN MOSCOW 20 JANUARY, 1945.

A. ANNEX TO ARTICLE 1.

The Hungarian Military Command shall hand over to the Allied (Soviet) High Command within a period fixed by the latter all the information at its disposal regarding the German armed forces and the plans of the German Military Command for the development of military operations against the Union of Soviet Socialist Republics and the other United Nations, and also the charts and maps and all operational documents relating to the military operations of the German armed forces.

The measures provided for in Article I of the Agreement regarding the internment of nationals of Germany now in Hungarian territory do not apply to nationals of that country of Jewish origin.

B. ANNEX TO ARTICLE 3.

The assistance specified in Article 3 of the Agreement shall be taken to mean that the Government and High Command of Hungary will place at the disposal of the Allied (Soviet) High Command, for use at its discretion during the armistice, in complete good order and with the personnel required for their maintenance, all Hungarian military, air and river fleet installations and buildings, ports, barracks, warehouses, airfields, means of communication and meteorological stations which might be required for military needs.

C. ANNEX TO ARTICLE 11.

The Government of Hungary will withdraw and redeem within such time limits and on such terms as the Allied (Soviet) High Command may specify, all holdings in Hungarian territory of currencies issued by the Allied (Soviet) High Command, and will hand over currency so withdrawn free of cost to the Allied (Soviet) High Command.

The Government of Hungary will not permit the disposal of external Hungarian assets or the disposal of internal Hungarian assets to foreign governments or foreign nationals without the permission of the Allied (Soviet) High Command or Allied Control Commission.

D. ANNEX TO ARTICLE 12.

The precise nomenclature and varieties of commodities to be delivered by Hungary to the Soviet Union, Czechoslovakia and Yugoslavia in accordance with Article 12 of the Agreement and also the more precise periods for making these deliveries each year shall be defined in special agreements between the respective governments. These deliveries will be calculated at 1938 prices with an increase of fifteen percent for industrial equipment and ten percent for other goods.

As the basis of calculation for payment of the indemnity foreseen in Article 12 of the Agreement, the American dollar is to be used at its gold parity on the day of signing of the agreement, i.e. thirty-five dollars to one ounce of gold.

In connection with Article 12 it is understood that the Government of Hungary will immediately make available certain food and other supplies required for relief and rehabilitation of the population of those Czechoslovak and Yugoslav territories which have suffered as a result of Hungarian aggression. The quantities of the products to be delivered will be determined by agreement between the three governments and will be considered as part of the reparation by Hungary for the loss and damages sustained by Czechoslovakia and Yugoslavia.

E. Annex to Article 16.

The Government of Hungary will ensure that wireless communication, telegraphic and postal correspondence, and correspondence in cipher and by courier, as well as telephonic communication with foreign countries, of embassies, legations and consulates situated in Hungary will be conducted in the manner laid down by the Allied (Soviet) High Command.

F. Annex to Article 18.

Control over the exact execution of the armistice terms will be entrusted to the Allied Control Commission to be established in conformity with Article 18 of the Armistice Agreement.

The Government of Hungary and its organs shall fulfill all instructions of the Allied Control Commission arising out of the armistice agreement.

The Allied Control Commission will set up special organs or sections entrusting them respectively with the execution of various functions. In addition, the Allied Control Commission may have its officers in various parts of Hungary.

The Allied Control Commission will have its seat in the city of Budapest. Moscow, 20 January, 1945.

DOCUMENT 9

ANNEX I TO THE POTSDAM PROTOCOL[1]
TEXT OF A LETTER TRANSMITTED ON JULY 12 TO THE REPRESENTATIVES OF THE U. S. AND U. K. GOVERNMENTS ON THE ALLIED CONTROL COMMISSION IN HUNGARY.

In view of the changed situation in connection with the termination of the war against Germany, the Soviet Government finds it necessary to establish the following order of work for the Allied Control Commission in Hungary.

1. During the period up to the conclusion of peace with Hungary the President (or Vice-President) of the ACC will regularly call conferences with the British and American representatives for the purpose of discussing the most important questions relating to the work of the ACC. The conferences will be called once in 10 days, or more frequently in case of need.

Directives of the ACC on questions of principle will be issued to the Hungarian authorities by the President of the Allied Control Commission after agreement on these directives with the English and American representatives.

2. The British and American representatives in the ACC will take part in general conferences of heads of divisions and delegates of the ACC, convoked by the President of the ACC, which meetings will be regular in nature. The British and American representatives will also participate personally or through their representatives in appropriate instances in mixed commissions created by the President of the ACC for questions connected with the execution by the ACC of its functions.

3. Free movement by the American and British representatives in the country will be permitted provided that the ACC is previously informed of the time and route of the journeys.

4. All questions connected with permission for the entrance and exit of members of the staff of the British and American representatives in Hungary will be decided on the spot by the President of the ACC within a time limit of not more

---

[1] *A Decade of American Foreign Policy, Basic Documents*, 1941-49 (Washington, 1950), pp. 47-48.

than one week.

5. The bringing in and sending out by plane of mail, cargoes and diplomatic couriers will be carried out by the British and American representatives on the ACC under arrangements and within time limits established by the ACC, or in special cases by previous coordination with the President of the ACC.

I consider it necessary to add to the above that in all other points the existing Statutes regarding the ACC in Hungary, which was confirmed on January 20, 1945, shall remain in force in the future.

DOCUMENT 10
NOTE OF THE HUNGARIAN GOVERNMENT TO THE BRITISH, SOVIET AND UNITED STATES GOVERNMENTS CONCERNING THE EXPULSION OF THE GERMANS FROM HUNGARY.
Hungarian Ministry for Foreign Affairs

130/res.—Bé.
1945
Sir,

Certain news items published in the Press indicate that those competent to settle the problems of Central-Europe are misinformed about the number of Germans in Hungary and, what is more, about the number of Germans who may be expatriated from Hungary under the principles adopted by the victorious Great Powers. For this reason the Hungarian Government consider it as their obligation to inform His Britannic Majesty's Government about the following:

Census figures of 1941 indicate that the number of people of German vernacular on the territory of Hungary amounted to 477,057, while those of German nationality amounted to 303,419.

The difference between the two figures is considerable and due to the fact that amongst those of German vernacular were numerous elements of Jewish or non-German descents; moreover many of German descent and German vernacular entered their name on the census sheets as being of Hungarian nationality. This latter attitude meant their definitive rupture with Germanism and open confession on the side of Hungary in 1941, the heyday of German victories, just in the period of increasing German pressure and terror. Indeed, there is a considerable number of people of German descent and German vernacular who were willing to share the fate of Hungarians even in the period of the severest German oppression, many of them having participated also in the resistance movement of the democratic parties. And, indeed, while the special procedure undertaken in order to investigate the political reliability of Germans was under way, it was proven that in most cases only those can be penalized who gave confession of their being of German nationality.

Investigation of the German population as to their national loyalty takes place by means of district committees formed especially for that purpose under decree no. 3820/1945. M.E.

These district committees, after having taken into consideration the local conditions, and after a thorough and scrupulous pondering of all available data relating to the general attitude and individual status of persons under investigation, may ascertain the following facts:

1. They may ascertain that the person under investigation played a leading part in some Hitlerite organization, or by his own will joined an *SS* formation (par. 1., art. 4.).

2. They may ascertain that the person under investigation was a simple mem-

247

ber of a Hitlerite organization (par. 2., art. 3.).

3. They may ascertain that the person under investigation, although not being a member of any Hitlerite organization, still supported its aims (par. 3., art. 4.).

4. They may ascertain that the person under investigation was neither a leader, nor a member or supporter of any Hitlerite organization (par. 4., art. 4.).

Besides that, they may establish under art. 6 of the decree that certain persons of German nationality gave testimony of their patriotism and democratic spirit in spite of Hitlerite terror.

30,000 out of the total 303,000 persons of German nationality are living in towns, so that the investigation undertaken by the district committees affects 273,-000 persons living in villages. Investigation returns from 96 communities indicate that 10% of the village population of German nationality were *Volksbund* leaders or *SS* soldiers, 28% members of the *Volksbund* or the *Hitler Jugend*, 32% supporters of the *Volksbund*, and 30% had no connection whatsoever with the *Volksbund*. Estimates in accordance with these data make it probable that 38% of the Swabian nationality, that is 103,000 persons, are to be punished by confiscation of their property under decree no. 3820/1945. M. E. As it is well known, this number comprises the members and leaders of Hitlerite organizations. Even adding to this figure the Germans having supported the *Volksbund*, the number of Germans to be expatriated will hardly exceed 200,000. Considering the fact that the most compromised Germans, and especially a considerable part of the German male population, left the territory of the country together with the beaten German army, it seems to be probable that 200,000 to 250,000 will prove to be a realistic estimate of the German population to be expatriated, as it has been intimated in the note of the 26th May, 1945 addressed by the Hungarian Government to the Government of the Soviet Union.

The Government of democratic Hungary avail themselves of this opportunity to state that it would be contrary to their conviction that Hungarian citizens should be expatriated solely on account of their ethnic origin. They are averse to this as well as to any kind of collective punishment. For this reason they consider it desirable that only those Germans should be expatriated who were manifest traitors to the cause of Hungary by their attitude of having served Hitlerism. The expatriation of these people is, however, considered to be absolutely necessary by the Hungarian Government, and they have the honour to request it, since this would be one of the pledges that German spirit and German oppression shall never be able to dominate this country again.

I avail myself of this opportunity to express to You, Sir, the assurance of my high consideration.

Budapest, December 1st, 1945.
(signed) Gyöngyösi.[1]

---

[1] Identical notes were sent to the United States and Soviet Political Representatives.

DOCUMENT 11
NOTE VERBALE OF THE HUNGARIAN FOREIGN MINISTRY TO THE BRITISH AND UNITED STATES POLITICAL MISSIONS IN BUDAPEST CONCERNING THE EXPULSION OF THE GERMANS FROM HUNGARY.

139/res.—Bé.
1945.
Budapest, December 15th, 1945.

Note Verbale.

The Hungarian Government present their compliments to His Britannic Majesty's Government and have the honour to communicate the following:

According to the point of view expressed repeatedly by the Hungarian Government up to the present, only those Germans were to be transferred to Germany who had joined the *Volksbund* or the *SS*, or who committed in the course of the war, an act of disloyalty against Hungary. The Government never planned, however, a transfer based on the mere fact of German origin, or speaking German as the mother tongue, which would mean a removal equalling collective punishment.

Considering, however, that from certain news items published in the press one could draw the conclusion that the Allied Powers are planning to oblige Hungary to remove 500,000 Germans, the Hungarian Government have the honour to request the kind communication of His Britannic Majesty's Goverment's ultimate position concerning this question.

Note No. 130/res/Be of the Hungarian Ministry for Foreign Affairs dated December 1st 1945, contains detailed particulars regarding the number of Germans in Hungary.

L. S.[1]

---

[1] An identical note was sent to the American Political Mission in Budapest.

DOCUMENT 12

MEMORANDUM OF THE UNITED STATES MISSION IN BUDAPEST CONCERNING THE TRANSFER OF NATIONAL MINORITIES IN CZECHOSLOVAKIA.[1]

In a note to the Government of that Republic in January of the current year the preliminary views held by the Government of the United States regarding the expulsion of Germans from the Czechoslovak Republic were expressed along the following lines:

1. Not only the needs of Czechoslovakia but also considerations of a general nature affecting future European peace and security, especially including the problems with which the occupation authorities of the Allies are faced in Germany, must be taken into account in solving this problem.

2. Minorities should only be transferred under the principles of international justice and in pursuance of international arrangements appropriate to that end.

3. In order to facilitate the settlement of transferred persons in an orderly way, they should be transferred by gradual processes.

4. No one nation should take action to effect the transfer of large groups of human beings pending the conclusion of international arrangements as above advocated.

The principles set forth in the note above mentioned to the Government of the Czechoslovak Republic are considered by the United States as being no less applicable with regard to the expulsion of minorities of Hungarian-speaking people from Rumania or Yugoslavia as well as Czechoslovakia.

The Governments of those states are primarily concerned with the matter of responsibility of these Hungarians for crimes against the state of which such Hungarians are citizens. The United States, however, would not consider it justified to deal with all members of an ethnic group who constitute a minority as criminals against the state and as subject to expulsion from its territory, only because of their ethnic origin.

It will be recalled that in the matter of the proposed organization of an international military court which will try major war criminals in Europe, the

---

[1] *Hungary and the Conference of Paris,* Vol. II, pp. 4-5.

Government of the United States proposed that a procedure be adopted which would make certain both a speedy and a just trial of important individuals and organizations who stand accused of war crimes and atrocities in European countries. The Government of the United States is not disposed to consider as included among such organizations entire minority groups of a single racial origin. On May 21, 1945, the Minister for Foreign Affairs of the Czechoslovak Republic who was then at San Francisco, California, said that punishment would be imposed only upon Hungarians who had conspired against the Czechoslovak Republic and who had fought on the side of the Nazis, but that those Hungarians who had shown friendliness to the cause of Czechoslovakia might remain in that country with the full rights of citizens of that Republic.

It may be added, that when reference is made in the foregoing to the Hungarian minorities it is not intended to include recent immigrants and displaced persons but only permanent residents of the countries mentioned belonging to the Hungarian-speaking group.

Budapest, June 12th, 1945.

DOCUMENT 13
REPLY OF THE UNITED STATES GOVERNMENT TO VARIOUS HUNGARIAN PROPOSALS CONCERNING THE PROBLEMS OF THE HUNGARIANS IN CZECHOSLOVAKIA.[1]

Legation of the United States of America.   Budapest, Hungary, February 9, 1946

Mr. Minister,

I have the honor to refer to Your Excellency's Notes No. 120/res.-Be. of November 20, 1945 and No. 133/res.-Be., of December 11, 1945, in the matter of the Hungarian-Czechoslovak minority question and to inform Your Excellency, by instruction of my Government, in reply to those Notes as follows:

1. In present circumstances the Government of the United States does not consider feasible the formation of an international commission to examine the Hungarian-Czechoslovak minority problem or to supervise any exchange of population.

2. The Government of the United States cannot support a request for the establishment of international control of the districts inhabited by Hungarians in Slovakia.

3. The Government of the United States will recognize and support a humane settlement freely agreed to between the Governments of Hungary and the Czechoslovak Republic.

I take this opportunity to renew to Your Excellency the assurance of my highest consideration.

(Signed) H. F. Arthur Schoenfeld.

His Excellency
M. János Gyöngyösi,
Minister for Foreign Affairs.

---

[1] *Hungary and the Conference of Paris,* Vol. II, pp. 53-54.

DOCUMENT 14
REPLY OF THE BRITISH GOVERNMENT TO THE VARIOUS HUNGARIAN PROPOSALS CONCERNING THE PROBLEMS OF THE HUNGARIANS IN CZECHOSLOVAKIA.[1]

British Political Mission in Hungary.   Budapest, March 19, 1946.
No. 45 (4/73/46).

Your Excellency,

DOCUMENTS

I have the honour to refer to your communications No. 61/res.-Be. dated 14 September, No. 120/res.-Be. dated 20 November and No. 133/res.-Be. dated 11 December, 1945, regarding the Magyar minorities in Slovakia in which Your Excellency put forward a proposal that an international commission should be appointed to investigate the problems under dispute between the Hungarian and Czechoslovakian Governments and that, pending the appointment of such a Commission, the districts of Slovakia inhabited by Hungarians should be placed under international control. In the above communications it was also suggested that should exchanges of population be impossible, the transfer of Hungarians from Czechoslovakia to Hungary should be effected by the cession of the Czechoslovak territory in which the Hungarian minority resides.

2. The views expressed by Your Excellency on behalf of the Hungarian Government have been carefully considered by His Majesty's Government and I now have the honour, by direction from His Majesty's Principal Secretary of State for Foreign Affairs, to inform you that His Majesty's Government would be unwilling to participate in any international commission for the examination of the problem of Hungarian minorities in Czechoslovakia or for the supervision of any Czechoslovak-Hungarian exchange of population on the lines proposed by the Hungarian Government. His Majesty's Government are of the opinion that this question should be settled on a bilateral basis between the two Governments concerned. Further, they would not be prepared to try to persuade the Czechoslovakian Government to agree to any frontier rectification in favour of Hungary though they would not withhold recognition of any changes freely agreed to between the two countries concerned.

3. His Majesty's Government have taken note of the agreement recently negotiated in Prague for the exchange of population and I am instructed to inform Your Excellency that this development confirms His Majesty's Government in their view that the best method of making progress in this problem is by direct negotiation between the two interested parties.

I have the honour to avail myself of this opportunity to renew to Your Excellency the assurance of my high consideration.

(Signed) W. Mitchel Carse

His Excellency   Acting British Political Representative
M. Gyöngyösi,
Hungarian Minister for Foreign Affairs.

---

[1] *Hungary and the Conference of Paris,* Vol. II, pp. 54-55.

DOCUMENT 15
THE SPIRIT OF HUNGARY.[1]
LEADERS' EFFORTS TO ESTABLISH DEMOCRATIC STATE.
A REAL IF UNEASY COALITION.

Any British visitor's estimate of the present state of Hungary must depend on the direction from which he arrives in the country. If he comes straight from London to Budapest he will be depressed by the war damage, the economic hardships, and the general uncertainty. But if (like your Correspondent) he comes from Rumania he will have just the contrary impression. He will note the energy with which the people of Budapest are rebuilding their city. He can buy newspapers and periodicals expressing widely different opinions on controversial subjects. Above all he will be surprised by the vigorous intel-

---

[1] Excerpts from an article published in *London Times,* October 31, 1946.

lectual activity displayed both in print and in conversation. In comparison with the mental sterility and haunting fear prevalent in the Balkans, Hungary seems an oasis of culture and liberty.

This comparison is essential for an understanding of the Danubian situation as a whole. It should not, however, be taken to mean that Hungary has not her troubles. In fact she is faced with grave problems in internal politics, in economic life, and in foreign policy.

The Hungarian Government is a coalition, and, unlike Rumania and Bulgaria, a real coalition. . . .

It cannot be said that the coalition is working smoothly. There is constant friction in big and small matters. . . . The Communists and Small Farmers exchange accusations and insults in public. It is frequently said that "this cannot last" and yet somehow it has lasted, and may well last a long time yet. Neither the left block nor the Small Farmers are confident of their ability to rule alone. Reconstruction needs the united efforts of all. In the last resort almost every one prefers the present situation to a breach.

. . . The parties of the left, though feared by many Hungarians as aggressors, consider themselves on the defensive. . . .

In contrast to Rumania and the Southern Slav countries, it can be said of Hungary that, in spite of difficulties and mistakes, a real attempt is being made to build a democracy capable of maintaining friendship with both the Soviet Union and the Anglo-Saxon Powers. Whether it will succeed will depend, at least in part, on the west.

DOCUMENT 16

MEMORANDUM OF THE HUNGARIAN NATIONAL BANK ON HUNGARY'S REPARA-
TIONS, PREPARED FOR THE CONFIDENTIAL INFORMATION OF THE
BRITISH AND UNITED STATES MISSIONS IN BUDAPEST.

The pengo equivalent of the 300 million United States dollars of reparations to be paid by Hungary over a period of six years is equal to 1,400 million pengos on the basis of the 1938 parity, with small adjustments for price variations in the meantime. Of this, the reparations to the Soviet Union account for 933 million 1938 pengos (in the following pages, "pengos" are, in every case, to be taken as 1938 pengos). In estimating the actual burden which this represents, however, the following facts must be taken into consideration:

1. In valuing the goods to be delivered as reparations, the Soviet commission took world prices as the basis, and not Hungarian prices, which were much higher. In consequence of this the cost of producing or purchasing the goods to be delivered is in fact 2,000 million 1938 pengos.

2. The difficult conditions of delivery increase this sum by 15% to 20%.

3. The burden is greatly increased by the very heavy interest payable in goods in the event of deliveries being delayed—a possibility which must be taken into consideration in the present state of the country's productive capacity. This interest is *five per cent per month*.

With the additional charges which these factors represent the total value of the deliveries to be made to the Soviet Union may well be in the neighborhood of 2,500 million pengos. If the same calculation is applied to those for Czechoslovakia and Yugoslavia, the total reparations payable by Hungary must be taken as between 3,000 and 3,500 million pengos, or 500 to 584 millions a year, which represents between 19 and 22 per cent of the present national income.

In addition to this however there are the other services laid down in the Armistice Agreement. Under Clause 11 Hungary has to make payments and render services to the Soviet army and pay for the expenses of the Allied Control Commission, which are calculated at 238 million pengos a year. Under paragraph 2 of Clause 12 there is also compensation for the other Allied states and their nationals. Clause 13 provides that the legal rights and interests of the United Nations and their nationals on Hungarian territory are to be restored and their property returned in complete good order. It is at present impossible to express the value of this obligation in figures. There are, further, the country's pre-war foreign debts, which may be estimated today at about 2,300 million Swiss francs.

If Hungary is to make these payments and also effect any measure of reconstruction, the standard of living, which is already low, will be reduced to a disastrous level. The national income, which has already shrunk from the 1938/39 figure of 572 pengos to 289 pengos per head, would be further reduced by another 89 pengos. And the very heavy requirements of reconstruction would have to be met out of this national income of 200 pengos per head.

Even if these reparations, payments, and services did not have to be made, the present agricultural production of the country is insufficient to feed the population properly. The bread-cereals harvest was exceptionally poor, as a result of which we have only 6.2 million quintals of grain available instead of the normal requirements of 17.2 millions, and even if 6 million quintals of maize are used to replace it, there is still a clear deficit of 5 million quintals. There has been a very severe decline in animal products as well, owing to 60 to 70 per cent of the country's livestock having been lost. Even if the comparatively low requirements of the population are taken as the basis, there is a deficiency of 35.8% in calories, 16.4% in proteins, 64.9% in fats and 28% in carbohydrates. It is however, inevitable that the agrarian population will retain rather more than the average quota, so that the daily calory ration of the urban population will probably average 1,478 instead of 1,766, whereas the League of Nations puts the standard at 3,080. This situation would suffer a further serious deterioration if fats and cereals have also to be delivered as reparations or for the supplies of the Red Army. It further entails a dangerous diminution in output per worker and will to work, and if carried further may well end in the complete crippling of economic life.

The industrial goods to be delivered as reparations, the industrial exports necessary to obtain the raw materials for their manufacture, and the investments needed to get reparations production started up, if taken all together amount to very nearly the total value of the production of industry, 525 million pengos (without the foodstuffs industry). At the present level, reparations would mean that there is hardly anything left for home demand. Yet the latter cannot be left unsatisfied; if only 20 per cent of the pre-war figure is applied to the population's requirement of industrial goods, 200 million pengos' worth of the latter are required. It must be noted that if the farmers cannot be supplied with certain industrial goods, it is almost impossible to get them to part with their produce. There are, however, two other forms of demand which cannot be neglected in industrial production: reconstruction and exports. Unless the farmers can be provided with the agricultural implements and machinery that they require, unless transport and communications can be restored, and unless the industrial equipment which has been destroyed can be replaced, there is the danger of a further fall in production. If there are no exports of industrial products, it is impossible to obtain the foreign raw materials which are needed for production and reconstruction, because this is very largely a task for industry now that agricultural exports have necessarily fallen off. Our factory production is today barely 35 per cent of what it was before the war, and not even the surviving proportion of industrial capacity can be utilized to the full. The decline is caused by the exhaustion of stocks of raw materials, the difficulties of obtaining supplies, an insufficiency of labour and a fall in output per worker. If the causes of these difficulties are examined, it will be found that in most cases the food situation, transport and the inflation are at the back of the trouble.

The effect of reparations on the finances of the country may best be illustrated by the fact that reparations would absorb between 19 and 22 per cent of the national income, or if the expenditure for supplies for the Red Army is included, *31 per cent of it.* The fact that budget revenue in the years before the war did not take even 20 per cent of the national income will show that the above-mentioned burdens alone claim a higher proportion of the national income than the State could obtain before the war through taxation and the receipts of the various ministries. At the same time it should be noted that as a result of various causes the State is at present unable to cover more than a very small proportion of its own requirements by means of revenue. Whatever may be effected, however, in the way of improving the budget situation, until production can be increased very substantially, reparations and the other services due from Hungary can only be covered by the use of the bank note printing press.

Although it cannot be expected that the country would be freed at one stroke from its economic and financial troubles by a mere relief from reparations, there can be no doubt that if a temporary moratorium were given there would be the possibility, if every endeavour were made, for the country to attend to the economic and financial situation on the basis of a well-thought-out plan.

In view of the foregoing, it would seem unconditionally necessary for a reparations moratorium of at least two or three years, and further for an assurance that the country will be relieved of the duty of providing for the supplies of the army of occupation, which is at present estimated at one million men.

In addition to reparations, the other obligations of the country (service of pre-war foreign debts and restitution of Allied assets in the country) should be established *jointly and after consideration of the country's economic capacity.* If this principle were put into practice the probable result would be that there would be no foreign payments for a temporary period of two or three years; but during that time a degree of reconstruction could be achieved which would enable Hungary to begin the service of her foreign obligations without undue strain on the means of production.

(signed) Arthur Kárász
President of the Hungarian National Bank

Budapest, November 24th, 1945.

DOCUMENTS

DOCUMENT 17

EXCERPTS FROM THE MINUTES OF THE MEETING (No. 59) OF THE COUNCIL
OF MINISTERS HELD ON OCTOBER 12, 1945, UNDER THE CHAIRMANSHIP
OF PRIME MINISTER BELA DALNOKI MIKLOS.[1]

Present were:
Dr. Ferenc Erdei, Minister of Interior
Dr. Imre Oltványi, Minister of Finance was represented by Secretary of State,
Loránd Dabasi-Schweng
János Gyöngyösi, Minister of Foreign Affairs
János Vörös, Minister of Defense
Count Géza Teleki, Minister of Religion and Public Instruction
Imre Nagy, Minister of Agriculture
Ernö Gerö, Minister of Commerce and Transportation
Antal Bán, Minister of Industry
Ferenc Nagy, Minister of Reconstruction
Dr. Eric Molnár, Minister of Public Welfare
Dr. Sándor Rónai, Minister of Food Provisions
Dr. István Ries, Minister of Justice
Dr. István Balogh, Political Secretary of State to the Prime Minister
Dr. Gyula Kállay, Political Secretary of State to the Prime Minister
Dr. Ernö Bojta, Administrative Secretary of State to the Prime Minister, and
recorder of the meetings of the Council of Ministers

The Prime Minister opens the meeting of the Council and asks Dr. István
Balogh, Secretary of State, to make a declaration on his behalf.

Dr. István Balogh explains that the topic of this special session of the Council
of Ministers is the Soviet-Hungarian agreement on economic cooperation. He recalls that the Council of Ministers authorized the Minister of Commerce and
Transportation and the Minister of Industry to negotiate a trade agreement with
the Soviet Government. The majority of the Council of Ministers was of the
opinion that the named ministers were not authorized to sign any agreement other
than the trade agreement. The standpoint of the Prime Minister was that the
Provisional National Government could not assume responsibilities committing the
country's economy for five years or more. Since the Prime Minister felt that the
Provisional National Government had power only for temporary solutions and not
for such far-reaching basic agreements, the Minister of Commerce and Transportation submitted the text of the Economic Cooperation Agreement to the members
of the Cabinet and to the coalition parties. Thus all interested authorities are familiar with the text. The Prime Minister, on his part, recommends ratification of
the Agreement on economic cooperation signed by the two aforementioned ministers.

He is making this recommendation because the Soviet Union respects the
political independence of Hungary and does not intend to exert political influence. Besides, we are compelled to accept the Agreement due to overwhelming
circumstances. According to our experience the Soviet Union shows great understanding towards us and gives help wherever we need it, and never used political
pressure to impair our independence. If this were not the case the Soviet Union
could simply dismantle and remove all German properties which were turned over
to her by the Potsdam Agreement. According to the terms of the economic co-

---

[1] Count Géza Teleki gave the Hungarian text of these minutes to General
William Key, American representative in the ACC and to A.D.F. Gascoigne,
British political representative, on October 13, 1945.

operation agreement the Soviet Union would supply Hungary with badly needed raw materials. So far Hungary has not received any such promise from the Western powers. The agreement is helpful in connection with reparations. On the other hand if we would refuse ratification this would be an expression of mistrust towards the Soviet Union, and we would receive no favors from her. If we take into consideration the economic situation in the country a revolution would very probably be forthcoming in the spring. Therefore, he proposes ratification of the Economic Cooperation Agreement by the appropriate authorities and the *ex-post facto* vindication of the two ministers who signed the agreement in Moscow.

Nevertheless, the two following reservations are to be included in the covering letter in order to dispell the anxiety of the Hungarian public:

(1) The Contracting Parties declare that the Economic Cooperation Agreement is not exclusive in character towards the United States or any other countries.

(2) The Contracting Parties declare that the present Agreement concerns primarily those German properties which could be seized in Hungary by the Soviet Union in accordance with the Potsdam Agreement.

He wishes to note, however, that the Agreement could not be limited exclusively to German goods since the Soviet Union has a free hand as far as these properties are concerned; but the term "primarily" might give some comfort to the public.

Prime Minister: The essential thing is that the rights of the other nations notably those of the United Nations are not affected by the agreement.

Secretary Balogh: This is expressed sufficiently in the covering letter.

Prime Minister: The representatives of the political parties should make a statement concerning their stand on the matter.

Minister of Interior: He accepts the agreement in his own name, but he does not know the stand of the Peasant Party.

Minister of Reconstruction: Accepts the agreement in the name of the Smallholder's Party with the reservations included in the covering letter.

Prime Minister: He thinks it necessary that the Minister of Commerce and Transportation give detailed information about the Agreement.

Minister of Commerce and Transportation: He thinks that he gave detailed information when he submitted the Agreement to the Council of Ministers for the first time. He is convinced that he and the Minister of Industry were fully authorized to sign the Agreement. He points out that this is not a special Hungarian matter because Rumania and Bulgaria already have concluded such agreements with the Soviet Union. Thus it seems to be advantageous for Hungary to attain the same position. Moreover, when he signed the Agreement he was greatly influenced by the information concerning the Potsdam Agreement which had transformed German property into Soviet property. It is also important to consider that our economic position is very bad and obviously will be worse in winter. We are getting important material for the welfare of the public within the framework of the trade agreement, but it is not everything that we need. We can get certain material only through economic cooperation. For example, materials necessary for the production of aluminum can be obtained only from the Soviet Union. We have to consider that we can obtain certain favors through economic cooperation. We hardly have any rolling stock and means of transportation. These problems can be solved only through close cooperation. Another consideration was that a general world economic crisis is imminent. In this event we cannot remain without a secure market. It is a well-known fact that the great economic crisis of fifteen years ago was delayed in Germany for one year due to a Soviet order of 900 million marks. Later when political conditions changed in Germany and the Soviet cancelled their German orders and gave them to England, the result was that the economic crisis did not reach such depths in Britain as elsewhere. If we safeguard our economy against such a crisis we can overcome the difficulties. We must do everything not to weaken still further our capacity to produce. The Agreement is not of an exclusive nature. If we receive similar offers from other countries there is no obstacle to our accepting them. Therefore, it was the right thing to conclude the Agreement. The Council of Ministers in its decision should consider the interests of the country.

Minister of Industry: The political committee of the Social Democratic Party accepted the agreement, and, he himself, shares their views.

Minister of Foreign Affairs: Declares that he accepts the agreement in his own name as well as in the name of the Minister of Finance. He emphasizes this, because it is important that the agreement be accepted by all members of the Government. He shares the views of Secretary Balogh concerning the non-exclusive character of the agreement. Therefore, the first reservation of the covering letter is superfluous but it is still useful to dispel apprehensions. The essential thing is to give a proper political meaning to the agreement. As to the second reservation, he heard it now for the first time, and thus he could not discuss it with Envoy Pushkin. In his opinion it has no practical meaning. The Soviet Union wishes to make financial investments and to cooperate on a 50-50% basis at the most but by no means as a major partner.

This proportion means the establishment of common enterprises. This is a favor in the case of enterprises which were German properties and this favor leads us to conclude that the maximum Soviet ownership will be 50%, and possibly be even less.

Minister of Reconstruction: States that the Foreign Minister is not well informed because the Smallholders Party considers the second reservation important. A few members of the Cabinet negotiated directly with Marshal Voroshilov and Envoy Pushkin and both reservations were discussed with them. Thus they are not uninformed. One has to take into consideration the apprehension of the public, and this is expressed in the two reservations.

Minister of Foreign Affairs: Does not intend to raise difficulties and submits himself to the decision of the Smallholder Party. But he had to mention that he heard the second reservation for the first time.

Minister of Reconstruction: We gratefully and kindly accept the Agreement, but we have to clearly dispel the anxiety of the people.

Minister of Foreign Affairs: The covering letter is unimportant. The essential thing is the ratification of the agreement.

Minister of National Defense: His standpoint is that some provisions of the agreement are urgent and are to be executed immediately. Other provisions clearly fall under the jurisdiction of the government to be duly elected. The Provisional Government should not assume obligations for future governments, and should decide only urgent questions such as the liquidation of the German properties. The other problems should be left to the succeeding government which will have the responsibility for the execution of the agreement.

Secretary Balogh: Such apprehensions would be justified only if we would sign a detailed agreement binding for decades. But, the agreement is only a framework, a gesture, the expression of a trend. Its conclusion is definitely within the jurisdiction of the Provisional Government. A treaty to be concluded with the Soviet Union could make us an equal partner before the peace negotiations. We would have had similar desires towards other Governments as well, but we must accept such a helping hand in the interest of Hungary. Besides, he was informed that the negotiations on details would take place in Budapest. Thus, the entire government will have the opportunity to look into the matter.

Prime Minister: It should be left to us as to what extent we execute the agreements.

Minister of Commerce and Transportation: The agreement contains only principles, it is not binding for details.

Prime Minister: Thus, we can accept it with the reservations included in the covering letter.

Minister of Foreign Affairs: The agreement will make it possible that part of the goods to be removed from Germany, as properties of the Soviet Union, could be used in Hungary.

Minister of Defense: Recognizes the loyalty of the Soviet Union, but he still thinks that there is a difference between the questions to be executed by the Provisional Government and those to be executed by the new duly-elected Government. The liquidation of the German properties is clearly within the jurisdiction of the Provisional Government, and this is an important question for Hungarian industry. Other problems should be dealt with later. All governments are criticized later and usually the previous governments are blamed.

Minister of Foreign Affairs: This is a highly exaggerated view; after all, we may rightly consider ourselves better than the government of Szálasi.

Minister of National Defense: If this is considered as a joke I am obliged to leave the session of the council.

(The Minister of Defense walks out and his place is taken by the secretary of state in the Ministry of Defense, István B. Szabo.)

Minister of Religion and Public Instruction: He is not versed enough in economic questions to fully appreciate the implications and repercussions of the problem; however, he wishes to state his own opinion in the light of his recent experiences in economics and constitutional law. He considers that the conclusion and ratification of such an Agreement is not within the jurisdiction of the Provisional National Government. A National Assembly which was not duly elected, and a government formed under the known circumstances would give the impression that the Government wants to bind the interests of the Nation in one direction. In view of the fact that an ACC has been functioning in Hungary he raises the question as to whether the two other members of the ACC consider the conclusion of the Agreement appropriate and as to whether they have made a declaration to this effect. The fate of a nation does not depend on a winter; economic survival is not the primary question; political existence and independence are vital. He wonders whether we asked for the opinion of the two other members of the ACC, in order to get a negative or a positive answer. If we fail to do this, we may encounter political difficulties endangering Hungary's interests. He is neither an economist nor a party man, and thus considers the whole problem objectively. He came to the conclusion that we must ask for the opinions of the United States and the United Kingdom. He emphasizes that according to his knowledge their point of view is negative. One sided commitments, such as were those toward Germany, may be dangerous for the interests of the country.

Secretary of State Schweng: Shares the views of the Minister of Public Instruction. The ACC also interferes in much smaller matters. It would seem natural therefore, that the opinion and comment of the ACC should be solicited before the ratification of this very important agreement.

Minister of Commerce and Transportation: The Minister of Religion and Public Instruction is worried about the independence of the country and at the same time he wishes to ask questions which would touch upon the independent acts of the country. There is only one ACC in Hungary, and its Chairman is Marshal Voroshilov. Consultation with him is sufficient.

Minister of Religion and Public Instruction: The points of view of the members of the ACC may differ. Hungary has not yet concluded peace. She faces not only the Soviet Union but all those states with whom she concluded the armistice. In case of commitments she is obliged to protect equally the rights and interests of all those countries. Therefore, we have to know the standpoint of the two other governments. If, however, this has already been taken care of, he does not wish to continue the debate.

Secretary Balogh: The ACC was duly informed through Marshal Voroshilov. It is not up to the Provisional Government of Hungary to interfere with the solution of the problems within the ACC. This is an internal affair within the ACC, and it is not our business to direct their attention to such problems.

Minister of Religion and Public Instruction: He does not wish to comment on economic matters, but he thinks that the official standpoint of the two other governments has not been clarified—at least this point is not clear to the members of the Provisional National Government.

Secretary Balogh: We shall be envied because of this agreement, especially by the satellite countries. For the time being it means only economic benefits, and political sacrifices are not involved. Besides, it would be too hazardous to raise the suspicions of the Soviet Union by delaying the ratification. As far as he is concerned, he carefully pondered all the details, and according to his best conscience, he recommends ratification.

Minister of Interior: Accepts the agreement with the reservations to be included in the covering letter.

Minister of Foreign Affairs: He would formulate this in the sense that the Provisional National Government interprets the agreement according to the covering letter.

Secretary Schweng: Referring to his previous remarks, mentions that the ACC had to be consulted in connection with the release of new currency notes and the regulation concerning foreign exchange. In this much more important case, it would seem absolutely necessary to ask for the opinion of the ACC, and this is not a mere formality.

Minister of Religion and Public Instruction: Proposes that the government submit the question to the Chairman of the ACC, and ask for an official reply from the ACC concerning the conclusion of the agreement.

Secretary Balogh: States again that Marshal Voroshilov knows of the agreement, and through his person all members of the ACC are to be considered as informed.

Minister of Foreign Affairs: Confirms the statement of Secretary Balogh.

Minister of Religion and Public Instruction: If both the Prime Minister and the Foreign Minister would state that the Marshal negotiated about the conclusion of the Soviet-Hungarian Economic Cooperation Agreement in his capacity as Chairman of the ACC, and thus the representatives of the two other great powers were informed of the Agreement and gave their consent to it, he would for his part accept the Agreement.

Secretary Balogh: Declares for the satisfaction of the Minister of Religion and Public Instruction that Marshal Voroshilov as a matter of course negotiated on the matter of the Agreement as the Chairman of the ACC.

Minister of Foreign Affairs: This is only natural.

Minister of Religion and Public Instruction: Takes note of the declarations made in the name of the Prime Minister by Secretary Balogh and by the Foreign Minister.

Prime Minister: Declares the Agreement to have been accepted by the Council of Ministers with the reservations to be included in the covering letter. He wishes to add that we will have free hands in the forthcoming negotiations on details concerning the nature and value of the agreements to be concluded.

Minister of Commerce and Transportation: This latter statement is unnecessary because it is included in the Agreement and is a logical consequence of it.

Secretary Balogh: Does not think it necessary either, because we are concluding only an Agreement on principle.

The Council of Ministers accepts the Soviet-Hungarian Economic Cooperation Agreement with the following statement to be included in the covering letter:

(1) The Contracting Parties declare that the Soviet-Hungarian Agreement on Economic Cooperation is not exclusive in character towards the United States or any other countries.

(2) The Contracting Parties declare that the present agreement concerns primarily those German properties which could be seized in Hungary by the Soviet Union under the provisions of the Potsdam Agreement.

DOCUMENT 18
UNITED STATES MEMORANDUM ADDRESSED TO THE HUNGARIAN GOVERNMENT, OCTOBER 31, 1945, CONCERNING THE SOVIET-HUNGARIAN ECONOMIC COOPERATION AGREEMENT.

In the view of the Government of the United States, the economic collaboration agreement recently negotiated between the Union of the Soviet Socialist Republics and Hungary is contrary to the United States policy of nondiscrimination in economic and commercial matters as that policy has been evidenced in the treaty signed with Hungary on June 24, 1925.

Attention is invited to the following points in this connection:

1. Article X of the United States Hungarian treaty assuring most favored nation treatment to nationals of the United States would make it necessary that joint Soviet-Hungarian enterprises for reconstruction and development in Hungarian industry, agriculture, transport and banking should be established and operated in such a manner as not to impair most favored nation treatment to nationals of the United States. Particular importance is attached by the United States to receiving most favored nation treatment for United States nationals in the field of discovery of petroleum, as well as its exploitation, refining, processing and marketing.

2. Special concern is felt by the Government of the United States at the clause in the Soviet-Hungarian economic collaboration agreement which permits Soviet-Hungarian participation in "existing" plants since nationals of the United States have substantial interests both in petroleum and in other properties in Hungary. Hence, action adversely affecting these interests is considered undesirable by the Government of the United States which must point out that the proper recognition and protection of such interests is necessary.

3. With reference to the organization and development of river and ocean shipping, the Government of the United States believes that the Soviet-Hun-

garian economic collaboration agreement should not be so implemented as to prevent complete freedom of transit being granted as provided in Article XIII of the treaty between the United States and Hungary.

4. The Government of the United States believes, with regard to the operation of the undertaking on the part of the Hungarian Government to facilitate the processing of raw materials supplied by the Soviet Union for processing in Hungarian factories, that this undertaking by the Hungarian Government should not be so implemented as to deny for United States nationals unconditional most favored nation treatment as agreed to in Article VII of the treaty between the United States and Hungary.

In general, the Government of the United States considers the purposes of the United States Hungarian treaty of continued importance without reference to the present status of that treaty as a result of hostilities, since the treaty could be restored to full force and effect upon the conclusion of peace and perhaps replaced at a later date by a new treaty mutually granting even broader rights. Budapest, October 31, 1945.

DOCUMENT 19

BRITISH NOTE VERBALE ADDRESSED TO THE HUNGARIAN GOVERNMENT, NOVEMBER 19, 1945, CONCERNING THE SOVIET-HUNGARIAN ECONOMIC COOPERATION AGREEMENT.

No. 92   British Political Mission in Hungary.
133/116/45   Budapest, November 19, 1945.

NOTE VERBALE

His Majesty's Government desire to make reference to the proposed Russo-Magyar Agreement for Economic Co-operation and to remind the Hungarian Government that under Article 2 of the Anglo-Hungarian Commercial Treaty of 1926, Great Britain secured most favoured nation rights. Even if this Treaty is technically abrogated by the war, the conditions of the Armistice guarantee to Great Britain the restoration of pre-war rights. It would indeed be intolerable if, having won the war, Great Britain were asked to accept less extensive rights than those previously enjoyed.

For the information of the Hungarian Government it is pointed out that discussions on this subject between His Majesty's Government and the Central Government of the Union of Soviet Socialistic Republics in Moscow have not, in fact, been closed, and they will be resumed.

DOCUMENT 20

NOTE VERBALE ADDRESSED BY THE HUNGARIAN MINISTRY FOR FOREIGN AFFAIRS TO THE POLITICAL MISSION OF THE UNITED STATES OF AMERICA ON DECEMBER 20, 1945, CONCERNING THE SOVIET-HUNGARIAN ECONOMIC COOPERATION AGREEMENT.

145/res.—Bé.
1945.

NOTE VERBALE1

The Hungarian Ministry for Foreign Affairs presents its compliments to the Political Mission of the United States of America and, referring to the Memorandum handed over by His Excellency H. F. Arthur Schoenfeld on October 31st, 1945, to M. J. Gyöngyösi, Minister for Foreign Affairs, has the honor to communicate that the National High Council ratified in its session held today the Agreement concerning economic cooperation between Hungary and the Union of the Soviet Socialist Republics signed at Moscow, on the 27th of August, 1945.

The ratification will be exchanged in the near future at Budapest.

When deciding on the ratification, the National High Council took into consideration the resolution of the Political Committee of the National Assembly, according to which:

"The Political Committee of the National Assembly presents for ratification the Hungaro-Soviet Agreement on Economic Cooperation to the National High Council and takes cognizance of the Government's declaration stating that this Agreement by no means impedes the Hungarian State to conclude economic or commercial Agreements of any kind with other States."

The Hungarian Ministry for Foreign Affairs wishes to add to the aforesaid that, according to the Hungarian Government, the Agreement of Economic Co-operation concluded with the Soviet Union does not effect the validity of the "Most favored nation Clause" inserted in the Treaty of Friendship, Commerce and Consular Rights concluded between the Kingdom of Hungary and the United States of America at Washington, on the 24th of June, 1925.[2]

Budapest, December 20th, 1945.

---

[1] The same day the British political representative in Budapest received a note couched in identical terms which referred in its last paragraph to the Treaty of Commerce and Navigation concluded between the Kingdom of Hungary and the United Kingdom of Great Britain and Ireland in 1926.

[2] For the termination of this treaty one year notice was required. This notice was given to Hungary on July 5, 1951, and one year later President Truman ordered the Treasury Department to end all trade agreement benefits to Hungary.

DOCUMENT 21

EXCERPTS FROM THE HUNGARIAN NOTE OF AUGUST 14, 1945, ADDRESSED TO THE BRITISH, UNITED STATES AND SOVIET GOVERNMENTS ON THE PEACE AIMS OF HUNGARY.

HUNGARIAN MINISTRY FOR FOREIGN AFFAIRS

44/res.—Bé.   1945   Budapest, August 14th, 1945.

Sir,

The democratic Hungarian Government wishes to express its deep gratitude to His Britannic Majesty's Government for the good will they have displayed towards Hungary during the Potsdam Conference when our country's fate was being discussed.

The Hungarian Government is especially grateful for that part of the communiqué issued at the close of the conference which makes it possible for Hungary to conclude a peace treaty in the near future, foreshadowing, as it does, our eventual admission into the organization of the United Nations. This will enable the Hungarian people to join the community of democratic states. Hungary wishes to participate actively and without reservation in the work of the new world organization which is predestined to lead the nations towards a happier future.

At the time of the forthcoming peace negotiations the Hungarian Government does not desire to stress particular Hungarian interests. It is our wish that the peace treaties to be concluded should adjust the Hungarian problems with due consideration for the cause of world peace, bearing in mind the special interests of the Central European community. Hungarian interests will also best be served by a peace which brings tranquillity to the peoples ravaged by the war and which achieves satisfaction to the widest possible extent facilitating peaceful co-operation with foreign states, especially our neighbours.

Starting from this guiding principle the Hungarian Government recommends that the following general considerations should form the basis of the peace negotiations adjusting the political, territorial, cultural and economic problems:

(1) The preliminary requirements of the welfare of the small nations living in the Danube valley is that their close economic co-operation should be realized. It is a well-known fact that the cost of agricultural production in these countries is much higher—for reasons which cannot be enumerated here but which were thoroughly investigated by the Hungarian Government—than in the large wheat-growing countries which establish world prices. Similarly the production cost of most of the manufactured goods in South-Eastern Europe is higher than world prices. The nations of this region are so interdependent economically that they must be either enemies or friends.

Under these circumstances the prosperity of the peoples of South-Eastern Europe can only be put on a solid basis if their close economic co-operation and reciprocal trade is institutionally secured.

The Austro-Hungarian Monarchy was undoubtedly obsolete politically, but it was better equipped on account of its widespread borders extending from Passau to Pola and Predeal to assure the welfare of its peoples than the small succession states carved out of it. The latter being impelled by excessive chauvinism tried to achieve unsound autarchy and adopted an economic policy of mutual exclusion which proved to be extremely detrimental to the welfare of the peoples. . . .

This unsound and irrational economic policy paved the way for the German economic penetration which none of the states were able to withstand, especially during the recurring economic crises.

Therefore the peace treaties should strive to ensure institutionally that the small Danubian nations, complementary to one another in natural resources and economically dependent upon each other, pursue the policy of closest economic co-operation instead of economic isolation. This would materially minimize the political controversies and dissensions and at the same time benefit world economy. The economic advancement of the Danubian countries would also augment their importance as consumer markets.

Here it is necessary to point out that in the commercial agreement between the United States of America and Czechoslovakia in 1935, the United States agreed not to claim under the most favoured nation clause any benefits that Czechoslovakia would confer on Austria, Roumania, Hungary or Yugoslavia. Thus the Government of the United States acknowledged at that time the special relationship existing between the Danubian States.

In view of the aforesaid the Hungarian Government on its part deems it desirable that the Powers responsible for the territorial reconstruction of the Danubian region state their views as to how the effective economic co-operation of the Danubian states can be institutionally secured.

(2) In this connection the Hungarian Government requests that when the reconstruction of the Danubian region is undertaken the increased industrialization of Hungary should be made feasible.

Here is indeed the crux of the situation: Hungary as an agrarian state can only take care of the increase in her population through the thorough reorganization of her economic system. There is no doubt that the reorganization of her agricultural production will necessitate large-scale capital investment, considerable time and favourable economic conditions. But even with the reorganization of agriculture the greater part of the natural increase in population will still have to seek employment in other industries.

Between 1900 and 1941 the population of present day Hungary increased by

2,463,000; out of this only 373,000 could find employment in agriculture. Other industries, mainly manufacturing, had to absorb the rest, about 2,090,000. . . .

The industrialization of South-Eastern Europe could be made easier if some of the German industries to be discontinued were reassembled in this region. In this event the economic dependency of these countries on Germany would cease to a large extent, and German expansion to the East would be drastically checked. Formerly the German industrial expansion has been towards the East, so its re-settlement here would continue the natural trend.

When advocating this plan the Hungarian Government does not wish to advocate economic self-sufficiency. This would not be in accord with our previous remarks about the necessity of economic collaboration between the Danubian countries. Every South-Eastern European country should be given an opportunity to develop those industries which complement its natural resources. In Hungary for instance it would mean the establishment of industries connected with agri-culture and fruit growing, as well as of those industries which have the requisite raw materials for developed production (for instance bauxite, oil, natural gas) and the reconstruction and improvement of existing industries such as chemical industries, manufacturing chemists, etc.

(3) Economic co-operation however has certain ideological prerequisites. In other words public opinion in the South-Eastern European countries must be trained in the art of good neighbourliness instead of enmity as in the past. The last traces of racial theory created by German chauvinism must be eradicated to prevent the recurrence of the evil effects of racial intolerance throughout the world. One of the most important tasks of all nations should be the total elimina-tion of all Nazi doctrines from their ideologies.

Therefore in the opinion of the Hungarian Government it is essential that public education should be basically changed from that existing between the two world wars, as well as the press and all political publication in the Danubian countries, all of them preeminently exposed to German ideologies. Means should be found within the framework of the new world organization to prevent the spreading of Fascist doctrines and other fallacies through school books and the press, which only arouse hostile sentiments towards other people.

The chauvinistic principle dominating these countries was responsible for creating an atmosphere inimical to healthy international co-operation of any kind. In view of this one of the first tasks of the democratic Hungarian Government was to revise all school textbooks. The aim of this revision was to eliminate all Fascist concepts and any statements which would cause antagonism towards our neighbours in the minds of our youths.

Furthermore, the Hungarian Government is planning the publication of a whole series of tracts emphasizing the common cultural and historical bonds be-tween the Danubian peoples, which will also show that the economic co-operation between them is in the natural course of events.

Experience of the past indicates the unhealthy Fascist morality, tendenciously spread through school books, the press and political publications and capable only of hatred of other people, is the most serious obstacle to firmly founded international co-operation.

The Hungarian Government thinks it desirable with this in mind to set up international cultural commissions within the framework of the new world organization—or at least limited to South-Eastern Europe—which would under-take to investigate in a friendly spirit those biased statements and harmful tendencies appearing in the press, school books and political publications, which are liable to hamper international co-operation and good neighbourliness.

This commission could achieve positive constructive work by the promulgation of those tenets which would create a friendly atmosphere between the Danubian peoples. These principles could then be popularized by the different countries in their press, school books, and radio.

(4) As for the territorial settlement to be undertaken by the peace conference, the Hungarian Government hopes to see established a peace "which will afford to all nations the means of dwelling in safety within their own boundaries, and which will afford assurance that all the men in all the lands may live out their lives in freedom from want and fear."

The conditions so wisely outlined in Article 6 of the Atlantic Charter can be realized only by the widest application of the principles of nationality. No doubt the ideal state of affairs would be if the boundaries would lose their significance. Failing this, the cause of international reconciliation and co-operation would best be served if nationalities living on contiguous territories were to belong to the same state.

The Hungarian people had to pay a heavy price for the failure to achieve this after the First World War, as largely due to this fact no sound democracy could be developed in Hungary. The Hungarian reactionaries for 25 years were sustained by the fact that one third of the Hungarian people torn away from the mother country against their will lived under severe oppression in the neighbouring countries. Hungarian public opinion could never understand why the Treaty of Trianon, advocating the principles of democracy and nationality, found it necessary to distribute one third of their compatriots among foreign states when the majority of them lived in one block on territories adjacent to Hungary. Hungarian minorities amounting to more than 3 millions unfortunately were subjected to the despotism of exaggerated nationalism, which fact was used to advantage by the reactionary Hungarian press to create and foster an irredentist and revisionist mentality in the Hungarian public.

The most effective measure to counteract national antagonism, which is still rampant in countries corrupted by Fascist doctrines and constantly stirred by chauvinist elements, would be the delimination of boundaries according to the freely expressed wish of the population and to the principles of nationality wherever the nationalities live on contiguous territories.

From the time of the French Revolution the principles of nationality as a basis for settlement have been universally accepted. This was the driving force behind several European revolutions. This principle inspired the theory of self-determination advocated by President Wilson and is the dominating feature of Lenin's and Stalin's works as well as of the constitution of the Soviet Union.

The Hungarian Government is well aware of the fact that a settlement according to the principles of nationality is not sufficient in itself to solve economic problems. The economic problems of South-Eastern Europe cannot be eliminated by adjusting the boundaries one way or another but by extensive economic co-operation as mentioned in section 1. On the other hand if the boundaries are delineated in conformity with the wishes of the population concerned, this would bring about the political stability necessary to economic co-operation.

The idea of the transfer of population has been often suggested to facilitate the formation of homogeneous national states. The standpoint of the Hungarian Government is, in this respect, that the transfer of populations can be justified only when nationalities live in isolated fragmentary groups, that is to say, when it is impossible to reunite the national minorities with the mother country by redrawing the boundaries. What is more, such transfer of populations runs con-

265

trary to all rights of liberty as well as to the evolution of international law for the past 300 years, and can be considered as absolutely arbitrary in character. Major transfers of populations can be effected in the Danubian countries already overpopulated agriculturally only through corresponding territorial adjustments.

Finally, the Hungarian Government recalls that, as the example of the Greek-Turkish population transfer proves, such large-scale movements in population can be effected only by granting international credit and economic assistance. This is especially true in the case of Hungary, which is obliged to meet heavy reparation payments and considering that she has practically no transport facilities, her industries are in a deplorable state due to well known causes in connection with the war; furthermore, her agriculture cannot be expected to attain the prewar production level for five or six years due to the loss of 70 to 90 percent of her live stock and to the radical land reform recently undertaken.

(5) Since national minorities most probably will still be found outside the mother country, however the borders may be drawn, it is absolutely necessary to provide for their protection by means of some international machinery of the United Nations.

The protection afforded to minorities by the League of Nations undoubtedly justified certain adverse criticism, but at least there was some protection. In many cases the very fact that such machinery existed was sufficient to restrain governments planning oppressive measures against minorities. It will be an act of retrogression if even such protection is not granted in the future to national minorities.

When presenting the above the Hungarian Government felt obliged to reciprocate the good will of the Powers at the Potsdam conference by joining actively the spiritual community of democratic nations and by participating unstintingly in their constructive work. The Hungarian Government is firmly convinced that at the time of the forthcoming international negotiations the strength of its proposals will be the fact that the Hungarian Government did not espouse any cause which is not in the common interest of all genuinely democratic countries. So the appreciation of the just and lawful Hungarian standpoint will serve not only Hungary but the cause of the sincere reconciliation of all European nations and thereby further the interests of world peace.

It is the earnest wish of the Hungarian nation that at least a peace should be concluded which in conformity with their wishes would take into consideration the just claims of all the peoples living along the banks of the Danube. A peace settlement based on justice and morality taking into account the legitimate interests and fundamental rights of peoples will bring tranquility to the new world and will prevent another world-wide cataclysm.

I avail myself of this opportunity to renew to Your Excellency the expression of my highest consideration.

(signed) Gyöngyösi.

DOCUMENT 22

EXCERPTS FROM THE MEMORANDUM ADDRESSED BY STEPHEN KERTESZ TO PRIME MINISTER ZOLTAN TILDY ON DECEMBER 28, 1945, CONCERNING THE HUNGARIAN PEACE PREPARATIONS.

151/res.—Bé.
1945

The memorandum reviewed the peace preparatory work of the Foreign Ministry since 1943 and described the organization established in 1945, the general program and the actual achievements of the various government agencies, scholarly institutions and experts. It called attention to the technical difficulties, lack of financial means, and asked for immediate appointment of delegates for the peace conference. It dealt, moreover, with the special political difficulties inherent in Hungary's postwar situation, emphasizing the necessity of taking a stand in connection with the responsibility for war,[1] and for the defense of the Hungarian minorities persecuted in the neighbouring states. At this juncture it objected to the decree concerning the expulsion of the Germans from Hungary, issued on December 22, 1945, in the following manner:

"For a defeated small country, it is of fundamental importance, almost to the question of survival, to profess consistently certain fundamental moral, legal and political principles. Only in this way is it possible to win the support, understanding and respect of the civilized world.

"Therefore, the decision of the Hungarian government concerning the expulsion of individuals of German mother tongue or nationality, might have disastrous impact on the development of our international position. We repeatedly made solemn statements to foreign powers to the effect that all expulsions would be made on the basis of individual and not on collective responsibility.[2] Irrespective of these pledges, the government decided to promulgate a decree which entirely contradicted our former policy statements.

"This decision is all the more regrettable because the acceptance of the principle of collective responsibility might have a boomerang effect on the Hungarians living in the neighboring states. As a result, we shall miss in the future the principle which assured for us an unassailable moral superiority at the negotiations at Prague.[3]

"It is worthwhile to mention in this connection that the foreign policy of the great powers usually does not change basically, from one day to the other, in the fields of fundamental moral and political principles. A small and defeated country can afford such changes even less because its only strength lies in the consistent adherence to moral principles appealing to the whole civilized world.

"If the Hungarian government would continue to demonstrate such an unstable and inconsequent attitude in fundamental questions, then we would have no serious basis on which to build and the whole preparatory peace work might prove to be a useless endeavor. In any case, the government with this decision opened the way to the arguments which could be brought against us and with this step took the burden of an historical responsibility, yet of incalculable magnitude. *Videant Consules . . .*"

It was further pointed out that once the governmental policy decisions were made concerning peace aims, all public manifestations and the activities of the parties should be geared accordingly. The following passages criticized especially the lack of governmental experience of the coalition parties in the handling of foreign affairs and stated that:

"Their behaviour often produced the regrettable impression that the parties were more interested in party politics than in the vital problems of Hungary.

"Apparently a longer governmental experience is needed until the democratic parties discover that the viewpoints and means are quite different in domestic and foreign politics. Someone may be a good politician, an excellent organizer or propagandist, without understanding foreign policy or diplomacy, the agency charged with carrying out policies abroad.

---

1 Cf., pp. 167-168.

2 See, for example, above, Documents 10 and 11.

3 This reference was made to the Prague negotiations of December 2-6, 1945. Cf. pp. 123-124.

"The inexperience of the present government in the realm of foreign policy is particularly apparent in the following two respects:

"a. During the last few months, foreign policy was made in Hungary not only by the Foreign Ministry, but also by the office of the Prime Minister; the various other ministries, the political parties and the Speaker of the National Assembly. This state of things is in part connected with our reduced sovereignty under the terms of the armistice agreement, and partially with the inexperience of official authorities in matters of foreign policy. The result is, in any case, that authorities unable to understand or to evaluate the questions involved, acted in foreign political matters without giving previous notice to the Foreign Ministry. In some cases the Foreign Ministry was not informed at all of important negotiations and decisions concerning foreign policy. . . ."

"b. The other hardly comprehensible phenomenon is the fact that the parties wish to secure their influence in foreign policy through the appointments of their own party men in foreign service. One cannot admit the supposition that the parties intend to reward their own party men with diplomatic posts because this would mean the total moral degradation of our foreign service.

"In principle, it was proper to rejuvenate the personnel of the foreign service from the democratic parties. Afterwards, however, all party political intervention should have been stopped in connection with the appointments in the foreign service. Nowhere in the world do party politics influence the selection of diplomatic personnel, except the head of the diplomatic mission. . . . It is only natural that the parties in democratic countries exercise influence on foreign policy through the parliament, committees on foreign affairs and the government but not through officials in sub-altern positions. In our country, however, party political protectionism has never brought such a pressure on the Foreign Ministry as in the course of the last months. This situation notwithstanding, no party is satisfied with the proportion of its party men in the foreign service.

"This phenomenon is all the more regrettable because the foreign service officers should represent the whole nation and not the interests of the single political parties. Such foreign service officers are needed whose way of thinking, past, and whole form of life correspond to the requirements of democracy. As a result of the incessant party-political interferences . . . the officers will not concentrate their efforts on the fulfillment of their official duties but in the interest of their own promotions, will prefer the building up of party political connections and the passing of information to the parties . . ."

"It was necessary to lay stress on the foregoing in connection with the peace preparatory work because the realization of the most noble principles, aims and decisions, depend on men able to execute them. Professional preparation, talent and firmness combined with elasticity and in general the qualities of a good character are such essential requirements in the foreign service that they cannot be replaced by any party-political background.

"The selection of foreign service officers to be sent abroad is of particular importance. Without good connections and objective informative activities in foreign countries the whole peace preparatory work would be nothing but a device for our own education. The establishment of diplomatic missions could break through our isolated position only in case we send the right men abroad.

"These viewpoints are even more valid for the selection of experts and delegates to the Peace Conference.

"It would be necessary, moreover, that the emissaries of the various ministries and political parties who travel abroad, should ask, as a matter of course, the

Foreign Ministry for instructions. Otherwise, Hungarian activities abroad will remain disorganized, and will bring rather negative than positive results. It is to be mentioned in this connection that the reputation of democratic Hungary has been already greatly impaired by the fact that various official and semi-official emissaries used their trips abroad for foreign exchange and black-market operations. Such activities should be barred by severe measures of the Government."

The last passages of the memorandum enumerated the peace preparatory notes sent to the three major victorious powers and the conclusions summed up the most urgent governmental agenda in the following points:

"1. The Government's decision concerning our Peace aims and argumentations. Once such decisions are taken, we should manifest a consistent conduct with regard to accepted moral, political and legal principles.

2. The immediate appointment of experts to be sent to the Peace Conference so that they could begin the study of the material as soon as possible.

3. The establishment of an adequate Peace preparatory organization and of provisions assuring that the execution of the Peace preparatory work under the guidance of the Foreign Ministry should not have to be interrupted from time to time or limited to an insufficient framework because of technical reasons or constant lack of funds. Not only pengö, but also foreign currency must be provided for in time.

4. The Ministry of Industry as well as the Ministry of Finance should be advised by the Government to complete without delay their peace preparatory work.

5. All government agencies should be instructed with regard to our peace aims and accordingly an agreement should be made between the political parties aiming at uniform and consistent public policies under the guidance of the Foreign Ministry. The same unity of view should prevail on the radio, in the press and other publications, in the activities of the parties and in the course of official and semi-official travels abroad.

6. The elimination of petty personal and party political influences with respect to the organization of our foreign service and especially in connection with the selection of delegates to be sent to the Peace Conference.

"I ventured to mention above a few viewpoints which, in my modest opinion, are important in connection with the preparations for peace. I wanted to be absolutely straightforward in pointing out difficulties and causes of trouble because this is a primary duty to all those who took risks in difficult times for the establishment of a democratic Hungary.

"Finally, I would like to emphasize that Hungary, after a war which was lost politically, militarily, and to some extent even morally, is confronted with better prepared states whose diplomatic position is incomparably more favorable than ours. In addition, the rehabilitation of the country is being carried out amidst a great economic crisis and other difficulties by political parties which—without their own fault—have not, thus far, had any governmental experience.

"We must sincerely admit that the unfavorable diplomatic position of ours, and the difficult internal conditions of the country frequently hinder correct actions. Thus, it will not be easy to achieve success. Nothwithstanding difficulties, however, all of us, and first of all the responsible Government have to do all possible for the promotion of the Hungarian case at the Peace Conference. The future of Hungarian democracy depends largely on the success of this work.

Mister Prime Minister, I am awaiting your effective and urgent actions, and those of the Hungarian Government, and remain,

Respectfully yours,
(signed) István Kertész"

DOCUMENT 23

POPULATION-BREAKDOWN OF HUNGARY FROM 1910 TO 1941 ACCORDING TO MOTHER TONGUE

Year		Total population	Hungarian	German	Slovak	Ruthenian	Rumanian	Croatian	Serbian	Other
1910[1]	absolute number	18,264,533	9,944,627	1,903,357	1,946,357	464,270	2,948,186	194,808	461,516	401,412
	%	100.0	54.5	10.4	10.7	2.5	16.1	1.1	2.5	2.2
1920[2]	absolute number	7,990,202	7,156,727	551,624	141,918	1,501	23,695	36,864	17,132	60,741
	%	100.0	89.5	6.9	1.8	0.0	0.3	0.5	0.2	0.8
1930[2]	absolute number	8,688,319	8,001,112	478,630	104,819	996	16,221	27,683	7,031	51,827
	%	100.0	92.1	5.5	1.2	0.0	0.2	0.3	0.1	0.6
1941[2]	absolute number	9,319,992	8,657,172	477,057	75,920	4,582	14,161	22,269	5,444	63,387
	%	100.0	92.8	5.1	0.8	0.0	0.2	0.2	0.1	0.8
1941[3]	absolute number	14,683,323	11,364,839	720,291	270,467	563,910	1,100,290	128,740	164,755	370,031
	%	100.0	77.5	4.9	1.8	3.8	7.5	0.9	1.1	2.5

1. Territory of historic Hungary excluding Croatia-Slavonia.
2. Territory established by the Trianon Peace Treaty.
3. Hungary with the territorial changes of 1938-1941.

Source: Elemér Radisich (ed.), *A Dunatáj, történelmi, gazdasági és földrajzi adatok a Dunatáj államainak életéböl, Vol. III* (Budapest, 1946), p. 252.

INDEX

(In view of the detailed Table of Contents, this Index is confined mainly to names of persons.)